Abandoned Women
and Poetic Tradition

Women in Culture and Society
A Series Edited by Catharine R. Stimpson

Lawrence Lipking

Abandoned Women and Poetic Tradition

The University of Chicago Press
Chicago and London

LAWRENCE LIPKING, Chester D. Tripp Professor of Humanities at North-western University, is an editor of the *Norton Anthology of English Literature* and author of *The Life of the Poet,* which is published by the University of Chicago Press.

THE UNIVERSITY OF CHICAGO PRESS, CHICAGO 60637
THE UNIVERSITY OF CHICAGO PRESS, LTD., LONDON
© 1988 by The University of Chicago
All rights reserved. Published 1988
Printed in the United States of America
97 96 95 94 93 92 91 90 89 88   5 4 3 2 1

Library of Congress Cataloging-in-Publication Data

Lipking, Lawrence I., 1934–
    Abandoned women and poetic tradition / Lawrence Lipking.
        p.   cm.—(Women in culture and society)
    Includes index.
    ISBN 0–226–48452–1.   ISBN 0–226–48454–8 (pbk.)
    1. Poetry—History and criticism.   2. Women in literature.
3. Poetry—Women authors—History and criticism.   4. Love poetry—
History and criticism.   5. Feminist criticism.   6. Canon
(Literature)   I. Title.   II. Series.
PN1103.L56   1988
809.1'9352042—dc19   87–26963
                                                                CIP

for Joanna

Contents

Series Editor's Foreword

In "Walking Blues," Ma Rainey, that magnificent musician, tells of a wandering woman. A man has left her. The mailman brings no news of him. She now searches for the place, ". . . the town they call San Antonio," where he might be:

> Walked and walked till I, walked and walked till I almost lost my mind,
> hey, hey, hey,
> Walked and walked till I almost lost my mind,
> I'm afraid to stop walking, 'cause I might lose some time.

Although her head is "bowed down," Ma Rainey's heroine refuses to quiver and cower. Tough, defiant, she keeps going. She sings the blues.

These abandoned women in poetry, of poetry, are Lawrence Lipking's immense subject. They have stood, alone, in the poems of many cultures since the beginning of literature itself. Lipking is intensely sympathetic to their suffering and to the suffering the abandoned woman often symbolizes and encodes. However, his deserted women are more than their desertion. If abandoned, they have, in turn, abandoned convention, decorum, control, the ordinary mind. Free from such bondage, in their own time, they can explore ecstasy as well as grief. Their "unruly" travels subvert all authority except their own.

Lipking is a notable, powerful, far-ranging reader of poems. He is fluent, lucid, but subtle; restless, energetic, but at ease with several languages; self-conscious, self-scrutinizing, but purposeful. He refuses to claim that women and men are essentially different. Nevertheless, he shows how differently women (Emily Dickinson, for example) and men (Byron, for another example) have written for, and about, the abandoned woman. She has often taught men how to explore their feelings; women how to construct a feeling, speaking, writing self. Men, of course, have traditionally preferred their vision of the abandoned woman to those of women. Two of Lipking's crucial chapters are about Sappho and the successive (if only erratically successful) centuries of her readers. After Sappho defined the lyric of abandonment, male poets insisted on abandoning her for a "Sappho" more satisfying to their fears and needs.

As Lipking moves from text to text, from the *Epic of Gilgamesh* to St. John of the Cross to Tsvetayeva to the *New Portuguese Letters,* the abandoned woman becomes much more than pathetic figure and persistent theme. Perhaps she has not kept a man by her side. Aeneas does flee from Dido. The poetry of the abandoned woman, however, spins power from her powerlessness. Her language becomes that of a mind and sensibility too passionate, too electrifying, for the grids of culture. Necessarily, she stands beyond the authority of the literary canon as well.

Like many of the most vital critics today, Lipking does more than walk away from small-bored laws and theories of cultural authority. He wants to rethink the meaning of cultural authority itself. He asks what a less myopic, a less clouded, gaze at poetry might see. What might a new poetics be like? In 1928 and 1929, in *A Room of One's Own,* Virginia Woolf famously resaw literature by and about women. So doing, she imagined what women might have composed if their fathers, brothers, husbands, lovers, and rulers had permitted them to do so. Among her characters was Judith Shakespeare, William's sister, as gifted and as consumed with genius as he. Adapting Woolf, Lipking now foregrounds Arimneste, the blood sister of Aristotle, that magisterial founder of Western poetics. What, Lipking wonders, would have happened if Arimneste had been as logical, as analytical, as educated, and as free as her brother? What might she have written about metaphysics, ethics, and poetry?

Arimneste, *Abandoned Women* suggests, might have derived her laws of literature, not from dramas and stories about men, but from dramas and poems about women. If so, her poetics would not have been those of her brother. Indeed, she might have argued, as Madame de Staël did later, that the emotions, like those of the abandoned woman, *were* poetry. Reasonably, Lipking is no more willing to reduce poetics to a single law, poetry to a single mode, than he is to reduce the representation of women to that of the abandoned woman. A poetics that grows from and returns to the abandoned woman, however, would recognize how deeply poets write to express "care and desire." Such a poetics would tutor our reading of poems as well as our reading of poets. For it would instruct us in the ways in which poetry can resist masculine authority and the cruelties toward women that authority practices and condones. Although the abandoned woman is alone, she seeks to share her feelings, including her devotion to such resistance. She encourages a community between her words and their audience. Because she has broken codes, customs, and civilities, she cannot reassure us, as Aristotle did, that nature and art, imitating nature, are in harmony. On the contrary: ". . . the world can shift too fast to be imitated . . . the harmony of art is made to be broken" (p. 226).

In her poem, "Transcendental Etude," Adrienne Rich pictures "two women, eye to eye." She presages, from that unity, "a whole new poetry beginning here." Lipking hears an older poetry, not of women's unity, but of a lamentable, inspired solitude; however, Rich's poetry of "we" and Lipking's poetics of an "I" declare that culture has no more mind, and time, to lose by evading, erasing, and corruptly emending women's writings.

Catharine R. Stimpson

Preface

Why does someone—why does a *man*—write a book on abandoned women? An honest answer to such questions cannot be simple. As a chapter of this book points out, men have been writing about abandoned women as long as poetry has existed, from motives that range from sympathy and desire to fear and hatred of women, and we had better not take the reasons they offer for granted. I might tell many stories about the way I came to this subject. One story, for instance, would go back thirty years, to the prehistory of the women's movement, when I first read the chapter on "Woman in Love" in Simone de Beauvoir's *The Second Sex*—a book I have been arguing with ever since. Another story would describe some women I have known, whose accounts of their experience have contributed to my education. And other stories, both personal and intellectual, might each catch a part of the truth.

One story, however, rings truer to me than the others. It begins with a sense of insufficiency. While finishing my previous book, on the careers or vocations of great poets, I became acutely aware of a missing pronoun: those poets were always "he" and never "she." In principle this should have been easy to repair. One or two great women poets could simply be inserted, to function either as support for my arguments or as counter-examples. I tried to do this, but in practice it turned out not to be easy. To read those poets carefully, or even to read those male poets who seemed most concerned with women, required a whole new way of thinking about poetry—not necessarily antagonistic to the sense of poetic vocation experienced by men, but *different*. Somehow women did not fit the male pattern, even at its most radical or revisionary. Emily Dickinson and Walt Whitman did not belong in the same book. So another book would be needed to account for some of the ways that women figured in poetry and to restore the missing pronoun. It took ten years to think the problems through.

This story is by no means mine alone. It seems to me part of the larger history of literary studies in the past few decades, part of the interest of scholars and critics in writing previously thought marginal or beyond the pale. I do not mean by this that my book derives in any simple way from current fashions in feminism or theory (anyone who takes as long as I do to write a book has no choice but to try to write for the ages, as the present age and its concerns keep slipping by). Yet I do think that literary studies are changing, and that the changes have been generally misunderstood. They are not, by and large, the result of new jargons or the politicizing of literature. Rather, the steady growth of knowledge has alerted many scholars to a range of phenomena once beyond their horizons—not only writing by women but non-Western writing, folk and popular culture, and a host of texts once excluded from study because they did not fit the few standard "literary" genres. The disenfranchised and the dispossessed no longer remain outsiders in literary circles. But there are two ways of adjusting to this situation. One way is to take an interest in writings on the margin solely for their own sake, exploring them, interpreting them, and perhaps converting to their values and customs. Another way is to use them to reflect back on the center, that place where each field or culture defines itself partly through what it excludes. The Roman Empire has no room for Carthage; Dido teaches us that, and thus stakes out the mission of Aeneas. We map a territory by drawing the line that bounds it. Hence scholars have redrawn the map of literature by examining not only what literary studies have taken in but what they have refused to notice.

The figure of the abandoned woman raises such issues with exceptional force. Even the word "abandoned" once meant "exiled" or "outcast," and it still retains the meaning of "shameless" or "outside the law." Thus the poetry of abandonment tends to touch on the limits of what is permitted or what is repressed in ordinary, comfortable life. Much of this book is devoted to probing those limits and the passionate works that test them. Great poets like Rosalía de Castro and Marina Tsvetayeva live in extremity, both personal and poetic. It has been my special reward to learn their languages and communicate a very small part of their dearly bought understanding. But the aim of this book is not only to claim such poets for the canon but to use them to question its grounds. In one of Tsvetayeva's most famous poems, "An Attempt at Jealousy," she warns an ex-lover that without her love, its hysteria and divinity, his life will seem empty. As a matter of fact she was right; fifty years later, he still kept a shrine to Marina. This book suggests a similar logic in literary history. However much abandoned women may be suppressed or consigned to the edge of the canon, they keep coming back to its heart. Once the voice of their poetry has been heard, it will not be forgotten.

Fortunately I have not been forsaken while living with the abandoned. A circle of friends and colleagues and students has wrapped me round at Princeton, Northwestern, and the Wilson Center for International Scholars. A Guggenheim Fellowship enabled me to begin the book, and I finished it during a term at the Humanities Research Centre of the Australian National University. It has been a particular pleasure to benefit from the generosity of the community of scholars in women's studies. Even when those scholars disagreed with my views, as often happened, they were always ready to share their information. I have also learned much from the responses of audiences in many parts of the world, from California to Calcutta; their questions cost me many sleepless nights and gave me many new ideas. Closer to home, Joanna B. Lipking asked many more questions than I could answer and taught me more than I can record. I cannot mention here all those who have helped, but I am grateful for specific suggestions from Fiora A. Bassanese, Clarence Brown, the late J. V. Cunningham, Ralph Freedman, Judith Gardiner, Susan Gubar, Elaine Hedges, the late Phyllis Jones, Jane Marcus, Robert K. Martin, Jerome J. McGann, Judy B. McInnis, Emily Mitchell, Sarah B. Pomeroy, Lawrence Rosenwald, and Bei-ling Wu. The encouragement and advice of Jean H. Hagstrum and Catharine R. Stimpson have supported me throughout.

The final chapter of this book is a revised version of an essay published in *Critical Inquiry* 10 (September 1983) and reprinted in *Canons* (Chicago: University of Chicago Press, 1984). Pieces of other chapters have appeared elsewhere, recorded in my notes. All translations in the text are mine unless otherwise noted.

Introduction

This is a book about poetry and abandoned women. The relations between them seem almost as old as poetry itself. Indeed, in some cultures the role of women in literature has been virtually identified with abandonment. The work that first defined the nature of heroinism, Ovid's *Heroides,* is a set of variations on the theme of a woman whose lover has left her, from Penelope to Sappho; to be a heroine, for Ovid and his legion of followers, means being abandoned. A similar theme winds through traditional Chinese and Japanese poetry, with their lonely, longing wives and neglected concubines. Women and poetry and abandonment are associated in ancient Ur and modern Portugal. The association no longer seems inevitable; other options have opened to literary heroines and women who write. Yet abandoned women still retain their power over the imaginations of authors and readers. A history of poetry that left them out, like an *Odyssey* with no Penelope, would lose its sense of direction and sexual balance. Too many accounts of poetic tradition have done without women. This book tries to remedy a part of that exclusion by studying one sort of woman, or one poetic figure of a woman, as she comes down through the ages.

She has not remained the same. No single, universal explanation can exhaust the significance of abandoned women in poetry. They vary with the minds that conceive them, the needs that they serve in different times and cultures, the poetic forms that contain them, the languages in which they have their being. Many books would be needed to do justice to the full complexity of the figure. To begin with, one might attempt a formal history of abandoned women in poems, starting with their prototypes in ancient texts and tracing the evolution of such types through each succeeding generation. No one scholar could do this. Yet even a small part of the project would offer a scholarly challenge; for instance, rich studies might be written on the influence of the *Heroides* or on the abandoned heroine in Japanese literature. Another sort of book might view abandoned women as products of culture, shaped by the conventions, prejudices, and material conditions of their societies. A comparative study of the ways that such women have been imagined in different times and places would take us far into the codes through which cultures define themselves. Still another book might regard the abandoned heroine less as a historical or cultural reality than as an undying myth, the Heroine with a Hundred Faces. Paying particular attention to the oldest versions of her story, it would sketch an anthropological pattern or psychological configuration that underlies both the most primitive and most sophisticated retellings of the myth. Finally, a book concerned predominantly with theory might try to analyze the types of abandoned women or their implications for ideas about genre and gender. As a tool of criticism or a metaphysical category, abandonment might serve as the basis of a new poetics, an alternative to literary systems that ignore the issues of sex and male domination.

None of these ways of conceiving the subject is indifferent to me, and this book touches on each of them. But its heart is elsewhere. My first aim is to understand poems, and how abandoned women have functioned in poems. My final aim is to modify our understanding of the nature of poetry itself. I began this book, about ten years ago, by noticing a phenomenon for which standard literary histories offer no explanation: the perennial recurrence, in most of the literatures of the world, of abandoned women. The poetry in which they appear seemed impressive not only in its quantity and quality but in its crucial relation to larger works. The epic hero, for instance, tends to define himself by leaving a woman behind. I wondered why; I accumulated examples. Eventually such poetry became an obsession of mine. This book records that obsession. But I have not forgotten my starting place: my sense of wonder that so many great poems should return to a figure of abandonment. Why should so many poets, male as well as female, submit to this figure? What accounts for its power?

Those questions inform this book. So far as possible I have tried to think about them without preconceptions or dogma, without undue abstraction, and without limiting the investigation to any one time, place, or language. Nor does a single theory dominate this book. From chapter to chapter it deliberately varies the method and focus of its criticism in an effort to comprehend the full range of the material it surveys. I look at poems from many angles, and try not to sacrifice the individuality of a work of art to some constraining idea. Often I have gone far afield. To understand one part of the history of poetry sometimes requires speculating about poetry as a whole. Yet the book always comes back to what happens in poems when they imagine the situation of an abandoned woman. I do not claim to have solved all the problems I raise. I do hope to have asked some new questions, and to have found some new ways of answering them.

No line of thought can be free, however, from some prior assumptions and definitions, and mine had better be declared in advance. This book handles some explosive issues, and it will be easy to misunderstand. But the following principles ought to be kept in mind.

First, this book is about *abandoned* women. It is not about seduction and betrayal, or unrequited love, or loneliness, or victimization, or rebellion—though each of these sometimes comes into play. It deals instead with abandonment, abandon, the abandoned. But the word itself carries a double meaning in every dictionary: "Abandoned: 1. Forsaken or cast off; 2. Unrestrained or shameless." The abandoned woman, in common usage as well as in this book, is both physically deserted by a lover and spiritually outside the law. This dual sense occurs in other European languages as well as English, and it reflects a peculiar etymology. The term goes back to Latin, *ad,* "to," *bandon,* "power or control" (cognate with English "ban"). Originally it signified a submission to power, as in bowing to the will of a monarch; the person who owns you can also toss you away. But the same etymology, with a slight adjustment of the preposition, allows a totally opposite meaning: freedom from bondage. The exile or outlaw makes her own laws. Hence those who are abandoned may be *banished* by the one who controls them (given up *by*) or they may take the reins entirely into their own hands (given up *to*). This verbal duplicity hints at the roots of power beneath the desolation of abandoned women—are they chattels or do they belong to themselves?—as well as the uneasiness with which most cultures regard them. Those who are banished are also let loose; utter surrender resembles utter freedom.

This book would not exist without the folding together of those alternatives. Women who live in "abandon" are capable of sudden dangerous turns. They become the objects not only of pity but envy, not only of fear but attraction. Moreover, since neither the protection nor the inhibition of the law applies to them any longer, they constitute a potential threat to a well-ordered society. Poets and respectable people do not always know what to make of them. Perhaps this helps account for their enduring fascination. The abandoned woman, as this book defines her, is far from a stable figure. Victim or outlaw, powerless or powerful, she can change in an instant from the acted-upon to the actor. Hence each of the poems discussed by this book incorporates both senses of abandonment, the physical predicament and its spiritual consequences. The poetry of abandoned women evokes a love not quite like any other and begins at a moment when the woman is both forsaken and unrestrained. What happens next is a test of the poet's resources.

If the first principle of this book is to study the poetic meaning of "abandoned," however, its second principle is to study abandoned *women*. Abandoned men are not allowed equal space. Why should this be? The main reason is that abandoned men have proved much less important to the history of poetry. Like Arnold's Forsaken Merman they compose a pathetic remnant, usually more priggish than out of control. Even ordinary language seldom refers to "abandoned men" in the full double sense. Instead, in poems men tend to be *rejected:* dismissed by the lady before possession, and therefore kept on a string. Dante is not abandoned by Beatrice nor Petrarch by Laura. The male poets could hardly be given up by women who never took them in the first place, and in the aftermath of separation the man becomes not shameless but more and more ashamed. He is obsessed less by a sense of loss than by a sense of what he has never had. Significantly, such female Petrarchans as Louise Labé and Gaspara Stampa reverse the conventions they inherit from men. As women, they complain about absent lovers they once knew all too well, and thus add an unusually direct note of sexual passion to the usual Petrarchan longings. A similar effect occurs in troubadour poetry. A thousand lovesick males declare their hunger, an appetite that could be quenched by the merest morsel of the treat they desire. After enjoyment those men would take to the road. But female troubadours like La Comtessa de Dia tend to remember a consummated love that has now passed away.

A double standard mandates the difference, of course: women are not supposed to be so aggressive as to chase a man, though once the man has had his way it becomes them to lament. Hence poems about female abandonment often have an air of inevitability, as if the woman were discovering the fate that expresses her being, while poems about male abandonment tend to sound resentful or puzzled, as if the man could not understand how such an inappropriate fate could have happened to someone like *him.* The stereotype is so firmly established, in fact, that an abandoned man may begin to feel his sexual identity waver. Some cultures exclude the possibility of male abandonment. Traditionally, a male Chinese poet who wishes to write about his own abandoned feelings must put them in the mouth of a woman.

The artificiality of such conventions of gender provides the great Christine de Pisan with both the theme and the target of her poems about love. Christine was expert at exploring the feelings of a woman left alone; her most famous poem, the ballad "Seulette suy, et seulette vueil estre" ("Alone am I, and wish to be alone"), repeats the loneliness of the widow mourning her husband until the deadening monotony of the phrase casts a pall over everything she perceives. But Christine did not restrict herself to the woman's position. In *Cent ballades d'amant et de dame (A Hundred Ballads of a Lover and a Lady,* ca. 1410), a man and woman alternate in describing the development of their love, its consummation, interruption, and final decay. The poet has no trouble adopting the voice of the gallant and the lady in turn: his importunity, her trepidation; his pride in his success, her joy; his jealousy, her fears; his eventual fading away, her bitter unending sorrow. Each sex plays its proper part; in French, we recall, the word for gender is *genre*. Yet Christine's ability to capture the conventional distinctions between a man and a woman in love does not mean she approves them. Quite the contrary. As the bitter conclusion shows, the rules of a love affair (or "courtly love") consign the woman to heartache or degradation. Abandonment is the destiny written in her script. Hence Christine's ballads function as a warning against the conventions they exploit, a poet's vision of the desolation that lies in wait when the poetry stops. The sexes are not equal in power or justice; the woman will be the one who pays and pays.

When a man is abandoned, in fact, he feels like a woman. That is the import of one of the most poignant masculine indictments of the "strange fashion of forsaking," Sir Thomas Wyatt's "They Flee from Me." Here, if anywhere, is a model of male abandonment. The speaker harps on the past, accuses his lover of deserting him, and does not pretend to have found consolation for what he has lost. Yet in one essential respect the poem differs from most in which abandoned women speak: the man does not internalize his abandonment. Instead he regards it as strange or unnatural (as in the ironic "kindely") and concludes not with unending regret but with "manly" resentment. Much of the interest of Wyatt's lyric derives from its implicit reversal of sex roles. Thus the man remembers a special time of lovemaking when he was completely passive. Her gown fell off as if by itself, he was caught in her arms, was kissed, was asked how he liked it; in short, she took the initiative. The memory of that time haunts the present moment, when his "gentleness" has resulted in loss of power—his deer have gone in chase of other game. This sexual turnabout justifies his self-pity. But the pathos of the situation, like the sweetness of his memory, depends on assuming that men are *supposed* to be masters. In the poem that follows "They Flee from Me" in the Egerton Manuscript, the poet observes the agony of his "sweetheart," who complains that he no longer loves her: "With piteous look she said and sighed: / 'Alas, what aileth me / To love and set my wealth so light / On him that loveth not me? / Alas the while!'" Though tormented by her sobs and groans, he does nothing to relieve them. Evidently her sense of abandonment (even while in his presence) is *natural;* it becomes a lady in love. And this time the man feels no injustice that he must set right. A man learns to live with sorrow by watching a woman.

Most of the abandoned men in literature have similarly caught their sense of loss from women. A number of great poems, plays, operas, and novels represent this one-way traffic or process of education, in which abandoned women foster abandoned men. A short, eclectic list might include the *Oresteia* and *Hippolytus, The Tale of Genji,* the *Stabat Mater,*

Troilus and Criseyde, "The Ruined Cottage," *Eugene Onegin, Aida, Pierre,* and *Tristan und Isolde.* Despite their obvious differences, these works repeat a pattern: a relatively happy and privileged man encounters a woman whose depth of abandonment, at first unfamiliar to him, eventually opens a world of loss into which he plunges and which he will never afterwards escape. His intimacy with the woman is translated into identity with her desolation, and he catches the infection of her fate. Learning to feel, for such men, means learning to feel abandoned. The process as a whole might be called "the Diotima effect," after the woman who instructed Socrates (according to Plato) that love attains its purest form when the object for which it longs has disappeared, as well as after her namesake in Hölderlin's *Hyperion,* whose wasting away in sorrow over her absent lover reveals the heart of emptiness to him. Men glimpse the essence of love and deprivation by studying women. Part of the interest of works like these is their implicit comparison between the ways that the two sexes construe abandonment. *Troilus and Criseyde,* for instance, might almost have been shaped deliberately to pose the question, is Criseyde or Troilus the more abandoned? Whatever the answer, the question could not have been raised without the hero's conversion to the heroine's code of values. Men seldom discover such intelligence by themselves.

The figure of the abandoned woman, therefore, seems to dominate that of the abandoned man. Yet men as well as women have been fascinated by her. Perhaps men need her even more than women do, to remind themselves both of their power and their weakness. Almost every great male poet has written at least one poem in the voice of an abandoned woman; that is one of the best-kept secrets of poetic tradition. Often these cross-dressed poems have a crucial place, I shall argue, in the poet's development. Thus a third principle of this book is its interest in men as well as women who use the figure of abandonment. If the protagonist of the poem tends to be a woman, its authors and readers belong to either sex. The poetry of abandoned women reveals not only how the sexes differ in their dreams but also what they share.

Much of the character of this book derives from its critical and perhaps precarious balance between women and men, as figures of art, as readers, and as artists. I have tried to accommodate both. A study might be written that viewed abandoned women as a female literary tradition, separate from those of men, or as a male fantasy imposed on women, or as a poetic construct with no relation to gender. Each of these may be plausible, in some contexts, but none of them accounts for all the truth. To argue for only one would require bending the evidence. The view that severs female from male traditions, for example, must ignore the fact that we do not know whether a man or a woman wrote many of the best works of the kind. Most anthologies of women poets include the beautiful Anglo-Saxon "Wife's Lament" by an "anonymous woman," but the sex as well as the name of the author remains entirely mysterious. We had better not jump to conclusions. Similarly, the view of abandoned women as exclusively a male fantasy reduces the women who have written or read such poems to dupes or unwitting collaborators in their own oppression; but historical evidence suggests that women helped to create the tradition, and women themselves have often testified to the strength they have found in it. Neither sex monopolizes the figures of poetry. On the other hand, there is no denying that men and women have read different meanings in those figures. The interdependence of male and female traditions does not prove that gender has no bearing on literature. It only warns us not to think that distinctions between the sexes are absolute. Authors and readers can span them.

This book is on middle ground. To some extent my work participates in the large and growing field devoted to writing by women; and certainly I could not have conceived such a book without being indebted to those scholars who have already cultivated the field. Yet another part of the book examines a male tradition and masculine motives. Some readers may be disturbed by these shifts in perspective. Do I think that Woman is Other or do I not? The answer is that I do and I do not. It seems to me the only sensible answer. A man can hardly deny that historically much of "mankind" has defined women as the opposite sex, the contrary that represents whatever men love and fear and try not to resemble. Yet the ruthless logic of this polarity looks foolish when it confronts the diversity and illogic of human experience, where men and women do resemble each other and communicate in many ways, not all of them sexual. If the rhetoric of Otherness is inescapable, it is also absurd. This book explores both sides of Otherness: the conventional wisdom or prejudice about sexual differences, and the many situations where it breaks down. I accept definitions of gender not as eternally given, but as hypotheses to be tested again and again.

A persistent note in this book, therefore, is skepticism about the familiar archetypes of women to which critics have been accustomed: the Femme Fatale, the Great Mother, the White Goddess, the Eternal-Feminine, She. These models of womanhood do not live on my street. They agree on just one point: Woman represents the Other, the sex opposed or inaccessible to Man. She endures as the priestess of a cult, guarding her mystery as jealously as the Sphinx. A great many people have a stake in tending that shrine. Who can deny temptation by the Other? Even women find their identities in it, from time to time, defining themselves as everything that men are not. And men derive considerable advantage from imagining that women belong to another species. The opposite sex can draw man on, excite, inspire him, solace, serve his needs; the one thing a man cannot expect from a woman is to understand her. This can save men a great deal of effort. The Other can be pursued but cannot be known.

Thus several of the most noted studies of female archetypes have managed to winnow out any trace of humanity or compatibility with men. So long as one does not question the Other too closely, her reserve endows her with a pleasing air of profundity. She is Lilith, La Gioconda, Delilah, Medusa—dangerous to approach. Drawn near, La Belle Dame is revealed as sans Merci. The treatment of Keats's poem by such connoisseurs of the Fatal Woman and the White Goddess as Mario Praz and Robert Graves, for instance, is very instructive. Each critic assimilates the lady deftly to his theme, where she serves as an exotic temptress ("the subject is obviously that of Tannhäuser," according to Praz) or a sacred executioner (Death by Consumption, according to Graves). The cruel Other has shorn the knight of his strength. Certainly this emphasis on "the magical, painful mystery" of "La Belle Dame" cannot be refuted; the title itself warns us of her lack of compassion. Yet how might the woman herself have explained her motives? The question seems hardly to have occurred to anyone. Keats's knight never thinks to ask the lady what she is doing, how she came to be in the meads, or why she weeps and sighs. This lack of curiosity is shared by Praz and Graves. The Other speaks the enigmatic language of fairies and relates no story of her own. She is an archetype; she can be taken for granted.

Yet another interpretation of "La Belle Dame sans Merci" may also be possible. The wildness and sadness of the lady, her abandoned situation when the knight meets her, do not require a supernatural explanation. Perhaps some human care has made her weep; perhaps she has a past. And the knight's response, his withering to a haggard and woebegone torpor, need not be attributed to any sinister enchantment. Perhaps he has simply learned what it means to be left. Once having been abandoned, he will no longer ride around the countryside in ballad fashion, succoring damsels in distress, for now he will know a distress of his own. Knights are at risk when they begin to feel. A fading rose or a lily, the former hero suffers as passively as any seduced maiden. The lady has stolen his sex. But what oppresses him most may be not his thralldom but his sympathy with the alien state of a woman. The Other he longs for seems deeply a part of himself—no Fatal Woman, no White Goddess, but only another lost soul.

Abandoned women often teach men that awareness. Unlike the stereotypical Other, they tend to reveal their secrets. The situation may help account for this frankness: once the woman has lost her lover, she has nothing to gain from silence and mystification. Her whole existence depends on the one who has gone, her only hope consists of making that one respond and echo her feelings. She sends a stream of poems, pleas, and letters—often too many. These motives are so transparent, in fact, that even male poets find it easy to express them in the first person. But another reason for the abandoned woman's lack of mystery may be psychological: she does not acknowledge herself or her lover as Other. Her poems and letters assume that certain truths of loneliness and shamelessness go so deep that all humanity ought to be capable of recognizing itself in them. Poetry about abandoned women, therefore, often envisions a community of sexes. It does not regard gender as a prison or mystery but as a set of terms through which human beings discover what separates them—and sometimes brings them together.

Indeed, part of my incentive for studying the poetry of abandoned women is that historically such poems may constitute our oldest and richest literary resource for comparing the sexes. Prior to the rise of the novel, it seems the *only* sort of literature that attracted male and female authors equally, as coworkers and mutual admirers in a long collaborative procession. The spell that Sappho cast over both men and women (discussed in two of my chapters) offers a case in point. Sappho excited Ovid who excited Heloise who excited Pope who excited Madame de Staël . . . the sequence continues. Hence this kind of writing provides a rare opportunity to discern some ways that men have imagined women and women have imagined themselves. Adapting her voice to abandonment, the female poet probes some emotions that may be her bondage or freedom; adapting his voice to a woman's, the male poet muses how far it may be like or unlike his own. Each sex explores its illusions about the other. The process, like the illusions, has no ending. Such poems do not tell us everything we might like to know about the differences and similarities, across the ages, between male and female modes of imagination. Yet collectively they may well be the best evidence we have. The abandoned woman is a mirror that reflects the face of anyone who looks into it.

We may not like what we see in that mirror. Precisely because so many men have impersonated abandoned women, their poems document the omnipresence of attitudes of male supremacy. From one point of view the poetry of abandoned women may seem an instrument devised to keep women in their place. Many of the works most influential in defining the nature of female sexuality, schooling women in what they ought to desire, have always been dreamed up by men. If Ovid invented the heroine, Tolstoy and Flaubert perfected her. At their best such authors seem astonishingly knowing, able like Tiresias to comprehend both sexes in themselves. Yet some women think they know better. For all the seeming sympathy of the male writer with his heroine, perhaps he aims at last to issue a warning to every freethinking woman: you are a weak, defenseless

creature. The threat of satire, with its hint of a covert male superiority to
feminine concerns, lurks behind every one of Ovid's letters; Anna Karenina and Emma Bovary drown in their illusions. Thus Anna Akhmatova
speaks for many women in her outrage at Tolstoy's determination to
make his heroine pay for her breach of man-made codes and man-made
laws. It is he, not fate, that hurls her on the rails. The ratification of such
penalties (not without a few pitying tears at their consequences) might
be considered Tolstoy's ultimate purpose, and the source of most men's
interest in Anna and her kind. Seen in these terms, the poetry of abandoned women appears a means of subjugating women or reminding
them how much they risk when they forfeit the protection of a man.
That threat too is a part of my subject. As a tool for comparing the
dreams of men and women, abandonment also touches their struggles
for power.

The method of this book, then, is comparative. It compares the ways
that abandoned women have been defined by poets in different ages, by
both sexes, by cultures widely separated in time and tradition and language. Above all it compares poems. That is my fourth and final principle. This book is organized not by chronology or ideology but by a set
of recurrent problems: the choices poets face in making poems. It follows
those problems through the whole world of poetry. The poems discussed
range from the beginnings of recorded history to the present, from East
to West, from "high" art to "low." This scope is deliberate. Too many
studies seem to offer vast generalizations about women on the basis of a
single period or genre—for instance, the nineteenth-century English
novel. Such studies have their own virtues; nor am I unaware of my own
limitations both as a scholar and as a custodian of the values of a white
male Western literary critic during the late twentieth century. Yet one
advantage of living in this age is the availability of works from many
times and cultures. The world is smaller than it used to be, and libraries
are larger. While no one can be acquainted with literature as a whole,
everyone should be conscious that there is more than one way of making
literature or thinking about it. I have taken that as my premise and my
burden.

This ambition may cause some readers to feel uneasy. They may suspect this book of divorcing poems from history, of implying that abandoned women embody a "natural" category detached from any specific
social context, of erecting a cosmic archetype that forces all women into
a single mold, or generally of trespassing beyond its competence. I share
their uneasiness; comparative methods are always in danger of distorting
works by emphasizing what makes them similar rather than what makes
them unique. But this book tries to guard against that danger. My main
expedient has been to tie each speculation to the analysis of a particular

poem, and to analyze that poem with full attention to relevant historical, social, and biographical contexts. The example takes precedence over the type. When some pet theory of mine conflicts with the details of a poem, I have tried to correct the theory, not to fudge the details. For similar reasons I have been reluctant to discuss any work that I could not translate. This book devotes itself to poetry, and poetry lives in details.

The focus on poems may also account for some things that this book does not do. It does not take a position, for instance, on the heated issue of whether biology or culture explains the patterns of female behavior better. Do feelings of abandonment fulfill something in woman's "nature," or are they culturally and socially conditioned? I suspect that the opposition is false and the right answer is "both," but my book offers no opinion. The fact that abandoned women appear perennially in poetry throughout the world does not prove anything about the nature of women, since one might attribute the fact just as plausibly to widespread literary conventions and social institutions. Readers who want to settle this argument had better look elsewhere; here they will find not ammunition but poems. Similarly, this book has relatively little to say about the legal and economic status of abandoned women in various societies. That is an important subject, but it is not mine. Undeniably poems about discarded courtesans or impoverished widows may be intended to expose real social evils, and poets perform a service by bringing such evil to light. But good intentions do not guarantee good poems, and poems are my business here.

Nor does this book pretend to tell readers, especially female readers, whether they ought to see themselves in abandoned women. It neither recommends nor dismisses abandonment as a model. If this book is correct, poetry about abandoned women has pervaded many traditions and dominated many imaginations; it is part of the history of humankind. That suggests that we must understand it in order to understand how many women in the past have envisioned their lives and read their stories. Since traditions persist, it also suggests that a sense of abandonment may continue to influence writers and readers, even against their wills. Yet not all literary women are abandoned. Some heroines, like Britomart, ride out to take control of their fate; some poets refuse to dwell on love and its discontents. Those models of female identity offer women alternative, positive ways of conceiving their lives. It is not surprising that many women now prefer them. This book has no quarrel with them. Abandoned women haunt the poetic past, but we need not live in the past.

Yet abandoned women also live today. By emphasizing poems rather than social issues, this book does not mean to set the ideal realm of literature apart from the world in which we feel and grow and act and have our being. Some theorists now define poetry as an autonomous order of words, related only to other words in an endless, hermetic circulation of language that refers to nothing outside itself. I am not one of them. This book does not consider abandoned women to be nothing but verbal signs or pure figments of imagination. Neither does it treat them as a theme, an image, a symbol, an archetype, a myth, an idea, a conceit, a fiction, a metaphor, a trope, a class, or a social problem. Instead it refers to the "figure" of the abandoned woman. The term is borrowed from Erich Auerbach, who required it to explain that Dante's Beatrice is not only a miraculous, disembodied allegory of divine truth or a fleshly living woman but both at the same time: an incarnation or "figural" representation (after "figura" or "plastic form"). I use the term to retain the same double possibility: that abandoned women exist within poetry and also sometimes outside it. The relation between the two is the heart of the figure. Like definitions of gender, such relations alter from time to time; they cannot be taken for granted. Hence this book does not attempt to resolve the inherent tension between the use of abandoned women as rhetorical figures and the persistent reality that they represent. To choose between the two would mock the power of poetry. Imagined figures sometimes compel real people to change their lives.

A few words should be added on the structure of this book. To begin with, it does not provide a continuous historical narrative or a single theoretical argument so much as a series of different perspectives. The first chapter takes the widest view. As a preliminary survey of abandoned women and their role in poetic tradition, it sketches the subject of the book, traces its significance for many cultures, and offers some reasons for its endurance. The second chapter is another sort of introduction, far more circumstantial. It unfolds one celebrated passage (Donna Julia's letter in Byron's *Don Juan*) in order to place the figure of an abandoned woman in the context of one poet's life and in the important but little-known tradition to which it belongs. The third and fourth chapters are historical. By studying translations and adaptations of one famous poem (Sappho's "Second Ode"), they draft a microcosmic history of European poetry, its starts and shifts, with particular attention to the separation and interconnection of male and female traditions. The fifth chapter takes up one part of that strand, examining the motives of male poets who write in the voices of abandoned women. What do men want from the figure? The sixth chapter takes up the other part of the strand, the special problems of women in finding a voice or a place in tradition and establishing their identities as poets. Does a sense of abandonment help them or harm them? The final chapter moves to a theoretical perspective. It tries to imagine a poetics that would be adequate to account for the poetry of abandoned women, a poetics that might supplement our usual ways of thinking about poetry.

Each chapter, as its title indicates, revolves around a single figure: Ariadne, Donna Julia, Sappho before and after her descent, the Sibyl of Cumae, Gaspara Stampa, and Arimneste (Aristotle's sister). Each abandoned woman is solitary, and each is different. Yet if the book works as a whole, the figure that emerges should be composite—a complex but unified likeness made of many parts. That likeness has not been easy to catch. The abandoned woman remains elusive and restless. She can be both pitiably weak and terrifyingly strong, both all-too-human and quasi-divine, what poets hope for most and what they fear. Even when we see her everywhere, we see her best as an outsider. We may not always want to look at her, or like what we see. But I hope that readers will recognize in her and in this book a part of themselves.

1 Ariadne at the Wedding: Abandoned Women and Poetic Tradition

ARIADNE'S REPROACH

At the center of his great epyllion on the marriage of Peleus and Thetis, Catullus presents the happy couple with a very strange wedding gift: a rich tapestry, decking or shrouding the bridal bed, that pictures the agony and fury of the deserted Ariadne. Naked on the beach, she hurls her curses after her fleeing lover. We are not told how the newlyweds reacted; they were not too abashed, at any rate, to get on with their fated task of conceiving Achilles. But the poem itself is divided. Two emotions struggle to possess it: the joy of marriage and the despair of abandonment. Like an uninvited guest at the wedding, Ariadne reproaches the poem and reader for their sense of well-being and threatens to stop the action. The story of her desertion occupies so much space, in fact, that we wonder (as in "The Ancient Mariner") whether we shall ever reach the ceremony. Eventually we do. But the form and spirit of the poem never quite recover from the intrusion. Catullus cannot make up his mind to join the party. He seems haunted by the obstinate image of Ariadne—her static and fruitless passion.

Much of the greatest poetry, ancient and modern, has been occupied with a similar image: the figure of the abandoned woman. Her abandonment begins with a lover but eventually takes in the world. She is barred from happiness and everyday decencies; she becomes the outcast of society and God. It is as if a woman deprived of her beloved were automatically outside the law. The pillar that sustains her falls away, and all conventions of behavior lie in ruins. Even the laws of nature no longer apply, it seems, when love is denied. Medea kills her children, Dido herself; Laodamia tries to copulate with the shade of her husband, and Eloisa with the castrate she mistakes for her Lord. As Ariadne gazes after Theseus, according to Catullus, her garments slip from her body into the waves. "Off, off, you lendings!" In the face of such passion all other motives, even self-respect or the distinction between good and evil, seem to shrink to petty evasions or rationalizations. An abandoned woman has nothing left to lose. She reminds us that even the ground we stand on can shift like sand.

Nor can we forget her. From earliest times, in virtually every culture whose literature has survived, the figures of abandoned women insist on a hearing. They are as old as Sumerian tablets, as new as a popular song. Ariadne will not be stilled. From Sappho to Nadezhda Mandelstam, from the love letters of Ovid's *Heroides* through the letters of the medieval Heloise, the *Letters of a Portuguese Nun,* the letters of Pope's Eloisa and Rousseau's *New Heloise,* to the *New Portuguese Letters* of our own time, the message of some abandoned woman has always been cherished. Even when critics snub her, the public responds; many tears have been shed in secret on her behalf. Some of the works devoted to her have been maudlin or claptrap, some—a very short list might include, in addition to Sappho, parts of the *Ramayana,* the *Song of Songs,* and the *Gitagovinda,* the *Second Idyll* of Theocritus, Dido's lament in the *Aeneid,* the yearning songs of Ts'ao Chih, Li Po, and Li Ch'ing-chao, the *Spiritual Canticle* of St. John of the Cross, the "Gretchen-Tragedy" in *Faust,* "Sappho's Last Song" as imagined by Leopardi, the lyrics of Emily Dickinson, Rosalía de Castro, and Marina Tsvetayeva, and much of Rilke's *Duino Elegies*—among the most beautiful poems ever written. However often the theme may be repeated, it never seems to lose its freshness. The poetry of abandoned women lives within literary tradition like the voice of Ariadne at the wedding, unforgettable and piercing.

It is also a scandal. Confronted with such an unruly guest, genteel people tend to avert their eyes, and so do most literary scholars. The figure of the abandoned woman has seldom been studied. Indeed, an astonishing number of the texts in which she appears have been suppressed or accused of illegitimacy. Sappho's poems were burned in the Middle Ages. Theocritus's *Second Idyll* and Ovid's "Sappho to Phaon" have suspicious backgrounds. The Portuguese nun did not write her own letters, most scholars say; a few also have their doubts about Heloise. "Sappho to Philaenis" has been rejected from the Donne canon because of its lesbian theme. Two and a half centuries passed between the writing of Lady Mary Wortley Montagu's daring "Epistle from Mrs. Y—— to Her Husband" and its first publication. Swinburne was ostracized for "Anactoria" and the "Sapphics." Emily Dickinson did not publish. The poems of Akhmatova and Tsvetayeva have been subjected to periodic Russian freeze and thaw, and the Portuguese government itself had to totter before the three Marias could come to light.

The catalogue might go on. Whatever the specific circumstances behind each of these cases (clearly they involve a wide range of textual, social, religious, and political problems), together they suggest the difficulty of accommodating the poetry of abandoned women to any received notion of poetic traditions or canons. The authorities are not comfortable with such poems. An air of the forbidden, of something potentially explosive or beyond control, hovers around them. As abandoned women stand shamelessly outside convention, so do the equally shameless works that lend them a voice. What they represent, therefore, seems less a poetic tradition than an implicit reproach or alternative to tradition, a principle of resistance to literary standards that smolders within literature itself.

Indeed, the poetry of abandoned women is highly subversive. It poses a threat to two of the most ancient and respectable assumptions about poetry (at least in the West): the rule of action and the status of the canon. Poetry, as Aristotle defined it, consists of action. The entelechy of a work of art requires a series of events brought to their natural and logical conclusion—an achievement, a closure, a resolution. Epic and dramatic poems must arrive somewhere, and so must their heroes. And even lesser kinds of verse must contain some principle of action, some object of desire or final purpose, that drives them to a close. Hence the one situation that must be rigidly excluded from poetry, according to Matthew Arnold, is that "in which the suffering finds no vent in action; in which a continuous state of mental distress is prolonged, unrelieved by incident, hope, or resistance; in which there is everything to be endured, nothing to be done." Arnold was true to his theory; it led him to suppress his own best poem, *Empedocles on Etna*. And William Butler Yeats, though hardly an Aristotelian or an Arnoldian, agreed that "passive suffering" was unfit for verse. The power of art depends on its momentum; it cannot afford to turn back on itself. Nor can the heroes of art refuse to act. If Aeneas had stayed with Dido, if Faust had lingered in Gretchen's prison, Rome and the *Aeneid* would never have been accomplished, the Faustian spirit and play would have been damned forever to inactivity.

Yet Dido and Gretchen supply a different perspective. From their point of view, the fact that "there is everything to be endured, nothing to be done" is the central fact of life. "Passive suffering" becomes them; they are caretakers of inaction, prima donnas of pain. (Many of the great arias in opera, it might be noted, belong to abandoned women.) Their fates are not in their hands. Nothing they do will bring the hero back, nothing they say has power to affect the plot. The best they can hope to achieve is to retard the inexorable forward motion of events. Yet they do succeed in giving the reader pause. Somehow we remember Dido and Gretchen. Even after they have vanished and the hero has moved on, their ghosts return, unappeased, in spite of the plot, and inspire him with longing. Abandoned women subvert the rule of action. Often the best part of the poem concerns their memory and feelings (as with the Wife of Bath), despite the theorist who would maintain that well-wrought works of art have no "best parts." Readers know better. Dido's suffering lingers in the mind long after Aeneas's plotting and piety have faded. The stubborn inertia of abandoned and desolate passion, however ineffectual, however opposed to action, can acquire a power of its own.

Consider again the role of Ariadne. Simply by looming so large in Catullus's miniature epic, I have suggested, she disrupts the heroic structure. Moreover, she might be thought to menace the very conception of the classical warrior hero, since conceiving the heroic Achilles is exactly the purpose for which Peleus and Thetis have been brought together. Interruption of their action would cancel the *Iliad* and the future of civilization, or at least the part of it that depends on men and their exploits. Ariadne in her passion seems quite capable of revenging herself on all mankind. She calls attention to the faithlessness of warriors and heroes, the insignificance of mere activity, the need for plots to take account of feelings; she lays her curse upon the "deeds of men" (*facta uirum,* line 192). The repudiation of masculine heroics looks still more striking if we accept the view, popular among some anthropologists, that the true or "historical" Ariadne may have been the last of the great matriarchs or White Goddesses of preantiquity. As queen of Crete, the magnificent though dying civilization ruled by women, she presides over timeworn mysteries that men have always failed to understand. Theseus represents a crude new breed, a male usurper. He stands for a world that scorns womanly wisdom. The hero pursues his own history and shuts his ears to the cries that would remind him of what he has lost. Whatever the matriarchal lineage, he is determined to reduce the woman to a mere episode in his own epic *Thesiad.* Yet poetry has not been able to ignore Ariadne. Her weakness moves us more than Theseus's strength and distracts Catullus from his mission. Ariadne demands to be heard—not because she represents some idea or myth or the solution to a problem, but simply because she suffers.

That pain has its own authority. Poets and readers recognize abandonment as a source of deep personal interest. Most of us know far more about suffering and loneliness, after all, than about being heroic. Moreover, since most men and almost all women have traditionally been discouraged from engaging in significant action, the rule of action tends to exclude the vast majority of the human race. Poetry based on suffering claims a larger constituency. While the gods make merry at the wedding of Peleus and Thetis, human beings will pay for the sport with their blood. Here at the festivities (as Colluthus would tell the story in *The Rape of Helen*) Paris will make his choice of Love, setting in motion the events that will bring down so many, not least Achilles himself. Nor will the weak and innocent be spared. That text of future suffering is folded within the happy chronicles of gods and kings and heroes. Great deeds and epics always involve an aftermath of pain for ordinary people. Hence

Arnold's own practice, if not his precepts, acknowledges that actions pass and suffering remains. The touchstones of his criticism, specimens of "the very highest poetic quality," return compulsively to a sense of loss, concluding with Milton's lines on the loss of Proserpine: ". . . which cost Ceres all that pain / To seek her through the world." The story we remember is not how Dis took action and found a wife. What moves us is the seeking and the pain.

Much of postclassical literature has depended on a similar emphasis: the prolonged, continuous state of mental distress that shadows abandoned women. For instance, the work that has been called "the first modern psychological novel," Boccaccio's *Fiammetta* (1343–44?), spends almost all its considerable length on a situation without hope or issue: Fiammetta's lover Panphilus takes his leave and does not come back. That is the plot. But of course we do not read such works for the plot. We read them for the sentiment, the moral, the psychological insight, the anatomy of a woman's heart. And the skill of the author consists of finding ways to retard the action, to raise hopes in order to frustrate them, to make the woman suffer. Fiammetta feels exquisite pain. Nor can it be accidental that she concludes her elegy by comparing herself to many other famous abandoned lovers, and finally to Ariadne. Boccaccio turns the epic inside out. Focusing on the woman whose passion threatens to stop the action, he makes that passion itself the center of interest. Many later authors have learned the same trick. Modern literature would hardly exist without its Princess of Cleves and Julie, its dreaming Annas and Emmas and Blanches, its Miss Havishams and Yermas. Indeed, the development of techniques for thwarting suspense, for waiting with Ariadne rather than following Theseus on his adventures, might be regarded as one of the defining characteristics of modern fiction. Historically such techniques seem to have originated with the poetry of abandoned women. A kind of verse must be possible, despite what Aristotle, Arnold, and Yeats preached, in which suffering finds no vent in action. And such verse will prescribe another way of writing about poetry, another set of literary assumptions.

CRACKING THE CANON

The abandoned woman threatens the authorities even more strongly: she cannot be placed in a canon. No hierarchy of values constrains her, no single literary genre, no standard of achievement, no language or culture, no historical period, no social class, no faith in traditional wisdom or the common good. She lives among the folk and the literati, the ancients and moderns. Much of the poetry that gives her a voice could be rendered into almost any language, by a clever translator, and seem at home there.

Tonight as I sleep alone
I am on my bed of tears
like an abandoned boat
on the deep sea

With a few changes of phrasing this little poem would fit into Egyptian hieroglyphics; the Greek of Sappho; biblical Hebrew; a Tamil anthology from the first century; modern Berber or Eskimo; a Sanskrit religious lyric; a fragment of Anglo-Saxon; the classical Chinese of Li Po or Tu Fu; a troubadour's Provençal; a lullaby in Gaelic; a courtly Italian sonnet of the Renaissance; a spinning song from the Luba; the Spanish of Gabriela Mistral; a classic blues. The author might have been a great poet with a famous name, an illiterate folksinger or group of singers, or a solitary unknown woman improvising to herself. As a matter of fact the author cannot be named; the lines come from an anonymous, traditional geisha song, translated from Japanese. But the song would sound just as convincing in the mouth of Prince Genji at the imperial court (geisha have often adapted the words of ancient classics). Emotions like these break down the artificial separations between sexes, classes, and peoples. They move freely from high art to low, from the winner's point of view to the loser's. And by refusing to accept such distinctions, they erode the authority of the canon.

When Lady Gregory set out to collect ballads from the west of Ireland at the turn of the century, for instance, her intention was truly subversive. What she hoped to find was a "great discovery," some words that would crack the canon by proving the Irish peasantry, like the Hebrew people who put their sorrow into the *Song of Songs,* fully equal to sophisticated English men of letters. One poem did satisfy her hopes. "There are some verses in it that attain to the intensity of great poetry, though I think less by the creation of one than by the selection of many minds." This ballad is called "The Grief of a Girl's Heart," in Lady Gregory's translation.

"O Donall og, if you go across the sea, bring myself with you and do not forget it; and you will have a sweetheart for fair days and market days, and the daughter of the King of Greece beside you at night.

"It is late last night the dog was speaking of you; the snipe was speaking of you in her deep marsh. It is you are the lonely bird through the woods; and that you may be without a mate until you find me.

"You promised me, and you said a lie to me, that you would be before me where the sheep are flocked; I gave a whistle and three hundred cries to you, and I found nothing there but a bleating lamb.

"You promised me a thing that was hard for you, a ship of gold under a silver mast; twelve towns with a market in all of them, and a fine white court by the side of the sea.

"You promised me a thing that is not possible, that you would give me gloves of the skin of a fish; that you would give me shoes of the skin of a bird; and a suit of the dearest silk in Ireland.

"O Donall og, it is I would be better to you than a high, proud, spendthrift lady: I would milk the cow; I would bring help to you; and if you were hard pressed, I would strike a blow for you.

"O, ochone, and it's not with hunger or with wanting food, or drink, or sleep, that I am growing thin, and my life is shortened; but it is the love of a young man has withered me away.

"It is early in the morning that I saw him coming, going along the road on the back of a horse; he did not come to me; he made nothing of me; and it is on my way home that I cried my fill.

"When I go by myself to the Well of Loneliness, I sit down and I go through my trouble; when I see the world and do not see my boy, he that has an amber shade in his hair.

"It was on that Sunday I gave my love to you; the Sunday that is last before Easter Sunday. And myself on my knees reading the Passion; and my two eyes giving love to you for ever.

"O, aya! my mother, give myself to him; and give him all that you have in the world; get out yourself to ask for alms, and do not come back and forward looking for me.

"My mother said to me not to be talking with you to-day, or to-morrow, or on the Sunday; it was a bad time she took for telling me that; it was shutting the door after the house was robbed.

"My heart is as black as the blackness of the sloe, or as the black coal that is on the smith's forge; or as the sole of a shoe left in white halls; it was you put that darkness over my life.

"You have taken the east from me; you have taken the west from me; you have taken what is before me and what is behind me; you have taken the moon, you have taken the sun from me; and my fear is great that you have taken God from me!"

Few poems have ever expressed a sense of abandonment so fully. It is an old, old story. The young man has taken everything she had—not least her maidenhead. But above all he has robbed her of her relation to the world, its order and proportion. Each of the homely details of domestic life—hearing a dog bark, milking a cow, going to mass, watching a coal on the forge—has lost its meaning, or has been absorbed into the single, monotonous, overwhelming meaning of loss. The amber shade in his hair blots out the world. At one time the presence of the young man could abrogate the laws of nature, transforming his sweetheart into Helen of Troy and Ireland into a rich and prosperous country. Now everything is false; the Passion itself is only a screen for love. In the distance between the opening of the ballad, with its hope that the young man may still return to her, and its close, with blackness settling over her life like a shawl, the girl has grown into a woman and has learned the worst fate that can befall a woman: to be utterly abandoned. Even her sense of self has been left as empty as a plundered house. All consolations fall away. She no longer believes any promises or accepts any authority.

A more subversive attitude, however, emanates from the ballad itself: its acquiescence in the view that nothing in the world—not duty, not propriety, not God, and certainly not literature—ranks in importance with the grief of a girl's heart. Her love destroys all distinctions. Over the course of generations, according to Lady Gregory, the peasants have "instinctively sifted away by degrees what was trivial, and kept only what was real, for it is in this way the foundations of literature are laid." The ballad conveys an implicit judgment about the essence of poetry, a judgment that mocks the triviality of fine ladies and fine anthologies. Reality lies elsewhere. External actions are not real, and neither are canons; but feelings are. And the feelings that are most real of all, so universal that they attain the intensity of Homer or the Hebrew psalms, belong to abandoned women.

What accounts for this universality? If the poetry of abandoned women is indeed so resistant to authority that it challenges the canon, so hardy and pandemic that it represents not merely one more poetic tradition but an insidious countertradition or alternative to traditional ways of thinking, then the causes of its popularity must lie deep in patterns of culture and human nature and the nature of poetry. Perhaps no single explanation can do justice to such a phenomenon. But several partial explanations may help trace its dimensions, at least in a preliminary way. They fall into five different kinds.

OPPRESSED AND INJURED

One brutal fact demands attention first: abandoned women exist. They have existed as long as women have depended on men. The testimony of history, the statistics of contemporary societies convey a grim reminder of how many women have been cast out of their communities or have fallen through the net of respectability into the gulf below. Their lovers or husbands desert them; they lose all social status; they turn, to support themselves and often their children, to any profession, however sordid, that offers a purchase on life. And even women whose circumstances are less desperate may spend a life mourning the one who has gone. Historians and sociologists have begun to gather the evidence, in recent years, of a situation that most women have always known about: the financial, political, and emotional dependency that keeps them down. The poetry of abandoned women, subversive and irrepressible through the centuries, reflects that truth. It is more than a literary invention.

Nor is it naive to emphasize the factual basis of so many sad and sentimental verses. The girl who grieves for Donall og has lost her name and turned into an archetype, but we cannot ignore the possibility that such a girl once existed. Indeed, she *did* exist—she or the many women just like her, across the ages in Ireland, who watched their men depart over the seas and waited in vain for a return. Those women have known their own truth. They have sung it, and listened to others sing it, and sometimes written it down. Such songs record a reality that gives the lie to some comfortable myths about women—above all the myth that men have always taken care of them. Abandoned women have learned they must live without shelter.

Myths do not die so easily, however. If the historical victimization of women provides a factual basis for much of the poetry of abandonment, the poems themselves often channel those facts into a safer outlet. Few readers have wanted to look at Ariadne face to face or to wonder how she makes a living. Male readers in particular prefer to keep her at a distance; Theseus has never stopped running. Hence much of the poetry of abandoned women exiles its heroines from common humanity, painting them as inhumanly "good" as Griselda or inhumanly "bad" as Medea. A wash of sentiment or fear covers the actual unpleasant situation of the woman. In practice, most artists deal with Ariadne by reducing her either to a poor lost soul or to an avenging virago. (The color of her hair, blond or brunette, is usually an index to her temper.) Other literary women, when abandoned, have conventionally been assigned to one of the same two types, the waif and the fury—Penelope and Clytemnestra, Cio-Cio-San and Katisha, Ophelia and Grendel's mother. The myth allows only two resources, to waste away and die or to retaliate with savage, terrifying vengeance. A heroine who declines to cast herself into the deep blue sea must make a pact with the devil. It seems a sad choice. Presumably such stereotypes originate more in fantasies than in the nature of actual women, whose repertoire is seldom limited to a thin consumptive cough or a scream of rage. Doubtless men must take the blame. Projections of male anxiety and guilt seem responsible for abandoned women in more ways than one. Yet the persistence of the stereotypes indicates how much both sexes need to come to terms with the facts of abandonment—if only to exorcise them, in the best Aristotelian fashion, through a discharge of pity and fear.

Nevertheless, many women are unwilling to be exorcised. Despite the lure of myth, poets in every age have managed to convey some of the naked truth about abandoned women. Much of the vitality of this poetry turns on the refusal of the victim to accept her fate in silence. Precisely because the abandoned woman has nothing left to lose, she is free to describe her feelings with an honesty and candor that other verse seldom approaches. Thus poets like Sappho, Gaspara Stampa, Emily Dickinson, and Marina Tsvetayeva seem to wear their abandonment like a badge of honor or a pledge of authenticity. Tsvetayeva named her firstborn "Ariadna." When asked whether the name did not put too heavy a burden on the child, she replied, "Precisely for that reason." Society must not be allowed to turn its eyes away from Ariadne. The victim speaks back, in verse, and so do her sisters. Whether or not the poetry of abandoned women has been successful in recording and protesting the victimization of women, at least it has offered relief.

Sometimes a poet can break through the wall of injustice and silence. In 1724 a juicy scandal piqued the interest of London. Some spies of the "gallant schemer" and libertine William Yonge caught his wife, the former Mary Heathcote, "in naked Bed" with a lover. The discovery cannot have disturbed him much; for some time the Yonges had lived apart. But through skillful use of this tidbit he parlayed it into a fortune, first by suing the lover for adultery and then by petitioning for divorce, from which he collected his wife's dowry and most of her money (a matter of 12,000 pounds). Mrs. Yonge did not contest the action. The Houses of Parliament, which approved the confiscation of her assets, concluded that "her Silence gave Consent." Immediately after the divorce she remarried, and no more is heard of her. But one person did object. In an "Epistle from Mrs. Y—— to her Husband," Lady Mary Wortley Montagu allows the imaginary author to raise all the arguments that the real woman had been denied. The epistle is fired by outrage—contempt for the marriage laws that condemn wives to "daily Racks" and "eternal Chains," for the double standard that punishes in women what it tolerates in men, for the social hypocrisy of those who damn her desire with their lips but acquit it in their souls, and not least for Yonge himself, who has managed to turn his own inadequacy as a husband into such profit.

> This wretched Out-cast, this abandonn'd Wife,
> Has yet this Joy to sweeten shameful Life,
> By your mean Conduct, infamously loose,
> You are at once m'Accuser, and Excuse.

The assault on propriety also takes in the conventions of verse. An Ovidian or "heroic" epistle is supposed to express the love of a famous historical or mythological woman who has been deserted. But the passion inspiring "Mrs. Y——" and Lady Mary is hardly love. Nor does the poem, like a standard heroic epistle, wrap its scandal in the charm of distance, the safe historical remoteness that titillates the reader by suggesting that even the loftiest woman, a Penelope or Heloise or Queen Elizabeth, is after all only a woman. Mrs. Y—— is not distant or lofty. Moreover, she does not want her husband back. Nothing could make her happier than to be totally forgotten and ignored by him. Why then does she write her epistle? It is not to move him; she knows that he cannot be moved. It is not to influence public opinion; in fact Lady Mary did not choose or dare to publish the poem. The answer must be simply that the poet insists on giving the victim a voice. That is the first motive not only for this poem but for many of the poems of abandoned women. The reality of how they have been treated and what they feel cannot be dismissed by a conspiracy of silence. Mrs. Y—— does not expect justice, but she does claim a right to talk.

> But this last privilege I still retain,
> Th' Oppress'd and Injur'd always may complain.

The Politics of Abandonment

Not all the oppressed and injured, however, are abandoned women. The sense of injury reaches beyond any one sex or any one situation. Perhaps that is a second reason for the widespread appeal of songs of abandonment: they speak for oppressed people everywhere. The poetry of abandoned women flourishes wherever those who hear it are reminded of their own subjection and alienation, of everything that is missing from their lives. Hence the girl who yearns from Donall og (like the girl who cries for her absent lover in the *Song of Songs*) may well be voicing the sorrows and oppressions of her race: the Irish people, mourning for a past glory but condemned to a bitter present of deprivation, filling the empty time with empty defiance, gifted at keening. "Man is in love and loves what vanishes"—and woman does too, in that country. The oldest Irish poetry keeps an honored place for its Deirdre and Emer, its ladies of accustomed sorrow. Indeed, the story of "The Grief of a Girl's Heart" might be summarized under the same headings as the history of Ireland: the Loss of Home Rule; Emigration and Depopulation; the Hunger of the Survivors; Division in the Church; Absentee Ownership. Such are the lullabies that a mother of Aran still sings to her child.

Abandonment, that is to say, cannot be set apart from politics. The abandoned women in Verdi's early operas, distraught about their missing lovers and fathers, rehearse a second theme for those who listen closely: *O Patria mia!* The lover's features merge with Italy's. By allegorizing the longings of his captive nation under the yearnings of a heartsick woman, Verdi smuggles his patriotic message past the censor. A similar theme arises almost everywhere when people are forbidden to discuss their complaints openly. Abandoned women complain for everyone. The mode of political allegory is especially well established in traditional Chinese literature, where love songs were often interpreted as petitions for advancement. The poet or minister who is out of favor may not approach his emperor directly, but etiquette allows him to invent a deserted wife or neglected courtesan to make his plea in verse. Much of the most aristocratic Chinese verse employs this device. But popular songs can use the same indirection. The geisha's gentle songs of blighted love, like Lorca's poems of women buried alive, convey a powerful social protest to anyone willing to listen. Oppressors do not understand such songs, or think that they express a merely personal grievance. The oppressed and injured know better.

Thus much of the poetry of abandoned women is written in a code, and sometimes the codes are lost. A striking example has occurred in the past few decades. Though blues and the black women who sing them have recently been swept up on a tide of popularity, one crucial exception stands out: the songs in which women are victims, imploring their two-faced lovers to come back and mistreat them again. The raw humiliation and subjection of women that seem inherent in the form have proved deeply embarrassing. Without such songs the blues would hardly exist. But many women, understandably enough, no longer want to hear them. One way to keep them alive would be to stress their latent sexual politics, the awakening of women to how badly they have been used by men. Thus Gwendolyn Brooks, in "Queen of the Blues," artfully modulates from the words of a song—"Show me a man / What will love me / Till I die. / . . . Go 'long, baby. / Ain't a true man left / In Chi."—to the thoughts of the singer as she realizes that the men in the audience show her just as little respect.

> Men are low down
> Dirty and mean.
> Why don't they tip
> Their hats to a queen?

The message is quite persuasive. But a singer who has learned to think that way will eventually blame the songs, too. Why should a self-respecting woman grieve for a no-good man?

In fact some codes have been lost. At the turn of the century, when the blues began to develop, the burden of such songs was usually protest: a container for all the grief and outrage that black people (especially black entertainers) were not supposed to express. Blues and trouble were linked from the beginning, and a woman without her man could sing about the freedom that she did not have, sharing her troubles with those who knew how to hear. She was singing about a man who was not only absent, as Ralph Ellison and others have since taught us, but *invisible*—deprived of a place to be himself. And she became invisible in turn, so powerless that even her identity was threatened. Ma Rainey and Bessie Smith, the genuine queens of the blues, were expert at knowing how much of themselves to show. Flashes of power alternate, in their songs, with the low-down misery of a woman whose whole being depends not just on a man but the Man—the white system that rewards a queen for her meekness.

Those singers cry dangerous tears. Their blues can cover a depth of secret protest and defiant self-assertion, like a file in a jailhouse cake. Black audiences of the time did not misunderstand the political implications. But politics has changed now, and so have the blues. We want a more active protest; we are not content to accept the oppression of women as merely a *symbol* of other oppressions. And those who do not want to identify with or enter the feelings of abandoned women may shut off the queens of the blues.

Our impatience with such feelings, however, may put us out of touch with a good deal of the world. In a curious way, an ability to understand the songs of abandoned women and the truths that they imply marks a difference between East and West, or between the people of the third world, acquainted (thanks to their masters) with passive suffering, and the privileged Western world that believes in action. A poignant moment in Forster's *A Passage to India* may help to illustrate the point. At the end of the tea party with which Fielding hopes to bring East and West together, the Brahman Professor Godbole is prevailed on to sing. His performance has a strange effect: "It was the song of an unknown bird." Though the Indian servants gather round to enjoy it, the English ears remain baffled. Afterwards the Professor explains in detail.

> "It was a religious song. I placed myself in the position of a milk-maiden. I say to Shri Krishna: 'Come! Come to me only.' The God refuses to come. I grow humble and say: 'Do not come to me only. Multiply yourself into a hundred Krishnas, and let one go to each of my hundred companions, but one, O Lord of the Universe, come to me.' He refuses to come. This is repeated several times. . . ."
>
> "But He comes in some other song, I hope?" said Mrs. Moore gently.
>
> "Oh no, He refuses to come," repeated Godbole, perhaps not understanding her question. "I say to Him, 'Come, come, come, come, come, come.' He neglects to come."

The milkmaiden, whose attempt to entice Krishna is a recurrent motif in Hindu ritual, may qualify as an abandoned woman through her shameless pursuit of the god and her failure to gain his presence. But the effect of the passage depends on something else, the inability of Mrs. Moore and her friends to gather the point of the song. The milkmaid knows how to live with frustration; thousands of years and many reincarnations may pass without her lover coming. But Western songs rely on another cadence, on an expectation that the ending will be, if not more happy, at least more conclusive. The English in India are addicted to action. Not even the sympathetic Fielding and Mrs. Moore prove able to grasp the lives of abandoned women. Nor does Forster himself totally reject the Western view. (It is one of the subtlest judgments of the novel that near

the end, when Krishna does come at last to Professor Godbole in a moment of revelation no less decisive for its modesty, He takes the form of
Mrs. Moore and her wasp. She herself provides the closure for which she
had hoped.) Yet the milkmaid commands a truth that oppression teaches
and the English will never learn: the lover may not want to come. Abandoned women, like subject nations, are very resourceful at waiting.

Divine Abandonment

Yet waiting for Krishna does not bring earthly rewards. Though
the situation described by Forster undoubtedly carries political implications, and even signifies the inevitable bafflement of the Empire and decline of the West, its tenor derives from religion. If God is not dead, he
certainly seems in hiding. Hence a third explanation for the universality
of poetic abandoned women may be that they express an eternal religious
theme: the absence of God and the longing we feel for his presence. The
love for man translates to a higher, diviner love. In almost every culture,
some songs maintain a delicate balance between carnal and holy passion.
"Might I but moor / To-night in thee!" It hardly matters whether the
missing companion of Emily Dickinson's "Wild Nights" is Christ or
God or merely some human lover; desire and prayer enlist the same vocabulary. Hence the language of abandoned women seldom distinguishes
Eros from Agape.

Virtually every lyric ascribed to the great Hindi poet Mira Bai
(1498–1547?), for example, throbs with erotic worship of the beloved.

> Sleep has forsaken me.
> I watch the night pass
> waiting for my love.
> Friends cautioned me,
> I closed my mind to them.
> While he is gone I cannot rest
> yet I am not resentful.
> My body wastes away, I twist and turn,
> my lips keep calling the one word of "love."
> No one can ever understand
> the agony of parting,
> the pain carved in my heart.
> The rainbird supplicates the clouds,
> the fish yearns after water.
> Mira is restless, abandoned,
> numb to the world.

The poet harps on one note only, like the *chataka,* or "rainbird," an Indian cuckoo supposed to live only on raindrops and to beg the clouds for

rain with every cry. Mira thirsts for her lover; she is so obsessed by his person that when he is missing all her senses fail. Yet without the biographical tradition that tells of this princess-priestess's devotion to Krishna (her insistence on wooing him like a milkmaiden, beneath her caste, scandalized her relations), an innocent reader would have no way of knowing what sort of lover is involved. Saint Mira the mystic is also a favorite of those whose love songs adore a vanished sweetheart or a distant movie star. At night, when yearning comes, it dissolves the borders between desire and prayer. The whereabouts of God are mysterious as a traveling salesman's. Men may think Him a king, but women perceive Him differently, more personally, through the pain of separation. The whole world proclaims His absence.

Historically, indeed, one might argue that the feminine understanding of God as an absent lover has provided the main alternative to the image of God as patriarch or power. The divine insomnia of Mira Bai, her inability to rest without Krishna by her side, finds an echo in many cultures. Perhaps no figure embodies the relation between God and his people better, in the Old Testament, than a woman whose lover is distant and who endlessly cries for his coming. Jerusalem remembers and Jeremiah laments. That longing seems inscribed at the heart of Hebraism (as opposed to the Hellenic or Arnoldian worship of action); it sustained the Jewish people through thousands of years of a seemingly unreciprocated love that expected a final return. If the patriarch gave Judaism its law, it was the abandoned woman who gave it a soul.

Moreover, Christianity inherited the figure. The scholastic moralizations of the *Song of Songs,* which allegorize the young woman and her young man as the Church and Christ or the soul and God, clearly respond to earlier Jewish readings. Most readers of the poem have always sensed the folding together of the sacred and the profane. So have readers of the so-called "Sanskrit Song of Songs," Jayadeva's great *Gitagovinda.* The connection between abandonment and religious longing is embedded in the holy books of many creeds. To be sure, not all religions interpret the figure in the same way. The medieval Indian rhetoricians, who distinguished seven types of abandoned women and four conditions of "love-in-separation," would have assigned most Christian allegories of abandonment to the fourth condition, *karuna,* or "mourning love." Death intensifies love; the *Stabat Mater* holds an honored place among love songs of the West. "In the European tradition the profane link between love and death as exemplified by the romance reflects the sacred link established in the Christian theology of martyrdom." By contrast, Hindu traditions prefer to end with the revivification or union of lovers. Yet whatever the differences in interpretation, theologians of many reli-

gions agree that knowledge of the soul's relation to God requires knowledge of the feelings of abandoned women. From Sappho to "Sunday
Morning" the theme recurs: an empty and lonely spirit invites the god.

The contrast between male and female images of divinity stems from
the beginning of recorded poetry. As early as the third millennium B.C.,
two major poems (or poetic collections) present the archetypal abandoned woman from radically different points of view. The dispute revolves around Ishtar, a goddess of love and war. (Ishtar is the Semitic or
Akkadian name for the Sumerian goddess Inanna.) Seen from a male
point of view, she appears at her most terrible in the great *Epic of Gilgamesh.* Foiled in her attempt to seduce the hero, the passionate abandoned
goddess avenges her frustration by setting loose the "Bull of Heaven"
(tablet 6), precipitating a chain of events that results in the death of Gilgamesh's best friend, Enkidu (tablet 7). In every version of this story,
early and late, there is no mistaking the hostility toward Ishtar. The fury
of a spurned female divinity has blighted the earth.

But the woman's version is different. In a series of eighteen poems
called *The Exaltation of Inanna,* the princess-priestess-poetess Enheduanna (ca. 2275 B.C.)—the first author known by name in the history of
literature—celebrates her goddess as the most wise and righteous, the
principle of fertility, "great lady of ladies." It is true that Inanna can also
be warlike, vengeful, and fearsome. Yet we do not see Enheduanna's lady
through the eyes of men. The priestess identifies directly with her goddess, and the poetry pays homage not to heroic deeds resisting the divine
will but to the faithful worship of woman by woman. At the beginning
of her peroration (tablet 16) Enheduanna seems to describe her creation
of the sequence as a "giving birth." Yet her labor pains, like those of
Virgil's Sibyl, require no prior masculine act of love. The goddess of love
herself has inspired the songs in her praise.

Much of *The Exaltation of Inanna* consists not of praise, however, but
lamentation. The "argument" of the sequence, its middle portion, re-
counts a falling away from the worship of the goddess. Enheduanna the
priestess is cursed and banished from Ur, and mortals and lesser gods
challenge Inanna's supremacy. We do not know exactly what happened.
It seems probable that this section documents an actual historical occur-
rence, perhaps a rebellion against King Sargon, Enheduanna's father, that
ended with his triumph and the reinstitution of Ishtar/Inanna (Sargon
attributed his rule to Ishtar's love). Whatever its precise political and
theological significance, at any rate, the despair of the priestess darkens
her songs. Banished to a leper's hut, she sits amid the dust storms till
sand chokes her "honey mouth." Even the moon god Nanna, Inanna's
father, turns against his high priestess.

Me who once sat in triumph
>   he has driven from the sanctuary.
Like a swallow in flight through a window
>   he cast me, my life is consumed.
He thrust me forth to walk
>   in bramble on the mountain.
He stripped me of the crown
>   befitting the high priesthood.
He gave me a dagger and sword—
>   "these become you," he said.

The unfaithful male god and the apostate people of Ur encourage the poet to kill or defile herself. Murderous enemies threaten to seize the temple. Only Inanna can save her.

Enheduanna and her goddess rise together from their term of trial. The prayers of the abandoned woman are answered; Inanna the all-powerful restores her priestess and herself to power. In the series of hymns and triumphal songs that bring it to a close, *The Exaltation of Inanna* places its two heroines—the worshipper and the worshipped—back on the throne they deserve. "She was robed in womanly beauty. / Like the light of the rising moon, how splendid was her array!" Is it the goddess or the priestess that shines here? The fates of the two are so closely linked, as one scholar notes, that "she" might refer to either one. Simultaneously the poem slips from first- to third-person narration, as if to emphasize the exaltation or promotion of Enheduanna herself. Women rise to the top. And the sequence defines itself, through that ending, not as a series of adventures but as an extended hymn of praise. The actions of men have less importance, for this poet, than the vision of a proper hierarchy and the female passions that correspond to the periods of its fall and rise. Hence the final exaltation is not only a religious ceremony but an exaltation of spirit.

Many details of Enheduanna's story are still obscure, and it would be idle to build a theory of women's literature or sexual difference on a work whose background and meaning must remain matters for speculation. (In other versions of the Inanna myth, for example, Gilgamesh is not her antagonist but her brother and helper.) Yet the intensely female perspective of *The Exhaltation of Inanna* cannot be mistaken. Whatever the poem "means," it shows us a woman's sorrow, a woman's joy. And the much-discussed relation of Sumerian writings to later religious texts, above all to the Old Testament, suggests that such a woman's point of view may contribute its spirit or "typology of divine exaltation" to many of the sacred books of mankind. God the patriarch, God the lawgiver draws much of his power from the longing of his people—their sense of being

forsaken, their hope for a final reunion with the One they love. Historically women have tended to express that longing best. Thus Enheduanna
stands as the first of women poets not only chronologically but spiritually: the priestess who knows that the godhead depends on a love surpassing the love of men.

The Psychology of Abandonment

She is also, however, a witch. The divinity of Inanna manifests itself not only in love but in her terrible glances, her curses, her dark unspeakable will; and her prophetess shares that intimacy with magic. According to the poem itself (lines 118–19) Enheduanna practices
oneiromancy and perhaps blacker arts as well. In this respect too she
serves as a type of abandonment. Long before Christianity, even before
the coming of Dionysus and the Eleusinian mysteries, abandoned
women were associated with magic. The curses that Ariadne hurled after
Theseus almost immediately found their target, Catullus relates, in the
death of the hero's father, the hapless Aegeus. Abandoned women know
how to cast spells. They take part in the most primitive religious rites
and enjoy power over gods and the future. Not only Ariadne but all her
sisters dabble in sorcery: Phaedra, Medea, Cassandra, Simaetha, Oen-
one, Dido, Deianira, Laodamia, Electra, Lamia, and, by courtesy, Sappho. Men seldom understand that lore unless some woman condescends
to teach it. Even that archmagician Virgil needed the Sibyl (Apollo's own
abandoned) to help him prophesy. And many more recent female poets,
like Emily Brontë or Sylvia Plath, carry on the line of magic, however
ironically.

> Herr God, Herr Lucifer
> Beware
> Beware.
>
> Out of the ash
> I rise with my red hair
> And I eat men like air.

If Ariadne and Lady Lazarus cannot force men to notice their pain, at
least they can touch them with fear.

Indeed, the attention paid to abandoned women in so many cultures
may well be a product of fear. Men are afraid of women and sometimes
turn them into demons. But both sexes fear the abandoned—not because
they are Other but because they seem all too familiar. The emotions that
we quarantine in the course of daily, complacent life come back to infect
us at night. Hence a fourth reason for the prevalence of abandoned
women may be psychological: they remind us of our own fears. However
ruthlessly men flee from Ariadne, the universality of her poetry confirms

that their flight is vain. Her feelings will always pursue them and blend with their own. From this point of view the poetry of abandoned women may signify the return of the repressed. Ariadne descends to haunt us when we are happy; the darkness over Eloisa's life blots out the sun of healthy enlightened times. Evidently no age or country is immune from the blight of such women. They infiltrate their pathologies into our parties and daydreams, and bring our secret terrors into the open.

One anxiety above all runs through song after song: the fear of being abandoned. Though men do not talk about this fear very much, at least in public, their actions and thoughts confess it. Perhaps no love affair or intense relationship, not even the relations among parents and children, can ever wholly escape it. The ones we care for leave us. They graduate, or move, or find someone else, or die, or simply grow away. Our letters return unanswered. "Parting is all we know of heaven, / And all we need of hell." Each time the door closes behind parents or lovers, the threat arises that they may not come back. Children often fantasize that they will be lost or forsaken, left by the side of the road, and grown-ups also worry about being left alone. It does happen—and not always to other people. The lucky ones make a new life; the unlucky ones spend a lifetime reliving the moment and emotions of abandonment. And so do poets like Emily Dickinson. The fear of being abandoned is the guilty secret of many marriages and poems. Both men and women feel it, and they have expressed it since the beginnings of literature by responding— sometimes with compassion and sometimes with defensive scorn—to the figure of the abandoned woman.

The oldest poetry plays on those emotions. Consider that founding myth, the story of Oedipus. Despite Freud's imaginative disclosure of primitive or infantile male hostilities that civilized people have since learned to recognize in themselves, despite the ingenious analyses of kinship rules by structural anthropologists, until recently almost no one seems to have commented on the act that sets the story in motion: the abandoning of the infant hero by his parents. Oedipus did not *want* to kill his father and marry his mother. So far as he knew, Laius and Jocasta were strangers. But ordinary rules of behavior do not apply to a world defined by abandonment. Rejected by his natural parents, and driven away from his adopted parents by the prophecy that he misinterpreted to mean that he would destroy them, Oedipus cannot know who he is; he is completely abandoned. All the rest follows from this. The outcast, according to a currently popular reading of the myth, is born to be scapegoat or victim. Freudian interpretations of the Oedipus complex have yet to come to terms with the full implications of Oedipus's predicament: his inability to discover where he came from, what name he was given, to whom he owes his allegiance, the nature of his relations. The hero does not belong to Thebes or anywhere. That isolation both precedes and causes his final tragedy. Moreover, his suffering reflects a reality that is both subjective and objective: Oedipus feels abandoned because he has been abandoned. Perhaps the power of the myth has more to do with such feelings than with the buried aggressions coaxed out by Freud. Women as well as men can recognize themselves in Oedipus. Whether or not most of us from infancy regard our parents with rivalry and desire, most of us certainly fear to lose them. The consequences of such a loss, the derangement of society as well as the self, may be the deepest lesson of Oedipus's story.

Not everyone is willing to face that lesson. Men especially do not acknowledge their fears, or contrive to project them on women. Abandoned feelings are suspect. Oedipus exerts all his masculine force, in Sophocles' drama, in order to prove that he is not personally touched by the situation. Of course the effort fails, but the audience appreciates the strength of his self-control. Jocasta understands the catastrophe before he does and suppresses it better. Prudent people are supposed to disguise their emotions. And that is why the abandoned woman commands such threatening and fascinating power. No feelings are too strong or too shameful for her to express. Hysteria, carnality, self-loathing, infatuation, fury, abasement, longing—these are her daily bread. Even in her quiet moments she lives at a pitch of despair obliterating everything that does not feed her passion. Yet the very intensity of her shamelessness, so destructive of good taste or everyday good manners, confers a special kind of knowledge. The abandoned woman has an educated heart. She accepts the weakness that most of us try to conceal, the irrational flood of anger and regret. She learns from it and nurtures it; she makes men see it too.

Many of the greatest poets, particularly women, have shaped their sense of abandonment into a world. In the work of Rosalía de Castro (1837–85), for instance, it seems an accepted principle that men will go—abscond or die or emigrate—and women will stay and grieve. One should not confuse this sexual fatalism with indifference. Rosalía had been abandoned at birth by her own father (a seminarian), and she was well aware that sorrow may be rooted in injustice. "Poetry, for Rosalía de Castro, was fundamentally the expression of a painful existential reality and a cry of social protest." In her native region, where she is still regarded as a legend and a saint and an archetypal Galician, her work functions to defend the Galician language and people against persecution or assimilation by the rest of Spain. She was also an early feminist. Like Sylvia Plath, Rosalía imagines herself a Lady Lazarus, bringing the news that, after centuries of embalmment, women are alive and writing. Yet all these forms of protest take their peculiar character from a deep mood of abandonment or what Galicians call *morriña*—"the passionate dark longing for something loved and absent." This mood is not a withdrawal from life and its troubles. For the poet it is life itself.

> *Cando penso que te fuches,*
> *negra sombra que m'asombras,*
> *ô pe d'os meus cabezales*
> *tornas facéndome mofa.*
>
> *Cando maxino qu'ês ida*
> *n'ò mesmo sol te m'amostras,*
> *y eres á estrela que brila,*
> *y eres ò vento que zoa.*
>
> *Si cantan, ês ti que cantas;*
> *si choran, ês ti que choras:*
> *y ês ó marmurio d'o río*
> *y ês á noite y ês á aurora.*
>
> *En todo estás e ti ês todo,*
> *pra min y en min mesma moras,*
> *nin m'abandonarás nunca,*
> *sombra que sempre m'asombras.*

> When I think that you are leaving,
> somber shade that shades me over,
> at the corner of my bedside
> mocking shadow, you return.
>
> When I dream that you have vanished
> in the sun itself you flourish,
> and are of the star the shining,
> and are in the wind the moan.
>
> If they sing, you are the singing;
> if they weep, you are the weeping:
> and the murmuring of the river
> and the night and break of dawn.
>
> In all things you are, you are all,
> for me, in me more than member,
> nor will you abandon me,
> shade that shadows me forever.

Such lyrics are beyond translation. Even the reader without Portuguese or Galician can recreate some of the effect by mouthing the echoing sonorities of the original, as in the obsessive *m* and *n* sounds of line 14 ("for my and in my very self you dwell") or the dark reverberating stresses of the final line, where the blending together of the words "sombra . . . sempre . . . asombras" (shadow, forever, shadows) weds the darkness that haunts the poet to eternity. But the special quality of this poem consists of its union of utmost simplicity with rich complexity of tone and implication. This is partly a matter of rhythm: the eight-syllable lines might seem jingling or monotonous, like a lullaby of gloom, were it not for the constant and subtle variation of stresses. It is partly a matter of diction: all the words and phrases are drawn from ordinary language, but the poet gives many of them an extra spin (i.e., *asombras*, "shadows," also carries the meanings of "frightens" or "haunts" or, in association with *sombra*, a literalistic "beglooms"). It is partly a matter of sound, remarkable not only for the repetitions we have noticed but for a skillful intermixture of brighter notes (for instance, the reiterated *y*, "and") that keeps the effect from becoming too cloying. Only the finest of lyric poets could pack so much alliteration, rhyme, assonance, and grammatical patterning in so few lines without sacrificing any weight of thought.

Above all it is the figure of the shadow itself, however, that generates the richness of the poem. At once familiar and infinitely strange, immanent and transcendent, the black gloom of the poet can perch like a cat "there at the foot of my bed" (line 3) or appear to her mystically as a darkness within the sun. Should we regard it as nothing but a mood? The poem itself carefully preserves two possibilities, that the shadow is a spirit inhabiting nature—the melancholy truth at the heart of things—or a personal fixation, in the poet's very self, that she projects on all around her. In any case no importance is attached to choosing between these possibilities. A psychological gloom is just as real, for this poet, as a metaphysical gloom or a change in the atmosphere. Yet a more difficult question is whether to consider the shadow an occasion for homage or mourning. On the one hand it undeniably represents Rosalía's misery, the specter of lost love and failed hope and ever-present physical pain and gathering death that never stops brooding over her and mocking her efforts to live. On the other hand it confers a sort of magnificence on her life, not only because its presence is so beautiful and mysterious and powerful but because it is so dependable. Unlike others she has loved, it will never abandon her. The line might be perceived either as threat or pledge. But for this poet the two come together. The shadow is her addiction but also her fate, and if it were to leave her she would lose her reason for being and the spell that allows her to write. The poem itself is the proof of how well gloom becomes her. She can rely on black.

What are the consequences of living always under a shadow? Doubtless it can result in a morbid state of mind or surrender to dejection. Confronting Rosalía's ever-present "negra sombra," many therapists would insist on opening the blinds and filling the room with light. Abandoned women dwell on the past and often seem to prefer the pain of remembering to any possible present glint of hope. Thus one of the most famous poems by Annette von Droste-Hülshoff (1797–1848), the much-admired German poet, observes New Year's Eve by agonizing over the death of the old year without so much as mentioning the new. No one would call this attitude heartening or wholesome. Yet living in the dark does enable certain poets to develop a rare perceptiveness. Even at daybreak Rosalía de Castro can sense the underlying persistence of a shadow beneath the encroaching light. If this is morbid, it is also acute and at times, perhaps, wise. Such poets understand how much of life looks backward, how much our feelings of abandonment can explain. Refusing to be consoled, they face the reality of what they feel and take some strength from it. Sometimes they may even come to believe that, compared to the depth of abandonment, no other way of life makes any sense.

> Once drinking deep of that divinest anguish,
> How could I seek the empty world again?

The function of poetic abandoned women, therefore, seems largely to provide a channel for feeling—especially for the shadowy, self-pitying, immoderate fears that the unabandoned work so hard at suppressing. Pathological but inextinguishable, the thought of Ariadne legitimates our anxieties. Catullus can find no reason to stop the wedding, but some uneasiness within him clearly insists on a protest. He turns then to another part of his soul; the forsaken woman authorizes him to express what he really feels. And abandoned women often set poets and readers free in similar ways. Their songs may not fit every mood or minister to every human need. Yet in times of trouble, in times of sorrow, nothing else seems to do. Men in particular seem incapable of voicing their darker passions except through the voices of women. A male poet may spend most of his life without confessing his weakness, frustration, or fear of being alone. Then, at moments, his fears are wrenched from him. When Crazy Jane began to speak through Yeats, at first he was shocked and appalled by the words she put in his mouth. He set out to exorcise her and eventually succeeded. But like other people he could escape his abandoned woman only by acknowledging her feelings and incorporating them into his own. She is the shade that shadows us forever.

THE POETRY OF ABANDONMENT

Indeed, it may be that the abandoned woman is also the archetypal poet. That is a fifth and final reason why poets tend to be so fond of her. If the verse of Enheduanna of Ur and Rosalía de Castro and Mira Bai and Ariadne depends on sympathetic magic, the conjuring up of something sadly missing, then many current literary theories would define poetry itself as a kind of magical thinking. In practical terms such theories point to the sense of loss that often attends the creative process. Somehow the

pursuit of the finished poem only confirms its absence, as the very attempt to recapture the original inspiration or depict an imagined reality
pushes them back into an ever-receding past or a fading vision. The pathos of abandoned women, on this account, lies on the surface of a deeper
metaphysical pathos: the divorce between conception and execution.

> Between the conception
> And the creation
> Between the emotion
> And the response
> Falls the Shadow

Every fire foreshadows its own ashes; every lover is always partly missing. Thus ever since the romantics (if not since Plato) successive critical
schools have gathered around one version or another of a poetics of want:
the incommensurability of Nature and Art or Nature and Mind, the en-
croachment of nothingness on being, the impossibility of communication, the frustration of the primal power of imagination by the belated-
ness of influence, the secret buried life. Modern literary theorists cherish
a sense of abandonment so much that they have inevitably identified the
poet's surrogate in the *Aeneid* as Dido, or as Satan (God's jilted lover) in
Paradise Lost. Only when presence dissolves into absence can the work of
the poet begin.

Some theorists might go further and locate the figure of the abandoned
woman in the figures of language itself. According to a deconstructionist
or poststructuralist line of thought, the ultimate pathos stems from our
necessary but often crippling delusion that words refer to something outside themselves: some external reality, some intention or human agent,
some act of speech, or even some determinate meaning. Hence we feel
that the substance of language is always *somewhere else*. But in fact that
substance is always already there. Whatever meanings we attribute to
written words, whatever contortions and recombinations we force them
to undergo in the effort to tease out significance, were already planted in
the letters with which we began, mere specks of ink except for the system
of differences that holds them together. The system outlives its users, as
love survives long after the lover has gone. We cannot bring our words
back. Hence the Paradise of an absolute unambiguous signification is always already lost. Like Rasselas in the Happy Valley, the deconstructionist perceives that Paradise itself has no meaning in the absence of something to which to compare it. Paradise hinges on Hell or the world
experienced by ordinary people; without the system of alternatives it
would be nothing. Only the play of differences abides. And like Rasselas,
the deconstructionist takes solace from this awareness of the meaning-

lessness and futility of human choices of life only by feeling "some complacence in his own perspicacity."

To phrase the matter more imperially: the goddess of deconstruction is an abandoned woman. Like Zarathustra (if not Nietzsche and others who speak his language) she counts herself both dissociated from humanity and shameless—beyond man, beyond God, beyond the pleasure principle, beyond good and evil. Every presence, for her, marks the place of an absence. Moreover, she spends her life exposing, like a deconstructionist critic, the inner contradictions of every attempt to subjugate language and achieve an unequivocal, harmonious whole. An abandoned woman knows better; the plot could always be told in a different way. Ariadne interrupts the wedding, Dido reveals the emptiness of empire, Tatiana reduces Onegin to a disconnected scribble, and Emily Dickinson pokes through the holes in Emersonian optimism. They rend and fray the traces on the page. The experience of loss, however devastating, confers a skeptical insight about interpreters who congratulate themselves on feeling one with the author. Abandoned women understand that marriages and meanings are not made in heaven, and that it is always possible to misinterpret the intentions even of those to whom we feel closest. No reading lasts forever. Hence the powerless always retain the right to deny legitimacy to the most powerful reading. Outcasts of the social and linguistic community, abandoned women speak an abrasive language of their own. The loss within them forces out a voice not quite like any man's, and sometimes nearer to a cry than to intelligible speech. But no one who has heard that voice will ever think that poetry can ignore it.

If abandoned women have a special affinity for poetry, however, their demands upon poetry may change its definition. The harmony and regularity of verse, the time-honored conventions that equip it so well for celebrations of the social order, can sound like mockery to those who have been excluded. Male poets who try on a style of abandonment often associate it with wildness and derangement, the distraction of Ophelia or the foul mouth of Crazy Jane. The art of the exercise consists of knowing which rules to break. But female poets have tended to regard their own shows of art with irony and detachment, as so many pretty illusions draped over a corpse. A poetic abandoned woman lacks patience with the seductive Muse or the powers that be. Her skepticism toward authority often extends to the medium she herself employs—"I too dislike it." Hence the verse she writes may urge a stripping away. In the brilliant sonnet in which Sor Juana Inés de la Cruz "tries to refute the eulogies inscribed on a portrait of the poetess," her disenchantment includes not only the work of the painter and the eulogist but her own art as well. Closely examined, the colors of rhetoric peel away to reveal the bare

canvas and aging flesh beneath—"corpse and dust, shadow and nothingness." Nor does she spare the poem. Sor Juana defines her art as the life-
and-death struggle of truth with illusion, the constant, exhausting strain
on language to correct the fallacies that its own ingenuity has created. It
is no accident that her best translator is Samuel Beckett.

Not every poet of abandonment is so unsparing. In the absence (real
or imagined) of the beloved, the discipline of art may become a consolation, an obsession, or the instrument of a new, fulfilling kind of passion.
Sometimes poetic rules can serve to build a fortress against an empty,
inchoate world. But more typically poems of abandoned women tend to
embody the emptiness within them, putting conventions of verse and
language on trial. The tensions between proprieties of form and the
woman's anguished, impatient cry force the poem to be self-conscious
about its means of expression. Abandoned art tests art itself. Its authors
are always searching for some way to break through the form and reveal
a pure, unmediated surge of feeling. They cannot succeed, of course.
Only art can provide the means to intensify art, only a master of verse
can persuade a reader that verse has effaced itself. Yet a sense of the inadequacy of poetry may be necessary if poetry is to be renewed. Abandoned women demand that words do more than words can do. In this
respect they manifest the insatiable desire of every good poet.

Certainly no one could accuse Li Ch'ing-chao (1083?–ca. 1151), China's foremost woman poet, of rebelling against art. A highly cultivated
woman, wellborn, capable of assembling (with her husband) one of the
best collections of her time—paintings, calligraphy, inscriptions in
bronze and stone—she took a fierce pride in her skill at versification. A
critical essay on *tz'u,* her favorite genre, ridicules many of the writers
who have failed to master its intricacies. *Tz'u* are "words for singing,"
lyrics composed in strict obedience to the form of a given tune. Hence
the author must fit words to a preexisting grid: a set number of lines
(usually of unequal length) and syllables, a fixed rhyme scheme, a pattern
of tones (the "flats" and "sharps" that characterize Chinese), and a repeated rhythm. In addition, Ch'ing-chao insists on observing the sequence of subtones, moods, and stresses. When we join to this the rich
texture of word associations, images, and allusions to earlier works that
every traditional Chinese poet must command, not to mention the proprieties and sensitivities of manners and class, it ought to be obvious that
no master of *tz'u* can be scornful of art. Even the "confessional" modes
in which Ch'ing-chao specializes—love songs, poems of parting and
separation, and poems of widowhood—were quite conventional long before her time.

Yet even a crude translation can suggest the extent to which her art

yields to abandonment and her words imply the insufficiency of words.
The verse retards to suit its melody, "Slow Song."

> Search search seek seek
> Chill chill lone lone
> Sad sad grief grief ache ache
>
> A sudden warmth and now the cold,
> this is the restless season.
> Three goblets of light wine, then more
> cannot stand up to gusts of evening wind.
> Wild geese pass over, harrowing my heart,
> though one among them is an old acquaintance.
>
> The ground is heaped with piles of yellow flowers,
> withered, haggard.
> Who cares to pluck them now?
> Waiting by the window
> alone, how will I last until dark?
> The plane tree thickens with fine rain
> at dusk, drop by drop by drop by drop. . . .
> What word can take this in,
> what can I do with "sorrow"?

Each element of the lyric functions both as an "objective" description of
autumn and a "subjective" record of personal feelings. Thus the alterna-
tions of warmth and coldness refer equally to weather and the speaker,
whose emotions allow her no rest; her tipsiness becomes apparent only
through external agents, as if it were the wind that made the goblets
stagger; the migrating geese, traditional messengers who now carry no
message for her, fly overhead as well as through her memory; the wasted
chrysanthemums reflect the one person left to notice them, the aging
woman whose beauty is as faded and unused as theirs; darkness gathers,
the sad tree grows sadder, raindrops fall inside as well as outside. She is
the autumn, autumn is in her. The poet allows no distinction between
nature and consciousness, between a season of the year and of the soul.

The beginning and end of the lyric, however, do not rely only on direct
presentation of the "thing." There words call attention to themselves.
The repeated disyllabic compounds of the opening, especially intense in
Chinese because "their reiterated short vowels and aspirate affricates"
suggest "shivering and clenched teeth," convey a mood so unrelieved
that any specific reference to its cause would violate it. Pain and consciousness feed on each other. Such effects are often called musical, since
they subordinate the descriptive powers of language to its patterns of
sound, and certainly Ch'ing-chao's *tz'u* aspires to music. But repetition

also makes nonsense of language, as when one repeats a word so many times that its meaning dissolves. The close of the poem extends this possibility beyond language. The repetitiousness of natural phenomena—the geese keep flying, the flowers will bloom and fade whether or not anyone wants them, the dusk insists on rehashing itself each day—culminates in the most notorious of repetitions, the dripping water-torture imitated by words (*tien tien ti ti* in Chinese). The poet has come full circle, back to the echo that mechanically represents the monotony of her feelings but can never express what it feels like to feel. The series of images always falls short. One would have had to know the presence—of the lover, the life, chrysanthemums in bloom—to appreciate the meaning of absence. Nature cannot supply such a presence. Neither can words. And the poem ends by noting the futility of words.

The abandoned woman can never complete her poem. Technically, the *tz'u* is not realized or whole without its melody, the music that precedes language and lingers in the air when it has gone. Spiritually, the poem does not exist until it has been recreated in the sensibility of the listener, who can never be sensitive enough to bring every nuance to life. Something—or someone—will always be wanting. That is a sorrow inherent in love and poems, a sorrow made vivid by the insufficiency of the word "sorrow." Abandoned women have no monopoly on this effect, to be sure. As Chinese poets never tire of noting, the beauties of poetry are elusive and intangible as the moon shimmering in the water. Every kind of poetry and every poetic figure must come to terms with what lies beyond them, the limits of what can be expressed. But abandoned women do not have to study a poetics of want; it is want itself that calls them into being. Hence they stand, in almost every culture, for all the inexpressible yearnings that poetry alone can begin to approach. "Search search seek seek . . ." At the heart of language, abandonment uncovers what language leaves out. A lover of language needs this reminder; without a sense of unfulfillment, lovers might grow too fat. The abandoned woman speaks in poetry and scorns the contentment of prose. No wonder that poets love her.

REMEMBERING ARIADNE

She magnifies and ramifies. Perhaps it seems by now that she is everywhere. A record of the oppression of women, an emblem of all oppressed people, the instrument of religious love and yearning, the voice of repressed psychological fears, the archetypal poet and figure of poetry—an abandoned woman meets us wherever we turn. Can we put any limits on her? This chapter began by suggesting that abandoned women represent an implied reproach or subversion of poetic tradition. Having come this far, a reader might suspect that abandoned women *are* poetic tradition, or at least so all-encompassing that no one could over-look them. Yet they *have* been overlooked. However ubiquitous, how-ever important, the figure of the abandoned woman continues to be ig-nored by critics and other authorities. Her role in tradition may even depend on this peculiar status, her capacity for being at once always pres-ent and always outcast. Does all the blame for deserting Ariadne rest on Theseus, who might have installed her as his queen, or is there some quality in Ariadne herself that resists the possibility of a happy ending and public recognition? How far can tradition accommodate a sense of abandonment?

Let us return once more to Catullus's little epic. Critics have always been challenged by its core, the massive presence of Ariadne within the wedding. What is she doing there? Many ingenious explanations have been offered. Catullus was translating some unknown Greek original, or splicing together two or more separate poems, or satisfying the artificial rules of a genre, or simply letting himself be carried away. Scholars who find no better principle of unity than these have tended to consider the poem an artistic failure. But other scholars regard it as Catullus's master-piece, and for them the story of Ariadne interpenetrates with the story of Peleus and Thetis. The most plausible reading concludes that the poet himself identifies with Ariadne (perhaps associating Lesbia with Theseus) and contrasts his own unhappiness ironically with the ideal union of the mythical happy pair. This biographical speculation has much to recom-mend it. But Catullus could not have communicated his personal sense of abandonment so powerfully unless a proper mask had been available to him: Ariadne and all she stood for. The male poet needs an abandoned woman to inhabit. He also needs to understand the sources from which that figure draws her power.

No simple formula can explain the relation of Ariadne's tapestry to the wedding. But two points seem especially important to Catullus. The first is the theme of forgetting. In this version of the story Theseus leaves Ariadne on Naxos not out of conscious malice but because she has slipped his mind. Such absent-mindedness seems truly heroic, and we may have difficulty accepting the crime of ingratitude as unconscious or unintentional. But Catullus is quite explicit; he repeats variations of the word "immemor" again and again. Moreover, Theseus's punishment perfectly fits his crime, since he kills his father by forgetting to hoist the white sail that would announce a safe return. Heroes tend to be forgetful of those they are supposed to love, but abandoned women will not let them forget with impunity. The theme of forgetting comes back at the end of the poem. After the Fates have blessed Peleus and Thetis, the poet sadly concludes that the days of such divine promise have passed forever, because men no longer remember how to pray and the gods have lost interest in mortals. Now it is we who are abandoned. The passion of Ariadne, her reproach to the faithlessness of men who forget, gradually spreads its darkness over the poem.

Thus Catullus uses Ariadne partly to frustrate the ritual of happiness or to mark the suffering that the joy of others can provoke. But she also serves a second purpose. Like some pictures on Attic *kraters,* the tapestry is designed in three scenes: Theseus departing on one side, Ariadne at the center, and on the other side Dionysus (or "Iacchus") arriving. Catullus brings his lengthy interlude to a sudden, violent climax. One moment Ariadne is weeping; the next, "euhoe bacchantes, euhoe!"—here is the god. A ritual orgy invades the poem, accompanied by strident music that thumps and screeches in onomatopoeic verse. Thus Dionysus takes the woman who has fired his love. The formal wedding a bride like Thetis expects, with gifts and solemn songs and catering and high society, is not for the likes of a castaway Ariadne. Yet one might argue that the arrival of Dionysus is just what weddings are about. The ceremony would be hollow without its kernel of passion and frenzy, the wild love-making when the couple unveil and lose themselves. Ariadne is no stranger to this moment. In that respect she represents the wedding within the wedding, shameless, abandoned, and utterly out of control. Her fury and loneliness cry out to Dionysus. Meanwhile the guests are embarrassed. But without that spark the marriage would seem rather tame, and so would the poem.

Apparently epics require abandoned women. Yet Ariadne functions not to speed the plot but to drag against it, to remind and remind and remind us of what is left out. She will not tolerate forgetfulness or stand on ceremony. She will not stop lamenting. And eventually her feelings wind their way through every stitch of the tapestry and the poem. Catullus deepens his story of a happy marriage by taking in a principle of resistance and reproach that finally persuades us that marriage is an occasion for weeping. Much of poetic tradition works in a similar way. If abandoned women were acknowledged, the action would slow to a halt; Peleus and Thetis would never marry and never conceive Achilles. If abandoned women were omitted, the action would never look back; Peleus and Thetis would marry, move to the suburbs, and live happily ever after. But poetic tradition neither acknowledges nor omits abandoned women. Instead it allows them in the back door as uninvited guests. They then try their best to spoil the party, and end by saving it.

Tradition cannot be rid of Ariadne. Dionysus is on her side and she is strong—stronger, according to poets, than any man. Women who write have never tired of her strength. She serves them as a model of the ultimate survivor, a female Crusoe. It is as if abandoned women alone had discovered, through their extremity, how to call up the god that they need. Dionysus appears to those who give themselves wholly and do not count the cost. Hence abandoned women sometimes enter a state in which the primary senses of abandonment—"forsaken" and "shameless"—yield to the older sense of "ecstatic" and "free." Even the lover, at such moments, seems absurd—how can a mortal person compete with the idol of love within the woman's heart? The conversion of the beloved to an inner possession is the obligatory scene of every extended narrative of abandoned women. We shall meet it frequently in the chapters that follow.

Yet what does Dionysus signify? The answer, I think, is clear. When an abandoned woman loves long enough and hard enough, when all her time is spent recreating that love, intensifying it, worshipping it, imagining it more vividly than life, then at last she will conjure up something better than a man. Perhaps it looks like a woman, perhaps like a god. Her vision will not bring comfort. The god who inspires abandoned women is also the god of fertile chaos; he speaks with a wild and savage voice. But Dionysus appeals to the woman's experience. He does not promise her a false security but only a stronger sense of the chaos that rules her life. In her new love she will not cease to be abandoned. Yet she may achieve a sort of immortality (on Naxos, Ariadne and Dionysus were worshipped together). The songs of abandoned women go on forever, until their harshness makes all the sweet chimes of Apollo sound cloying. Catullus cannot do without Ariadne's passion; it echoes on when the wedding has been forgotten. Perhaps we too require that touch of chaos. The time of abandonment has not ended yet.

2 Lord Byron's Secret: The School of Abandonment

Where did you learn all these secrets?

DONNA JULIA'S LETTER

The letter of Donna Julia began as an afterthought. When Byron read parts of canto 1 of *Don Juan* to Shelley in summer and autumn of 1818, the episode of young Juan's "earliest scrape"—the affair of a sixteen-year-old boy with a beautiful, passionate, and unhappily married woman of twenty-three—had ended in comedy: the discovery of Juan in Julia's bed, his naked escape from her husband, "the pleasant scandal" of divorce proceedings, and the rapid departure of the young hero abroad. But Julia was too strong a character to be wasted. By December Byron had thought of another ending, quite different in tone. "Julia was sent into a nunnery, / And there, perhaps, her feelings may be better / Shown in the following copy of her letter." The fate of the woman was no longer to be slurred over. Instead her heart would be entirely exposed to view, in a passage that became one of the famous set-pieces of romantic poetry.

"They tell me 'tis decided; you depart:
    'Tis wise—'tis well, but not the less a pain;
I have no further claim on your young heart,
    Mine was the victim, and would be again;
To love too much has been the only art
    I used;—I write in haste, and if a stain
Be on this sheet, 'tis not what it appears,
My eyeballs burn and throb, but have no tears.

"I loved, I love you, for that love have lost
    State, station, heaven, mankind's, my own esteem,
And yet can not regret what it hath cost,
    So dear is still the memory of that dream;
Yet, if I name my guilt, 'tis not to boast,
    None can deem harshlier of me than I deem:
I trace this scrawl because I cannot rest—
I've nothing to reproach, nor to request.

"Man's love is of his life a thing apart,
    'Tis woman's whole existence; man may range

The court, camp, church, the vessel, and the mart,
  Sword, gown, gain, glory, offer in exchange
Pride, fame, ambition, to fill up his heart,
  And few there are whom these can not estrange;
Man has all these resources, we but one,
To love again, and be again undone.

"My breast has been all weakness, is so yet;
  I struggle, but cannot collect my mind;
My blood still rushes where my spirit's set,
  As roll the waves before the settled wind;
My brain is feminine, nor can forget—
  To all, except your image, madly blind;
As turns the needle trembling to the pole
It ne'er can reach, so turns to you, my soul.

"You will proceed in beauty, and in pride,
  Beloved and loving many; all is o'er
For me on earth, except some years to hide
  My shame and sorrow deep in my heart's core;
These I could bear, but cannot cast aside
  The passion which still rends it as before,
And so farewell—forgive me, love me—No,
That word is idle now—but let it go.

"I have no more to say, but linger still,
  And dare not set my seal upon this sheet,
And yet I may as well the task fulfil,
  My misery can scarce be more complete:
I had not lived till now, could sorrow kill;
  Death flies the wretch who fain the blow would meet,
And I must even survive this last adieu,
And bear with life, to love and pray for you!"

This note was written upon gilt-edged paper
  With a neat crow-quill, rather hard, but new;
Her small white fingers scarce could reach the taper,
  But trembled as magnetic needles do,
And yet she did not let one tear escape her;
  The seal a sunflower; "*Elle vous suit partout,*"
The motto, cut upon a white cornelian;
The wax was superfine, its hue vermilion.

No part of *Don Juan* was more admired on its first appearance. If Donna Julia herself heroically managed not to drop a single tear on her letter, few of her readers seem to have been so strong. Indeed, even readers like Francis Jeffrey, who detested *Don Juan,* acknowledged the letter's power—all the more hateful because of its diabolical beauty. "All

this is merely comic, and a little coarse:—But then the poet chuses to
make this shameless and abandoned woman address to her young gallant,
an epistle breathing the very spirit of warm, devoted, pure and unalter-
able love—thus profaning the holiest language of the heart, and indirectly
associating it with the most hateful and degrading sensuality." Such indignation testifies how deeply Jeffrey had been moved; Byron must have
enjoyed the tribute. But the praise that meant most to him undoubtedly
came from Shelley, who had admired and encouraged the poem so much
from the beginning, and whose letter of 26 May 1820 supplies my theme.
"The love letter, and the account of its being written, is altogether a
masterpiece of portraiture; of human nature laid with the eternal colours
of the feelings of humanity. Where did you learn all these secrets? I should
like to go to school there."

Byron never satisfied Shelley's curiosity. But the question is a good
one, and deserves an answer. Where *did* Byron learn all these secrets? The
matter is worth investigating in some detail; for the answer, I believe, can
tell us a good deal not only about Byron but about some of the best-kept
secrets of poetic tradition.

BYRON'S SCHOOLING AND MADAME DE STAËL

Like most good questions, Shelley's can be answered at least two
ways. First, as with any question about the origin of a poem, the answer
may be given that it comes from earlier poems. Here we can be specific,
for Byron frequently told us where he went to school. The blunt fact is
that he learned the secrets of Donna Julia's letter from Pope, and particularly from the epistle of "Eloisa to Abelard." If Shelley or modern students of romanticism had spent more time reading Pope, they could
hardly have missed the source. "Eloisa to Abelard," the most celebrated
poetic love letter of the eighteenth century, returns to life in Julia's and
Byron's hand. The "shameless and abandoned woman" in her convent,
forever separated from her lover yet still madly blind to everything but
his image; the pathetic revelation of her innermost feelings; the rending
dialectic between passion and constraint, rebellion and obedience,
memory and desire, the lot of man and the lot of woman; the role of
tears; the showy emphasis on the physical appearance of the letter itself;
even verbal echoes like the trembling taper—all come from Pope. Nor
could anything be more natural than such borrowing, for Byron had set
out to evoke a consuming passion, and as he himself wrote, "If you
search for passion, where is it to be found stronger than in the epistle
from Eloisa to Abelard?"

Even the most convincing source study, however, usually runs up
against a familiar problem: there are always more sources than one.
Whether or not they know it, all those poets who have imitated "Lyci-

das" have also been imitating the poets whom Milton imitated, right back to Theocritus (if no further). When Byron went to school to "Eloisa," he was also conning lessons from a whole tradition, including not only such obvious sources as the twelfth-century Heloise or Rousseau's much-admired *New Heloise* but the thousands of letters and poems that lay behind them. And Byron knew that very well. The most extended of his comments on "Eloisa" demonstrates a clear sense of the tradition to which it belongs. "Never was the delicacy of Pope so much shown as in this poem. With the facts and the letters of 'Eloisa' he has done what no other mind but that of the best and purest of poets could have accomplished with such materials. Ovid, Sappho (in the Ode called hers)—all that we have of ancient, all that we have of modern poetry, sinks into nothing compared with him in this production." Is Byron declaring Pope's "Eloisa" the best poem ever written? Even though I rejoice to concur with a better critic than Byron, Samuel Johnson, who called the epistle "one of the most happy productions of human wit," I do not think we have to go quite so far. The choice of names suggests that Byron is thinking of a specific *kind* of poetry, a kind he associates with Ovid and Sappho.

What is that kind? Narrowly defined, it may be identified as the heroic or Ovidian epistle (named after Ovid's *Heroides*): a versified love letter, involving historical persons, which dramatizes the feelings of a woman who has been forsaken by husband or lover. Perhaps the most famous of all such epistles is "Sappho to Phaon." Adapting Sappho's own lyrics, and especially her so-called Second Ode (the subject of my next two chapters), Ovid impersonates a woman's style in order to dissect the anatomy of passion. No one learned that anatomy lesson better than Pope, whose brilliant early translation of "Sappho to Phaon" clearly influenced his later "Eloisa." In this respect, strangely enough, Pope may have been recapitulating history; some medievalists have argued that the original "letters of Eloisa" were a literary invention based primarily on Ovid. At any rate the *Heroides* and their imitations have been celebrated in almost every age but our own. They were probably the most popular classical poetry of the later Middle Ages; spawned many Renaissance best-sellers, including Daniel's "Complaint of Rosamund" and Drayton's *England's Heroicall Epistles;* took a new lease on life in the late seventeenth century, thanks to a complete English translation supervised by Dryden and to the sensationally successful *Letters of a Portuguese Nun* (see chapter 6 below); and with the help of Pope, Rousseau, and other idolators, were still being memorized and bewailed by romantic readers. As recently as 1814, only four years before Julia's letter, even Byron's archenemy Wordsworth had made his own try at naturalizing Ovid in his curious "Laodamia" (see chapter 5). When Byron asserted Pope's superiority to "all that we have of ancient, all that we have of modern poetry," therefore, he knew just what he was saying. The poet in search of passion must find his way through the Ovidian epistle, and there Pope was master.

Beyond the specific genre of the heroic epistle, however, a larger school exists where poets can learn secrets of feeling. It is the School of Abandonment, or what I have already called the poetry of abandoned women. Byron was well acquainted with that school. When he opened the heart of Donna Julia, what he saw there was the residue of many old scripts, the dramas and novels that had fashioned the modern forsaken woman into a type. Any reader of sentiment would have met her likeness before. For this reason, indeed, Donna Julia's letter fails to qualify as a regular heroic epistle, since Julia seems less a historical person than Everywoman—a model of abandoned feeling. Pope's effort to imagine Eloisa in a medieval setting and state of mind is replaced by Byron's effort to free his heroine from every circumstance except her essential feminine nature. Hence the letter contains almost no detail to localize or individualize its author; it could be translated into virtually any time or language. Byron subordinates all else to feeling. He thus associates his abandoned woman with a class of literature that one of his friends had described: "There are some writings, such as the letters of Abélard, works by Pope, *Werther,* the *Portuguese Letters,* etc., and a unique work, *The New Héloïse,* whose chief merit is eloquence of emotion. Though their theme may often be moral, what stands out above everything else in them is the all-powerfulness of the feelings. Such works of fiction are in a class by themselves. In a hundred years we find only one mind, one genius, that can create them." Byron would not have objected to joining that class.

The author who wrote those words was Germaine de Staël (in her *Essay on Fiction*), and Madame de Staël had aided the schooling of Byron. Some of her influence on Julia's letter may have been quite specific. A hostile reviewer, Alaric Watts, charged that much of the third stanza ("Man's love is of man's life a thing apart, / 'Tis woman's whole existence") had been plagiarized from *Corinne;* and though the charge is surely exaggerated, there seems little doubt that Byron had Madame de Staël on his mind. As an alert scholar has noted, the opening of the stanza echoes a sentence from *The Influence of the Passions:* "Love is the story of the life of women; it is an episode in that of men." Who could be more expert on the secrets of a woman's heart, after all, than the woman Byron thought the cleverest he had ever known, "the first female writer of this, perhaps, of any age"? The books of Madame de Staël had revealed the inner workings of feminine passion to any man willing to pay attention; and as Byron liked to complain, even men *not* willing to listen were forced to endure her lectures on the subject in conversation. Byron himself sometimes listened.

He had a personal reason, moreover, to be fascinated with Madame de Staël. She was his "feminine counterpart." As he had created the Byronic Hero, so she had created the Romantic Heroine; and the two have been linked by critics from that time to this. "For literary women," Ellen Moers has argued, "Corinne was the female Childe Harold, and Byron owed something, as he and his contemporaries recognized, to Mme de Staël." Certainly Byron admired *Corinne;* and the glamor attached to his own dark, moody heroes, their isolation, their exotic allure, their pride, and their infallible ability to attract all eyes even while seeming to spurn them, may well owe something to that model of "performing heroin-ism." But in one respect he had not lived up to his model: he had never created a convincing heroine. Even in *Don Juan,* most of the women seem all too obvious projections of male desire and fear—innocent crea-tures for pleasure or bluestockings who deny their own hearts. Hazlitt was not the only critic to perceive this weakness. "Lord Byron makes man after his own image, woman after his own heart; the one is a capri-cious tyrant, the other a yielding slave." The letter of Donna Julia seems almost a calculated response to such reproaches. This time at least, Byron would imagine a superior woman, carried away by passion yet honest and intelligent enough to know herself. For one brief moment Julia is a heroine not to be patronized. And the verbal echoes from Madame de Staël show that Byron knew where to look for such a woman.

In surrendering himself to the mind of a heroine, however, he had also inherited the problems attached to such conceptions. Above all there was the disparity between the strength of the woman and the passivity of her situation. Julia must sit and suffer. Love is her whole existence, and her only resource is to play the victim with one man after another. The fact that these lines originate with a woman, Madame de Staël, rather than a man is hardly likely to console a woman who reads them today. They stick in the craw of anyone who wants to make something of her life. The knowing and dogmatic distinction between the lives of men and women, so often quoted as the acme of conventional sexual wisdom, encourages a helpless fatalism that Julia's own actions—or lack of them—confirm. Such heroines merely teach women to stay in their place. I shall return to these lines. For the moment, it may be sufficient to point out that Byron himself was aware of the dangers. He once de-scribed to Lady Blessington a conversation in which he and Madame de Staël accused each other's works of immorality—to the outrage of the lady, on his account, and to his own amusement. His central point at least deserves consideration: "how dangerous it was to inculcate the belief that genius, talent, acquirements, and accomplishments, such as Corinne was represented to possess, could not preserve a woman from becoming a victim to an unrequited passion, and that reason, absence, and female pride were unavailing." The same accusation might be levelled, of course, at Donna Julia. What use is heroism if the fate of every heroine is to be abandoned?

Rather unfairly, Byron does not record Madame de Staël's side of the argument. But fortunately we need not speculate about her line of defense, for she was quite capable of speaking for herself. The first major literary critic of her sex, and not coincidentally the first critic of either sex to write intelligently about abandonment, she often expressed her opinions about literary morality and the modern heroine. The unique contribution of modern writing, she maintained in her important work *On Literature* (1800), was precisely its ability to capture the feminine passions. The ancients, despite their accomplishments, had not understood the quality of love or women: "sorrow, tender and lasting grief, was not in their nature; it is in the hearts of women that enduring memories dwell. I shall often have the occasion to note the changes wrought in literature since the time women began to share the intellectual and emotional life of men." Since the essence of literature is its "capacity to affect us emotionally," stirring the mind with eloquence until virtue "becomes an involuntary impulse, a movement that courses through one's blood, and sweeps one along irresistibly like the most powerful passions," the superior discrimination of women in matters of feeling gives them a natural advantage in perceiving literary *nuances*. "A vague and profound sensibility is one of the greatest beauties of some modern works. And women, knowing nothing of life but the capacity to love, have transmitted their tenderness to the style of some writers." Moreover, works of such delicate sensibility could never produce an immoral effect, because "genuine feelings" always elevate the character. "Human nature is serious, and in the silence of thought one seeks only works of reason or sensitivity. It is in this *genre* alone that literary renown has been won and in which its true influence can be recognized." *Corinne* could not be immoral. Like all great works, it had revealed "what is most heroic in devotion and most moving in sacrifice. To study the art of stirring men"—and women—"is to probe the secrets of virtue."

Those secrets were not Byron's study. Nothing irritated him more than women who spoke of their virtue, especially when they confused it with their feelings. Indeed, *Don Juan* was inherently opposed to such fine feminine professions. According to Byron, he stopped writing the poem precisely because the woman in his life, Teresa Guiccioli, could not stand his assault on everything women held dear: "it arises from the wish of all women to exalt the *sentiment* of the passions—& to keep up the illusion which is their empire.—Now D.J. strips off this illusion—& laughs at that & most other things.—I never knew a woman who did not protect *Rousseau*"—or did not hate *Juan*. Even the name of Julia is probably intended as a sly thrust at "the cant of sentiment." By associating his heroine with Rousseau's Julie, the high priestess of sentiment, and by filling her thoughts with high aspirations to virtue, Byron calls attention to the real situation underneath the "vague and profound sensibility" of *The New Heloise*. Julia is another name for an adultress. And though Byron admired the novels of Rousseau and Madame de Staël, he also relished a more ancient sort of writing, less vague and less profound. *Don Juan* would make fun of women.

Except in one instance. On the surface, at least, Donna Julia's letter adopts the style of Rousseau and the aesthetic of Madame de Staël. It seeks to move the reader through an acknowledgment of love so unqualified and a devotion so resolute that they scorn disguises. The frank passion of the woman acquires a positive moral force; no man could be capable of such sacrifice. In context, moreover, the letter seems still more striking. No passage in the first canto, with its mockery of literary and female pretensions, has prepared us for such literary and female eloquence. Up till this moment Donna Julia has been most notable for deceiving her husband and herself, adept at the double-talk that never calls anything by its right name ("And whispering 'I will ne'er consent'—consented"). *Così fan tutte*. Yet abruptly she and the poem change. The Julia who once canted about "Platonic love" now names her love and guilt directly; the Julia of wiles and humbug now persuades us that she has a soul. Moreover, the woman can write. Despite the earlier statement that "not a line had Julia ever penned" (unlike the scribbling Donna Inez), the letter reveals a master author. Julia's education in feeling has made her eloquent, as Madame de Staël would have predicted. A woman requires no other art than "to love too much." And if we object that Julia has already used many other arts, and that even her letter is artful, the fact remains that most readers have been astonished by its truth to life. "Everything eloquent is true," according to Madame de Staël, and the letter belongs to that select company of works (like *Julie*) that seem to see straight into the heart—without vanity, without illusion.

Thus Byron had learned from literature the secret of writing as if literature did not exist. The passions of abandoned women held the key. The force of such poetry, I have already argued, depends partly on its claim to stand outside convention, shamelessly subverting all the pieties of normal, complacent people. Abandoned women care nothing for art or decorum. Byron enjoyed pretending that he did not either. And Donna Julia's letter erupts into the artificial social comedy of the narrative like a spot of blood on the page. The sincerity of her despair allows no consolation. She understands that her time is over, that the plot will quickly move on. How much room can be given to a single abandoned woman, after all, in a story about Don Juan? Yet just that sort of knowledge makes her real. In her last moment on stage she vies with her own author and compels him to see the situation from a woman's point of view. The hero pursues his illusions; the woman sees through them. Her letter sealed, Julia steps out of literature forever. She is condemned to life.

Even this effect, of course, might be called an illusion. Literature cannot abrogate literature, and the poetic abandoned heroine is no less an artificial creation than is the wandering hero. Byron has made them both. Yet the poetry of abandoned women has always traced a fine line between art and life. The heroic epistle, for instance, does not describe the heroine or narrate her story. Instead it purports to give us her own words in her own hand, a relic or artifact of history rather than a work of art. For this reason, presumably, the heroine must be a historical figure, someone who actually existed and might have written this actual letter. Only the versification is false to life. Significantly, heroic epistles in prose, like the letters of Heloise or the Portuguese nun, have often been taken (or mistaken) for authentic historical documents rather than products of art. Fictitious love letters look just like facts. And a similar dissolving of the borders between art and life accounts for much epistolary technique. Donna Julia's repeated reference to the "sheet" on which she traces "this scrawl," for example, serves to remind us of the near-identity between the page she writes and the page we read. She even reads along with us: the word "love" is no sooner put down than viewed as "idle" and semi-retracted. But nothing creates the illusion of reality more strongly than our sense that the letter is not intended for our eyes. Reading another's mail is impolite; we look at it guiltily over her shoulder. The effect seems unusually intimate. Most literature, by comparison, keeps a proper distance. Abandoned women tend to violate that distance between author and reader or art and life, and draw us into a shameless complicity with their affairs.

It was just such a complicity, Madame de Staël thought, that lay behind the ultimate triumphs of fiction and the new romanticism. For the special province of the best modern literature was exactly to bring the author and reader together in a paradoxical sharing of solitude. The abandoned woman, in her aloneness, persuades the rest of us that we are not alone. No works could ever mean more to feeling readers. "Let these passionate and sensitive souls enjoy such works—they cannot make themselves heard. The feelings that move them are hardly understood. Ceaselessly condemned, they might believe themselves alone in the world and might soon come to abhor their own character that isolates them from others, did not some impassioned and melancholy works enable them to hear a voice in the desert of life and to find in solitude some rays of happiness that elude them in society. This pleasure in withdrawal gives them peace from the vain efforts of disappointed hope." Here was the final lesson of the School of Abandonment: the sensitive all feel abandoned. Corinne and Donna Julia suffer from nothing other than the human condition, and by feeling at one with them the reader and author can share a communion. The act of reading itself consoles the spirit, on this analysis, through demonstrating how much sympathy can quicken moments of solitude and withdrawal. Hence the poetry of abandonment helps to cure the very isolation that it represents. The secret is fellow feeling. Byron speaks for the soul of Donna Julia; and Julia speaks for the soul of each of us.

INSIDE JULIA

But how does a man—especially a proud and selfish man like Byron—learn to feel like a woman? Does it not require a heroic labor of self-effacement, of self-abnegation? In fact it does not. In practice, many male poets have been able to impersonate abandoned women very credibly. And here I touch on Byron's second secret. He did not have to go to school to Pope to study passion, or to Madame de Staël to study the heart. He found much better examples nearer home. If literature had given him the means to express the torments of women, the insight had come from life. Nor did he need to consult women themselves to discover their innermost feelings. His own interior was quite mysterious enough. To put the matter crudely: the secret of Lord Byron's ability to feel like Donna Julia is that in every important respect he *was* Donna Julia. That is a second answer to Shelley's question. Byron simply looked into himself. He learned all those secrets by going to school to his past.

The particular moment he required from the past was the time of his own first love. Juan, the hero of love, deserves a sweet initiation. And Byron loads on the sweetness, with six stanzas that enumerate all the sweet things of life (in a parody of stanzas 72–74 of Smart's *Song to David*) while Juan enjoys Julia discreetly off stage. The climax is saved for original carnal knowledge.

> Dear is the helpless creature we defend
> Against the world; and dear the schoolboy spot
> We ne'er forget, though there we are forgot.
>
> But sweeter still than this, than these, than all,
>   Is first and passionate love—it stands alone,
> Like Adam's recollection of his fall.

The choice of examples makes clear that the author remembers his first love with some misgivings. However passionate the savor, it is associated in retrospect with betrayal ("there we are forgot") and a fall. "The tree of knowledge has been pluck'd—all's known— / And life yields nothing further. . . ." The weary poet looks back on his younger self indulgently but with a touch of rue. Somehow the sweetness of first love has left a bitter aftertaste.

The moment that Byron was remembering can be dated with some confidence, as it happens. Though he had already formed several childish attachments to girls, his first "official" passion for a woman belongs to the summer of 1803. "Those were days of romance! She was the *beau idéal* of all that my youthful fancy could paint of beautiful; and I have taken all my fables about the celestial nature of women from the perfection my imagination created in her—I say created, for I found her, like the rest of the sex, any thing but angelic." Mary Chaworth did not return his ardor. An older woman of seventeen to his fifteen, she flirted with him, laughed at him, kept him from returning to Harrow, and finally rejected him (according to Byron's own story, one night he overheard her telling her maid, "Do you think I could care any thing for that lame boy?"). But she also performed one service for him that changed his life: she inspired him to write verses. "I never wrote any thing worth mentioning till I was in love," Byron told Thomas Medwin, and Mary Chaworth had played Beatrice to his Dante. First love and first poetry were one and the same.

Poetry was also working its mischief in that summer of 1803. Byron read one book of juvenile love poems over and over, that year, until he knew it by heart: the so-called *Poetical Works of the Late Thomas Little*. As he later complained to the author, his friend Thomas Moore, "Heigho! I believe all the mischief I have ever done, or sung, has been owing to that confounded book of yours." Obviously the poems had stirred the fifteen-year-old would-be lover not only with sexual yearnings but with a whole romantic vocabulary through which to perceive them.

> Oh! while this heart delirious took
>   Sweet poison from her thrilling eye,
> Thus would she pout, and lisp, and look,
>   And I would hear, and gaze, and sigh!

The lady who inspires such instructive sentiments in "Little" bears a familiar name: Julia. Not only the object of love but the author of some verses herself, this Julia has just that insipid perfection that young men crave; and she also poses prettily for a scene of farewell.

> But must we, must we part indeed?
>   Is all our dream of rapture over?
> And does not Julia's bosom bleed
>   To leave so dear, so fond a lover?

The point need not be belabored. "Little" is not Byron, nor is Julia Donna Julia. Yet fifteen years later, when the poet sought to recapture the thrill of adolescent love and the misery of parting, he did not have to

read Pope or Madame de Staël. Very inferior verses had already done his
business. He still knew the feelings and even the phrases by heart.

> Once more my sweet Girl, Adieu!
>   Farewell, I with anguish repeat,
> For ever I'll think upon you,
>   While the Heart in my bosom shall beat.

His heart took a long time to heal. The mixture of love and treacly
verse first compounded in 1803 was stirred up again five years later,
when the twenty-year-old poet met Mary Chaworth-Musters with her
little daughter and highly unsatisfactory husband. Byron was surprised
to find that time and pride had not "quench'd at length my boyish
flame." Even his verse suffered a relapse.

> 'Twould soothe to take one lingering view,
> And bless thee in my last adieu;
> Yet wish I not those eyes to weep
> For him that wanders o'er the deep;
> His home, his hope, his youth are gone,
> Yet far away he loves but one.

Byron's satisfaction in saying an anguished farewell, not only to Mary
but to anyone else who catches his fancy, can hardly be overestimated.
His adieus to Mrs. Musters echo throughout his early work, particularly
the beginning of *Childe Harold*. All these may be regarded as dry runs for
Donna Julia's letter. Yet Donna Julia is not *that* sentimental. By the time
Byron cast himself as an abandoned woman, he had grown up. His crush
on Mary Chaworth had eventually been cured, in fact, when in 1814,
separated from her husband, she made overtures that much alarmed the
poet. The last thing he wanted was to allow an actual, faded woman to
interfere with the bright poetry of his memories. He ran for his life.

In a peculiar autobiographical fragment of 1816, "The Dream," Byron
composed the final pages of his romance with Mary Chaworth. Here is
the whole story in a thin poetic veil: his childish infatuation, his rejection,
his eventual disillusionment. The scene of parting deserves a special emphasis, for what it describes is the writing of a letter.

> Within an antique Oratory stood
> The Boy of whom I spake;—he was alone,
> And pale, and pacing to and fro; anon
> He sate him down, and seized a pen, and traced
> Words which I could not guess of; then he lean'd
> His bow'd head on his hands, and shook as 'twere
> With a convulsion—then arose again,
> And with his teeth and quivering hands did tear
> What he had written, but he shed no tears,

And he did calm himself, and fix his brow
Into a kind of quiet. . . .

The lady of his love comes in, but does not understand the "tablet of unutterable thoughts" on his face; they part, perhaps forever. Byron did not finish his letter, in 1804. In 1816 he could not even guess the words. Yet the boy was to have his revenge. The time would come when the lady would finish the letter, and take it, word for word, from his dictation.

For Byron would think of Mary Chaworth once again. Juan's first love is tangled in the bittersweet memories of his author—convulsion, betrayal, and fall. Mary, to be sure, was not Julia; she had not fallen. But neither was Juan Byron. The poet's ironic distance from his hero, which closes only in the later cantos, probably reflects a circumstance that also prevents the rest of us from coming too close: Juan has no flaw. In fiction as in life, physical perfection attracts us more than it engages our sympathies. Not even poets identify with such creatures. Nor can we ignore the mending of reality by which a lame poet gives birth to a perfect boy. This time first love will be different. There is nothing in Juan for the older woman to reject, and naturally she falls. And what could be more natural than that she, in turn, should become the helpless victim of the affair? In Byron's vision of first love, as when it had occurred in his own youth, the parties divide into a winner and a loser. But this time it will be the woman, not the man, who pays the price of longing, and who is condemned to write the letter of farewell.

Yet Byron did not gloat at his revenge. He knew too well that his heart would always sympathize with the loser. *Don Juan* itself insists on this identification. The reference to the cornelian, for instance, should remind us of the poet's sentimental attachments to his own cornelians, the subjects of two early verses. But the decisive evidence that links Donna Julia to her author consists of her motto: *Elle vous suit partout*, "she follows you everywhere." Byron himself owned a seal with this motto. By giving it to Julia, he was also confessing himself her alter ego. And surely the reversal of sexes was extremely elegant. A motto that once might have stood for the haunting of a man—his inability to escape his dream of a lost love wherever he might flee—was converted instantly into a woman's wistful pursuit of an unattainable moving target, her quest as instinctive as the turning of a sunflower toward the sun or a magnetic needle toward the north. Byron combines that woman with that man. In the economy of the motto, *elle* and *vous* are potentially equal losers, unable to escape their fate whether fixed or moving. Indeed, the doubleness of the phrase even testifies to a curious sexual equality. Man and woman, it implies, suffer from the same condition: one hearkens outward, the other yearns back. The only point they cannot attain is to come together. For then there would be no longing, and eventually no passion.

This hint that the sexes share a common predicament may be seen in the letter as well. On the one hand, Donna Julia clearly suggests an absolute distinction between the lives of women and men. "Man may range / The court, camp, church, the vessel, and the mart, / Sword, gown, gain, glory, . . . / Pride, fame, ambition." The life of man, as described here, certainly does teem with incidents and professions, not to mention metonymies and synecdoches. "And few there are whom these can not estrange." Yet the very facility of this list of "resources" may well cause disquiet. They fill man's heart, but do they quench the thirst of his soul? Or do they rather "estrange" him, alienating him not only from unhappy memories but from himself? If man's love is a thing apart from his life, we might infer, so much the worse for man. Condemned to be restless, he realizes his humanity only at those moments when a woman is present to tell him what he feels.

On the other hand, much of the letter seems to work against this separation of the sexes. The feminine heroism practiced by Donna Julia surprisingly resembles that heroism taught on the playing fields of Harrow—not to cry when hurt, not to complain, not to boast, not to be a poor sport or a bad loser. Women have no monopoly on masochism. Surely it is a man rather than a woman who believes that "Death flies the wretch who fain the blow would meet" (the spectacle of a warrior trying desperately but unsuccessfully to die in battle occurs far more often in Byron's imagination, one would guess, than in life). A very subtle critic might suggest that Julia is working on Juan's feelings by couching her feminine ordeal in terms of his masculine experience; her blood rushes before the wind, for example, just as the waves roll from the ship that is bearing him away. But Byron was seldom that subtle. What did he understand, with a fierce and unrelenting clarity, was that every sensitive man, like every sensitive woman, spends a lifetime trying to forget the past—and always in vain. Hence the oft-remarked passivity of his heroes. For all their energy and glamor, Byronic rebels are sentenced to a perpetual scourging by memory, and arrested in the act of saying good-bye. The past enchains them. "What is Poetry?" Byron once asked his diary, and responded to his own question: "The feeling of a Former world and Future." By this standard both Julia and her creator, like most men and women, deserve the name of poet. Neither can live in the present.

If men and women are distinct in Julia's letter, therefore, their emotions diverge no more than two sides of a single coin. Both suffer from restlessness and estrangement; both carry a disease past curing. According to Byron's logic of the heart, woman represents man in a pure state, distilled to one memory and one hope. "Man has all these resources, we but one." The line that follows, in Byron's revised manuscript, offers remarkable evidence that he cared much less about what that resource might be than that there should be only *one*. He wrote, in fact, three different lines.

To love again, and be again undone.

To mourn alone the love which has undone.

To lift our fatal love from God to Man.

And in the margin, for the printer's benefit, he left an insouciant note: "Take that which of these three seem to be the best prescription." Woman was the creature with one resource—*which* resource hardly mattered.

As usual, the line chosen was the line that sounded best. Unquestionably "To love again, and be again undone" has a certain ring. Nor need it be disqualified as inappropriate for a lady in a convent; the doors of convents were notoriously capable of revolving for highborn wives. Yet perhaps the alternatives suit an abandoned woman better. They sketch, indeed, the major options of the literary situation. For Julia as for Eloisa, the most acceptable behavior would doubtless be "To lift our fatal love to God from Man." Unfortunately it does not rhyme well. An inability to take the step, to become truly the bride of Christ rather than of some Abelard, Alfonso, or Juan, tightens the screws not only on Pope's Eloisa but on many of her sisters. "One" and "Man" make an uneasy pairing when God comes between them. And a more likely alternative consists of the second choice, "To mourn alone the love which has undone." Most of the poetry of abandoned women points to this one resource. Sequestered in her gloom, the lost soul devotes her life to mourning and hallows her love into an idol. The process requires a good deal of patience from readers as well as authors; women seem more capable than men of such devotion. Yet in the best poems of the kind the undone woman discovers secrets inaccessible to men. The loved one vanishes, the love remains.

Yet Byron tended to choose another line. "To love again, and be again undone" nicely expresses the pattern of his own affairs. With each new woman, as well as some boys, he recreates the unfaithfulness of Mary Chaworth, the sequence of infatuation and betrayal. A love without betrayal would lose much of its savor for him. The repetition compulsion avowed by Donna Julia, in this version, gains more in pathos than it gives away in self-pity. To catch a whiff of future abandonment at the very moment of passion lends an exquisite sadness to love, like the sensation that the spirit we are clutching is swaddled in mortal flesh. Byron had learned that secret early, at the time of his own first love. A connoisseur of abandonment, he shares it with all his lovers. Julia passes her misery on to Juan. In the fatality of loving and being undone, again and again, men and women are indistinguishable.

TEARING THE SEAL

If my argument so far carries any conviction, however, if Byron knew Donna Julia's feelings because they were his own, the question remains: why did he add that final descriptive stanza? Does it not subvert all Julia's pathos, warning the reader not to be too absorbed? To this last question one of Byron's best editors, T. G. Steffan, and one of his best critics, George Ridenour, join in a resounding yes. "Is there not at the end some penetrating laughter at the delicate postures of sentiment in the little ironies about the 'gilt-edged paper' and 'neat little crow-quill,' her sunflower seal of 'superfine' vermillion wax, with its motto 'cut upon a white cornelian'—*Elle vous suit partout*'?" And Ridenour comments that Steffan "is, of course, perfectly right in seeing irony here. It is not savage irony, to be sure. The tone is one of quiet, almost tender mockery. But Julia is not permitted to be merely pathetic. The rather indulgent self-pity of the letter itself and the elegance of its appearance suggest that Julia is well aware of the dramatic possibilities of her situation and is determined to play the part to the hilt. One hardly blames her very much, but one is not taken in." Indeed, he goes further: the letter represents nothing less than the final stage in "the decline and fall of Donna Julia."

Since I have already expressed respect for both these scholars, it is with some trepidation, but great firmness, that I offer a contrary opinion: both of them are perfectly wrong. The coda to the letter does not falsify Julia's statements, it confirms them. She says that she will not cry, and she does not. She says that her soul trembles like a magnetic needle, and her fingers unconsciously verify it. To be sure, her *situation* is dramatic, and *Byron* plays it to the hilt, but she herself does not indulge in theatrics. What good would they do her? Everything she says is true. She does not expect to see Juan ever again, she has no way of calling him back, and in fact he will not come. She is left with the truth of abandonment, and she accepts it. Far from being the moment of Donna Julia's "fall," this is her finest hour.

Why then the elegant details—the gilt-edged paper and the superfine wax? A complete answer to this question would take us far afield. First, one might point to the aesthetic need for establishing some distance between the passion of the letter and the flippancy of the sequel; not even Byron is cavalier enough to break in immediately with "This was Don Juan's earliest scrape." Next, a historical explanation might emphasize how much contemporary readers, brought up on Richardson, Rousseau, or Sterne, liked to be given the means of *visualizing* sentiment—projecting themselves into the scene. Clarissa was not allowed to die without particularizing every writing implement and piece of furniture, and Donna Julia's feelings deserve a similar graphic record. Nor should we think ourselves superior to this effect. If Georgian readers were not more sophisticated than we, they certainly surpassed us in the ability to construct and respond to mental pictures. Byron saw more than we do.

The crucial point, however, is surely a matter of disparities: the disjunction between words in the heart and words as they look on the page; between the act of writing and its effect; between the gesture of sealing a letter and the finality of sealing a life. Reality itself derides our feelings. Byron was painfully sensitive to such disjunctions. His poems return obsessively to the ultimate mixed metaphor of spirit and clay, the mismatched companions who are bound together to death (as a spirited man may walk through life in shackles). The body is the prison of the soul. Hence the distance between the sentiment of Donna Julia's letter and its physical appearance strikes us as absurd because it represents the indifference of paper to the hand that writes upon it—an absurdity neither greater nor less than the physical facts of human existence.

With the full recognition of this absurdity behind it, the final line of the passage appears one of the most delicate in all Byron's work. First, for the undiscerning, it presents merely an irrelevant detail, ironic because of the commercial coloring of "superfine" and, perhaps, the very faint hint in "vermilion" that Julia will remain a scarlet woman in the eyes of the world. The power of this reading depends on the way that the author deliberately averts his gaze from the sufferings of his alter ego. But another reading is also possible. In the cold and deadly appearance of the seal an observer might just perceive a tiny flush, vermilion on white, like the semitransparent rush of blood in the cheeks of a very fine woman. One sees such chilling faces in a wax museum. This effect can be no more than an optical illusion, of course; a letter is not a person. But that is precisely the point. The nearest approach of a sympathetic reader to the sufferings of another human being still falls far short. The hearts of others are sealed from us; we glimpse no more than a portion of the envelope. All Donna Julia's eloquence, therefore, serves only to remind us of the limits of communication. She remains alone. Time and the sea carry Juan away, and the reader will turn the page.

As a man or woman survives the death of his or her ideals, however, so a letter can survive the breaking of its seal or the heart of the person who sends it. Julia's letter outlasts Julia. In the second canto of *Don Juan,* in fact, it dwindles to a heartless stage prop. First it is pressed into service to show the tyranny of the body over the mind. Juan's devout rereading of the letter on shipboard is interrupted by a higher power than love: mal de mer. The scene is pure low comedy: "'Beloved Julia, hear me still beseeching!' / (Here he grew inarticulate with reaching.)" But a still more grisly fate awaits the letter. Fifty stanzas later, the ship has wrecked and the survivors are dying of hunger: "The longings of the cannibal arise / (Although they spoke not) in their wolfish eyes." They resolve to draw lots,

> But of materials that much shock the Muse—
> Having no paper, for the want of better,
> They took by force from Juan Julia's letter.

The letter is torn into strips, the lot falls on Juan's tutor Pedrillo (did he choose the scrap with "I had not lived till now, could sorrow kill"?), and the feast commences. So ends the story of the letter.

The earliest readers of this passage could hardly stand it. Thus Jeffrey comments that Byron seems purposely to show "how possible it is to have all fine and noble feelings, or their appearance, for a moment, and yet retain no particle of respect for them—or of belief in their intrinsic worth or permanent reality." Just so. And even Shelley, after his praise for Byron's knowledge of the heart, goes on: "I cannot say I equally approved of the service to which this letter was appropriated; or that I altogether think the bitter mockery of our common nature, of which this is one of the expressions, quite worthy of your genius." These critics were not misreading. Byron persecutes the body of the letter with a thoroughness that must be related to his own temptation by its "fine and noble feelings." An ideal cannot live in this world. So Byron knows, and so Juan must be forced to learn. Even the finest letter is cased in a frail shell of paper; even the noblest abandoned woman must quickly be cast aside.

MAN'S VERY SYMPATHY

Yet the swiftness of Byron's vengeance—on his own ideals as well as Julia's—may well raise doubts not only about his sympathies but about the whole poetic school of abandoned women. Are men to be trusted on such subjects? Do they really have the patience and understanding to enter the feelings of women without violating them or exploiting them? Once again Byron has left an acute observation.

> But as to women, who can penetrate
>   The real sufferings of their she condition?
> Man's very sympathy with their estate
>   Has much of selfishness and more suspicion.

Lord Byron's secret, I have argued, is that Donna Julia was himself. A similar secret informs almost all the best works of the kind. Catullus's secret is that he is Ariadne; Pope's, that he is Eloisa ("He best can paint 'em, who shall feel 'em most"); Swinburne's, that he is Sappho; Madame

Bovary, *c'est* Flaubert; and the secret of the *Duino Elegies* is that Rilke is all the abandoned women who ever lived. But the monotony of this repeated secret may warn us how much selfishness goes into the sympathy. When male poets imitate female voices and female hearts, they always turn out to be thinking about themselves.

A still darker suspicion may intrude. Perhaps the reason that a poet like Byron lavishes so many of his own traits on a woman like Julia is that he wants to cut them out of himself. The letter performs an exorcism. It gathers a heap of faded memories, some scraps of adolescent writing, an old cornelian, a few favorite quotations, an attitude, a motto, in order to dismiss them as "womanish." The man shows his superiority to feminine weakness and sentiment. Certainly Byron himself held consciously to a double standard. "A woman without sentiment is not a woman," he declared. "I should hate a woman who could laugh at or ridicule sentiment." But that only confirmed his own right to laugh at sentiment wherever he found it. How better to prove he was manly? By first imagining and then rejecting Julia, he dominates the woman in his own heart.

He was also getting Juan out of a scrape. The "scrape" that the poem refers to may involve Alfonso's revenge, but perhaps it stands more directly for Julia's love. Don Juan cannot afford to be entangled. Many versions of the legend stress that seduction can be easier than extrication. Nor can a contemporary audience mistake the aspect of sexual anxiety and hostility in the Juan legend—specifically men's fear of women. Even today, in our own liberated age, a mature beautiful strong outspoken passionate lonely woman seems more than most men want to handle. Her very virtues suggest how hard she will be to satisfy and how much she will demand. Not even Don Giovanni is sexually confident enough to tarry with Donna Anna or Donna Elvira. As Byron himself puts the matter, with a characteristically knowing air,

> Alas! the love of women! it is known
>   To be a lovely and a fearful thing;
> For all of theirs upon that die is thrown,
>   And if 'tis lost, life hath no more to bring
> To them but mockeries of the past alone,
>   And their revenge is as the tiger's spring,
> Deadly, and quick, and crushing; yet, as real
> Torture is theirs, what they inflict they feel.

And he is also enough of a gentleman to place the blame squarely where it belongs: "They are right; for man, to man so oft unjust, / Is always so to women."

In short, men are not to be trusted. Even the man who goes to school to abandoned women may be nursing an ulterior motive: to spy out their secrets. Byron had no illusion about his motives. Fear, injustice, and even contempt had defined his relations with women. Insofar as he had ever succeeded in evoking the opposite sex, he told Lady Blessington, it was only because he had temporarily put aside the corruptions of his maturity and remembered what it was like to be young and pure. "To describe woman, the pen should be dipped, not in the rainbow, but in the heart of man, ere more than eighteen summers have passed over his head; and, to dry the paper, I would allow only the sighs of adolescence." He had followed that formula exactly with Julia's letter, echoing the letter and the spirit of his own fifteenth summer. That was Byron's cleverest secret. Shelley, in asking his question, had doubtless meant to pay tribute to his friend's worldliness and knowledge of manners, but the true answer was unexpectedly simple: men learn to impersonate women by forgetting the hardness of heart that experience brings. Julia was a more innocent Byron. If a man is not to be trusted, a woman can sometimes remind him of his better self. Adam needed Eve to teach him that love can survive a fall.

Yet Julia's letter conveys another secret of which Byron may have been unaware. Women are not so innocent. The complexity of emotion in the letter, the intelligence that it brings to bear on what might have remained a rhetorical exercise, give the lie to the conventional assignment of sex roles to which Byron himself subscribed. Julia has strength of character. The poets who have schooled her, from Sappho to Madame de Staël, have taught her to express her emotions with a clarity that Juan himself never equals, and Byron seldom (certainly not in his early untutored Farewells). Abandoned women can speak with a force above men's. That is not to deny that Byron is the author (a characteristic glibness in the versification, for instance, especially in the facile alliterations, clearly displays his hand). But something else had also authored the lines: the school of abandonment whose power had descended through so many poets. Byron had touched on secrets beyond his knowing. And what he passed on, through Julia, was more than an innocent version of himself. He had helped to invent, as it happens, the modern woman.

PUSHKIN AND BYRON'S SECRET

The plausibility of this assertion, if not its indisputable proof, can be established by tracing a specific line of influence. The trail winds through Pushkin. The role of *Don Juan* in inspiring *Eugene Onegin*, the great fountainhead of modern Russian literature, is a commonplace of literary history—though like other commonplaces it is open to doubt. Pushkin himself changed his mind. His first announcements claimed that *Onegin* "is in the genre of *Don Juan*," but later, offended at being called a satirist, he went so far as to insist that *Juan* "has nothing in common with *Onegin*." The truth, as we might expect, lies somewhere between; the two poems are related by antithesis as well as similarity. But Pushkin's most interesting comment on the relation is this one: "if one really must compare *Onegin* with *Don Juan* it should be done in one respect only: who is more winsome and more charming, *gracieuse,* Tatiana or Julia?" This injunction may be thought self-serving, since the Russian surely wins this particular competition. Yet the comparison also points to a central artistic problem: Pushkin's attempt to conceive a heroine (as well as a hero) who would incorporate and surpass the best that Byron had to offer. Julie and Julia stand behind Tatiana. That was the school where Pushkin learned his secrets.

The School of Abandonment, in fact, provides a major thread of *Eugene Onegin*. Pushkin brilliantly works his criticism of the tradition into the poem itself. Consider Tatiana roaming and reading in the woods, "Dreaming herself the heroine / of her beloved novelists— / Clarissa, Julie, or Delphine" (Madame de Staël's epistolary novel of abandonment):

> She sighs, and having made her own
> another's anguish or romance,
> by heart she whispers in a trance
> a letter to the leading man.

Even before becoming an abandoned woman, the heroine preps for the role. Donna Julia does not enter her imaginings, if only because at this precise moment (midsummer of 1820, in fictional time) the text of *Don Juan* was not yet available in Russia. But obviously Tatiana is ready to *be* Donna Julia. Pushkin cannot protect her from her reading matter. "Tatiana, dear Tatiana! Now / I weep with you. It is too late. / A fashionable tyrant's hands / now hold, with your consent, your fate."

The "fashionable tyrant" here is Eugene Onegin. But Byron himself would serve quite well in his stead. Indeed, distinguishing the two is not always easy. That is what Tatiana herself discovers in the magnificent scene of chapter 7, when she spies out Onegin's soul by poring through the very few books he has left in his library. *Don Juan* is there now (in June 1821), and its margins have been well marked. Gradually Tatiana understands with whom she has fallen in love.

> This angel, this high-flying fiend,
> who is he? Can he be a fake,
> a phantom substanceless as smoke,
> a Muscovite in Harold's cloak,
> a gloss on others' fads and freaks,
> a lexicon of slang? Maybe . . .
> or just, in fact, a parody?

Onegin is nothing but a secondhand Byron. And Tatiana, though still in love, now begins to suspect what many readers of Julia's letter must always have guessed: the man to whom she has sacrificed herself is not worthy of her love. Lord Byron's secret consists of emptiness and the exploitation of women. What place did Onegin's pencil mark? We do not know; but few men of his type could have resisted "Man's love is of his life a thing apart."

Yet the irony goes deeper still. Pushkin's criticism or deconstruction of Byron's abandoned mode extends even to the structure of *Onegin*. Unlike the sprawling *Juan*, the Russian poem has an elegant shape. It has been described schematically by the formalist critic Viktor Shklovsky: "Tatyana falls in love with Onegin and nothing comes of it. Then he falls in love with her and nothing comes of that. End of novel." What might be added is that the symmetry of emotion corresponds to an exact duplication of forms: the two love letters. The whole plot suspends between Tatiana's letter to Onegin (3:31) and Onegin's to Tatiana (8:32). Once his letter has been read, indeed, the work has nowhere else to go and ends. It is as if Pushkin had consciously decided to found his poem on Donna Julia's letter, dividing it among the two principal characters and allowing each of them to express their fullest passions only there. The episodes do not matter. *Eugene Onegin* revokes the structure of *Don Juan*, its endless adventures and distractions, and compresses the abundant, picaresque landscape into the space between two epistles. Nothing matters except the lonely heart. Onegin, unlike Juan, cannot escape from his "scrape." She follows him everywhere.

Pushkin pursues Julia's letter to each of its secrets. Tatiana (as well as her author) is acquainted with Sappho, Ovid, and Madame de Staël. Most of all, she faithfully quotes *Julie,* and her hesitation to seal the letter is borrowed, as Nabokov notes, from Julia herself. Even the Gallicism of the epistle—Pushkin claims to be translating it from the original in French—may be associated with *Juan,* since Pushkin read that too in a French translation. Onegin is less familiar with the secrets of abandoned women. Yet his letter also fulfills its place in the tradition: Pushkin adopts both phrases and the tone from Saint-Preux's correspondence with Julie. Indeed, Eugene may well have profited from his reading of *Juan,* since what he most wishes from Tatiana, in his own phrase, is to "follow you everywhere." He also follows her reading: between the lines of the books intended to distract him, other lines intrude—"secret traditions / of the heart's dark past; / . . . or a young maiden's letters." Pushkin comprehends that his shallow hero has no other way to develop his heart than by imagining the heart of a woman. Moreover, the poet himself shared this secret. Like Byron, Pushkin made both his hero and heroine from parts of himself—Onegin from the man-about-town and Tatiana from the sensitive poetic soul. But more of him went into the woman than into the man. Lord Byron's secrets were second nature to him.

The ultimate secret of *Eugene Onegin,* however, lies well beyond Byron. It is that a whole world can be made from abandonment. Onegin's
first indifference to Tatiana's love, Tatiana's later refusal of Onegin's, are
not incidents in the story but the story itself. Love never arrives in phase.
Hence Julia's letter, as Pushkin reads it, contains more of the truth about
human passion than does all the rest of *Don Juan.* "I loved, I love
you"—the overlapping tenses do not represent a continuity so much as
an inevitable failure of synchronization. We live in the past; it is there we
have missed our chances. And the present moment only confirms the
impossibility of a reciprocal love. An abandoned woman stands for the
whole of humanity. Pushkin grasps this story so firmly that he need not
even consummate the "affair" between the "lovers" before parting them;
the pathos of a fallen or adulterous woman would only distract us from
the unconditional sense of abandonment in every soul. Not even first love
is exempt from feelings of loss. Byron had shown that, despite his effort
to cover the wound with a layer of sentiment. Pushkin peels off the cover.
There, in the innermost heart, each lover recognizes the truth of being
alone and abandoned. Tatiana and Onegin, like Julia, have only one resource: not "to love again, and be again undone," but to love again and
not have love returned.

The Russian novelists all went to school to Pushkin. Behind the great
nineteenth-century heroines—Turgenev's Elena (in *On the Eve*) whose
diary exposes her soul, Dostoevsky's Dunya and Aglaia (whose letter and
its reception bring *The Idiot* to a peak of futility), Tolstoy's Natasha and
Anna Karenina—the figure of Tatiana sparkles and broods like the Eternal Feminine herself. Even the structure of many novels seems made in
the image of *Onegin:* a long preparation for the moment when a passionate heart shockingly reveals its secrets, often through a letter that fails to
induce the wished-for response. Those novelists did not keep their reliance on Pushkin a secret. From Gogol to Nabokov an unbroken stream
of tributes has sprung from *Onegin's* fount. Many male authors have admitted that they learned about women through Tatiana—and so have
many women. The schooling continues. If the spirit of Julia lives again
in Tatiana, the spirit of Tatiana has been renewed in heroine after heroine
all over the world.

Not everyone, to be sure, reads her in the same way. The distance
between Turgenev's "light" *Onegin* and Dostoevsky's anguished Slavic
madonna has been repeated, in the twentieth century, by the critical debate between those (like Shklovsky and Nabokov) who emphasize Pushkin's pervasive irony and those who cannot separate the emotions of the
poem and its characters from life itself. To some extent, we might note,
this debate reproduces the argument about whether Byron enjoys some
irony at Donna Julia's expense; and both arguments have a similar tech-

nical cause. Abandoned women can hardly be judged from outside. Their
isolation removes them from the social world where conventions of morality apply; not even the author intrudes on them at will. Loneliness
follows laws of its own. Hence a necessary mystery often surrounds an
abandoned woman, and when she breaks her silence and reveals her secrets, the author allows her words to stand alone. Both Byron and Pushkin reserve comment on their heroines' letters, as if slightly in awe of
their own creations. (Pushkin insists that his "translation" from the
French is feeble in comparison with the original.) Julia and Tatiana convert all appearances relentlessly to their own points of view. Thus even
the smallest external authorial gesture—the gilt-edged paper, or the che-
mise that slips from Tatiana's charming shoulder—may be seized on as a
clue to meaning. At such a distance, irony and compassion look oddly
the same. The outsider is free to respond according to his own bent. But
things seem different from inside. A few readers, at least, have taken
abandonment so deep into themselves that it has become their own nature. Many of those readers are women.

Marina Tsvetayeva first encountered the "love" of Tatiana and Onegin,
she tells us in "My Pushkin" (1936), at the age of six. She never recovered
from it. "That first love scene of mine foreordained all the ones that followed, all the passion in me for unhappy, non-reciprocal, impossible
love. From that very minute I did not want to be happy and thereby
pronounced the sentence of *non-love* on myself." What Tatiana had communicated to her was the terrible power of abandoning and being abandoned, the lure of self-sacrifice that prevails over love itself. "A lesson of
courage. A lesson of pride. A lesson of fidelity. A lesson of fate. A lesson
of loneliness." Indeed, according to Tsvetayeva that embrace of loneliness, of "the fullness of suffering" over "the emptiness of happiness,"
had presided over her birth, since her own mother had chosen to sacrifice
love to marriage.

> Thus, Tatyana not only had an influence on my whole life, but on
> the very fact of my life: if there had been no Pushkin's Tatyana, I
> would not have come into existence.
> For women read poets *that way* and not otherwise.

If women read the poetry of abandoned women differently from men,
however, not to discover the secrets of the opposite sex but to draw on a
pattern of living, then perhaps a different study is needed for their kind
of understanding. What Byron and Pushkin learned from literary tradition and from projecting their own intense individuality into a female
form, Sappho seems to have been born knowing. Abandonment comes
as no surprise to women. Shelley could have learned its secrets from either of his wives, had he thought to ask them. The sources of Donna

Julia go far back, to the lives in which women have been schooled from ancient times and to the poetry they have made from those lives. Men know those sources only at second hand. " 'Tis woman's whole existence" or, in Madame de Staël's more accurate version, it is "the story of the life of women." That story, if properly told, would take into account not only the transmission of a school of abandonment from women to men to women, but also the misunderstandings and distortions that enter at every stage. Like any secret passed down from person to person, Lord Byron's knowledge of the passions of women had only a distant relation to the original text. But not all the texts have vanished. We still can trace the secret to its source.

The story begins with Sappho.

3 Sappho Descending: Abandonment through the Ages

> *"O Törin! warum stieg ich von den Höhn,*
> *Die Lorbeer krönt, wo Aganippe rauscht,*
> *Mit Sternenklang sich Musenchöre gatten,*
> *Hernieder in das engbegrentze Tal,*
> *Wo Armut herrscht und Treubruch und Verbrechen?*
> *Dort oben war mein Platz, dort an den Wolken."*
> "O fool! why did I climb down from the heights
> That laurel crowns, where Aganippe roars
> And choirs of muses harmonize the stars,
> Down to the depths of this constricting valley
> Where hardship rules and broken faith and crime?
> My place was there above, there in the clouds."

Sappho Ascendant: The Second Ode

Sappho stands on the heights. No other lyric poet since the world began has ever drawn such praise. She is our *perfect* poet: the Tenth Muse, as Plato himself called her, or the idol and nonpareil of John Addington Symonds: "Of all the poets of the world, of all the illustrious artists of all literatures, Sappho is the one whose every word has a peculiar and unmistakable perfume, a seal of absolute perfection and inimitable grace." And Sappho stands alone. Indeed, even in the ancient world that was a part of her function: to keep to herself, slightly off from the others; half priestess and half legend; the only mortal muse among the immortals; and not incidentally, the one great woman poet. "My name is Sappho," according to the epitaph by Antipater of Sidon, "and my songs excel those of women as Maeonides those of men." As Homer was "The Poet," for Aristotle and his contemporaries, so was Sappho "The Poetess," and Aristotle adds that "the people of Mitylene have honored Sappho, although she was a woman."

The "although" may give us pause. Is it possible that all this emphasis on the exceptional quality of Sappho, singling her out, serves only to patronize women by marking the peculiarity of their genius? Yes, it is possible. Horace's ultimate word of praise for Sappho, we may remember, was *mascula* (manlike or strong); and the man-woman inevitably has an air of the freakish. *Roget's Thesaurus* puts the matter with its usual

57

inexorable logic: "exceptional; eccentric, anomalous; non-uniform; homosexual, lesbian, queer; epicene, androgenous, gynandrous; mongrel, hybrid." The Poetess is someone special. An object of both worship and fear, she reminds us of proper bounds through her very act of going beyond them; she joins a masculine power or readiness to make demands with a feminine openness of feeling; she fascinates both sexes; and she warns all women, everywhere and for all time, how much they hazard by trying to rise above their sphere. She is not only a perfect poet, therefore, but a perfect example. If Sappho had not existed it would have been necessary to invent her.

Perhaps she *was* invented. The small collection of verses and fragments that escaped the public burning of her poems, the somewhat larger but thoroughly contradictory muddle of biographical traditions, do not inspire much confidence that the Sappho we know is anything but a fiction. Of the 462 pages in the expansive survey of her career by Édith Mora, a generous estimate might conclude that ten, exclusive of footnotes and quotations, would hold all the hard facts about the actual poet. The title of chapter 2 may epitomize the whole: "Sappho? Sapho? Psappho? Psappha?" Most of us still prefer to call her Sappho. But the magic of the name ought not to delude us into thinking we know what it stands for. Sappho is too perfect to be true, nor does she hold together as a person.

Indeed, each age invents its own Sappho even more surely than its own Homer. Facts do not bar the way. Hence the image of the Poetess, shining and unflawed as a mirror, gives each generation back an image of itself—its idols and fears. More than a poet, or less, she is also a goddess, a source of poetry. That view of Sappho has been implicit from earliest times, in her honorary title of the Tenth Muse: an inspirer as well as a creator. Nor has she been less generous than the other muses in bringing new life to her devotees. A history of lyric poetry could be written by following the ways that later poets have adapted her lines to their own purposes, and a survey of changes in Sappho's reputation could result in a whole history of social attitudes toward ambitious, creative women. Those histories might not be altogether pleasant. Sappho on her heights, divine and unassailable, seems to breathe a rarer, finer air; but Sappho on her long descent into history, where her very name for centuries meant "whore," is no better than the many minds she passed through. Yet we ought to follow her down. The journey leads us through the art of one great poet to the depths where rooted ideas about poetry and gender are tangled together.

We begin with a poem. To focus the investigation, nothing will do but the best: the text once known commonly as the Second Ode and now, in our computer age, as L.P. 31 (after the Lobel-Page edition). "The best" has long been its name. If critics and poets had been polled, through the centuries, to choose the greatest lyric of all time, this one might head the list. Even its survival, in fact, depends on its status as "the best," since the author of *On the Sublime* preserved it exactly to show how sublime a lyric could be. And a multitude of later authors have paid it the frankest of tributes by imitating or stealing its words. It seems almost too high a thing to capture in print. But here is the text as we have it.

φαίνεταί μοι κῆνος ἴcoc θέοιcιν
ἔμμεν' ὤνηρ, ὄττιc ἐνάντιόc τοι
ἰcδάνει καὶ πλάcιον ἆδυ φωνεί-
cαc ὑπακούει

καὶ γελαίcαc ἰμέροεν, τό μ' ἦ μὰν
καρδίαν ἐν cτήθεcιν ἐπτόαιcεν·
ὡc γὰρ ἔc c' ἴδω βρόχε', ὤc με φώναι-
c' οὐδ' ἒν ἔτ' εἴκει,

ἀλλ' ἄκαν μὲν γλῶcca †ἔαγε†, λέπτον
δ' αὔτικα χρῶι πῦρ ὑπαδεδρόμηκεν,
ὀππάτεccι δ' οὐδ' ἒν ὄρημμ', ἐπιρρόμ-
βειcι δ' ἄκουαι,

κὰδ δέ μ' ἴδρωc ψῦχροc ἔχει, τρόμοc δὲ
παῖcαν ἄγρει, χλωροτέρα δὲ ποίαc
ἔμμι, τεθνάκην δ' ὀλίγω 'πιδεύηc
φαίνομαι†

ἀλλὰ πὰν τόλματον, ἐπεὶ †καὶ πένητα

To me he seems an equal of the gods
that man who sits opposed to you
and listens close, hanging on
your sweet voice

and luring laughter that startles
the heart in its cage. For when
I look at you suddenly I have no
power to speak

my tongue falters, a thin
flame runs quickly under my skin
my eyes see nothing, thunder
spins through my ears

cold sweat pours down on me and trembling
rushes over me and greener than
grass and on the brink of dying I
seem to myself

The physical immediacy of these lines is shattering. Passion breaks over the speaker and reader like an invisible wave. Not even a flat translation can spoil the effect. And the music of the Greek has always been thought incomparable (though no one today knows quite how to recite it). But what the poem *means,* or even what it *feels,* continues to mystify critics. To some extent we might say that Sappho's words abide in the category of pure signs, like some ancient language whose Rosetta stone has been lost. Indeed, the comparison would be singularly apt, since the word and concept "sign," as semioticians have lately been reminding us, originally derive from medical symptoms. A sign is related to meaning as a symptom to a disease; both are external manifestations of something that cannot be viewed directly. And the list of symptoms precisely defines Sappho's poem. Most ancient commentators ignore its literary value, in fact, and refer to it as a textbook medical diagnosis of a seizure—the symptoms of love according to Plutarch; according to Lucretius, of fear.

A similar conflict of diagnosis lies behind the main critical debate about the poem: is the poet's excitement kindled primarily by looking at the woman or by imagining herself in the place of the man? "We have to choose, in short," says Denys Page, "whether the emphasis falls on *love of the girl* or on *jealousy of the man;* and there is no certain clue to the correct choice." Page himself does not doubt that jealousy is the answer. In this respect he agrees with a reading of the poem that has long been popular—at least among men. Ever since Catullus, Sappho's ode has been staged as a classic triangle, a playlet with three characters: the girl, the man, and the poet. But the triangle is acutely angled. At the short end the girl and man sit together, intent on each other; and far away, at degree zero, the poet watches and suffers. She is the third party, the unwelcome "member of the wedding" whose presence could only interrupt the other two. This scenario has been adopted by almost everyone. Even though Wilamowitz's notorious theory that Sappho designed the poem to be an epithalamium, recited at a wedding ceremony, has tended to be ridiculed of late (imagine the puzzled reactions of the happy couple!), the majority of critics still accept his direction. The man and the poet are rivals; they compete for a girl. And the emotion of the poem results from its confession that the poet—the woman—has lost.

One current diagnosis of the poet's seizure, in fact, would analyze her symptoms as evidence not of love but of an "anxiety-attack" brought on by her "fear of loss and despair at the impossibility of competing with the man." The intimacy of the couple forces the speaker to recognize her own impotence. She succumbs to "phallic awe," a hopeless envy of the male organ, and lapses into paralysis. The godlike man can never be displaced. Moreover, the guilt and jealousy associated with homosexual desire have communicated their panic to every part of her body. Hysteria reigns like death. No less an authority than K. J. Dover subscribes to this diagnosis, though not without some uneasiness at the way he must use the poem both as evidence of "female homosexual emotion" among the Greeks and as a text to be read in the light of that evidence. It is a classic "hermeneutic circle," in which a particular interpretation of a text is employed to establish the context by which the text will be interpreted: sapphism explains Sappho who exemplifies sapphism which explains . . . not very much. Furthermore, as any lover of Sappho might point out, this circle is especially vicious because it projects a modern hypothesis about "lesbianism," stressing "anxiety" and "penis envy," onto the Greek originals. The theory implies the presence of a man in every erotic relation between women. Even when physically absent, he reminds them of what they are missing. No wonder he seems like a god!

Is there any other way to read the poem? I think that there is. If we take the first line to mean not that the man is *fortunate* as a god (privileged to woo the girl) or *potent* as a god (capable of loving her as a woman never could) but *invulnerable* as a god (able to endure the girl's presence), our whole interpretation changes. Now the subject of the poem turns from rivalry to ecstasy—specifically, the terrifying annihilation of self sparked by the nearness of the loved one, like Semele in the presence of Jupiter. To paraphrase: to me he seems strong as a god, because he can sit close to you without dying, while *I,* when I approach, feel myself extinguished by the force of your beauty. Note that this reading would function just as well if the man were reduced from a person to an abstraction; that is, "*anyone* able to sit close to you seems like a god to me." Nor does the grammar forbid it. Once we eliminate the man as a major character, indeed, the poem makes much better sense: the curious rivalry between the sexes yields to an unequivocal androgynous declaration of love. The one we love affects us like a divine messenger, reminding us by contrast of our mortality—we can hardly endure it. Hölderlin read Sappho this way, and so do I. Yet whether or not we incline to this manless, woman-to-woman reading, it must be acknowledged that history has recorded a different verdict. For most of the thousands of poets and critics who have prized these lines have not wanted Sappho to be a straightforward lover. They have wanted her to be an abandoned woman.

THEOCRITUS

The figure of the abandoned woman, that is to say, has proved stronger than Sappho herself. Very few heroines or noted female poets have escaped being pressed to its mold. Hence Sappho, as the prototypal Poetess, must also obey the prototype of all supremely gifted women—the Ariadne strain. Loneliness, frustrated desire, and the oddity attributed to the social outcast pursue her reputation like furies. However

various the feelings she once expressed, convention dictates that they all
be interpreted one way, as symptoms of abandonment. A poetess must
have been crossed in love. This reconfiguration of the historical Sappho
seems to have taken place within a century of her death. Although we
do not know exactly how the six (or more) Athenian comedies named
Sappho chose to treat their heroine, the likelihood is that neither fame nor
learning kept her from being mocked—perhaps as the third person in a
triangle. Older women in comedies tend to be disappointed. Moreover,
they are often aggressive and lascivious. The Greeks had a word for such
women: Lesbians. In antiquity the word did not denote homosexuality
so much as any brazen sexual behavior (fellation, for instance, or ogling
one of the couple at a wedding). Sappho was a Lesbian. Whether her
poetry gave her countrywomen their reputation or, as seems more likely,
their reputation led to a certain reading of her poetry, she could not elude
the scandal visited on almost any woman whose name has become public
property. One ancient debate revolved around the question of whether
to call her *publica*—a Latin word for whore. An iron logic grips the
woman poet: poetry equals abandonment and abandonment equals
shamelessness. Quite early Sappho fell under the spell of this logic.

She thus evolved into an image of wanton female sexuality. The process of absorbing the Poetess into the bawd may be seen at work in one
of the most remarkable of all Greek poems, the great *Second Idyll* of Theocritus (ca. 275 B.C.). As the abandoned Simaetha implores the moon to
help her conjure back Delphis, her philandering lover, she remembers
the moment when he first crossed her threshold, and Theocritus deliberately recalls the symptoms of Sappho's ode:

> πᾶσα μὲν ἐψύχθην χιόνος πλέον, ἐκ δὲ μετώπω
> ἱδρώς μευ κοχύδεσκεν ἴσον νοτίαισιν ἐέρσαις,
> οὐδέ τι φωνῆσαι δυνάμαν, οὐδ᾽ ὅσσον ἐν ὕπνῳ
> κνυζεῦνται φωνεῦντα φίλαν ποτὶ ματέρα τέκνα·
> ἀλλ᾽ ἐπάγην δαγῦδι καλὸν χρόα πάντοθεν ἴσα.

> Then I froze to the marrow, colder than snow,
> and from my brow sweat began to trickle like dew,
> nor could I speak a word, not so much as a baby's
> whimper in sleep crying to its dear mother,
> but all my fair white body grew stiff as a doll's.

No problem of diagnosis attends these symptoms. Simaetha is in heat
(as Gow notes, the word for her whimper "is properly used of dogs").
In spite of the decorative similes that convert her physical excitement
into something as innocent as dewdrops, a baby, a doll, she and her
body know exactly what they want; she worships a man, not a god.
The effect is not so much erotic or ecstatic as voyeuristic. Each of the

embellishments of Sappho's text serves to accentuate the extreme self-consciousness of the woman's desire. In this respect the last line carries an extra charge. Theocritus observes Simaetha in the act of observing her own lovely body, as if narcissism were at the root of her condition. Still more cleverly, the image of the doll reminds us of the sorcery or love magic that Simaetha has practiced throughout the poem, and the stiffening of her body in preparation for love may alert us to her habit of usurping the role of the man (it is she who is the aggressor, she who will pull Delphis down onto her couch). This woman does not take abandonment lying down.

Sappho has never recovered. Theocritus did not invent the caricature of a rapacious, sex-haunted woman, and in all probability he was not the first to associate that caricature with the greatest woman poet (since the *Second Idyll* may well have been influenced by Hellenistic comedy, and since Sappho may well have been a stock figure of that comedy, it is quite possible that Simaetha derives from a theatrical tradition of the Poetess). Yet by reading the Second Ode as a conventional expression of female lust—an aphrodisiac rather than a libation—the male poet brings his muse abruptly down to earth. Whether or not Theocritus intended to parody Sappho's words by adapting them to a coy and carnal seizure, whether he means us to laugh at Simaetha's fury or to admire it, the effect is to make such passion all too human. A lovesick woman craves a man, in this man-centered reading; his entrance relieves all her symptoms. Without him she would be as helpless as a baby without its mother or a doll without someone to touch it. Moreover, Theocritus also degrades the notion of a woman poet. The sorcery and jealous rage that move Simaetha belong, by extension, to Sappho as well; the Poetess is a witch. The *Second Idyll* exchanges the mystery of a divine encounter for a knowing look at feminine behavior. It defines the woman entirely through her reaction to a man, and translates her verse into an attempt to catch a man's attention.

CATULLUS

The androcentrism or reengendering of Sappho soon went a step further. No one has ever translated her better than Catullus did, in his version of the Second Ode, nor adjusted her attitudes more clearly to those of a man.

> *ille mi par esse deo uidetur,*
> *ille, si fas est, superare diuos,*
> *qui sedens aduersus identidem te*
>   *spectat et audit*
> *dulce ridentem, misero quod omnis*
> *eripit sensus mihi: nam simul te,*

Lesbia, aspexi, nihil est super mi
 [Lesbia uocis]
lingua sed torpet, tenuis sub artus
flamma demanat, sonitu suopte
tintinant aures, gemina teguntur
 lumina nocte.
[otium, Catulle, tibi molestum est:
otio exsultas nimiumque gestis:
otium et reges prius et beatas
 perdidit urbes.]

He seems to me the equal of a god,
he seems, if it could be, above a god,
who sits opposing you and over and
 over looks and hears
sweet laughter [unhappy me!] which rips
out all my senses; for as soon as I
see you, Lesbia, nothing is left me but
 Lesbia's voice,
my tongue thickens, a thin flame trickles
under my skin, with their own sound
my ears jangle, twin night
 covers my eyes. . . .

Catullus's homage to Sappho goes very deep. He renders not only the
meaning of her lines but some of their beauty—"a more beautiful translation there never was and never will be," according to Swinburne. One
great poet bends his verse to another, adopting an alien manner of writing. Most decisively, Catullus casts his Latin into the difficult Greek form
of the sapphic stanza (perhaps the first sapphics he had ever tried) with
its rapid and breathless short lines. Nor is it a small thing that, addressing
his own love, he should christen her "Lesbia" (the name was presumably
coined for this poem, the first of the sequence to Lesbia). Only a Lesbian
maid, or one who can be associated with the great original Lesbian, deserves sapphic tribute. Catullus internalizes Sappho's sexual preferences
as well as her symptoms. This man identifies his interests with abandoned women.

Nevertheless, Catullus 51 represents a fall for Sappho—a fall into a
masculine world. The conversion of the speaker from a woman into a
man, and hence from unconditional passion into the usual heterosexual
heats, is only the most obvious of many significant distortions. The first
has already been hinted. In place of the delicate situation imagined by
Sappho, where the man is so lightly touched that he may be only a figure
of speech, Catullus puts an equilateral triangle with all its edges firm.
That man, that man boosted extravagantly by the added second line into
more than a god, enjoys a privileged position not only in space but in

time, since he looks as well as listens "identidem"—again and again. He is a full-fledged character, and a full competitor. As a result the poet is "misero"—a rival, rejected suitor. The sense of competition seems to lend the poet's feelings not only their intensity but also their spice. How much less interesting the situation would be if the other man were not there! To win this lady Catullus will have to break all records for the high jump, soaring above the above. It has been well said, I think, that the author of this poem is "the first troubadour, avowing his desperate and despairing love for a great lady, with nothing to offer but himself and his poetry." He gains, of course, the pleasure of the chase. A man's love surely thrives on competition, though perhaps not every woman would want to call it love.

Catullus departs from Sappho, moreover, in a second crucial respect: he suppresses the whole of her fourth stanza. The weak Alexandrian elegance of his climax, "gemina teguntur / lumina nocte" (twin night covers my eyes), can hardly substitute for the powerful accumulation of details—sweat, trembling, pallor, death—that precisely defines the original structure. The reason for so drastic a change might be debated. (Only a very rash scholar would rule out the possibility of a stanza missing from the manuscript—though not a scrap of evidence remains to prove it.) But the effect cannot be debated: the Latin version utterly spoils Sappho's rhythm. Nor is this only a matter of poetic rhythm. Though posterity has diagnosed the symptoms of the ode in many ways—as jealousy, ecstasy, fear, or anxiety—a more specific physical diagnosis might also be offered: the rhythm of a sexual swoon. Only one scholar, so far as I know, has referred to Sappho's condition by the word "orgasm," and that is in the decent obscurity of a Latin commentary. But almost every poet or critic who has turned a hand to these lines, from Theocritus to the present, has had to find some means to register the sex—Sappho's own "dying fall." The association of "dying" with "coming" is so deeply engrained in so many languages that not even the most literal translation of the ode can avoid it. Many later ages, we shall see, found Sappho's swoon uncommonly suggestive or prurient. But Catullus dodges the issue. He distorts the poem thoroughly with his premature climax, and commits a sort of poetess interruptus. A man could scarcely be more insensitive to a woman's rhythm.

It is the additional stanza in Latin, however, that really gives the masculine game away. The hammer blow of otium, twice repeated, drowns out the woman's seizure with lassitude. Catullus reverses Sappho's direction, not to mention his own, so completely that many scholars have always suspected the stanza of belonging to some other poem. No textual evidence supports this. One solution might be to connect the lines with the final dangling line attributed to Sappho: "but all must be endured. . . ." Perhaps Catullus is merely translating a stanza we have lost. Unfortunately no one has ever been able to relate the Latin stanza convincingly to the line of Greek. Another, highly ingenious solution posits that Catullus added the stanza at a later time, after he had been disillusioned by "Lesbia." But that argument only converts the leap of logic into a leap through time. In any case the text does represent a typical male attitude, a way of looking at Sappho's poem that must have occurred to many men, even if few have expressed it in public. All this concentration on love, all this obsessive introspection about one's feelings, eventually produces a reaction. Passion is a waste of time, especially when frustrated or unconsummated. There is something *effeminate* about it; one wants to get on with one's business.

> Ease is my plague; ease makes thee void,
>   Catullus, with these vacant hours,
> And wanton: ease, that hath destroyed
>   Great kings, and states with all their powers.

The author of this translation knew what he was talking about, for he spent his life combatting *otium* and wantonness and building the state; he was no less a person than the Right Honorable William Ewart Gladstone.

Gladstone was very interested in abandoned women. He often picked them up in the streets. Yet the nature of his interest in Catullus, like Catullus's in Sappho, may serve to draw a sharp distinction between men's and women's conceptions of abandonment. It is the distinction between an interlude and a way of life. Male poets and male statesmen often sympathize with abandoned women and adopt their point of view. As we have seen with Byron, they may even identify their own most cherished secrets of feeling with the secrets of women. Yet such feelings are also disabling. One possible reading of Catullus's final stanza would gloss *otium* as impotence, thus diagnosing the condition of the poet as enfeeblement brought on by too strong an infatuation with the woman he adores (in that case he might be nerving himself to resume the fray). Gladstone, more confident of his powers, does not consider such an interpretation. Instead he deplores the ennervating effect of dalliance; bills might be passed during those hours of sitting around. But both men agree in regarding the time spent in the presence of women as dangerous—distracting or incapacitating. Men need to reach some conclusion. Dido furnishes Aeneas not only with an interlude but with a threat to his whole career. The teleology of the Roman Empire and the *Aeneid* pull him away from her; Italy and book 12 lie in wait, and the *otium* of love is only a pause between two heroic wars. Most ambitious men have beaten the same retreat from abandoned women. They allot no more than a stanza or two to such lulls in the action. Gladstone vacationed in Greece, and Catullus in Sappho.

Very few female poets have been privileged to keep such a safe distance from the abandoned woman. Her heart is where they live. Not a day went by, in the long poetic devotions of Emily Dickinson, when she did not inhabit her fated abandoned role. And the same might be said of many other great women poets. Abandonment appears to them not as a game or interlude but as the reality that sheds its truth on every other human relation. Even their careers as poets obey its logic. To conceive of Catullus's final stanza in the mouth of a female poet, therefore, almost defies imagination. The "plague" or "void" he fears has been, from Sappho to Tsvetayeva, a source of life at its most intense. For the figure of the abandoned woman seems historically not an *alternative* to heroic behavior, for women, but the ultimate sum and substance of being a hero.

OVID

The evidence for this assertion may be given quite succinctly, in the title of the work that set the terms of feminine heroism for almost two thousand years: Ovid's *Heroides* (or *Heroic Epistles*). The heroine, as Ovid presents her, is always an abandoned woman: Penelope, Phaedra, Dido, Ariadne, Medea, Laodamia—or Sappho. Separated from her lover, empassioned, and often betrayed, she pours out her sorrow in a letter (frequently stained with her tears), rebuking or cajoling him, hoping above all to coax him back. She never succeeds. But she endures. All the history of eminent women, in myth and literature, is encompassed by this situation. Even the arrangement of the *Heroides* suggests this. It begins with Penelope, the first great heroine of classical literature, and ends with Sappho, in whom the myth of the abandoned woman enters historical time and the first real woman whose poems have been preserved.

Yet Ovid's heroine is also a fallen woman. The epistle of "Sappho to Phaon" marks a decisive stage in Sappho's long descent. No one but Lucifer himself has ever fallen quite so far so fast. The story involves, to begin with, a literal fall: the heroine's leap from the Leucadian rock to the waves below. Ovid himself is not responsible for the legend of Sappho's suicidal effort to rid herself of passion for a handsome young ferryman. Menander had referred to the leap in a play that may also have influenced Theocritus's version of Sappho. Moreover, one scholar has plausibly conjectured that the poet herself originated the myth in a poem, associating her own plunge for Phaon with Aphrodite's for Phaethon (the Evening Star retrieving the sunken Sun) and thus claiming a godlike immortality. But Ovid makes her motives thoroughly mortal. The vividness and psychological credibility of his portrait of abandonment have never been forgotten; they rival, and eventually came to overshadow, the contrary evidence about Sappho's proclivities that we find in her own poems. The poetess self-destructs—with some masculine help. It is amazing how

many later poets have preferred Ovid's Sappho to Sappho herself, as if
not even the feelings of a woman could be authenticated except through
the witness of a man.

But worse yet happens; for Sappho falls further in reputation than from
the cliff. She descends into sluttishness. The aging, burning woman of
Ovid's epistle has lost her *pudor* (not only chastity but shame); she is
radically impure as a poet and a person. Here Sappho assumes her second
career, as a poet-whore. To say this is not to say that Ovid does not view
her with sympathy and amusement—as well as more than one touch of
autobiography. If ever a poet proved capable of appreciating and collabo-
rating in sluttishness, that poet was Ovid. Indeed, he obviously builds
up his Sappho with considerable affection. Like many a famous actress,
she never seems more lovable than when, with superannuated flirtatious-
ness, she makes her interminable farewells. But history did not accept
such refined distinctions, and the Sappho passed down by Ovid was very
fallen.

The critical tumble of Ovid's poetess, however, is her descent into self-
consciousness. Theocritus's hint of narcissism spreads over all her language. The poet Sappho loves to look at what she loves; the Ovidian
Sappho loves to watch herself in the act of loving. Probably no two figures in literary history better illustrate Schiller's distinction between the
naive and the sentimental, between direct presentation of a subject or
emotion and the self-dramatizing effort to load that subject with personal
significance. Every word of the epistle reeks of "Sappho." The opening
lines set the tone.

> *Ecquid, ut aspecta est studiosae littera dextrae,*
> *protinus est oculis cognita nostra tuis?*
> *An, nisi legisses auctoris nomina Sapphus,*
> *hoc breve nescires unde veniret opus?*
> *Forsitan et quare mea sint alterna requiras*
> *carmina, cum lyricis sim magis apta modis:*
> *Flendus amor meus est; elegi quoque flebile carmen;*
> *non facit ad lacrimas barbitos ulla meas.*

> Say, looking at this hand's keen characters,
> did your eyes spy at once that they were ours?
> Unless you had read the author's name, Sappho,
> would you have known whence came this billet-doux?
> Perhaps you'll ask me why these couplets fetter
> my song, when lyric measures suit me better:
> My love's for sighing; elegiacs sigh;
> No lyre of mine was ever made to cry.

The sentiment (so nicely caught by Pope's famous translation) should not
keep us from noticing the sheer *vanity* of the Latin. Reproaching her lover
proleptically for failing to recognize her distinctive literary and calli-

graphic style, Sappho calls her hand "studiosae"—not only eager but learned. The contrast of pronouns, in the second line, is also a contrast of persons: his eye is familiarly thine (*tuis*) but her letters are regally ours (*nostra*). Nor does Ovid's heroine dignify her lover's name by mentioning it along with her own. Phaon is just the sort of illiterate who will need a literal signature to identify a great poet, and who will not find her words "brief" (*breve;* in fact this is the longest of the epistles). In the next quatrain Ovid cleverly points to his own daring in ascribing elegiac couplets (alternating hexameters and pentameters) to Sappho. Unlike Catullus, *this* Roman poet refuses to bend his versification into a Greek mode. An abandoned woman must be pathetic, and elegiacs are right for pathos. The female poet is forced into Latin. At the same time she self-importantly reminds us of her fame; love does not make her forget whom sapphics are named after. Phaon and her own pride contend for supremacy within her divided mind.

Yet Sappho is not in control. Ovid slices her in two, and reveals the pathetic woman beneath the masterful poet. The couplets neatly parcel her emotions into a series of oppositions. Her mind and body, her scorn and submissiveness coexist uneasily in the mixed medium of declamation and love letter. Thus even the swoon of her senses, as adapted by Ovid, must culminate in an equal and opposite reaction.

> *cum mihi nescio quis "fugiunt tua gaudia" dixit,*
> *nec me flere diu nec potuisse loqui;*
> *et lacrimae deerant oculis et verba palato,*
> *adstrictum gelido frigore pectus erat.*
> *Postquam se dolor invenit, nec pectora plangi*
> *nec puduit scissis exululare comis,*
> *non aliter quam si nati pia mater adempti*
> *portet ad exstructos corpus inane rogos.*

> When someone said to me "Your joys have flown,"
> I could not speak for hours, I made no moan,
> and tears forsook my eyes and words my tongue,
> with cold constricting ice my breast was wrung.
> But when my grief rose up, shameless despair
> beat on my breast and, howling, rent my hair,
> as when a mother ravished of her child
> bears the dead body to the funeral pile.

The symptoms of ecstasy recorded by Sappho—already mere clichés in Ovid's day—here turn into theatrical shock, a calm before the storm. Like an actress rehearsing a play, the heroine shifts from dumb to strident, tearless to tearful, in rapid alternation. The economy of the Greek lyric yields to a catalogue of hysterical sensations, and all the emotions seem calculated if not posed. Passion itself, for Ovid, obeys a dialectic.

Indeed, the rigid compartmentalization of states of feeling, as rigid as the distinction between the ways that men and women are supposed to behave, even extends to the heroine's love. The essence of the scene is that Sappho plays it to herself. The absence, not the presence, of her lover brings on this torrent of abandonment, and it requires no audience for its effect. To be sure, one might argue that she has acted out her grief precisely for the purpose of reporting it later to Phaon. But a likelier explanation is that she and Ovid are working it up for the sake of poetry. Sappho performs on the stage of her own imagination, where Phaon becomes almost irrelevant. To enter her part more fully, she fancies herself a mother whose infant has died (here as well as elsewhere, Ovid reminds us that Phaon is young enough to be her son). Imagination prevails over life. It also seems to dominate in sex. While the seizure has almost no sexual element, in Ovid's version, the following passage (123-34) explicitly brings in the missing part: calling Phaon back to her in dreams, Sappho masturbates to a climax. Ovid will not allow her any love that is not selfish. Nor does he allow this poet, even for an instant, to forget herself.

The lesson proved irresistible for the future. Significantly, even the Greek author of *On the Sublime,* quoting the Second Ode in Greek, praises Sappho for "contradictory sensations, freezing and burning" (something barely hinted in the text he cites), as if he cannot read the poem except through an Ovidian screen. But the major lesson for posterity was still more devastating. When Ovid reconceived his heroine as a pathological case of sex-in-the-head, an abandoned woman in whom ambition, intelligence, poetry, sexual fantasy, and a death wish were inextricably combined, he created a chain of associations that still fetters many minds. The fear of women and the fear of imaginative freedom still join in a potent coupling. What can those women be dreaming about? Black magic, or poetry, or sex—some kind of witchcraft. Witches are burned at the stake. And so it happened to Sappho—not Ovid's Sappho, who served so well as a warning to women, but the Poetess herself. No famous poet has ever burned brighter; not a single manuscript survives intact. We are left with the shards. And ambitious women, for thousands of years, have drawn the proper morals: poetry is dangerous. It encourages one to think about oneself. Women had better not dabble in it. Griselda needs patience, not poetry, to trick her husband into taking her back. But Sappho and Griselda cannot live in the same world together. The Middle Ages knew no other Sappho than the one that Ovid had invented. A sinkhole of history swallowed the fallen poet. The perfect one became common: a common noun, an epithet or curse without a single poem attached to it. Sappho lay hidden in the depths.

RONSARD

She surfaced again, in the Renaissance, almost as an emblem of the
problem: is it possible to be a respectable woman and also a serious poet?
For women poets the question meant life or death. Hence the revival,
along with Sappho, of the ancient theory that *two* Sapphos had existed:
one a virtuous matron and author, the other a courtesan. The double
tradition often proved convenient. By separating the creature of dubious
legend from the shining Tenth Muse, writers of the sixteenth and seventeenth centuries could restore the name of Sappho to its full perfection.
Renaissance poets were eager to find a pure and untouched classic. Thus,
from the moment of its rediscovery in 1554, the Second Ode inspired a
host of imitators and translators. Robortello's edition of Longinus not
only restored the poem to the canon (by quoting it) but certified it as a
model of sublimity. Moreover, the vigor and physical immediacy of
Sappho's description seemed to offer a useful alternative to the passive,
immaculate clichés of Petrarchan love. Even before the Ode was published, we shall see in a later chapter, Gaspara Stampa seems to have
grafted it on to her own version of Petrarch. A return to the ancient
source, bypassing Ovid, could sanction new symptoms of love and a new
poetic technique.

By 1556 the Prince of Poets, Pierre de Ronsard, was searching for some
way out of his own apprenticeship to Petrarch. He turned, like others, to
Sappho.

> *Je suis un demidieu quand assis vis à vis*
> *De toy, mon cher soucy, j'escoute les devis,*
> *Devis entrerompus d'un gracieux soubrire,*
> *Soubris qui me detient le coeur emprisonné,*
> *Car en voyant tes yeux je me pasme estonné,*
> *Et de mes pauvres flancz un seul mot je ne tire.*
>   *Ma langue s'engourdist, un petit feu me court*
> *Honteux de sous la peau, je suis muet et sourd,*
> *Et une obscure nuit de sur mes yeux demeure,*
> *Mon sang devient glacé, l'esprit fuit de mon corps,*
> *Je tremble tout de crainte, & peut s'en faut alors*
> *Qu'à tes pieds estendu languissant je ne meure.*
> I am a demigod when, seated opposite
> To you, my precious care, I listen to your chat,
> Chat intermingled with a gracious smiling,
> Smile in which my imprisoned heart is wound,
> Because in looking at your eyes I faint, spellbound,
> And my poor breast finds not one word availing.
>   My tongue grows numb, a little fire begins to run
> Blushing beneath the skin, I am deaf and dumb,

And a gloomy night sinks down upon my eyes,
My blood is turned to ice, the soul flies from my flesh,
I tremble through and through with fear, and on the edge
While stretching languid at your feet I nearly die.

Petrarch contends with Sappho. To be sure, a modern reader might conclude that Petrarch has won the struggle. By replacing "that man" with himself and by blending the unapproachable loved one with a familiar sweetheart, Ronsard prettifies and conventionalizes the original. Perhaps he even turns it into nonsense. The logic of Sappho's poem depends on *contrasting* the godlike man and all-too-mortal speaker; one can endure the presence of the beloved, the other is annihilated. Ronsard collapses the two into one and spoils the logic; the end of the first stanza refutes its beginning. How can he have failed to notice this? The answer lies in Petrarch and his successors. Two centuries of poetry had exploited the paradoxes of love, its sweet bitterness, divine hellfire, delectable agony. Hence a Renaissance poet was not likely to find anything illogical about a demigod rendered powerless by a mortal. So many demigods behaved that way, in sixteenth-century verse, that vulnerability to love might be interpreted as their defining characteristic. Ronsard's speaker may announce himself as a demigod, that is to say, just *because* he is in a position where he is doomed to suffer. Love abrogates the rule of consistency.

Sappho is softened still more. By substituting his own formulas for the Greek symptoms, Ronsard purchases sweetness at the cost of precision. Too polite to laugh, the beloved merely smiles; the lover's heart, like most Petrarchan hearts, is held prisoner. Nor is there room in French for sweat or the homely detail of grass. Worse yet, Sappho's fierce pace becomes slack. Ronsard reduces the four stanzas of Greek, each with its own climax, to a double sestet with rhymes and balances. More accurately, one might call the French poem an abbreviated or retarded sonnet. The typical sonnet structure of systole and diastole, one stanza of rising and one of falling, controls the tempo. To this Ronsard has added his own ingenious retards. The first line lingers over internal rhymes ("suis . . . assis vis à vis"), the words that end the second and third lines come back when the next line begins, and similar echoes and repetitions throughout delay the reader. Even the last line pauses to sketch a description, as if to suggest a leisurely interval in the midst of the seizure. The effect is more luxurious than desperate. As the poet swoons, he retains enough composure to select the most picturesque place to fall.

In one respect, however, Ronsard prefers Sappho to Petrarch: there is nothing spiritual about this experience. The symptoms do not point to a higher world; they *are* the world of the poem. Hence the demi-sonnet might be regarded as an experiment with a new sort of love—without morality, without divinity, without Plato, and even without Petrarch. A still more daring experiment was tried by Sir Philip Sidney. In one of Cleophila's songs in the *Old Arcadia* (ca. 1578), the poet defies the conventions of English verse by adapting Sappho's symptoms to a quantified measure, borrowed from Anacreon, that imposes its own strong beat.

> My muse what ails this ardour?
> My eys be dym, my lyms shake,
> My voice is hoarse, my throte scorcht,
> My tong to this my roofe cleaves,
> My fancy amazde, my thoughtes dull'd,
> My harte doth ake, my life faints,
> My sowle beginnes to take leave.

Sidney stresses the *monotony* of the experience. Abjuring rhyme, syntactical variety, or any other source of poetic gratification, he intentionally jars the ear by grating consonant against consonant ("throte scorcht," "roofe cleaves," etc.). No Latinate melody will be allowed to alleviate Sappho's barbarous fit. The song imitates the sense of nausea it describes, and reduces the Ode to a medical report. The experiment did not catch on. But it does represent an extreme case of Hellenized English, of an effort to superimpose Greek accents on a modern voice. Sidney does not allow Ovid or Petrarch to intrude between him and Sappho. Instead he tries to tune himself directly to the pure beat of her verse—or Anacreon's—poet to poet.

Yet the Ovidian Sappho kept its own adherents. Long after the Renaissance recovery of the authentic poet had been completed, the mention of her name could still provoke a smirk. Indeed, a new pornographic genre developed around comic epistles from "Sapho to Philaenis," in which Phaon metamorphoses into a female whore (her name taken from Martial) who stirs the poetess to passionate confessions of lesbian desire. Men seem to have been especially amused by this equation of women's poetry with homosexuality and self-love. The masterwork of the genre, Donne's "Sapho to Philaenis," frankly compares the love of woman for woman with looking in a mirror: "Likeness begets such strange selfe flatterie, / That touching my selfe, all seemes done to thee." Sappho's verse, it is hinted, may derive from the same sort of onanism. Donne and the Restoration wits who followed him can hardly bring together the idea of a poem and the idea of a female author without leering. Nor could the Second Ode itself be immune from lewd associations, as Byron, the last of the Restoration wits, makes all too clear.

> Catullus scarcely has a decent poem,
>   I don't think Sappho's Ode a good example,
> Although Longinus tells us there is no hymn
>   Where the sublime soars forth on wings more ample.

But for women the double tradition was no laughing matter. When Madame Dacier defended Sappho's honor from the attack of the great skeptic Pierre Bayle, in a celebrated war of words at the end of the seventeenth century, she thought the honor of literary womanhood to be at stake. Women required a champion. It was a rare female poet in those days, after all, who was *not* called Sappho, and the woman who received such a tribute had a right to inquire whether the name meant Poetess or Slut.

DE SCUDÉRY AND BOILEAU

Not even a queen could be indifferent to the answer. When John Lyly wrote *Sapho and Phao,* a comedy staged for Queen Elizabeth herself in the early 1580s, he did not scruple to represent the monarch allegorically through his heroine, the Princess of Syracuse, "Sapho, faire by nature, by birth royall, learned by education, by gouernment politike, rich by peace: insomuch as it is hard to iudge, whether she be more beautifull or wise, vertuous or fortunate." The queen could hardly have felt offended by such comparisons. But the playwright was playing with fire. Endowing his heroine with the fever of love and the name of Sappho, he prompted his hearers to think about royal affairs. Lyly handles the situation with great delicacy. By drawing on the double tradition, he separates the two Sapphos so firmly that no trace is left of the strumpet. The disinfecting of the Second Ode is managed with particular skill. "When Phao commeth, what then? wilt thou open thy loue? Yea. No! Sapho: but staring in his face till thine eies dasell, and thy spirites fainte, die before his face: then this shall be written on thy Tomb, that though thy loue were greater than wisdome could endure, yet thine honour was such, as loue could not violate." Here the heroine's seizure of love ingeniously works to preserve her virtue. Sappho conquers Cupid and endures with honor. But the price she pays includes her reputation as a poet. Lyly suppresses any hint that Sappho is a writer. Amorous verse would not become a queen. And a perfect woman must be willing to sacrifice literary ambitions to more suitable feminine virtues.

The battle over Sappho's name continued in the seventeenth century. To those who opposed an education for women, a famous Poetess could only be a harlot; to women who fought for learning, the Poetess served as a proof of what women could be. Each side enlisted Sappho in its cause. No one had better success, or identified more with the name, than "the foremost advocate of the learned woman," Madeleine de Scudéry. In one of the most popular books of the century, *Artamenes; or, The Grand Cyrus* (1649–53), Scudéry shapes the romance of Sappho and Phaon into a definitive portrait of the ideal *femme savante.* Much tact was needed for this performance, not least because the author herself was known as "Sappho." Scudéry does not give herself the worst of it; she loads her paragon with all the charms, including beauty. Yet the essence of the heroine's superiority is the lightness and grace with which she carries her learning. Despite Sappho's fame as a poet, no one ever sees her reading or writing, and her conversation is guided by an "infallible Maxime, that though I would have Women to know more then generally they do, yet I would not have them talk as if they were knowing at all." Modesty keeps her rigidly "within the Sphere of her own Sex." Hence the plot of this idyll revolves around two false interpretations of proper feminine learning. The first is that of Damophile, a vulgar, pedantic imitator of Sappho and the star of a rival salon, who hungers for the public recognition that is the bane of truly learned ladies. Sappho knows that female poets shine best in the dark: "there is nothing more troublesome than to have a good wit, and to be treated accordingly; if one have any birth, and nobleness of heart." The second misunderstanding is that of Phaon, who initially suffers from the "conceipt" or prejudice that "it was a thing almost impossible for a woman to be learned and not ridiculous, or at least not troublesome." Phaon learns better, and so do Scudéry's readers.

Unfortunately, however, a learned lady must put more confidence in the taste of her readers than they deserve. Scudéry's Sappho is forever being misread. Since her way of life depends so much on concealing what she knows and hiding her genius, it is not surprising that literal-minded people should misjudge her. The crisis of the story hinges, in fact, on a false interpretation of the Second Ode. "She admirably described the sweetness of Looks, the trembling of Heart, which a sudden surprize useth to cause, the disorder of the Countenance, the agitation of the Spirits, and all the motions of a passionate Soul." When Phaon chances upon the poem, he immediately jumps to a wrong conclusion: "*Sapho* could never write those verses unless she were in love with some or other." The Ode is read as if it were a diary, and the jealous lover suffers torments over a rival who turns out, of course, to be himself. One might blame Phaon's narrow and sexist mode of reading, which assumes that female poets never invent but only confess. Yet Sappho herself must share a part of the blame. By veiling her feelings so well behind refined social graces, she makes it impossible for her lover to connect the passion her poem expresses with the woman he knows; and indeed her reserve prevents her from easing his doubts until the situation has been milked for the maximum discord. Scudéry's Sappho shows not one outward sign of being a poet. The cost of her charm is utter repression: the learned woman cannot afford to reveal that she is anything but a lady.

Thus Scudéry scrubs Sappho clean. The question, however, is whether one can believe that such an inhibited creature could ever have written such poems. Certainly Nicolas Boileau did not believe it. The portrait of Sappho in *The Grand Cyrus* drove him to satiric frenzy. A leaden lump,

Scudéry's "dread" and "horrible" volume is wielded to begin the famous
"Battle of the Books" in canto 5 of *Le Lutrin* (1683). But Boileau had
taken a more subtle revenge in his *Dialogue of the Heroes of Novels* (1665).
There Sappho herself comes forward to speak, assuming the identity and
language of Scudéry. With exquisite double-talk, she draws a portrait of
Tisiphone, a Fury whose loathsome appearance is polished rhetorically
into a sort of beauty. Readers of *The Grand Cyrus* would have recognized
the source: the endless, dainty catalogue of Sappho's features that transforms the traditionally dark and dumpy poetess into a femme fatale.
Boileau's parody of this effect is cruel. It ridicules not only Scudéry's
precious prose but also, by implication, her feminine charms. Yet the
main point of putting Scudéry's words in Sappho's mouth is to deny that
they belong there. Sappho did not talk that way. Indeed, the picture of
Greek society in *The Grand Cyrus* parodies itself with its salon mentality
and obsession with etiquette—Sappho in the guise of Miss Manners.
Boileau calls down a curse on romance conventions and revokes Scudér-
y's right to the name of Sappho.

He also made a Sappho of his own. When Boileau published his translation of Longinus in 1674, he not only helped to create an enduring
vogue for the Sublime but fixed an image of the Second Ode that retains
its influence, in France, to the present day. It is, in more ways than one,
a classic version.

> *Heureux! qui prés de toi, pour toi seule soûpire;*
> *Qui jouït du plaisir de t'entendre parler;*
> *Qui te voit quelquefois doucement lui soûrire.*
> *Les Dieux dans son bonheur peuvent-ils l'égaler?*
>
> *Je sens de veine en veine une subtile flame*
> *Courir par tout mon corps si tost que je te vois:*
> *Et dans les doux transports où s'égare mon ame,*
> *Je ne sçaurois trouver de langue, ni de voix.*
>
> *Un nuage confus se répand sur ma vûë.*
> *Je n'entens plus: je tombe en de douces langueurs;*
> *Et, pâle, sans haleine, interdite, éperduë,*
> *Un frisson me saisit, je tremble, je me meurs.*
>
> *Mais quand on n'a plus rien, il faut tout hazarder, etc.*

> Happy! who near you, for you only sighs;
> Who takes his pleasure listening to you talk;
> Who sometimes meets your sweetly smiling eyes.
> How can the gods themselves equal such luck?
>
> I feel a subtle flame from vein to vein
> Run through my flesh when first I see your face:
> And sweet transports perplex my wandering brain,
> I cannot find my tongue then, nor my voice.

A shapeless cloud spreads down upon my sight.
I hear no more; in languor sweet I sway;
And pallid, breathless, discomposed, distraught,
I tremble, shivering, I die away.

But one with nothing still must hazard all. . . .

Boileau sets out to restore the passion and artistry of Sappho. Unlike his immediate predecessors, he avoids recasting the poem as a conventional, heterosexual love duet (the "happy" man is not identified with the speaker). Moreover, like Longinus he emphasizes the excess and violence of the emotion, and the rapidity with which one symptom follows another. The climax in lines 11 and 12, for instance, makes Ronsard seem pallid by contrast. Nor could Scudéry's Poetess be capable of anything so outspoken and intense. Here Sappho recovers a "virile," formal perfection.

Indeed, Boileau has labored to *improve* the classic form of the original. Embroidering Longinus, he claims that Sappho has found an "infallible secret" of greatness in choosing the right details and blending them into an ensemble. Hence the French poem goes well beyond the Greek in tying things together. Partly this is a matter of prosody; Boileau's symmetrical quatrains, with their alternating rhymes and full fourth lines, convey a sense of balance very different from sapphics, whose abbreviated fourth lines work against regularity and closure. Yet the French also contrives other means of harmonizing its details. In the first stanza, for instance, repetitions and parallels occur on the level of the phrase ("prés de toi," "pour toi"), the line ("Qui jouït," "Qui te voit"), and the stanza as a whole (where the good fortune of the gods is saved for line 4, to counterpoise the "happy one" of line 1). A lengthy Jakobsonian analysis of grammatical and sonic patterns would be necessary to do justice to Boileau's stitchwork; as another example, note that each stanza contains a variation on "doux." The effect is an elegant unity quite different from the Greek. To be sure, Sappho's lyric creates its own sort of unified "ensemble." One might argue that much of its brilliance stems from the contrast of a headlong rush of particular symptoms (paratactic construction) with a highly ordered pattern of sounds; a famous example of the latter is the chime of the opening words, *phainetai moi,* with the last complete line, *phainom' [em' autai].* Hence the form of the Greek is at once linear (one item after another) and cyclic (a moment of experience held in suspension). Yet Boileau substitutes a far more even form, based more on equilibrium than momentum. That was the way he trained his successors to hear Sappho.

Thus Sappho became more tasteful. Despite his contempt for Scudéry's preciosity and his effort to capture the stark high style of Greek, Boileau might also be accused of reducing his muse to a lady. He even knew that himself. In notes to his translation he remarks that the expressions "pale as *grass*" and *"cold sweat"* could never be *agreeable* in French. Moreover, modern ladies (as in Ronsard) are not so coarse as to *laugh;* instead, they merely *smile.* The problem goes beyond poetic diction. It reflects a general problem of the age, the reluctance of literary men to acknowledge the rights of women not only to education but to plain speech, especially speech that mentions the naked facts of corporality. Women must be sheltered from a knowledge of what goes on beneath their clothes. It is not so much that Boileau is a misogynist. It is that even his worship of Sappho's sublimity falters when he tries to imagine a poet as a woman. He does not have a language to render her sensations—or rather, to render them without comedy or bad taste. The excellence of the Second Ode, for Boileau, requires that it be uncontaminated by any thought of a living woman. Can the two traditions of Sappho be kept apart? The more that authors tried, the harder it became to keep the Poetess pure.

RACINE

Not many men did better. In a curious way the problem seems to lie at the very heart of classicism, especially French classicism, with its alternate worship and fear of the passions of women, its *agon* of honor and love. That sense of the classic was given its consummate definition, most critics agree, in the *Phèdre* of Racine. But only a few critics have noticed the crucial role of Sappho's Ode. Racine admired his friend Boileau's translation so much, a few years before the play, that he said he "had seen nothing more vivid or beautiful in all of antiquity." He saved this precious remnant for a special occasion. At the end of act 1, scene 3, the tortured heroine at last confesses the source of her illness. It had burst upon her at the first sight of Hippolytus, her "superb enemy."

> *Je le vis, je rougis, je pâlis à sa vue;*
> *Un trouble s'éleva dans mon âme éperdue;*
> *Mes yeux ne voyaient plus, je ne pouvais parler;*
> *Je sentis tout mon corps et transir et brûler;*
> *Je reconnus Vénus et ses feux redoutables,*
> *D'un sang qu'elle poursuit tourments inévitables.*
> I saw, I blushed, one look and I turned pale;
> Confusion rose in my distracted soul;
> My eyes were blind, I could not speak; in turn
> I felt my body chill all through and burn;
> Venus! I recognized her deadly flame,
> Searing the blood she hunts with fatal pain.

One by one the Sapphic symptoms and Ovidian oppositions fall into place, except for the final swoon. Yet in this death-haunted play the missing element seems most important of all. Phèdre's whole confession explicitly pleads the necessity of her dying; and when she does die at the end, with a poison inherited from Medea, it cannot be accidental that the fire tormenting her blood repeats exactly the symptoms of love.

Two observations may help to clarify the effects that Racine imported from Sappho. The first is the precision, the analytic detachment, with which Phèdre regards her own seizure. Though captured and broken by passion, her mind remains cool and her rhetoric keeps its balance. This effect reflects a quality in the Ode that many critics have thought its most remarkable feature: "the uncommon objectivity of her demeanour toward her own extremity of passion," or the mixture of uncontrolled feeling with supremely controlled expression. Fire and ice. Sappho takes her own pulse; she records the moment when it fails. And Phèdre does the same. In one respect, in fact, her composure exceeds that of Sappho, since she is able to recognize and even pronounce the name of her illness (if I cannot see, cannot speak, and am burning inside, the logic runs, this must be Venus). Such effects notoriously do not translate into English, where ability to discriminate among passions is thought a form of snobbery. Significantly the nearest English approximation, Pope's "Eloisa to Abelard," derives from Sappho, Ovid, and the French. In French the analysis of passion has long seemed second nature. Such analysis furnishes men with an accepted method of understanding women—or thinking they understand them—by giving their feelings a name. Magnificent, *mascula* Sappho! who feels like a woman and thinks like a man. Much of French classicism depends on that inheritance of sexual discrimination. When Racine put Sappho's words into the mouth of Phèdre, therefore, he was paying homage to the greatest classic of all: the eternal Frenchwoman in all her glory.

Yet he also was putting her down. What Racine appropriated from Sappho, in the second place, was not only a mechanism of passion but its context: the triangle lurking behind it. Phèdre suffers above all from *guilt*. Her seizure at the sight of Hippolytus, she discloses, occurred immediately after she had been bound to his father by the strictest laws of Hymen. Theseus lurks behind this vision of love as the forgotten, injured party. Even when looking at his face, the woman confesses, she sees Hippolytus there. Nor does Phèdre disguise her self-condemnation. Unlike Sappho, whose ecstasy seems not to admit a single tremor of blame, the wife of Theseus wears guilt like a shroud of black dye; it colors and winds into every thread of her passion. Even her sexual longing takes on its coloration. (As Catholics especially like to comment, a pleasure untouched by guilt would seem not only improbable but insipid.) Thus the poisonous love that fills the veins constitutes its own punishment. A sexually aroused woman is polluted with fluids like a sewer and deserves to die. Racine, as we know, subscribed to the Jansenist tenet that every sexual act recreates the fall of Eve and puts the soul in peril; the sinfulness of love perpetually violates the hard bargain of grace. The words of Sappho and Phèdre, therefore, represent a sort of antigrace or anti–conversion experience—sudden, arbitrary, and fatal. (The effect of arbitrary fatality dominates the French text far more strongly than the Greek, since Phèdre, unlike Sappho, is describing love *at first sight*.) Even the physiological details contribute to the sense of damnation by reminding the woman of the flesh that binds her soul. Perhaps what Phèdre ultimately realizes, to her own shock and horror, is simply that she lives in a body.

A proper Christian woman could not have spoken such words. If the true plot of *Phèdre* consists, as Roland Barthes has suggested, less of actions than of the difficulty of *speaking*—the three successive confessions wrung out of the heroine—then Racine finds a highly ingenious way to let the woman speak. Phèdre owns no words to confess her love, but luckily she can quote the words of Sappho. The beautiful pagan poem, whose origin allows the reader both to worship the speaker and cheerfully send her to hell, enables the playwright to keep a respectable distance. He transcribes the lines of another, without commitment. The Greeks must take the blame. In this way Racine can express both the attitudes toward women without which his play could not exist: the pure soul and the raging body, or what has earlier been called the Poetess and the Slut. Phèdre is both. She represents both the pathos of abandoned women, as men see them, and their sexual witchery or, to use the two key words of the play, their *fate* and *blood*. Racine warns women of the ancient poison that infects the blood of even the best of them. The symptoms are universal. Hence he succeeds in bringing Sappho still lower than Ovid had managed, by adding a single fatal touch: the sense of original sin.

EIGHTEENTH-CENTURY SAPPHOS

Yet Sappho would not stay down. Women would not allow it. They needed a genius of their own: a mother poet whose work survived any criticism and was not obliged to any man. And men, on the whole, were willing to be converted. During the course of the eighteenth century the reputation of Sappho, both as a poet and as a respectable woman, steadily ascended. One of the most important turning points, in that resurgence, was the praise of Addison, whose *Spectator* papers 223, 229, and 233 (1711) transformed the poet to a lady. Sappho could be accepted in polite society, he assured his readers, though only just barely. "I do not know, by the Character that is given of her Works, whether it is not for the Benefit of Mankind that they are lost. They were filled with such bewitching Tenderness and Rapture, that it might have been dangerous to have given them a Reading." Remarks like these seem certain to guarantee a best-seller. And Addison was quick to satisfy the appetite he had whetted, by providing some translations (the work of Ambrose Philips) "written in the very Spirit of *Sappho,* and as near the *Greek* as the Genius of our Language will possibly suffer." Here is the Second Ode.

> Blest as th'Immortal Gods is he,
> The Youth who fondly sits by thee,
> And hears and sees thee all the while
> Softly speak and sweetly smile.
>
> 'Twas this depriv'd my Soul of Rest,
> And rais'd such Tumults in my Breast;
> For while I gaz'd, in Transport tost,
> My Breath was gone, my Voice was lost:
>
> My Bosom glow'd; the subtle Flame
> Ran quick thro' all my vital Frame;
> O'er my dim Eyes a Darkness hung;
> My Ears with hollow Murmurs rung:
>
> In dewy Damps my Limbs were chill'd;
> My Blood with gentle Horrours thrill'd;
> My feeble Pulse forgot to play;
> I fainted, sunk, and dy'd away.

However namby-pamby to modern ears, this version retained its immense popularity for over a century. It lends itself nicely to dramatic performance, with the voice dropping ever lower until breath fails at the last words. Women especially loved to recite it. Nor need we seek far for the reason. In Philips's gentle translation, as in few others, a wash of sentiment covers but does not distort the enduring sexual rhythm. Note, for instance, the crucial placement of that highly suggestive word "sunk." Yet at the same time the diction preserves a rigid decency. Cold sweat dissolves to "dewy Damps," and no one will mistake a "vital Frame" for a living body. The core could hardly be softer. But it is not altogether a blunder, I think, that a recent pornographic picture book, luridly illustrating snatches of Sappho, chose the Philips version as its text for the Second Ode. Such poets know the value of teasing. Nor could eighteenth-century ladies have been entirely innocent, giving themselves to these lines, about exactly what they were enjoying.

What they enjoyed most of all, however, was pathos. The Sappho revived and raised to Victorian times might fall, now and then, but only to extract a tear. She suffers with exquisite grace. When Philips shifted the attack of passion from the present to the past tense, he lost the immediacy of the Ode but made a new story possible: the story of a woman haunted by what she has lost. Her love exists in memory or dreaming, not in sensation, and she speaks to us from the other side of the grave. Even the detail of the "Youth" adds to the pathos by suggesting that the speaker has been displaced by a younger competitor (as in Ovid's and Pope's version of "Sappho to Phaon"). The distance between the old lover and the object of her love becomes a matter of time as well as space. The past cannot be recaptured; this woman seems truly abandoned. Hence Philips's heroine acts out a scene that takes place only in her imagination and will not lead to any future. The love poem combines with a poem in love with death.

Throughout the eighteenth century the death wish of Sappho grew along with her reputation. She is victim, never aggressor. If abandoned women conventionally belong to one of two opposing camps, defined in my first chapter as the waif and the fury, or sparrow and harpy, then the Sappho perceived by the Age of Sensibility seems every inch a sparrow. Physically frail and distracted ("My feeble Pulse forgot to play"), often on the brink of madness like the much-imitated Ophelia, a compulsive lover of song and unfaithful men, she is much too weak for this world. Yet her weakness suited the times. In the 1740s, when a flood of grave-yard poetry spread out from England across Europe, the deathly poetess became an exemplary figure, an archetype of the sensitive, lonely poet described by Young, Gray, and the Wartons. Not even the case-hardened Tobias Smollett could resist the fashion. Putting the Second Ode into the mouth of Roderick Random (1748), he inflated the final line into a turgid lament.

> Condemn'd to nurse eternal care,
> And ever drop the silent tear,
> Unheard I mourn, unknown I sigh,
> Unfriended live, unpitied die!

Self-pity, in such verses, seems a stronger emotion than love. The Sappho the ancients had known, that intensely social being surrounded by lovers, disciples, and rivals, has faded away to a wraith. Indeed, it hardly matters whether or not the speaker writes poetry, since no one will ever hear it—"Unheard I mourn, unknown I sigh." The paradox is characteristic of mid- and late-eighteenth-century verse: the most poetic souls are too sensitive to communicate their woes, and die without publishing. Hence the high prestige of the Poetess came to be associated less with her genius than with her capacity for grief. She learned to forget that she was a poet.

At the same time, she became a celebrity. The implicit tension between the poet and the victim is made explicit in the work of Mary "Perdita" Robinson. An actress in her youth, she took her sobriquet from the role

in which she captivated the Prince of Wales (George IV); but later she
played the role of an author, "the English Sappho." Hence aspects of
autobiography, her royal affair and abandonment, are incorporated into
the forty-four sonnets that tell the sad story of *Sappho and Phaon* (1796).
Sonnet 4 adapts the Second Ode to an explanation of Sappho's loss of art.

> Why, when I gaze on Phaon's beauteous eyes,
>   Why does each thought in wild disorder stray?
>   Why does each fainting faculty decay,
> And my chill'd breast in throbbing tumults rise?
> Mute, on the ground my Lyre neglected lies,
>   The Muse forgot, and lost the melting lay;
>   My down-cast looks, my faultering lips betray,
> That stung by hopeless passion,—Sappho dies!

The lyre is here neglected in more ways than one. Robinson redirects the
attention from inner physical symptoms to outward theatrical ges-
tures—stage directions for an actress who must remember to express her
tumults in rising throbs of the breast, to cast down her looks, to betray
her emotions by fluttering her lips. The poem is an actress's dream, a
mad scene and death scene at once. But the essence of such acting must
be a seeming indifference to the audience. Sappho forgets her muse so
that she may impersonate a "wild disorder." The detail of the neglected
lyre, therefore, adds a necessary touch by reminding us of something that
the speaker herself is not allowed to notice: her identity as a poet. That
celebrity status reinforces the pathos; the heroine has thrown herself
away. In the end, it is less important for Robinson that the woman is
Sappho than that Sappho is only a woman. All abandoned women are
sisters in the dark.

ROMANTIC SAPPHOS: FOSCOLO

By the height of the romantic period, in fact, the sacrifice of Sappho
was nearly complete; her name no longer meant poet but suicide. A new
poetic genre grew out of the final line of the Ode, the genre of Sappho's
Last Song. Felicia Hemans has described the sketch (by the younger
Westmacott) that inspired her own effort: "It represents Sappho sitting
on a rock above the sea, with her lyre cast at her feet. There is a desolate
grace about the whole figure, which seems penetrated with the feeling of
utter abandonment." Three stanzas from Hemans's "Last Song of Sappho" (ca. 1830) may be enough to convey an entire age of pathetic verse.

> Sound on, thou dark, unslumbering sea!
>   My dirge is in thy moan;
>   My spirit finds response in thee
> To its own ceaseless cry—"Alone, alone!"
> . . . .

> Sound on, thou dark, unslumbering sea!
>   Sound in thy scorn and pride!
> I ask not, alien world! from thee
> What my own kindred earth hath still denied.
> ....
>   I, with this wingèd nature fraught,
>   These visions wildly free,
>   This boundless love, this fiery thought—
> *Alone* I come—oh! give me peace, dark sea!

The heroine of such a poem will go to any lengths, in answer to Racine's charge against women, to deny her own body. Nature, not Phaon, has betrayed her, and resists her desperate attempts to read her own emotions into it—her moan, her feeling of having been scorned, her need for peace. Even her own physical nature or "kindred earth" remains alien to her. She prefers to be wingèd and will soon try stepping into the air. When she surrenders everything she has to the sea, by offering her consciousness—"This boundless love, this fiery thought"—the lack of a final response only confirms the heroine's isolation from any human or natural community. (In the one unquestionable masterpiece of the genre, Leopardi's "Ultimo canto di Saffo" [1822], even a pool into which she tries to dip her foot "disdainfully runs away.") The romantic Sappho stands *alone*.

Nor does her death contain the slightest overt hint of sexual dying. Here the fainting and sinking feelings attributed to Sappho by Philips are repressed into pure death wish, a violent header by the spirit out of its bodily state. The woman poet courts extinction. The same exacerbated sensitivity and sense of being unloved that have made her a poet have made her a suicide. She tears the creature out of her. Our word for this effect, of course, is sublimation—the thoughts fly up while eros stays below—and indeed the death scenes of *Sappho,* in the celebrated tragedies of that name by Madame de Staël (1811) and Grillparzer (1817), aim to be very sublime. Yet they almost entirely dispel the acute sensory and bodily perceptions of the Greek poet. The ultimate symptom, dying, precludes all the others; it alone relieves her spiritual ache. And in the characteristic romantic estrangement attributed to Sappho—abandonment not only by the lover but by nature, the body, poetry, sex, and life—the poet Sappho is also estranged from herself.

Hence Sappho entered into a new double tradition, in which the famous poet is always shadowed by her alter ego, the anonymous suicide. Not many admirers of the Lesbian could bring themselves to ignore her appointment in Leucadia. Yet the two figures inhabit the same reputation with some unease. Like other romantic heroines, the romantic Sappho often seems schizophrenic—sometimes the epitome of Greek health and elegance, sometimes a sallow hysteric. To some extent this division might be thought to embody romanticism itself. One of the first paintings to generate a controversy over the word "romantic" was Gros's unsettling *Sappho at Leucate* (1801), in which moonlight veils and irradiates the haunted woman, arrested at the moment of her leap. The work was greatly admired and greatly condemned. As one critic later wrote, "it was a fundamental deviation from the principles of Greek art to undertake the painting of despair." Yet many romantic artists experienced the same deviation and attempted the same fusion of opposites. "Romantic classicism," like "moonstruck sanity" or "anonymous celebrity," may sound like a contradiction in terms, but the phrase serves inevitably to describe the work of Hölderlin, Berlioz, Byron, and Delacroix. They live in an imaginary ancient world, a mental Greece that is the home at once of temples and ruins, of perfect beauty and morbid dreams. And Sappho stands for both—the glory, the decay. Romantic artists make her one with them.

The complexity of this response is particularly vivid in the work of that most romantic of authors, Ugo Foscolo. Like the other great Italian poet of his time, Leopardi, Foscolo identified with Sappho. Born on the Ionian island of Zante, he grew up speaking Greek as well as Italian, and from earliest times he associated his own poetic gifts with the classical poets. "My cradle was in that sea / where the naked spirit / of Phaon's girl still wanders." (Zante is 60 miles from Leucas—on the other side of Ithaca.) He was also well acquainted with suicide. Both of his brothers killed themselves, and the novel that made his reputation, the *Last Letters of Jacopo Ortis* (1798), ends with the suicide of a young man oppressed by love and politics. In one crucial scene in that novel, Ortis is moved to ecstasy by hearing his beloved sing; what she sings are his own translations of Sappho's odes. Foscolo, like Goethe writing about *Werther,* confessed his indebtedness to the English graveyard poets. *Ortis* is prefaced by a line from Gray's "Elegy" ("Ev'n from the tomb the voice of Nature cries"); and Foscolo's later poetic masterpiece, *The Sepulchers* (1806), might be regarded as the culminating classic of the graveyard line. Yet the other side of his heritage, a proud Greek classicism, balances the morbid modern strain. If Sappho is Phaon's pathetic, drowning girl, she is also an active, passionate artist whose vitality puts modern poets to shame.

Foscolo translated the Second Ode three times. The last and best of these versions, published in an appendix to *Essays on Petrarch* (1821), conveys his admiration not only for the intensity of the Poetess but for her craft. He criticizes all other translators (including Boileau and Philips) for lacking her fire and her knowledge of the heart. "A modern Sappho, more skilled in displaying the interior anatomy of her feelings, exhibits them rather to the understanding, than to the eyes and hearts of her readers: but they who can coolly dissect their passions, cannot excite the sympathy of others." This passage is aimed at Madame de Staël; Foscolo had reason to regard Corinne's long "improvisation" as a plundering of his own *Sepulchers*. He owns the copyright on Sappho. But he especially values his own translation of the Ode for preserving the meter as well as "the contrasts and gradations of the original."

> *Quei parmi in Cielo fra gli Dei, se accanto*
> *Ti siede e vede il tuo bel riso, e sente*
> *I dolci detti e l'amoroso canto!—*
> > *A me repente*
>
> *Con più tumulto il core urta nel petto;*
> *More la voce, mentre ch'io ti miro,*
> *Su la mia lingua: nelle fauci stretto*
> > *Geme il sospiro.*
>
> *Serpe la fiamma entro il mio sangue, ed ardo;*
> *Un indistinto tintinnio m'ingombra*
> *Gli orecchi, e sogno; mi s'innalza al guardo*
> > *Torbida l'ombra.*
>
> *E tutta molle d'un sudor di gelo,*
> *E smorta in viso come erba che langue,*
> *Tremo e fremo di brividi, ed anelo*
> > *Tacita, esangue.*

That one seems lifted to heaven among the gods, when near
You he sits and views your beautiful laughter, while feeling
Your gentle effusions and love-inspiring song!
> Suddenly in me

Rising in tumult the heartbeat batters my chest;
The voice dies away, as long as I gaze at you,
Upon my tongue: through a throat drawn tight as a string
> My sigh gasps for breath.

A serpent of fire enters my bloodstream, and burns there:
An indistinct tinkle and jangle encumber
My ears, and I daydream; there rises in me at the sight
> A cloudy shadow.

And soaking all through with a sweat that freezes,
And pallid in face as grass that withers away,
I tremble and shiver with shudders, and yearning I languish
> Silently, bloodless.

The Italian is technically brilliant. Without forgoing the elegant style and introspective imagery he had learned from Petrarch, Foscolo restores the sapphic measure. But what he prided his version on most was its ability to discriminate four different movements of passion. The first stanza, according to his analysis, expresses ecstasy without delirium, a gentle sensual fulfillment; the second breaks away abruptly to tumult and transports; the third is pervaded by "a more glowing ardour," confused and visionary; in the fourth, "the tumult—the ardour—the perturbation, disappear in a languor that approaches the icy chills of dissolution." Foscolo reads the Ode as an anthology of moods, each precisely distinguished from the others. Hence each stanza employs a different rhythm and a new stock of images. The translator seems less concerned with the literal sense of the words than with the shifting emotions of which they are signs. Indeed, he was so sure of having decoded the Ode that he had no doubt of how it must have ended: "Sappho finished like Phaedra in Euripides, by profound reflections upon the misery of desperate love." Foscolo views himself as a reincarnation of the classical lover; her spirit lives in him.

Perhaps a romantic lover lives there too. In order to convey "the contrasts and gradations of the original," a modern poet must heighten the details. The "voice" of the Greek girl divides, in Italian, into two separate functions, talking and singing; one Greek word for trembling requires an onomatopoeic set of three Italian words. Nor is the translation content to expand such details; it also makes them more violent. Sappho's "thin flame" is twisted into a serpent, and the "nothing" she sees turns into a gloomy shadow. Foscolo strives (perhaps too hard) to impress the vividness of the images upon modern readers, to shock us out of our stupor and carry us back to the fresh observations of classical art. But the paradox of such striving is that it can succeed only by enhancing the classic text with all the resources of turbulent modern art. Our senses are now too dull to respond to something as pure and simple as Sappho's lyric; it needs to be kindled first by romantic fire. Thus Foscolo serves as incendiary as well as translator. He recreates Sappho's spirit by projecting his own complexities into her, reading her poem as compounded equally of antique Greek precision and impulsive Italian hot blood. The mixture is very charming—worthy of Verdi. Yet no one would ever mistake this hybrid heroine for a woman of ancient Greece.

She also remains "Phaon's girl." As Foscolo interprets the symptoms of the Second Ode, they stand not only for love but despair. The woman who tosses among such passions is just one step from suicide; another brief stanza would finish her off. Thus she records what she hallucinates as well as what she feels. By emphasizing the variety of emotions rather than the momentum of a single seizure, Foscolo's version readies us for one more leap, this time into the abyss. Moreover, the heroine is self-conscious. She has time to dream and luxuriate in her sorrow, time to observe a shadow that foretells her death. In this way the translation, unlike the original, asks for our sympathy. Romantic glamor and gloom surround the heroine's preparation for suicide. Foscolo does not exaggerate this effect. Unlike other translators, he resists most of the sentimentality that blights the romantic Sappho. Divided though she may be, this heroine does not lack energy; she may be an abandoned woman, but she is not a waif. There are no tears in Foscolo's version, only one panting sigh. In this respect he shows a restraint unmatched by his contemporaries. But after him came the deluge.

BAUDELAIRE

During the course of the nineteenth century, the pathetic, suicidal, and outcast Sappho became constantly more estranged: a perfect symbol of the artist too good for this world. She bears a sorrow that cannot speak its name. Frustrated sexual passion, especially when lesbian in nature, might be the name of that sorrow. But much of the time she seems to suffer rather from her intelligence, which has unsuited her to play a proper feminine role. She is not a good mother or wife. Even when domesticated for middle-class consumption, as in the lovely, saccharine version of the Second Ode with which Tennyson concludes his "Eleänore" (1832), Sappho never seems at home. Victorian poets are ready to pity her, or to use her as an occasion for self-pity, but seldom to pay attention to her symptoms. They translate her into a shy or tongue-tied sweetheart. Certainly Tennyson admired the Second Ode. He took its first two lines as an epigraph for "Fatima" (1832), which also adapts the description of fire in the blood. Young Tennyson had no trouble envisioning himself as an abandoned woman; variations on that theme inform his career. Yet the extended version of the Ode in "Eleänore" surpasses even the capacity of Matthew Arnold (in "A Modern Sappho") for masculine self-absorption, since the cause of the speaker's swoon is not the sight of his beloved but the sound of his own name on her lips—presumably crooning "Alfred." Tennyson is known to have had a weakness for that sound; he found it very lulling. At any rate, his "languid fire," "brimm'd with delirious draughts of warmest life," does not burn with the sexual intensity of the Greek. The young male poet lowers the temperature. Displacing the feeling from ecstasy to intoxication, he resorts to Sappho's lines precisely to mark her distance from himself. The cosiness of his own musing, like a glass of good port, becomes still more warming when compared to the barbaric symptoms of that odd unhappy Greek person.

The ultimate sacrifice of Sappho, however, was performed by the hands of Baudelaire. From the beginning of his career the French poet betrayed his unease at the image of the Poetess—"burning Sapho, that patron-saint of hysterics." One of his earliest publications, probably written in collaboration with friends, parodies the Second Ode as it might be rendered in a modern sentimental play (a *Sapho* by Arsène Houssaye had recently been announced):

> *Oui, Phaon, je vous aime; et, lorsque je vous vois,*
> *Je pers le sentiment et la force et la voix.*
> *Je souffre tout le jour le mal de votre absence,*
> *Mal qui n'égale pas l'heur de votre présence;*
> *Si bien que vous trouvant, quand vous venez le soir,*
> *La cause de ma joie et de mon désespoir,*
> *Mon âme les compense, et sous les lauriers roses*
> *Étouffe l'ellébore et les soucis moroses.*
> Yes, Phaon, I love you; and, seeing you close,
> Take leave of my sense and my force and my voice.
> I suffer the ill of your absence all day,
> An ill that your presence alone can outweigh;
> So that, when you come in the evening, you share
> The cause of my happiness and my despair,
> My soul is rewarded, and under the holly
> The hellebore smothers and my melancholy.

Oleanders ("les lauriers roses") duel with hellebore in a mix of poisonous perfumes. Presumably the target of this travesty is not Sappho so much as the stale idolators who have turned the fire of her passion into sniffles and an honest lesbian into a clinging coquette—Manon in the guise of a Greek. Written in 1845, the parody anticipates a legion of Sapphos to come: the soft and languishing bird of passage painted by Gustave Moreau, modernized in fiction by Alphonse Daudet, and set to music by Gounod, Massenet, and Puccini. She lacks the energy even to die.

Yet Baudelaire's uneasiness comprehends the real Sappho as well. Brilliant, poetic women, women not content to remain passive vessels of his fantasies, rasp on his nerves. In a later tribute to Marceline Desbordes-Valmore, the "greatest" female poet of France (alas!), he praises her above all for her good taste in never rivalling men—least of all as an artist. "Madame Desbordes-Valmore was woman, was always woman and was absolutely only woman; but she was to an extraordinary degree the poetic expression of all the natural beauties of a woman." Against this paragon of ardent artless sentiment, Baudelaire deliberately places a horrid counterimage: the ambitious literary woman who would strive for "sacrilegious pastiches of the male mind." Authors like George Sand, consumed by the "impious wickedness" of writing like men, inevitably fall into "those masculine absurdities which in the woman take on the proportions of a monstrosity." Sappho herself could not escape this charge; she had tried to rise too high. Nor can Baudelaire, any more than Racine,

endure the possibility of a love without sin. The free pure Sappho, the
ideal of a perfect poet—that one must be dragged in the mud.

He dragged her down in "Lesbos." On its surface that poem (banned
by the censors in 1857) appears the most sympathetic of any of Baudelaire's excursions into the lesbian world. Here he portrays an island of
lush loving women, not the vampires or "damned women" of the lurid
companion poems. Moreover, the whole last part of the poem consists
of an homage to Sappho, specifically associated with the poet himself,
who has been chosen to "watch from the summit of Leucadia, / Like a
sentinel," for the return of her "adored cadaver."

> De la mâle Sapho, l'amante et le poète,
> Plus belle que Vénus par ses mornes pâleurs!
> —L'oeil d'azur est vaincu par l'oeil noir que tachette
> Le cercle ténébreux tracé par les douleurs
> De la mâle Sapho, l'amante et le poète!
> Of manly Sappho, the lover and the poet,
> Fairer than Venus through her pale repose!
> —The azure eye is conquered by the black eye's fret
> Around the shadowy ring traced by the woes
> Of manly Sappho, the lover and the poet!

Cleverly adapting Horace's word of praise for the Poetess, *mascula*, into
a *mâle* that strikes exactly the right false note, Baudelaire insinuates his
unease into the vehicle of celebration. A masculine shadow falls over Sappho. Her uncanny strength—both as an author and as a woman brave
enough to love other women—depends upon something perverse, less
homosexual than hermaphroditic. She competes with Venus precisely by
rejecting any sign of health or sexual pleasure. Indeed, it is even possible
that the "dismal pallors" and eyes ringed by shadow that Baudelaire pro-
fesses to find so attractive belong to a corpse. Floating in the sea for more
than two thousand years does wonders for the complexion! Nor can all
the beauty of this Sappho conceal that her sex is rotten.

The reason for such insinuations becomes clear only at the end of "Lesbos," when Baudelaire springs his trap. The desolation of the island, the
cruelty of the sea, the failure of lesbianism in the modern world—all
these are Sappho's fault. They began on "the day of her blasphemy," the
day when manlike Sappho yielded herself to a man.

> —De Sapho qui mourut le jour de son blasphème,
> Quand, insultant le rite et le culte inventé,
> Elle fit son beau corps la pâture suprême
> D'un brutal dont l'orgueil punit l'impiété
> De celle qui mourut le jour de son blasphème.
> —Of Sappho who died the day of her blasphemy,
> When, insulting the rite and cult of her own creed,

> She made her fine flesh the fodder most high
> Of a brute whose pride avenged the impious deed
> Of her who died the day of her blasphemy.

Suddenly we perceive that the whole poem has enacted a ritual intended for this moment: the sacrifice of the heroine. All Lesbos cries for her death. Ignoring the standard biographies of Sappho, which had given her a husband and child, Baudelaire converts her to the high priestess of a Lesbian cult. By taking a man, like Bellini's Norma she has betrayed her kind. The poem collapses the story of Phaon and the Leucadian leap into a single day (as if the cliff were on Lesbos) and interprets the remission into heterosexual love as supreme sacrilege. Manlike Sappho has doubled the sin of Eve, transgressing against her sex as well as the divine command. At that very instant the beauty of Lesbos faded. Her weakness has blighted the earth.

Moreover, the poem itself performs the ritual sacrifice that it describes. The implacable movement of the verse, notable both for its enjambments and for the brutal succession of monosyllables in line 3, culminates with a shock at "celle." For the only time in the poem, Baudelaire varies the last line of the stanza from the first, specifically to wipe out the name of Sappho and reduce it to "her." The Poetess had thought she could be more than woman, reversing the cycle of sin and damnation and championing a sex without guilt. But her own legend refutes that heresy. No woman can escape her flesh, fodder for a brute—named Phaon or Baudelaire—who teaches her that even her best songs exist to be desecrated by men. Deprived of a name, the eternal She merges with the first woman, whose insistence on using her own mind and asserting independence from her husband led immediately to death. Vengeance is mine, saith Baudelaire; henceforth Sappho and Eve must stay in their place. Let manlike women beware! "Lesbos" is a cruel poem. It victimizes the woman poet and blames her for her own victimization. And its beauty depends on the idea that Sappho—like every other heaven-storming poet—achieved her heights only by violating nature.

SWINBURNE

The theme was taken up by a poet who had studied at the feet of Sappho as well as Racine and Baudelaire, and had learned from them above all the virtues of being unnatural. Algernon Charles Swinburne paid them back in kind. In "Sapphics" and "Anactoria," his two brilliant exercises in the Lesbian mode, he finds a voice for Sappho that carries the poet's alienation from nature to its apotheosis—if not to the destruction of the gods. Phèdre's craving for death and Baudelaire's fear of women here reach immaculate expression; no poet has ever made more out of Sappho. To be sure, one might also call Swinburne absurd. His notion of lesbianism, compounded of equal parts of sadomasochism, violent rhetorical attack, cannibalism, games of domination, sentimentality, devil worship, infantile orality, and the promiscuous coupling of identical units of sound, might well offend the most tolerant reader. If a modern sapphist insisted on thrusting these poems into the flames, not many critics would risk burning their fingers to snatch them back. Nevertheless, however deplorable, "Anactoria" is unmatched in its worship of the Poetess. Anyone who wishes to see Sappho in all her glory must learn to read her with Swinburne's eyes.

He read her, to begin with, with boundless reverence, as "beyond all question and comparison *the very greatest poet that ever lived.*" Among the "whole world of verse" no poem could rival Sappho at her best, the "Ode to Anactoria" (as Swinburne called the Second Ode). How then might a male poet match it? A sense of inadequacy haunts Swinburne's description of the process that led to his own "Anactoria." "I tried, then, to write some paraphrase of the fragment which the Fates and the Christians have spared us. I have not said, as Boileau and Phillips have, that the speaker sweats and swoons at sight of her favourite by the side of a man. I have abstained from touching on such details, for this reason: that I felt myself incompetent to give adequate expression in English to the literal and absolute words of Sappho; and would not debase and degrade them into a viler form. . . . The descent is immeasurable from Sappho's verse to mine, or to any man's." The divinity of the ode bars any direct access. Yet Swinburne solves his problem (with the aid of Browning) by recreating the Poetess from within, in an extended dramatic monologue—not translation but transubstantiation. "I have striven to cast my spirit into the mould of hers, to express and represent not the poem but the poet." Greater than a god, we might say, he seems to Swinburne, that man allowed to think himself close to Sappho. Such proximity makes him faint. But the male poet willing to undergo this ordeal will be rewarded by seeing the whole world in a new way. Terror hardens the soul. Passed through the mind and words of Sappho, history and the universe itself become sapphic—permeated by her spirit.

The technical means of this permeation has no precedent in literature, so far as I know. At one point or another in "Anactoria" Swinburne translates virtually every fragment of Sappho known in his time—except the "Ode to Anactoria" itself. That alone, the author's note explains, he will not debase into English. Yet from another perspective *all* "Anactoria"— all 304 lines—derives from the Ode. Nor should this be understood merely in the vague sense of "influence." The sequence of the Ode precisely determines the structure of Swinburne's poem. He paraphrases Sappho's symptoms again and again, projecting them into every aspect

of nature and thought. Formally "Anactoria" might be considered a set
of variations on a theme never explicitly stated (as in Elgar's "Enigma
Variations"). But a more nearly accurate description, I believe, would
compare the poem to a great passacaglia, built over the foundation of a
repeated ground bass—the measures of Sappho's Ode—that never stops
sounding. Swinburne drums his favorite lyric into our ears so insistently
that eventually everything we hear assumes the same beat.

The opening lines of "Anactoria" may help to make this procedure
clear.

> My life is bitter with thy love; thine eyes
> Blind me, thy tresses burn me, thy sharp sighs
> Divide my flesh and spirit with soft sound,
> And my blood strengthens, and my veins abound.
> I pray thee sigh not, speak not, draw not breath;
> Let life burn down, and dream it is not death.

Almost every detail of the Ode—the pounding heart, the failure of sight
and speech, the division between bodily agitation and the observing
mind (or flesh and spirit), the burning, the veering toward death—recurs
in this passage. Without quoting any phrase verbatim, Swinburne nevertheless manages to communicate a precise sense of the original seizure.
But already one difference emerges: *this* Sappho has lost her objectivity.
Unlike her Greek counterpart, she knows just whom to blame for her
torment. The blinding and burning, for instance, occur not as agents of
a force too strong for any but a god, but rather as direct consequences of
Anactoria's own exercise of power—"*thine* eyes / Blind me, . . . thy
sharp sighs / Divide my flesh and spirit." Note also the one-to-one relation between cause and effect, as when eyes "blind" eyes. A sympathetic
magic seems implied, as if Anactoria's ceasing to sigh, speak, or breathe
could repair each of those falterings in Sappho. Hence the poetess stands
ready to turn on her persecutor, reversing the flow of bitterness until it
poisons the killer. Suicide verges on murder.

This reciprocity of pain, a sadomasochism that Swinburne apparently
considers the essence of lesbianism, dominates the next 150 lines of "Anactoria," through many versions of the sapphic ode. "Yea, all thy beauty
sickens me with love"—the emphasis should probably fall on "sickens."
It reaches a climax with the sadistic recoil of the pangs of love back upon
love's object.

> O that I,
> Durst crush thee out of life with love, and die,
> Die of thy pain and my delight, and be
> Mixed with thy blood and molten into thee!
> Would I not plague thee dying overmuch?

> Would I not hurt thee perfectly? not touch
> Thy pores of sense with torture, and make bright
> Thine eyes with bloodlike tears and grievous light?

The modes of torture continue for many more lines. Despite appearances, however, Swinburne has not merely let his fantasies run away with him. Instead he is trying to imagine love as it would be if the Second Ode told all the truth about it. If every seizure of love followed the same pattern, then Sappho's swoon into dying would have to be recognized not as a side effect of her passion but as its essence. The loved one would then be regarded not as an innocent bystander but as an instrument for inflicting pain, and the lover as a lover of pain. Swinburne pursues this logic to its end. Thus he recites the symptoms over and over, at an ever more feverish pitch, until they yield the secret that only Sappho knew: how love would have to be conceived if what we desired from it, both giving and taking, amounted at last to death.

Yet Swinburne has saved a still darker secret for his finale. Sappho survives not only as a lover, he reminds us, but as a creator; and ultimately her cruelty stems from her rivalry, as the greatest of mortal poets, with the first Creator:

> were I made as he
> Who hath made all things to break them one by one,
> If my feet trod upon the stars and sun
> And souls of men as his have alway trod,
> God knows I might be crueller than God.

If the creative acts of poets reflect, as the Neoplatonists thought, the primal creation or Logos, then God himself must be responsible for the tragic sense of human suffering that informs the best poetic creations. "The mystery of the cruelty of things" abides in creation itself. Hence Sappho's capacity for wounding and being wounded declares her the archetypal goddess-poet. God himself might envy her ingenuity at inventing torments. As Swinburne follows this thought out, he discovers an amazing implication in the Second Ode. Perhaps its story of a living god or godlike man who sits face to face with a breath-taking or death-dealing power yet seems immune to death is an allegory of that other god who made his son face death. Like Virgil's Fourth Eclogue, in this reading, the Second Ode predicts the coming of Jesus in atonement for the curse laid on woman. Sappho demands retribution.

> Hath he not sent us hunger? who hath cursed
> Spirit and flesh with longing? filled with thirst
> Their lips who cried unto him? who bade exceed
> The fervid will, fall short the feeble deed,
> Bade sink the spirit and the flesh aspire,
> Pain animate the dust of dead desire,

> And life yield up her flower to violent fate?
> Him would I reach, him smite, him desecrate,
> Pierce the cold lips of God with human breath,
> And mix his immortality with death.

The Crucifixion pays for Sappho's swoon.

Indeed, the woman revenges herself thoroughly in Swinburne's gospel. Her passion not only anticipates Christianity but exposes it, since by insisting on the cruelty of the Incarnation and Crucifixion she reveals the presence of sadism at the heart of Christian love. Sappho "loves" Jesus by identifying with his pain. Yet she also claims priority in suffering. In this respect "Anactoria" redresses a balance. On many occasions throughout history, in the poetry of abandoned women, abandonment by the lover has been used to symbolize divine abandonment. "My God, my God, why hast thou forsaken me?" But only in Swinburne's reading does the sense of being abandoned by God appear as a sort of plagiarism or belated imitation of the primal abandoned woman poet. Sappho knew martyrdom first; no man or manlike god can rival her poem. It is literally Swinburne's bible.

The rest of "Anactoria" borders on anticlimax. Yet Swinburne succeeds in extending the symptoms of the ode into an entire theology or metaphysics. He projects the swoon beyond the Cross into nature, which turns barren and sick as the pain of Sappho infects it, and into an estrangement or entropy that brings down the stars. Nothing can assuage those symptoms, the poet concludes,

> Till time wax faint in all his periods;
> Till fate undo the bondage of the gods,
> And lay, to slake and satiate me all through,
> Lotus and Lethe on my lips like dew,
> And shed around and over and under me
> Thick darkness and the insuperable sea.

Even the Leucadian leap, Swinburne hints, anticipates the apocalypse or the end of time itself. If Sappho retains some of her nineteenth-century pathos, at the close of "Anactoria," the reason is not her "frailty" but the limitations placed on the highest human life. Darkness and the sea will eventually surround her like the obscurity that has blotted out all but a few fragments of her poems, because our memories have failed. Mankind (and perhaps womankind too) has not kept faith with its archetypal poet. We have allowed nature and history to separate us from the ecstasy of the Second Ode, and we have confused it with our own deaths. Hence Sappho grows weary. Yet the pain and loneliness that spurred her song (and that of every lesser poet as well) pass down to us as our universal human heritage. When Swinburne looks at the sky, he sees her face.

Thus Sappho remounted the heights—infinitely above the rest of her species. Nor has that vision faded even today. In the past hundred years the sapphophilia and sappholatry of classicists have hardly wavered. An amusing test of this phenomenon occurred at the turn of this century, when a number of fragments from Sappho were discovered in the scrap-paper lining of some ancient Egyptian coffins. For a generation of scholars raised on Symonds's dictum that every word of the Poetess had a seal of absolute *perfection,* the findings excited considerable tension. Would some of the words, or parts of words, turn out to be slightly flawed? The scholarly world held its breath. But at length, after the new evidence had been sifted, a happy fanfare blew abroad to the nations: these words and pieces of words were also Perfect. "Out of the dust of Egypt there came one beautiful fragment after another to justify the opinion previously held." Swinburne and Symonds had been right after all: the Poetess did belong to a higher species.

4 Sappho Descending:
Abandonment to the Present

> "You are all men, you bastard, and just like the others—
> no-man Odysseus so clever at cutting and running
> or my own husband, whoever he might be—you
>   never existed."
>
> "Sappho to Phaon"

CALLING ON SAPPHO

A poet on the heights is out of reach. Hence, for one part of our species, the idolization of Sappho—the glass case and signs of Do Not Touch enclosing each of her fragments—has never seemed quite satisfactory. A pedestal discourages conversation. And what women have asked from Sappho, in the past several hundred years, has not been an image to worship but a speaking voice. Indeed, the tradition of women's poetry in the West (at least until the twentieth century) might very nearly be identified with the transmission and rehabilitation of Sappho. Hers is the voice that speaks when others fall silent—the founding muse, the mother of us all. Once and for all time she proves the genius of women. And if only other women could communicate with that genius—converse with it, build on it, take it in—they might engender a poetry of their own.

Yet the genius of Sappho has seldom been easy to live with. Her reputation precedes her and dictates a role. At times she has loomed as a stifling and warning presence: the one acknowledged type of woman poet, who forces every other to take her stamp. Hence almost every female author, for centuries at a time, has been squashed by the same comparison: Louise Labé, the "Sappho Lyonnaise"; Aphra Behn, who held the title of the English "Sappho" against many challengers; die Karschin, "the German Sappho"; Madame du Boccage, the "modern Sappho" of France; Eurica Dionigi, the "Sappho Lazia"; "Carmen Sylva," not only Queen of Rumania but the Rumanian Sappho; Ada Negri, "the proletarian Sappho"; the American Sappho, Sara Teasdale; or Renée Vivien, "Sappho 1900." The list could be multiplied by ten, and no doubt a bit more research would uncover the Polish Sappho, the Arkansas Sappho, and the Sappho of Ultima Thule. Certainly many women have sought the honor. We can only imagine what feelings were stirred on that occasion, for instance, when "one evening in 1827, as the story goes, the great

Manzoni in the presence of Lamartine called La Palli, the happy-hearted
Italian poetess, a 'Saffo novella.'" Yet such women may also have felt
themselves clamped in a vise. We do not call T. S. Eliot, after all, a St.
Louis Virgil. A woman dubbed "Sappho" has received some subtle encouragement not to be her own imperfect self. No wonder, then, that
more than one woman poet has asserted her identity by breaking her ties
to Sappho. When Anne Bradstreet's poems were published in 1650, her
brother-in-law usurped Sappho's title by calling the book *The Tenth Muse
Lately Sprung Up in America,* but Bradstreet herself insisted that the Old
World and old myths had nothing to do with her. "The *Greeks* did
nought, but play the foole and lye. / Let *Greeks* be *Greeks,* and Women
what they are." Better an honest wife and childbearer than a transplanted
barren Sappho.

Yet most female poets have held out their hands to Sappho. Above all
they have wanted to touch her, joining hands not only with her genius
but with a tradition or community of literary women—a salute passed
down through the ages to each new sister in the muse. Just as juvenile
male poets, ever since Milton, have habitually begun their careers by
addressing some lines to Shakespeare—presumably hoping for a laying
on of hands—so ambitious young women have often called on Sappho.
Sometimes, as with the adolescent Christina Rossetti's lugubrious, much-
sighing "Sappho" (1846)—later suppressed by her brother William—
they have tried to establish a line of descent directly by entering her
mind. (When Virginia Woolf wrote that Christina "was about as good as
poetesses are made, since Sappho jumped," she picked exactly the most
appropriate praise.)

Sometimes the approach is more tentative. Consider, for instance,
what may be the first poem preserved by the teenaged Emily Brontë
(1836?).

> Cold, clear, and blue, the morning heaven
> Expands its arch on high;
> Cold, clear, and blue, Lake Werna's water
> Reflects that winter's sky.
> The moon has set, but Venus shines
> A silent, silvery star.

In more ways than one this poem represents the birth of an identity.
Specifically, it functions as a "birth stanza" for A. G. A., the queen of
Brontë's Gondal cycle, and claims "her birthright as a daughter of Venus." Venus presides over all great heroines of poetry, as once she had
presided over Sappho. Brontë deliberately avoids any masculine influence
(in fact, no male progenitor of A. G. A. is mentioned). Inventing the first
of her fictional kingdoms, she describes the cold English climate with

sapphic clarity and imagines the world as an enclosed space dominated by an ascendant female star. Nature is not allowed to interfere. Technically, the Wordsworthian picture of the sky reflected in the lake, where we might expect to see the morning sun, yields to a ghostly vision—no *reciprocity* between the mind and nature, as so often in Wordsworth, but an eerie supernatural light. Even the refusal of the last couplet to rhyme, thus eluding the conventions of ordinary English verse, restores the stanza to a timeless, unlocalized mode of speech, like some literal translation from the Greek. "The moon has set"—those words belong to Sappho. Brontë does not claim any direct descent. But when she tries to imagine a world formed by the desires of women—a world most unlike England—what she sees is a woman's star.

The silence and privacy of that birthright, however, may also call attention to a paradox of Sappho's influence: she teaches her later sisters that they are alone. The touch of Sappho brings no companionship but only intensified solitude. Thus Christina Rossetti can imagine only one end for her own pathetic heroine: "Living unloved, to die unknown, / Unwept, untended, and alone." The abandoned woman necessarily sings to herself; no other audience dare approach her. Hence Sappho, despite her fame, remains *unknown*. She has certainly never been skilled at conversation. Even the fragmentary nature of her work as it comes down to us, a few scattered pages blown away from the fire, reminds us of the irretrievable distance across which she speaks. The greatest woman poet is a lost soul. And any number of later women, hoping to found a tradition or at least a cult of Sappho, have run up against the same problem. The tradition of the female poet consists largely of outcasts, divided from themselves and each other: a "community" of isolated individuals. Each generation reinvents Sappho, and sometimes even Sappho's companions; but passing Sappho's *strength* from one generation to the next has proved almost impossibly difficult. Louise Labé, Felicia Hemans, Christina Rossetti, Rosalía de Castro, Ada Negri, HD, Marina Tsvetayeva feel most identified with Sappho when they feel most alone.

Teasdale as Sister and Daughter

A good deal of interesting poetry has dealt immediately with this problem. It is related, of course, to the issue of "sisterhood" (as we call it today); and few poems have discussed such issues more frankly and engagingly (if clumsily) than Amy Lowell's "The Sisters" (1922).

> Taking us by and large, we're a queer lot
> We women who write poetry. And when you think
> How few of us there've been, it's queerer still.
> ....
> There's Sapho, now I wonder what was Sapho.

. . . .
Ah, me! I wish I could have talked to Sapho,
Surprised her reticences by flinging mine
Into the wind. . . .
And listen, thinking all the while 'twas she
Who spoke and that we two were sisters
Of a strange, isolated little family.
And she is Sapho—Sapho—not Miss or Mrs. . . .

These lines would not be hard to ridicule. Anyone who takes a mental snapshot of Amy Lowell flinging off her garments in order to put Sapho at her ease (the image of stripping always fascinates Lowell) might be tempted to sketch a burlesque Beerbohm cartoon. But the reflex is surely unfair, for the difficulty and unlikelihood of such conversations suggest exactly Lowell's point. She tries to imagine a different poetic tradition. What would it be like to speak as a woman poet with no last name inherited from some man, with no Miss or Mrs. before her? What would it be like if female poets generated their own little family, sharing something beside their loneliness? What would it be like to live always with Sappho in the imagination, sharing her utter commitment to passion and poetry as a sister?

The situation would certainly be very queer. I take the word from Lowell, not limiting it to the modern restrictive sense (as if everything queer must conform to one kind of queerness!) but noticing that Lowell too inevitably associates female poets with something "strange" or sexually forbidden. Unbuttoned Sappho, prudish Mrs. Browning, and Emily Dickinson who "hoarded—hoarded"—these make up the trio of sisters whom Amy Lowell finds "marvellously strange, . . . frightfully near, and rather terrifying." Lesbianism does not terrify this poet. But a genuine anxiety strikes her at the thought that poetry and womanhood form an unnatural combination, or at the least require a sacrifice of ordinary human relations. "The strength of forty thousand Atlases / Is needed for our every-day concerns." Sappho's strength is frightening, not to mention her sexual preferences. Lowell does not mention them; the time had not yet come to fling certain reticences to the wind. Yet much of the interest of "The Sisters" derives from the author's mixed feelings as she regards the others of her species, conversing with them on her own terms but distrustful of theirs. Even the slack technique of the poem declares Lowell's reluctance to sacrifice too much of her own life to such very demanding muses.

An example lay near at hand. One almost-sister with whom Lowell liked to discuss her art was the American Sappho herself, the most popular female poet of the early twentieth century: the not-quite-forgotten Sara Teasdale. *She* had willingly given her life to Sappho. But Teasdale's love for her Greek sister and muse was never quite reciprocated. Constraints ringed her round: the demand for respectability that leads Teasdale always to insist on Sappho's purity and sexual orthodoxy; the painfully timid poetic technique and sentimentality that won so many early admirers who later wearied of such predictable effects; and perhaps even a denial of the poet's own sexual nature (as biographers have lately hinted, her "unsatisfactory" marriage may have been a futile attempt to disguise her preference for women even from herself). Her most ambitious effort to recapture the Greek spirit, a blank-verse monologue "Sappho" (1913), asks not for love but peace. "I wanted Sappho to be almost suave in her attitude and perfectly self-possessed," she told a friend. "I wanted to get away from the passionately hysterical Sappho that most people have done." Joyce Kilmer, an early reviewer, described the poem well as "stately." In order to identify properly with Sappho, Teasdale first must scrub her clean. And the voice that survives this treatment sounds very faint.

Teasdale's most interesting verses about Sappho directly confront the problem of how to approach her. Rather than force an entrance into that alien mind, they sidle around it, trying to catch glimpses through the eyes of friends and family. At her most honest, Teasdale views herself not as a reincarnation of Sappho but as an abandoned, would-be daughter. The poem "To Cleïs (The Daughter of Sappho)" unfolds this theme best.

> When the dusk was wet with dew,
>   Cleïs, did the muses nine
>   Listen in a silent line
> While your mother sang to you?
>
> Did they weep or did they smile
>   When she crooned to still your cries,
>   She, a muse in human guise,
> Who forsook her lyre awhile?
>
> Did you feel her wild heart beat?
>   Did the warmth of all the sun
>   Through your little body run
> When she kissed your hands and feet?
>
> Did your fingers, babywise,
>   Touch her face and touch her hair,
>   Did you think your mother fair,
> Could you bear her burning eyes?
>
> Are the songs that soothed your fears
>   Vanished like a vanished flame,
>   Save the line where shines your name
> Starlike down the graying years? . . .

Cleïs speaks no word to me,
   For the land where she has gone
   Lies as still at dusk and dawn
As a windless, tideless sea.

Despairing of any chance to look on Sappho bare, Teasdale seeks out an intermediary, someone to confirm her reality. The child is mother to the woman, and by touching her own sources of childlike wonder the poet hopes to recover her belief in preternatural genius. The goddess Sappho bore a human line. But the interrogation, unfortunately, leads nowhere. Cleïs is dead as her mother, and the last question fizzles, since its answer has already been anticipated: yes, the songs *are* vanished and Cleïs has vanished too. The sea of time and death lies motionless. Teasdale can find no way to be transported back to Sappho.

Nor is it clear that she genuinely wants to see her. The mother-muse descends not only in beauty but fear. Behind those questions about the frightening mother—"Did you feel her wild heart beat? . . . Could you bear her burning eyes?"—an earlier poem about creation, Blake's "Tyger," exerts its pressure. The passions of Sappho inspire Teasdale with the same dread as the cruelty of a beast. Whether we attribute that dread specifically to sex—the thought of being touched by Sappho—or to the uncontrollable energy of poetry itself, the modern poet can hardly endure the presence of the muse except at second hand. (Even the force of "The Tyger" is somewhat diluted, in "To Cleïs," by the aimless inquisitiveness of a common precursor, "Twinkle Twinkle Little Star.") Blake's poem marks his confidence, according to many critics, in his own powers of creation. The tiger cannot intimidate *him,* because a true poetic genius will not bow to any Nobodaddy or distant heavenly creator. But "To Cleïs" affords a disturbing comparison. Sappho's creations, her songs and her daughter, have both been effaced, and even the idea of female creativity seems threatening. Only a melancholy afterthought remains. Hence Sappho's lullabies serve the purpose of soothing the fears that her own presence had excited. Teasdale does not dare to come close. The woman poet should not spy out the primal scene of original creation, in her view, but instead lament her own inability to remember a mother. Poetry, for a woman, consists of being deprived. Only one thing could devastate Teasdale more than Sappho's gradual extinction: the return of Sappho herself.

Renée Vivien

A similar prayer echoes through the verse of many women: come, Sappho, come—but not too close. Thus much of the history of women's poetry could be allegorized as a version of the Second Ode, in which need and dread balance each other so perfectly as to induce a not unpleasing paralysis. Hundreds of poets repeat symptoms of the same condition: sapphophobia, or the fear of high poetic places. One method of treating it, the popular compromising line of Teasdale, undertakes to catch Sappho's inspiration without the sex, the passion, and the loneliness that traditionally accompany it—abandon without abandonment. Seventeen-year-old Jane Colman, daughter of the president of Harvard, expressed the common dream of a female poet in 1725: "O let me burn with *Sappho's* noble Fire, / But not like her for faithless man expire." But her marriage the following year to the Reverend Ebenezer Turell seems to have quenched the fire along with the apprehension. Sappho does nothing by halves. Young Elizabeth Barrett put the consequences ruthlessly in her "Vision of Poets": "And Sappho, with that gloriole / / Of ebon hair on calmèd brows— / O poet-woman! none forgoes / The leap, attaining the repose." The muse will not be satisfied by partial measures. "Who chooseth me must give and hazard all she hath." And the compromised version of Sappho's influence, whatever its charms, has tended more to evade than recover her strength.

A second method for coping with this dilemma—the need and dread inflicted equally by Sappho—would summon her authority to break through all the customary inhibitions that society imposes on literary women. Even a literal translation of the Second Ode can stimulate a new frankness toward sex. Hence the outburst of Victorian love poetry by women, a freedom of speech that greatly impressed Ellen Moers, may be attributed in part to a better distribution of Sapphic remains. How closely does one translate them? A daring young woman poet may well be suspected of wanting to go all the way. Thus the New York poet Mary E. Hewitt, in her "Imitation of Sappho" (1853), draws on the Second Ode to express irresistible passion.

> If when thou utterest low words of greeting,
> > To feel through every vein the torrent pour;
> Then back again the hot tide swift retreating,
> > Leave me all powerless, silent as before—
>
> If to list breathless to thine accents falling,
> > Almost to pain, upon my eager ear;
> And fondly when alone to be recalling
> > The words that I would die again to hear—
>
> If at thy glance my heart all strength forsaking,
> > Pant in my breast as pants the frighted dove;
> If to think on thee ever, sleeping—waking—
> > Oh, if this be to love thee, I do love!

The triteness of the verse should not be allowed to obscure the nerve of the poet's revelation: like Sappho, she has a body. Almost without exception, "there is no other poet at this time, male or female," according to

Emily Stipes Watts, "who dared to approach woman's sexuality this explicitly." Doubtless many modern readers will regret that Hewitt did not
go further. The feminine dependency and passivity of her images, her
"powerless" ardor, "all strength forsaking," confess her helpless submission to a man. Moreover, the inevitable reduction of all symptoms to
nothing but love robs the emotion of its sapphic ecstasy and mystery. Yet
clearly the ode has been enlisted in a good cause: the cause of woman's
freedom.

　More talented women also joined that cause. By the end of the nineteenth century a vogue of Sappho had spread across Europe, trailing after
it a fashion for Grecian costumes and phrases. Few educated women
passed through adolescence without adopting some sapphic poses. Male
homosexuals encouraged the style, and female homosexuals enjoyed a
new sense of liberation. Sappho no longer had to die in pain; sometimes
she lived happily ever after with her sisters. Much of the literature that
resulted from this vogue trivialized the original poetry past all recognition. But some authors paid deadly serious homage to Sappho, combing
her work for lessons in changing their lives. A few may even have succeeded in catching her spirit, drawing so close that all dread vanished. Of
these, the exemplary figure is Renée Vivien (1877–1909).

　No one can accuse Vivien, at any rate, of having given less than her all
to Sappho. Much of her life was deliberately modeled on a conception of
the Poetess. When the young Anglo-American woman Pauline Tarn
transformed herself into the French lesbian poet "Renée Vivien," the decisive influence was not only her friend and lover Natalie Barney but
Sappho's verse, to which Barney had introduced her. Sappho gave birth
to Vivien, and Vivien never left her. She studied Greek in order to capture every nuance of the poetry; she procured a villa at Mitylene; she
dressed and spoke in antique style, and gathered a circle of like-minded
women around her; and even her tragic early death (which today might
be attributed to anorexia) was predicted by many poems about the abandoned and desperate Sappho. In poetry, above all, Vivien tried to rein-
carnate her idol. Volume after volume witnesses the obsession. She edited and translated the texts with surprising fidelity, and then embellished
them repeatedly in a series of imitations, variations, monologues, and
dramas. Nor should one underestimate the quality of this verse. Unlike
many other disciples of Sappho, Vivien understands that true reverence
requires attention to a demanding legacy: an all-consuming devotion to
the craft of putting exactly the right words in exactly the right order.

　Yet Sappho was not always kind to her disciple. The Poetess that Vivien inherited had passed through many hands—especially the hands of
Baudelaire, Swinburne, and Verlaine—and their touch had made her
cruel. A woman poet who inherited the love of "pure poetry" would also
have learned that purity at its best is flavored by corruption—not least

the corruption of women. Vivien had studied those male masters well. Interpreting Sappho, she looks for the taint that must underlie apparent surface perfection; and of course she finds it. "Lesbians had the bizarre and slightly perverse traits of mixed races." Thus Sappho's charm reflects the hybrid nature of her breed, on that Greek island just off the coast of Asia Minor, where the "perfumed shadows" of the Orient and "the blue eyes of Greece" mingle together. It would be possible to read Vivien's analysis as the result of a typical Western obsession with the "decadence" of the East, or as an Anglo-American-French woman's attempt to project her own divided nature onto her idol, or even as a racial explanation of lesbianism (in which blue eyes and olive skin yearn for each other). All these seem plausible. But Vivien is most of all a poet, and what she seeks to find in Sappho's background is most of all the secret of her style, "Asiatic by the violence of the passion, and Greek by the rare chiseling and sober charm of the strophe." The trace of violence lends Sappho's purity its fascinating undertones. It also gives a peculiar edge to Vivien's fine version of the Second Ode.

ODE À UNE FEMME AIMÉE
L'homme fortuné qu'enivre ta présence
Me semble l'égal des Dieux, car il entend
Ruisseler ton rire et rêver ton silence,
        Et moi, sanglotant,

Je frissonne toute, et ma langue est brisée;
Subtile, une flamme a traversé ma chair,
Et ma sueur coule ainsi que la rosée
        Âpre de la mer;

Un bourdonnement remplit de bruits d'orage
Mes oreilles, car je sombre sous l'effort,
Plus pâle que l'herbe, et je vois ton visage
        A travers la mort.

ODE TO A LOVED WOMAN
The happy man made drunken by your presence
Seems equal to the gods to me, because he hears
Your streaming laughter and your dreaming silence,
        And myself, sobbing,

I shiver through and through, and my tongue shatters;
Subtle, a flame has passed across my flesh,
And my sweat trickles just like the bitter
        Dew of the sea;

A humming saturates my ears with the noise
Of thunderstorms, for I sink beneath the strain,
Paler than any grass, and then I see your face
        Crossed over by death.

Prosodically the verse is a triumph, one of the best examples of the sapphic stanza in French. Few poets have come closer to the sound of the Greek. Vivien's hendecasyllables, which may be heard as an abbreviated feminine version of Baudelaire's alexandrines, as an unstressed equivalent of Swinburne's English "Sapphics," or as an illustration of Verlaine's doctrine that rhythmic charm always requires something "odd," leave the reader with a "strange sensation of incompletion," intensified by the equally odd line of five syllables. The ear experiences a continually deferred closure, resulting in a mild, not unpleasant vertigo or "sinking." Hence Vivien communicates a sense of frustration through the verse itself.

The oddness extends beyond the rhythm, however. Each of Vivien's additions to the text she worships introduces a note of self-conscious impurity. Thus the lucky man, in her scenario, is *intoxicated* by the presence of the beloved; neither strong nor invulnerable, he coarsely enjoys his unfair advantage. By contrast, the poet herself luxuriates in exaggerated ill fortune. Rather than simply record her symptoms, she invests them with cosmic repercussions, comparing her inner tidings with the sea, thunderstorms, the face of death. Nor can they be interpreted as signs of ecstasy. The shocking end of the first stanza, "sanglotant" (sobbing), covers all the rest of the poem with a weight of grief. Moreover, it implicitly cuts the speaker off from her loved one, whose laughter and silence are brutally juxtaposed against the vocal agony of an unheeded love. Perhaps that rejection is just what Vivien wants. Unlike Sappho, she does not even *look* at the other woman until the very end, when the first sight of the face is superimposed on a vision of death. No medicine could assuage such melodramatic self-pity. One critic has diagnosed the condition of the French poem as "erotic manicheism," a duel between Eros and Aphrodite or God and Satan. At any rate the view of love is not simple. Even the title, "Ode à une femme aimée," suggests a signature by "une femme damnée."

Indeed, Vivien may have intended to emphasize her distance from Sappho, the impossibility of recreating, in the modern world, the ancient love between women. A sinister power has intervened to keep women apart and poetry impure. Part of the blame must surely fall on men—not only the "happy man" who blocks out the beloved but the male poets who had appropriated lesbian themes for their own dark purposes. "Lesbos" and "Anactoria" had taught Sappho hatred, and Vivien responds to that hate. The love of woman for woman is seldom unmixed, in her work, with a morbid need to be punished. It is as if the French poet had internalized the misogyny of her masters. But that self-contempt only makes her yearning more poignant. From this perspective we might read the "Ode" as addressed from Vivien to Sappho herself: the loved one forever separated from her lover by time, men, inhibition, and death.

Not even the devotion of a lifetime will bring Sappho back. Hence the genuine charm and beauty of Vivien's work depend on an absence: the muse adrift in the sea. Searching for purity, the French poet willingly renounces any society but that of women, any verse without feminine endings. At last she also sacrificed herself. But not even that gesture could restore the Second Ode. The Sappho of Vivien's imagination retains the sickly pallor with which Baudelaire had painted her; held too close, she takes on the color of death. And her failure to reciprocate the love of her disciple, or satisfy her needs, may lead to hostility. The daughters of Sappho have not always found her an ally. She asks too much; she walks under no one's banner. To love her as Vivien loved her can overburden a woman poet with a sense of inadequacy. Perfection, like any drug, addicts those who crave it until it consumes the rest of life. Learning to see through the eyes of Sappho, putting aside all dread of social constraints or suicidal feelings, Vivien eventually began to dread looking in a mirror.

HD

Not every literary woman has thought that sacrifice worthwhile. Those ambitious of some achievement larger than a perfectly chiseled lyric, in particular, have often begun their careers by revolting from Sappho. Thus thirteen-year-old Elizabeth Barrett, in the amusing and courageous preface to her epic "Battle of Marathon," rejoices to be living in an age when a female poet need not fear "being celebrated by her friends as a *Sappho*," and declares her allegiance instead to Homer. And more than a hundred years later, in the "Poem out of Childhood" that ultimately introduced her *Collected Poems*, Muriel Rukeyser similarly rejected the dead name of

> Sappho, with her drowned hair trailing along Greek waters,
> weed binding it, a fillet of kelp enclosing
> the temples' ardent fruit :
>
> Not Sappho, Sacco.

Both these poets base their ambitions on a community that includes men as well as women, that considers abundance as honorable as compression, and that has wearied more than a little of Sappho and the female sensitivities she emblemizes. Homer and Sacco play on a larger stage. Yet both Mrs. Browning and Ms. Rukeyser, one might note, eventually won recognition for lyrics about their experiences as women. Nor would it be difficult to trace the Sapphic themes and images in those lyrics. The Tenth Muse is a jealous goddess; she insists on descending even into those who might prefer to worship someone else. Ignoring Sappho has not proved much easier, for women poets, than coming to terms with her.

One final method for coping with the problem has been only rarely attempted. What if a poet were to make her need and dread of Sappho, her mixed desire for and resistance to a mother-muse, the source of her poems themselves? One author at least has built her career on this question, by using her difficulty in communicating with Sappho as a model of the difficulty of speech and of human relations in general. I refer to the poet HD. In six poems inspired by Sapphic fragments, as well as in pieces of many others, the young poet tests her own distance from Sappho by deliberately imagining herself as a reborn Greek spirit. HD could hardly avoid the comparison. Even her fledgling verses (influenced by the *Greek Anthology*) reminded people of Sappho, and Ezra Pound, her first suitor and mentor, was thrilled by the innate imagism and classicism that she personified. "H.D. has lived with these things since childhood, and knew them before she had any book-knowledge of them." For a brief period in 1912 and 1913, while Pound invented "H.D. Imagiste" and also modern poetry, she served as his Exhibit A: "Objective—no slither; direct—no excessive use of adjectives, no metaphors that won't permit examination. It's straight talk, straight as the Greek!" Sappho had come again. From that moment HD's reputation as a hard, pure lyricist and imagist was established—a reputation that has endured to the present.

Later it came to seem a misunderstanding. In the long run HD's talents were not those of an imagist, at least not according to any strict definition of the term. She saw herself rather as a mythographer, or more precisely as an interrogator of signs, someone who spent her life interpreting the visionary question marks she saw written on a wall: "another question, another question mark, a half-*S,* the other way round, *S* for *s*eal, *s*ymbol, *s*erpent certainly, *s*ignet, *S*igmund." The name HD itself was such a sign. So of course was the name *S*appho. Yet before HD could embark upon her final project of converting her personal history into an enduring, woman-centered epic, she had to subjugate the Poetess in herself. In part this meant turning away from the small, chiseled form of the lyric, with its ruthless drive toward a perfection that allowed no trace of anything merely human. The poet would have to come out of her shell (as in one of HD's favorite poems, "The Chambered Nautilus"). In part the struggle with Sappho also meant acknowledging her sexual nature. HD's early lyric achievements had been guided by men—Pound, Richard Aldington, later D. H. Lawrence. To some extent her identification with Sappho provided a refuge or female retreat where they could not follow. But that refuge also implied a coldness or sexual distance from men, if not explicit lesbian tendencies. The disastrous breakup of her marriage to Aldington, along with other desertions, led HD to associate herself with Ariadne and Ariadne with Sappho, the muse of unhappy love and abandoned women. Most of the "Fragments from Sappho" deal with this theme. Yet they offer a series of screens, in which painful heterosexual love is screened as love between women and love between women dares not speak its name. The thought of Sappho confuses HD. Perhaps the most honest of the fragments, "the deep center of her poetry," is "Fragment Thirty-six / *I know not what to do:* / *my mind is divided.*" The poet does not know whether to choose love or art; nor does she know whether she prefers women or men.

HD's most overt effort to resolve her ambivalence about Sappho occurs in an odd prose version of the Second Ode. In the unpublished novel *Asphodel* (1922), Hermione (a thinly disguised HD) declares her love for Fayne Rabb (Frances Gregg) and insists that their mutual passion requires no screens. "I don't want to be (as they say crudely) a boy. Nor do I want you to so be. I don't feel a girl. What is all this trash of Sappho? None of that seems real, to (in any way) matter. I see you. I feel you. My pulse runs swiftly. My brain reaches some height of delirium. Do people say it's indecent? Maybe it is. I can't hear now see anymore, people." Trashing the Second Ode, HD rebels against what she perceives as its anxiety, its screens, its failure of the senses. Why should Sappho begin by invoking a masculine rival? Because she *wants* to be a boy (in HD's reading); rather than face her lesbian love directly, she projects her desires onto a man and punishes herself with symptoms of terror and death. Hermione preaches a healthier love of woman for woman, a love that would enjoy the body's excitement as a heightening of life that shuts all other people out. Such love would free HD not only of Sappho but of her own ambivalence as a poet. She later told Freud that she might have been happy with Frances Gregg. But he denied it—"No—biologically, no"—and informed her that she *did* want to be a boy. Whatever we think of this analysis ("The Professor was not always right"), the fact remains that HD never eliminated the phantom male from her own poetry. She was bound to Sappho forever, by need and dread.

The first of the Sapphic lyrics, "Fragment 113," draws the issues most clearly. Though ostensibly an amplification of the tiny cryptic phrase "*Neither honey nor bee for me,*" the verse performs a set of free variations (as critics have noticed) on the Second Ode. HD approaches her text obliquely, with cunning and indirection. H. T. Wharton, whose edition of Sappho supplied her information, mentions the usual interpretation of the phrase as a proverb "referring to those who wish for good unmixed with evil." But the modern poet reads the words another way, as a rejection of any passion that might cloy the taste or touch with sweetness. Instead she craves something fierce:

> though rapture blind my eyes,
> and hunger crisp
> dark and inert my mouth,
> not honey, not the south . . .

The gift of flowers will serve her only as a sunscreen or lens, "withering the grass." In place of southern fragrances, she invites the shock of resistance.

> not iris—old desire—old passion—
> old forgetfulness—old pain—
> not this, nor any flower,
> but if you turn again,
> seek strength of arm and throat,
> touch as the god;
> neglect the lyre-note;
> knowing that you shall feel,
> about the frame,
> no trembling of the string
> but heat, more passionate
> of bone and the white shell
> and fiery tempered steel.

In one of its dimensions this is obviously a love poem (stubborn as Frost's "To Earthward") which hardens against the image of a feminine yielding or opening, as a flower awaits the "deep plunge" of a bee, and instead promises the lover a heat and resistance like steel. Men had often failed HD, and here she seems to recant the old desire for heterosexual love. Whoever takes her in future will not find her soft. At the same time we may read the lyric as an imaginary sequel to the Second Ode. The speaker—Sappho or HD—has passed through the weak phase of her sexual swoon and been tempered by it into a passion strong enough to endure a god. Indeed, she avows herself a goddess. The subtle fire beneath the skin has burned away the flesh, trembling no longer "seizes all my body," and any lover who dares to touch her may come away scorched. This poet is no worshiper of others but proud to the bone.

Yet the poem claims another dimension. The image of the lyre, consistently worked out through the final eight lines, marks the object of the lover's or reader's embraces as less a flesh-and-blood woman than an instrument or muse. The poet offers herself as a pure lyric spirit, purged of its human weakness. Who touches her touches a lyre. But no harmony, no lyre note or trembling string, will transpire from this contact. Instead the frame burns with heat as if the tempering of its steel were never to stop. HD renounces the song while claiming direct access to the passion that inspires it. Sappho lives not in her fragments or remains, on this reading, but in her originating act of renunciation: the lyre that refuses to play. Hence the vanished Sappho might be considered the speaker, from another point of view, and HD the lover who turns to her, striving toward the same condition of passionate silence. The modern poet satisfies her need by embracing dread. HD wants Sappho not for her beauty but her emptiness, a symbol of the vast spaces that separate any lovers and of the abandonment that declares itself visibly in the gaps within fragments and the breaks between lines. The poems of women know how to occupy such spaces. Deprived of flesh and blood, they sing along the bone.

HD was not content to give her life to fragments. But her early enchantment with Sappho has not been lost on men. They too have seized on bits of broken verse, resistant to interpretation or communion, as signs of a positive value. Even the scholarly editions of Sappho, Hugh Kenner has noted, have helped disseminate a poetic taste for ruptures in logic and discontinuous rhythms. A reader who has studied such editions, as Ezra Pound did, will not find Pound's *Cantos* so jarring. Nor will HD's reluctance to connect her thoughts to each other or Sappho baffle a reader who has learned to associate poetry itself with the avoidance of direct statement. We distinguish verse from prose by the amount of white space on the page, and few poets surpass HD at leaving the page uncluttered. Hence her work assumes the hardness of a classic—at least a modern classic. And the theme that her variations on Sappho return to so often—the theme of a love whose heat is fueled by absence and loss, a love without yielding or reciprocity, a love always disconnected from its object—may well be considered the classical modern theme.

T. S. ELIOT

Indeed, the influence of Sappho penetrates to the core of what we define as modern. Surely *The Waste Land* typifies the modern movement in poetry at its most intense, the climate and tone of voice that taught a generation what it felt; and no passage manifests *The Waste Land* more fully, according to many critics, than the lines to "the hyacinth girl."

> —Yet when we came back, late, from the Hyacinth garden,
> Your arms full, and your hair wet, I could not
> Speak, and my eyes failed, I was neither
> Living nor dead, and I knew nothing,
> Looking into the heart of light, the silence.
> *Oed' und leer das Meer.*

These lines have been linked to the Second Ode only once, so far as I know, not in a commentary but in Guy Davenport's version of Sappho: "I cannot speak, / . . . / My eyes cannot see . . . . / I am neither living nor dead and cry / From the narrow between." With the exception of the final clause, neither good Sappho nor good Eliot, Davenport simply translates one poet into the other. Nor did this require any special cleverness. At a later moment of *The Waste Land*, Eliot freely admitted his debt to Sappho. His casual reference to the Hesperus fragment at lines 220 and following—"This may not appear as exact as Sappho's lines"—

shows that he expected readers to notice the allusion. And any reader who knew that fragment from the standard edition, as Eliot did, could hardly have failed to know the famous fragment that just precedes it: "As on the hills the shepherds trample the hyacinth under foot, the purple flower to earth."

Whether or not they echo the Second Ode intentionally, at any rate, Eliot's lines compose a fascinating variation on the ancient sapphic seizure. Even the ambiguities that surround the experience—might the hyacinth girl have been a *man*? does the failure of the senses represent an ecstasy transcending the constraints of life and death, or a fatal inability to feel or communicate?—relate to the Greek poem. A hint of homosexuality or "sin," we have seen, has deepened the poignance of Sappho's words for many readers. Love is most nearly itself when it wants what it cannot or should not have. Eliot's speaker, like Sappho's, cannot bridge the divide. Moreover, both passages depend on the ironic identity between the symptoms of ecstasy and paralysis: the presence of the loved one reduces the lover to a kind of zombie. "Love is like the lion's tooth." Yet both poets imply that the love-death descending at such moments corresponds to religious abandon, enabling one to imagine the feelings of the gods or to look into the heart of light. Sublime possibilities come into view at the instant when the self is emptied.

Yet the experiences also differ. One way of accounting for the differences might focus on the retrospective or meditative aspect of Eliot's seizure. *Once* he knew nothing; *now* he knows too much. His awareness of rapture is belated, not immediate like Sappho's (who feels like this "whenever" she looks at the girl). Eliot stresses the distance of the emotion. His love-death happened once upon a time—prewar, one might say—and in all probability will never happen again. The shift of tenses from Greek present to English past seals the ecstasy in an irrecoverable sanctuary of time. Passion was then. Moreover, the final snatch from *Tristan*—"waste and empty the sea"—serves not only to frame the passage with Wagnerian longing but to return it to a brutal, endless present. The loss of the hyacinth girl will go on forever. In this respect Eliot's superimposition of Sappho on Isolde confirms the reading of the past several centuries. A dying fall is Sappho's only story. She looks over the sea for Phaon, he does not come, she plunges—and goes under like Wagner's lovers. The Leucadian leap claims us all. Hence Eliot's ecstasy, no less than his despair about modern love in the waste land, signals the death of romance. Transposed to modern times and poetry, all love poems must drown in nostalgia.

Another way of putting the difference between the two passages would be to observe that Eliot universalizes the sense of disconnection inherent in Sappho's transport. Both poets record an out-of-body experience. Sappho's ability to note her symptoms even while suffering them divorces her body from her mind, or at least her suffering-faculty from her recording-faculty. She floats outside her senses. And Eliot implies that his own seizure has transported him to another state of being, a moment detached from time and space or life and death. By registering so few of his symptoms, however, he effectively suppresses all sense of the body. Where is the sex in his swoon? If present at all, it has been etherealized into metaphors equally suitable for the Holy Ghost. Instead he values the disconnection itself. The height of his imagination, and his pleasure, culminates in an escape from the senses. So austere an enjoyment had not been desired by Sappho. Eliot tries to remake her into a purer spirit.

Yet his emptying of self always hovers on the verge of a spiritual emptiness as well. Note the exquisite transition from positive silence to negative "oed' und leer," with only a hair's breadth between them—the Dantesque heart of light suspended over an infinite empty sea of faith. The mixed effect is characteristic of Eliot, built into his technique of "montage" or the shoring of fragments. For no matter how faithfully he had reproduced the passions of Sappho, they would still remain only one among many possibilities, one among the sad varieties of love that Tiresias "sees." If the Poetess originally felt herself exploding into fragments, then Eliot chooses to exaggerate her fragmentation and add it to his collection. Indeed, he succeeds in making her lines still more "perfect" by separating them so far from their context that no reader can be quite certain whether they have been referred to at all. Sappho's historical "tragedy," the smashing of her canon, attracts Eliot far more than any whole great poem. Her brokenness stamps her as modern. And Eliot captures the Second Ode for his own art by purging it of the merely temporal Sappho that remains and incorporating it into the Mind of Europe.

Perhaps such universalizing goes too far. In general, *The Waste Land* might be criticized because it reduces all its different voices to variations on Eliot's; in particular, because it consistently shies away from the vision of the abandoned woman who keeps trying to intrude. Tiresias's monotone drowns out a host of such women: the Countess Marie; Philomela; poor Lil; the typist forsaken by her carbuncular clerk and "glad it's over"; the Thames daughter unresentful "after the event"; and she who fiddles music on her hair. Eliot does not allow them to express despair. In this respect his labors may be said to justify Ezra Pound's little joke about his own midwifery: "A Man their Mother was, / A Muse their Sire." A manly reticence controls the female passions. Despite that one outburst from Sappho, most of *The Waste Land* represents a failure, not an excess, of feeling. But perhaps the figure of an abandoned woman manages to intrude on the poem after all. I am thinking, of course, of the wife in "A

Game of Chess." She shows, if anyone can, the depths of abandonment that may afflict a woman even when her "lover" sits across the table. "Stay with me. / Speak to me. Why do you never speak. Speak."

> "Do
> You know nothing? Do you see nothing? Do you remember
> Nothing?"
>
> . . . .
>
> "Are you alive, or not? Is there nothing in your head?"

The questions cannot be dismissed. They interrogate, with childlike directness, not only the husband but the state of the Second Ode, that state of speaking, seeing, knowing nothing, of suspension between life and death; and once again they raise the paradox of "closeness": that the presence of the other person so much on one's mind can bring on a trance or stupor, a sense of being utterly alone. We cannot know another, or what another thinks. "What are you thinking of? What thinking? What?"

Allow me to hazard a guess. What the husband is thinking of, I suspect, is not rats' alley but the feelings of his wife; and what reduces him to such paralysis is the terrible fear and temptation of imagining those feelings as his own. To enter fully into her hysteria or "bad nerves," her all-too-justified dread of abandonment, her ghastly vivacity and pretense at conversation, would be only too easy; and it would mean being lost forever. Better to think about Shakespeare. If the sensibility of the classics has abandoned the modern world, if modern poets can no longer experience their feelings, in the way of Sappho and Donne, as immediately as the odor of a rose, then at least the pathos of the situation will strike many chords in *The Waste Land*. What would be the alternative? Perhaps one might identify not with Tiresias but with that ultimate abandoned woman who stands at the head of the poem, the Sibyl of Cumae, whose immortal barrenness points to a single desire: "I want to die." Better to think of Tiresias. He at least knows that female hysterics are boring. Better to think of control, *Damyata* and *shantih*. Yet thoughts do not always obey the poet's will. Behind *The Waste Land* a constant pressure exerts its force, steering the poem away from action and toward paralysis: the death in life or solitude in marriage. The Fisher King had a wife. When Eliot tries to imagine an emblem of modern life, his thoughts turn compulsively toward the figure of an abandoned woman, and much of the tension of the poem derives from his struggle to keep her from speaking.

William Carlos Williams

Even a male poet more sympathetic to women, however, may have trouble catching their tone. Sappho's mystery, like Sappho's words, resists translation into a foreign idiom or American grain. Yet poets continue to try. Thus William Carlos Williams, in his early seventies, labored to find an American voice for the Second Ode. He was fascinated by Sappho. More than half a century before, his best poetic friends had introduced him to her austere charm; and later, when "I abandoned the rare world of H.D. and Ezra Pound," she seemed to offer an ally in the great war against Eliot and tradition and the fixed foot and the European past. Born before history had begun, she talked straight as any American. And Williams pays her back in kind by striving to match her directness. "My purpose was to speak as I thought this remarkable woman meant to speak—not what the classic English students had done to her in their stilted translations. I had the poem read aloud to me, over and over, in the original Greek by scholars who knew how the words should sound so that I might catch the rise and fall of the beat." He took the task very seriously. In repeated comments he insists that "I want to dig around and find the concentration of everything that Sappho had to give," and that "I have been as accurate as the meaning of the words permitted— always with a sense of our own American idiom to instruct me." Moreover, Williams seems to have been proud of the result. His translation was issued in 1957 as a broadsheet in a series intended to represent the poet at his best; and the following year it assumed pride of place at the beginning of section 2 of *Paterson,* book 5.

> Peer of the gods is that man, who
> face to face, sits listening
> to your sweet speech and lovely
>   laughter.
>
> It is this that rouses a tumult
> in my breast. At mere sight of you
> my voice falters, my tongue
>   is broken.
>
> Straightway, a delicate fire runs in
> my limbs; my eyes
> are blinded and my ears
>   thunder.
>
> Sweat pours out: a trembling hunts
> me down. I grow paler
> than dry grass and lack little
>   of dying.

A reader must make some allowance for the difference between the will and the deed. Though clean and largely accurate, Williams's version remains at some distance from "our own American idiom." The "official British translations" lingered in his ear; and in view of his outrage at their "enormities" it is amusing to note how close his "rouses a tumult / in my breast" comes to Philips's "rais'd such Tumults in my Breast." Such diction communicates very little of Sappho's pounding heart and natural language. Indeed, to some extent the translation probably misses its intended effect, since the prefatory remarks by an academic (L. Arnold Post)—"She wrote for a clear gentle tinkling voice. She avoided all roughness."—seem not so much contradicted as confirmed by Williams's performance. It is doubtful that the poet wished to be seen agreeing with an academic in public. But several vigorous phrases redeem the lines from gentility. Not many translators have bettered the frankness of "Sweat pours out."

Sweating, in fact, probably supplies the key to Williams's reading of the ode. "Morals have nothing to do with art," he told John Thirlwall. "When Sappho was sweating for a woman, she put it down." He diagnoses a physical lesbian passion (like the one he had recorded, not without sympathy, in *Paterson* book 4). The beauty of the Greek words, which interests Williams most, runs together with his attraction to the rebel and outcast. Sappho is a "Beautiful Thing," and *Paterson* had already explained why her poems had had to be burned by the Church: "beauty is / a defiance of authority." Williams responds to her burning, her honest sweat. As she had defied convention in setting down her love, so he translates her partly to defy the Greek scholars and "the classic English students." Moreover, such devotion to poetry holds the promise, for the American poet, of a sort of counterreligion—pre-Christian, pre-European beauty. "As you know, I'm not even a heathen. If there is any possibility of reproduction in another world, it must consist in refinement as of a poet. The conventional terms of heaven and hell don't mean a damn thing." True immortality would recreate the pure defiant Sappho, a beautiful untouched thing like America at the moment when Columbus found it. Williams pares verse to its essence. "I'm always looking for a concentrate in one poem."

Yet something interferes with the effort. Technically, we might point to Williams's difficulty in adapting the literal meaning of Sappho's words to an American idiom (Americans seldom refer to "the gods"; American grass does not look pale, though Williams's insertion of "dry" improves the picture). Metaphysically, we might note (like Joseph Riddel) that any attempt to restore a poet to immediate presence will only confirm her absence. But the context suggests a more telling problem: Williams's attitude toward women, of whom Sappho functions as a representative example. In a word, he needs their mystery. Despite his canny physician's knowledge of the scars beneath their dresses, their life stories, their ordinary diseases, he also admits the wonder and confusion they cause him. The marvelous balance, in "Asphodel, That Greeny Flower," between two views of his wife—both a day-to-day companion and a mythologized Helen—recurs in *Paterson* book 5. Hence the version of Sappho is followed (after a sour dose of Pound's economics) by the lovely glimpse of "a woman in our town," seen and sought but never spoken to, and by Mezz Mezzrow's memories of Bessie Smith: "Every note that woman wailed vibrated on the tight strings of my nervous system: every word she sang answered a question I was asking." Williams vibrates the same way to Sappho's song. But he dares not approach too close. Significantly, the ancient urge to diagnose her symptoms and specify her condition does not stimulate his curiosity as a doctor or poet (we know his opinion only through a later interview). Beautiful things should never be explained; they hold back a part of themselves and do not tell their names ("Let them explain you and you will be / the heart of the explanation. Nameless, / you will appear"). Hence Williams lets Sappho keep her distance. He leaves the Second Ode as he found it, not quite assimilated to this continent or a man's way of talking. In an earlier draft of his translation, published in *Spectrum,* Williams had supplied a version of the fragmentary "extra" line: "I am another person." This rendering has nothing to do with the Greek but everything to do with the poet's own sense of the text. Sappho is another person to him. He respects her mystery, her otherness, and tries to make room for it in his own poetic scheme of things.

Yet Williams's respect for abandoned women, like Eliot's fear, divorces them from full humanity as men experience it. Even the most beautiful thing remains a thing rather than an agent. Thus most male poets prefer a Sappho they cannot quite understand, a creature who engages their admiration or pity rather than their self-definition. In his late lyric, "Sappho, Be Comforted," Williams acknowledges the limits of his sympathy with his usual disarming candor: "I, we'll say, love a woman / but truth to tell / I love myself more"—just as Sappho loves songs and girls but not men. Such love merely confirms one's loneliness, "each in his prison." Hence the postscript of Williams's Sappho, "I am another person," perfectly fits another cancelled line, once mused on by the silent husband in *The Waste Land:* "But it is terrible to be alone with another person." Male and female poets, like men and women in general, do not always share a community of values. The same text that gives a woman hope of affiliation and sharing may teach a man the desolation at the heart of love. Many men have learned that from Sappho. Imagining her, they see themselves alone.

Robert Lowell

Thus "mascula Sappho" returns in a masculine voice. In recent times few poets have strained harder than Robert Lowell to conceive the

Poetess in their own image. He seeks her out repeatedly, impatiently, as if to compensate for some part missing in himself. Lowell often imagined himself an abandoned woman. Though one of the most unmistakably masculine of poets, he spoke throughout his career in feminine masks: Anne Kavanaugh, Mother Marie Therese, Phaedra, Clytemnestra, and many desperate wives who "speak of woe that is in marriage." Not all those efforts were convincing, to be sure. Randall Jarrell's comment that "the heroine is first of all a sort of symbiotic state of the poet" applies to most of Lowell's women. "You feel, 'Yes, Robert Lowell would act like this if he were a girl'; but whoever saw a girl like Robert Lowell?" Yet Lowell did try to bend to that alien mold, even to the point of identifying with those wives whom he himself had victimized. Taken into his verse as a self-inflicted punishment, their pain feeds his sense of sin. He numbers his crimes, through them, and sentences himself to abandonment. To feel like a woman is torture, and that is what Lowell wants.

The process may be seen at work in his first, indirect version of the Second Ode, his translation of Racine's *Phaedra*.

> Hippolytus! I saw his face, turned white!
> My lost and dazzled eyes saw only night,
> capricious burnings flickered through my bleak
> abandoned flesh. I could not breathe or speak.

Compared to either the French or the Greek original, these lines show a kind of disdain for immediate sensual experience. Indeed, quoted in isolation they might be thought to describe an electric shock treatment more successfully than the onslaught of love. Not doom but alienation threatens Lowell's Phaedra. The extravagant second line (in place of the simple "my eyes could see no more"), the substitution of "capricious" for "redoubtable" flames, the two adjectives that disown the flesh even in the moment of its stirring, all turn the implacable logic of the French verse to a brilliant but arbitrary disconnection. The woman is *lost,* in more ways than one. Lowell himself praised Racine's verse for "the glory of its hard, electric rage," and clearly he has caught that effect. Yet the rage of his heroine seems motivated less by feminine passion than by the resentment of her spirit at being trapped in a woman's body.

When Lowell turned directly to Sappho, in *Imitations* (1961), his discomfort at impersonating a woman, and still more at imagining her sexual arousal, proved too great to master. He succumbs to his masculine instincts. As Sappho justly complains, in this version, "Refining fire purifies my flesh!" Hence the Second Ode serves as the first of "Three Letters to Anaktoria," which a headnote consolidates into a sort of playlet: "The man or hero loves Anaktoria, later Sappho; in the end, he withdraws or dies." The sheer audacity of this plot is stunning. Lowell pro-

motes "that man"—who may or may not exist in the original—into the
protagonist. Sappho writes *to* Anactoria, but *about* him. His unseen presence, like the hand of Lowell, guides her pen and her emotions. Under
the circumstances we should not be surprised that the second of the "Letters" stitches together some unrelated fragments, and the third transcribes a famous anthology piece ("The moon slides west") that Sappho
did not write. Lowell, like Ovid before him, defines the heroine as someone who has lost a hero, and imagines her only desire as the need for a
man. Thus the second "Letter" openly transposes a female lover into a
male. Lowell makes his own kind of sense from the Greek and does not
pretend to be Tiresias. Yet the cost of the sex-change operation is high.
Convention, sentimentality, and wryness flatten out Sappho's ecstasy;
sheer pathetic loneliness replaces the intensity of passion: "Anaktoria!
Pray / for his magnificence I once pined to share." The worst thing that
Lowell can imagine for a woman, it seems, is that she might be deprived
of him.

Seven years later, in his *Notebook* (1968), Lowell returned to his imitation. In a remarkable technical feat, he compresses the 45 lines of the
"Three Letters" into a single unrhymed sonnet. No form could be more
his own; but now the voice is a woman's.

> SAPPHO
> "I set this man above the gods and heroes—
> all day he sits before me face to face,
> like a cardplayer. My elbow brushes his elbow;
> if I should speak, he hears. The touched heart stirs,
> the laughter is water hurrying over pebbles. . . .
> He is the fairest thing on this dark earth;
> I hear him, a hollowness is in my ears,
> his footstep. I cannot speak, I cannot see.
> A dead whiteness trickles pinpricks of sweat;
> I am greener than the greenest green grass;
> I can easily make you understand this—
> a woman seldom comes to what is best:
> her child, her slaves, her simple household ache—
> the moon slides west; time gone; I sleep alone."

"To Speak of Woe That Is in Marriage." Lowell reduces the triangle to a
straight line, the threesome to a couple. Indeed, the art of this sonnet
consists largely of *unimagining* or demystifying the Second Ode. Thus
Sappho herself replaces the girl who sits facing the man, so that the seizure once precipitated by an act of imagination—casting herself into
the man's position—can now be attributed to simple proximity. His nearness overwhelms her. Similarly, the curious detail of the brushing el-
bows, presumably drawn like the anachronistic cardplayer from Cezanne,

helps to localize and specify the situation. An eerie literalness supplants an eerie vision; the strange perseverance of "all day" prolongs the sudden Greek stroke of love. And the object of the woman's love is entirely male. If Sappho had written this way, not even the most orthodox believer in home and family and female subordination would have needed to burn her.

The ultimate naturalizing and normalizing of the Second Ode occur, however, in the last four lines. Lowell selects fragments from his other imitations of Sappho in order to explain her seizure away: "I can easily make you understand this." A woman's worship of a man has nothing mysterious about it, considering what we all know about the lives of women: the domestic boredom, the lack of fulfillment, the accumulating inescapable loneliness. Nor can men be depended upon to share one's bed. Lowell's new ending for the ode does not leave much to the imagination. A capsule sociology resolves the woman's symptoms into the ordinary process of human affairs. A sonnet contains enough space to account for the "simple household ache" that most women feel. Hence the divine visitation that Sappho once endured corresponds to a sad heart in the supermarket: the given facts of female lives and female psychology.

Why did Lowell engage in such reductions? An outraged lover of the Second Ode might well charge him with a lack of imagination where women are concerned, as well as with being omnivorous and self-absorbed, the kind of poet never satisfied until he has transcribed or forged all previous poetry into a language that will fit above his own signature. But Lowell may also be credited with a better motive. Valuing honesty above all other forms of poetic eloquence, he tries to make Sappho an honest woman. He reads the Second Ode, that is to say, as a confession. Sappho herself, in Lowell's version, supplies the title of her song, and the quotation marks around it assure us that she speaks not as a disembodied artist but as a particular human being. The brilliance of the language, the physical immediacy of the symptoms, should not be allowed to obscure the directness with which she tells us what she feels and sees. No music sounds better than the truth. Lowell had learned that from women—not only the women in his life but the female poets of his time. A poet ought not to pretend; if pain and madness are what she experiences, then pain and madness are what she must report. Nor will such honesty compromise her verse or make it slack. Sylvia Plath's favorite word, according to Ted Hughes, was "ecstasy." And perhaps Sappho's legacy to modern poets was the knowledge that ecstasy could be described as frankly and precisely as anything else. Men need to know that at least as much as women do. Hence Lowell's imitation pays Sappho his ultimate tribute: he honors her for being down to earth.

MARGUERITE YOURCENAR

Sappho could hardly descend much further. If modern poets have generally treated her as aspects of themselves, Lowell takes one step more and reconstructs her as an ordinary person. The Tenth Muse comes down from Parnassus and slips into prose. Yet Lowell's assault on her singularity has not proved the last word on Sappho. She continues to inspire passions and satisfy needs: the need of men for mystery and for instruction in how to feel, the need of women for a precursor and companion. The Poetess still is a tutor. At the very least she offers poets the model of an uncluttered, "spare but musical" style. HD had learned that style from Sappho, at the urging of Ezra Pound; and many years later Pound sent Mary Barnard to the same tutor and was eventually rewarded by Barnard's translations of Sappho in the "fresh colloquial directness of speech." A daily exercise in Greek removes unsightly verbal flab. It can also inspire more ambitious technical efforts. Like his predecessors Leopardi and Foscolo, Salvatore Quasimodo identified with Sappho and found, in his lovely translations of her work, the possibility of "a new technique, foreshadowing a concrete language that would reflect the real, and displace the planes of rhetoric." A more austere Italian supplants the lavish ornaments of most Italian verse as well as Quasimodo's own earlier hermeticism. The student of Sappho is likely to lose any taste for excess or to be nauseated by a surfeit of words. When the American poet J. V. Cunningham published his own version of the Second Ode, he intended to illustrate a special kind of art, laconic but precise, where the gaps between words themselves draw out the meaning. The Poetess hovers over the shoulders of craftsmen, always encouraging them to leave out more.

Yet Sappho also offers something else. More than a professional consultant, she allows us to glimpse a way of seeing that is radically different from anything modern. To put the matter simply, Sappho seems to live among the gods. She talks with Aphrodite as a familiar and recognizes a god in the man who sits near her beloved. Nor should we be too quick to think of these as metaphors. Perhaps the language of love has been debased by centuries of confusion in which even the most trivial erotic passion appropriates the vocabulary of the divine, the heavenly, the angelic, the eternal. But Sappho does not seem to have taken such words lightly. In her poems a vision of love interpenetrates with the sacred, sharing its devotions and rituals. The gods preside over both, and for Sappho the presence of divinity is not only a way of speaking but a way of life.

What would it mean to live among the divine, to think of oneself as divine? No modern author has imagined the life of a human god more vividly than Marguerite Yourcenar. In her best-known work, *Memoirs of Hadrian* (1951), Yourcenar performs the astonishing feat of recreating a state of mind in which the human and divine are one. Not only does Hadrian believe himself a god, without sacrificing his humanity or rationality, he half convinces the reader. Yourcenar has described her own motivations in pursuing this ancient mode of existence. To some extent, early in her career, she was reacting against the facile projection of modern attitudes upon the gods, as in the entertainments of Offenbach or "Giraudoux, whose ingenious and Parisian Greece irritated me as something can when it is both very close and totally opposed to us." What she sought was something deeper: an understanding of sanctity that would not be opposed to the things of this world, or a love that would not lose its contact with the divine. "One thing that has always troubled me in the French notion of love, and perhaps in all European conceptions of love, is the absence of the sacred; somehow, . . . we have lost the sense that love, or, more simply, sensual bonds between two people, or for that matter ordinary everyday relationships, are sacred."

She found such a love in Sappho. The subject of Yourcenar's *Fires* (1936) is "absolute love, striking its victim both as a disease and a vocation"; and the last story deals with "Sappho, or Suicide." The setting is contemporary. As the title indicates, the heroine represents not the Poetess but the desperate, abandoned lover. An aging acrobat and lesbian, she tries to assume a feminine vulnerability in the arms of handsome young Phaon; but when he dresses as a girl she realizes that she cannot escape her ghosts. Death is her last resort, and she leaps from the highest trapeze. "But those failing at life run the risk of missing their suicide"— she is caught by the net. Yourcenar's story teeters between the sublime and the absurd. Indeed, that is its point. "This notion of mad, sometimes scandalous love that is nevertheless permeated by a sort of mystical power could only survive if it is associated with whatever belief in transcendence, even if only within a human being. If deprived of this basis . . . mad love quickly becomes nothing more than vain mirror play or sad mania." The modern Sappho, unable to find any principle higher than the top of the circus canopy or her own skill, resembles a clown. Yet her obsession does touch on "mystical power."

More than forty years later, Yourcenar came back to Sappho, translating her along with other Greek poets in *La Couronne et la Lyre* (1979). This time a modern sensibility does not predominate. Instead the translator strives to be faithful to the originals, catching their "sacred psalmody" or quality of incantation as well as their literal meaning. Yet the version of the Second Ode seems less true to Sappho than to Yourcenar's own long-standing meditations on love.

> ... *Il est pareil aux dieux, l'homme qui te regarde,*
> *Sans craindre ton sourire, et tes yeux, et ta voix,*
> *Moi, je tremble et je sue, et ma face est hagarde*
>   *Et mon coeur aux abois ...*
> *La chaleur et le froid tour à tour m'envahissent;*
> *Je ne résiste pas au délire trop fort;*
> *Et ma gorge s'étrangle et mes genoux fléchissent,*
>   *Et je connais la mort ...*
> . . . He is like the gods who looks at you, that man,
> Without fearing your smile, and your eyes, and your voice,
> But me, I tremble and I sweat, and my face is drawn
>   And my heart at bay . . .
> Now heat, now cold within my flesh holds sway;
> A mighty frenzy overwhelms my breath;
> And my throat strangles and my knees give way,
>   And I am versed in death . . .

The French is clear and straightforward, suggesting (though not replicating) sapphics, and chantlike in its ceremonious rhythms and rhymes. Yourcenar takes no interest in modernizing or heightening the Greek. If anything, she tends toward a sort of dry understatement, as in the sixth line ("I do not withstand an excessive delirium" or, less stiltedly, "I can hardly keep from raving out of control") or the suave conclusion. In the eyes of the translator, "Sappho's art has no trace of anything stale or slack or artificial."

Why then, a reader may ask, has Yourcenar both abridged and altered the Greek symptoms? The assault on Sappho's tongue and skin and eyes and ears has been deflected to the throat and knees or to a general frenzy, and the specific details that cast the spell of the Greek lyric—the thin flame under the skin, the pounding heart and pale grass—are quietly dropped. Moreover, the careful parallelism of the first French stanza obscures the dramatic situation of the Greek, where the man sits opposite the beloved and the speaker is *suddenly* stricken. The image of the heart at bay is piquant, to be sure, but it is not Sappho's. Why all these liberties? Doubtless the exigencies of meter and rhyme account for some of them, and the effort to keep the language fresh accounts for others. But Yourcenar must have had something else in mind.

Her object, it seems, was to convey a sense of "absolute love." According to her introduction, "for the ancients as for us, Sappho lives above all as the interpreter of the emotions peculiar to those in love," and a proper translation must catch those emotions. Yourcenar is not particularly concerned with the symptoms. What interests her is the diagnosis, and about that she has no doubt at all. In a word, Sappho is in the grip of "delirium." Love seizes her like a disease and a vocation, and nothing else matters. Yourcenar does not think it important to categorize this seizure as, for instance, specifically sexual or "lesbian." The use of the word "sapphic" to signify the love of woman for woman is the mark of "an age where people read the poetess less and less, but where people more and more feel the need to systematize human behavior." Such urges only distort the essence of love. Hence a fascination with the symptoms and varieties of passion reveals an age that no longer understands its nature. Sappho can lead us back to love in its pure state: indifferent to pleasure, overwhelming, indivisible, fearful, and sacred.

More subtly, the French translation tends to dismiss the *interiority* of the Greek poem. In place of the sequence of failing sensations within the body, Yourcenar presents an invading force that holds the heart at bay, swarms through the speaker, overcomes resistance, and finally hurls her down. The effect is not unlike that of Racine, the conquering ruling passion that sweeps all before it. Yet unlike Racine's antagonist, the devil in the flesh, the power described by Yourcenar is a divine visitation. It passes over its victim like a ravishing god, and leaves her with a new knowledge of the ways of the gods. Yourcenar does not mediate or explain this experience. It is not her business to teach us how to read our bodily symptoms. Yet what her version does transmit, against the grain of most modern translations, is precisely a sense of being visited. To feel the spirit of a god upon one does not make one less human. Yourcenar's Sappho is not a "real woman," if by that we mean someone, like Williams's or Lowell's Sappho, easy to understand in terms of her predilections and her sex. But to be a real woman may also imply a capacity for transcending the self, a love not composed of symptoms but itself a symptom of the everyday presence of the sacred in life. Such women need not believe in the gods in order to enjoy their visits. Yourcenar's Sappho is fashioned to show them the way.

Sappho Persisting

Thus Sappho reflects her readers, and sometimes exalts them. Even the scarcity of her remains appeals to the imagination. Each translator, each reader must make her anew. Moreover, like other gods she is very adaptable, willing to respond to all sorts of prayers and solicitations. The stronger the need, the more ruthlessly has she been enlisted in its cause. Her name itself can function as a motto. "We weave our minds round your Grecian words / Of the Mused collective consciousness: / 'Lesbians Love Now' / / Sappho, you must have been a 'Right On' woman." The final line has been pressed into service as the title of a book; and the Poetess will surely survive it, just as she has survived her transformations into a goddess, a slut, and a man. Each generation is entitled to its own

diagnoses of the Second Ode. Indeed, no generation can avoid the labor
of creating its own Sappho. She rises again, in modern poetry as throughout Western tradition, whenever poets need a lyric voice to express the
feelings of ecstasy and pain that lie just below the surface of life, like a
thin flame under the skin.

What accounts for such persistence? The history sketched in this chapter makes no more sense than history itself, except insofar as it records
a few recurrent themes: the interrelations of poetry and gender, the
varieties of misogyny in different times and places, and the struggle of
women to establish connections with the past and each other. The poetry
of abandoned women is involved with such themes, and my next few
chapters will try to explore them more fully. But Sappho's survival,
against so many odds, represents something more than her usefulness as
a scapegoat or heroine, a figure or example. It also testifies to some quality in her work that later poetry has not been able to do without, an
intensity beside which most verse seems pale. However traduced and
buried, that quality shines through her fragments. Without some spark
of it, no poet ever seems quite complete. We might call it abandonment.

To suggest what I mean, I must take an emblem from Sappho. One
part of the Second Ode has been largely ignored. At the end of Longinus's transcription, a single corrupt line drifts into space, generally believed the beginning of a lost stanza. Devoid of context, it might be rendered as "but all can be endured since . . . even a beggar" or "all has been
ventured." How did Sappho intend to finish her thought? Lacking any
conclusive evidence, the reader is in the dark. Catullus offers one way
out, and later interpreters another: a leap into suicide. But a proper answer will stem from the poem itself. Its subject, according to our initial
reading, is the terrifying effect of the beloved's presence, her godlike
power of life and death over the poet who views her. Most of us have felt
something close to what Sappho describes. By testing the symptoms
against our own bodies and memories, we imagine ourselves in her state
and diagnose it according to our own experience: as fever, love, delirium,
anxiety, or transport. But most of us, of course, eventually do manage
to come closer to those we love—at least to catch a glimpse of them
without dying. We temper our hearts; we learn to endure. And that, I
think, is what Sappho herself meant to learn. The final stanza would have
asserted that, for all the dangers, she intended to approach the girl, because nothing else in any case would have made life worth saving. At
worst she would die, at best become a god. And fortunately the latter is
what happened. She survived to write the poem.

The emblem applies, I believe, to more than the missing stanza. It
touches on the furthest reach of what abandoned women have always
endured and ventured. When such a woman loves, she enters an abyss

where nothing exists but passion. The loved one laughs and vanishes and must be made again within. Poetry begins in that moment. Like one of Rilke's "bees of the invisible," the poet converts mere mortal stuff into eternal substance—the honey of Sappho's poems. Descending to the perishable world of feelings and appearances, she restores them to pure significance, to symptoms whose meaning will never be exhausted. The beloved will never desert the one who holds the form in her heart. Such poets are strong. For only the truly abandoned know what it means to venture everything and to reach the other side of loss: the state of ecstasy where the loved one in all her terror is always immortally present. A number of women have gone there, and perhaps a few men. Such poets are tempered like steel; they seem to me hard as gods. And Sappho is sovereign among them. Even to come too close to her fills one with a sense of danger, a risk of viewing abandonment face to face. But poetry lives there with her. Sappho stands on the heights.

5 The Rape of the Sibyl: Male Poets and Abandoned Women

> What is the shape of the sibyl? . . .
> It is the sibyl of the self,
> The self as sibyl, whose diamond,
> Whose chiefest embracing of all wealth
> Is poverty, whose jewel found
> At the exactest central of the earth
> Is need.

THE SIBYL IN VIRGIL

Almost as long as poetry has existed, male poets have shared a fantasy: the dream of speaking with a woman's voice. Sometimes that fantasy has been embodied in the Muse, the beautiful virgin daughter of Memory who descends in the night, breathes into the passive, instrumental male, and allows him to take dictation. But often the dream is more active. The male poet who is not content to wait for a visit from a woman may forcibly pursue her, taking his muse by storm. Above all he strives to capture her way of speaking, to inhabit her like a demon or dybbuk and mold her voice to his will. Why should he need to do this? Evidently women know secrets that men are compelled to learn if they wish to be poets. A man by himself can speak with the voice of a hero; he knows about anger and travel and arms and the law. But a woman's voice can strike certain notes better: abandoned love, the fear of being lost. Her register is higher and more piercing than anything a man can reach. Hence male poets express those notes through women. By stealth or force, they borrow a different voice and find that they can speak a different language.

An emblem of this process has come down from Virgil. The Sibyl of Cumae, in book 6 of the *Aeneid,* presides over the ultimate mysteries of death and the future. A muse had sufficed to tell the cause of Aeneas's troubles in the world above. But the underworld requires another sort of guide: a woman with a male presence inside her. The Sibyl belongs to Apollo. A mad, immortal old virgin, she has looked into the darkness so long and known so much loneliness that only unintelligible ravings could be expected from her were it not for the god and master who pulls her strings. Virgil describes the coming of the god. The prophetess resists him; she struggles against the divine inspiration like a child fighting ether. But in the end Apollo wins his entrance: "he exhausts her maddened mouth, tames the wild heart, and presses her to the mold"; he "shakes the reins of her fury and twists the spur in her breast." The scene is brilliant and ugly—a sexless rape. The male god rides the fury of his priestess as if she were a wild horse he took pleasure in breaking. Yet his cruelty serves its purpose. The spectacle of the Sibyl's frenzy, her visible possession by an irresistible spirit indifferent to human pain, authenticates the truth of her words. Aeneas cannot doubt her authority; it combines the passion of a raving, tortured woman with the calm foresight of a ruthless unimpassioned masculine god. Prophecy never sounds more convincing than when an abandoned woman voices it. Her fury lends the proper air of mystery to Apollo's measured tones.

The poem requires her too. Poetically the Sibyl functions as an intermediary between two worlds: the human and divine, or life and death. Conducting the hero through Avernus, she shows how well she is acquainted with chaos, night, and false dreams, yet also with the basic information that a man needs in order to experience such things while retaining his sanity. She is both a mad old witch and a trusty guide. In this respect she resembles Virgil himself. Both sides of the Sibyl, the *vates* and the mentor, derive from ancient notions about the poet; and both were often associated with the author of the *Aeneid*. The poet's renewed invocation at the gates of Hades, addressed this time not to a muse but to the unseen powers and silent shadows that rule below, confirms his desire to know the Sibyl's secrets. To learn them he is willing to become part woman. Just as Tiresias's quest for forbidden sexual knowledge changed him to a hermaphrodite as the condition of his prophetic intuition, so any male poet who strives for the knowledge of passion may have to change sexes. The way to hell begins inside a woman.

Inside a woman is also where men take form. Aeneas and Virgil both make their descent in hope of renewing themselves, and so have many later male poets. Again and again men have turned to abandoned women during a stage of poetic self-definition. Ovid learns how to tell a story by taking the heroine's part; Fiammetta and Criseyde teach Boccaccio and Chaucer who they are; Juan de la Cruz becomes a poet by identifying with a cast-off lover; Wordsworth's great period opens with one vision of blighted female devotion, Margaret in "The Ruined Cottage," and closes with another, the doomed Laodamia; Baudelaire comes into full flower when he overhears the language (as he conceives it) of the lesbian and vampire; Valéry, after decades of silence, returns from the dead by tuning his voice to the "rich contralto" of a woman lost in memories, a "young fate"; and Yeats, in the instant when "life returned to me as an

impression of the uncontrollable energy and daring of the great creators,"
cries out through Crazy Jane. The imagined woman allows them to find
themselves. Whether her voice still rings true, refracted through husky
male attitudes and a masculine consciousness, might certainly be disputed. Yet whether or not male poets impersonate abandoned women
convincingly, the effort itself revives them. A man must visit the Sibyl
to read his future.

No special heroism seems needed for the journey. So many poets in so
many ages have traveled that road that the way has been worn smooth.
Every Chinese poet learns how to enter the feelings of the deserted courtesan or neglected wife, and every country-western singer knows the
words of careless love by heart. Men take those themes for granted. Indeed, in many cultures the feelings of abandoned women seem identical
with poetic feeling. Hence the ordinary practice of the blues or of Japanese verse will train a man in two delicacies, the delicacy of female sorrows and the delicacy of the poetic genres that express them. Each broken
heart obeys a formula. Perhaps such formulas suit male poets better than
female, since men can avoid a personal involvement with the woman's
memory of pain. Though Tennyson may well be grieving for himself
more than for "Mariana," he can keep the self-indulgence at a distance
by projecting it onto a woman. Men are permitted to pity the opposite
sex. And the conventions of poetry offer male poets many chances to
indulge in tears and take the woman's part.

Moreover, a man who borrows the voice of an abandoned woman does
not require special knowledge. Such women live alone. Their very abandonment, their separation from other people and normal social ties, relieves a man of the obligation to take account of the innumerable details
of behavior and speech that distinguish a woman's life. When Pär Lagerkvist imagines *The Sibyl,* for instance, he places her high on a mountain,
utterly divorced from humanity. Raped by a god who represents the Father as well as Apollo, nurturing an idiot son who eventually mounts to
heaven, she speaks a timeless idiom where the languages of Greeks and
Christians merge into one. In her world no one owns any possessions,
not even a name. Her situation is "pure." All that a man need imagine,
therefore, is her heart. Concentrating on the essential facts of love and
loss, the male poet puts aside the world of action or domesticity, of social
norms and external descriptions, that furnishes the interest of other poetic kinds. Instead he must capture the inner logic of grief. And poetry
offers the means. Simplified to a single passion, the abandoned woman
is ripe for translation into a man. She wears her heart on her sleeve, or
exposes it in arias and ballads, in love letters and soliloquies. Men have
not been slow to take advantage. No kind of poetry has proved more
nearly universal, so indifferent to time and place.

To a surprising extent, in fact, the poetry of abandoned women survives translation. Nuances of language or conduct can easily be lost in
passing from culture to culture or sex to sex, but the sense of abandonment lingers. It gives life to other traditions. Thus, when Ezra Pound
cited three historical sources for what he considered "the most interesting
form of modern poetry" (the dramatic monologue), he unwittingly
chose male imitations of abandoned women as all his examples: Theocritus's *Second Idyll,* Ovid's *Heroides,* and Li Po's "The River Merchant's
Wife." Those ancient poems seem modern. In fact, the last of them, like
Li Po's "The Jewel Stairs' Grievance" (Pound's other touchstone for Chinese poetry), is thoroughly conventional, modeled on songs that appear
in the earliest Chinese anthologies. Yet readers who do not recognize
those conventions have still found it easy to respond to the women's feelings: the loneliness of the wife (presumably the poet's own) as time
slowly passes beneath wait-for-husband-heights, the desolation of the
court lady who wanes with the moon. Abandoned women move us
across the ages. "Sole pride and loneliness:" Conrad Aiken observed in
his own *Letter from Li Po,* "it is the state / the kingdom rather of all
things."

Using Women: Li Po, Ezra Pound, Ts'ao Chih

Precisely because such emotions come so easily to a man, however,
a careful reader may well suspect the translation. If any male poet can
coax a reflex tear by impersonating an abandoned woman, we need not
conclude that sympathy for women is his chief concern. Perhaps he has
other motives. A look at Pound's version of "The Jewel Stairs' Grievance" may help show the complexity of these transactions between cultures and sexes.

> The jeweled steps are already quite white with dew,
> It is so late that the dew soaks my gauze stockings,
> And I let down the crystal curtain
> And watch the moon through the clear autumn.

Pound himself leaves no doubt about his understanding of the poem and
his motives for translating it. He regards it as a puzzle that he has solved.
"I have never found any occidental who could 'make much' of that poem
at one reading. Yet upon careful examination we find that everything is
there, not merely by 'suggestion' but by a sort of mathematical process
of reduction. Let us consider what circumstances would be needed to
produce just the words of this poem. You can play Conan Doyle if you
like."

His own imitation of Sherlock Holmes had already appeared in *Cathay.*
"Jewel stairs, therefore a palace. Grievance, therefore there is something
to complain of. Gauze stockings, therefore a court lady, not a servant

who complains. Clear autumn, therefore he has no excuse on account of weather. Also she has come early, for the dew has not merely whitened the stairs, but has soaked her stockings. The poem is especially prized because she utters no direct reproach." A brilliant piece of detection! The virtues stressed in Li Po obviously reflect Pound's own attempt to make a new English poetry: a dance of images, an exercise in seeing. "It is because Chinese poetry has certain qualities of vivid presentation; and because certain Chinese poets have been content to set forth their matter without moralizing and without comment that one labours to make a translation." The images themselves convey the message. No editorializing or sentimentality distorts the effect. We are not intended to *feel* for the lady but to *see* her situation, expressed as urgently as a telegram.

Yet another Conan Doyle might find another message. Even regarded strictly as a riddle, the poem may pose a question that Pound ignores: not simply "what is happening?" but "who am I?" Technically, the most striking device of the original is its refusal to locate a speaker. This trick of perspective emerges clearly when we imitate Pound's own source, Fenollosa, and gloss the Chinese word for word.

jade	steps	grow	white	dew
night	late	attack	gauze stockings	
let	down	crystal	blind	
glass-clear		watch	autumn	moon

The lack of a pronoun and of verb declensions (in Chinese as well as English) cuts the poem loose from any specific point of view. There is no way to tell whether some impartial observer or the lady herself is speaking; first- and third-person translations are equally valid ("I let down the crystal blind" or "she lets down the crystal blind"). But more important, there is no way to tell whether the details refer to the inside or outside, the lady's consciousness or the scene around her. Viewed subjectively, each poetic notation can mark an interior state of mind or feeling.

Let us play Conan Doyle again, this time with our eyes on the woman (I will take the role of Dr. Watson to the Holmes of some Chinese scholars). Jade, a conventional epithet for fine skin. White dew, therefore tears or age spots on her cheek. Also, White Dew stands for early September in the Chinese lunar calendar; therefore she grows old, as late night also implies. Crystal blind, therefore she sees through a screen of tears. Glass-clear, the scene mirrors her face. Autumn moon, therefore she feels old and lonely. The solution or translation is then elementary.

> SEPTEMBER SONG
> My jade skin tarnishes with age.
> Long nights dissolve the finest gauze.

Tears streak my lashes, but I see
as in a mirror how the moon grows old.

External reality, like a glass, returns the woman's image to herself. One
might add that Li Po is also addressing a well-known social injustice. The
neglect of Imperial concubines, who might spend a lifetime waiting for
a visit that never came, had long been a scandal. More than two hundred
years earlier, a poem by Hsieh T'iao had protested this cruel treatment
("I let down the beaded blind in the hall at night. / Fireflies fly around
and take rest. / Through the long night I sew gauze dresses. / How can
there be an end to my thoughts of you?"). Li Po's imitation of this poem
may well be a direct response to the critics who had accused him of "lack
of concern for the welfare of the people." Here at least the poet espouses
a cause. In this respect his verses are by no means "without moralizing."

I do not mean to claim that Pound's translation is wrong. Clearly he is
entitled to read the original in his own way and to make the best English
poem that he can. Yet the differences among Li Po's "The Jade Steps'
Grievance," Pound's "Jewel Stairs' Grievance," and my "September
Song" suggest that any male poet, when he claims to adopt a woman's
point of view, may be open to question. We cannot trust men on such
matters. Pound takes the woman's side in order to annex her to the imagist movement; I translate her into a prototype of the Abandoned
Woman. And Li Po himself may well have been moved less by compassion for the lady than by the chance to air some grievance of his own. He
gave the "river-merchant's" wife a voice, according to scholars, in order
to express his own loneliness; decorum required that the weakness of the
man be projected onto the woman. A similar analysis could be fastened
on many such poems. The portrait of a lady generally reveals more about
the man who paints it than about the woman who is painted. Thus the
poise of "The Jade Steps' Grievance" between inside and outside, a woman's and man's point of view, might be thought emblematic of the whole
tradition. The male poet who appropriates the voice of an abandoned
woman does not give up his privileges as a man. To put it bluntly, the
reason that most men imagine abandoned women is in order to use them.

The tradition of "women's grievances" in Chinese poetry supplies
some remarkable evidence for this proposition. Most Western readers,
encountering such poems in translation and out of context, are likely to
regard them as touching displays of sensibility. That reaction is valid but
also a little naive. Certainly the male poets of China devote themselves
to feminine emotions and perceptions, the educated heart of the lonely
and sensitive woman. Poetic mastery has been almost unimaginable,
throughout the East, without the sexual reversal that allows a man to
explore the tender and often lachrymose feelings barred to expression by
his sex. Western readers may resent the assumptions that lead to such

poetry: the silent strength of men, the restricted lives of women that afford them no alternative to enshrining some man as the center of all their desires. But at least the poetry voices the grievances of women. How delicately the great Ts'ao Chih (192–232), for instance, imagines the plight of a deserted wife, in one of his many influential treatments of the theme.

> The bright moon shines upon a high pavilion,
> Streamers of moonlight undulate and eddy.
> Upstairs, within, a melancholy woman—
> Her sorrows overflow in endless sighing.
> Venture to ask her, "Who is this that sighs?"
> And she will say, "I am a wanderer's wife.
> More than ten years ago my lord departed
> And now his wife, forsaken, nests alone.
> He is like drifting dust upon the road
> And I the mud that clots a turbid river—
> Floating or sinking, each to its element.
> When shall we cling together, be as one?
> I wish that I could be the southwest wind
> Flying away, far off, into his heart.
> His heart . . . but if it never opens to me
> Where shall I turn, what place will take me in?"

The heartache of the desolate woman survives translation. And even a reader made angry by the situation—the husband who has treated his wife so brutally yet is never reproached, the woman so oppressed that, like a clod of clay, she desires no better fate than to be stepped on—will probably concede the poet's skill at feeling like a woman. Or so it seems.

Yet appearances are deceiving. In fact Ts'ao Chih may have been using the woman to voice a grievance of his own. According to Chinese scholars the poem is a political allegory, meant for the ears of the poet's brother, the emperor Ts'ao P'i, and intended to convey frustration about the supplicant's lack of advancement and banishment from court. Ts'ao Chih requests an audience; the rest is protocol. Thus the imagery of dust and mud evokes not only the bond between man and wife but the common origin of the brothers, both made of the same substance despite the different states to which circumstances have brought them. Ts'ao Chih now humbles himself in the mire. The special mark of his humility is his willingness to assume a woman's position. Male poets practiced allegorical bowing, in those days. "In a feudalistic society like that of ancient China, . . . it was natural to compare the relationship between ruler and minister with that between man and woman or between master and slave." Hence the traditions of the neglected wife and the deserted courtesan, in Chinese poetry, almost always involve a politics of subservience. They are not alternatives to the masculine struggle for power but one of the main expressions of that struggle. The jade steps' grievance pleads Li Po's own cause. He speaks the yin that registers his yang.

To say this is not to deny that male poets can have feelings, in China and elsewhere. The ability of men like Ts'ao Chih and Li Po to put themselves in the place of a slave or woman remains an impressive act of imagination. But surely Blake's words also apply: "Pity would be no more, / If we did not make somebody Poor." Abandoned women are pathetic because men need them to be. They serve both as "allegories" of masculine frustrations and as the servile other self who reminds the male of his power. Hence their existence, in poetry as in real life, often obeys an iron law of victimization. Abandonment must fill their whole horizon, without the possibility of new scenery and occupations or another lover. The wanderer's wife must have no one else to turn to; the emperor's concubine must utter no reproach. In many such poems, one might argue, the abandoned woman is nothing more than a male conceit, shaped by a fantasy of absolute domination. A man who uses a woman defines himself.

THE MOTIVE OF SELF-DEFINITION

Indeed, the first, collective motive for male poets who impersonate abandoned women may be sexual self-definition. The pity of a man for a woman confirms his strength; the alternative to being abandoned is being found. Hence epic poems are always well stocked with abandoned women, the forsaken and mourning wives and lovers who vainly attempt to change the course of the action. The hero requires a foil to set him off. It is through Andromache that Hector knows himself a man, through Dido that Aeneas learns what it means to be a Roman. A careless eye might read such characters as distractions or subversions of the business at hand. "What's Hecuba to him, or he to Hecuba, / That he should weep for her?" But the question can be answered more precisely than Hamlet may be aware. What Hecuba represents to the man who identifies with her is just that sense of helpless and futile passion that spurs the man of action to his revenge. Hecuba is his other self—the self that suffers and does nothing. Recognizing himself in that passive victim, Hamlet of course feels ashamed. "O, what a rogue and peasant slave am I!" But the shame itself brings about his resolve, the clear and urgent pressure to do *something*. Hamlet is not Hecuba; he is a *man*. Unlike Ophelia, he will not lapse forever into grieving. Abandoned women show him the truth of his nature: the need for the actor to suppress everything womanish within him and perform his father's deeds. He weeps for Hecuba to goad himself.

Hecuba and Ophelia do not profit much from this motive. Insofar as the poetry of abandoned women has served to distinguish between heroes and heroines, opposing the strength and activity of one sex to the weakness and passivity of the other, it has been responsible for perpetuating some stale clichés about feminine helplessness. Many women would prefer that Ovid had never invented the heroine. And certainly the skill exhibited by such male poets at charting the infirmities of women in pain has not encouraged women to hope for a better life. The role of heroine preempts effectual action. Moreover, it doubtless tempts men into the illusion that they understand or sympathize with women. Ovid and Li Po impersonate abandoned women so brilliantly that all the female heart seems to lie open. Such poets are supremely *knowing*. And the insights of Ovid and a few other authors enabled their readers to feel equally knowing for almost two thousand years. Hence most medieval writers seem confident about their ability to unravel women's motives—at least so long as women exemplify the requisite weakness. Abelard taught Heloise what she was by moralizing Ovid for her—especially the *Art of Love*—and she learned her lesson so well that eventually she acted the role of a perfect Ovidian heroine whose letters imitate and supplement the *Heroides*. Nor could Chaucer have understood Criseyde without that Helen whom Ovid had opened like a book. Few readers will doubt that Chaucer was genuinely knowing. But stereotypes about abandoned women also passed down to the least and dullest of men. Fortified by the charm of the tradition, even a foolish Flute thinks Thisbe within his grasp. Men take some pride in their roles as abandoned women.

That pride, however, can easily turn exploitative. Even when most sympathetic to the problems of women, a male poet may view them through masculine blinders, if not as a text or pretext for reading himself. The greatest of poets may not be immune to such charges. Consider, for instance, Goethe's beloved Gretchen. Seduced and abandoned by Faust, cursed by the brother whose death is on her head, cast out of society, convicted of the murder of her child, yet still obsessed and faithful to her lover—she suffers as only abandoned women can. Few heroines in literature have attracted so much sympathy, and clearly the first of her lovers was Goethe himself. The "Gretchen Tragedy" originated, according to some accounts, in the poet's compassion for a woman on trial for infanticide, and he bends every effort to demonstrate her spiritual innocence, the loving frankness that the devil has seized as his prey. *Faust* itself shows us that Goethe worshipped Gretchen. Her virtue blends with the Holy Virgin's, a voice from above proclaims that she has been "saved," and in the great concluding scene of part 2, transformed into "a Penitent," she functions as the instrument or instructress of Faust's own redemption. A woman could hardly rise higher.

Nevertheless, the point of view is a man's. Even if we accept the reality of Gretchen as a creation (and not all critics do), the use to which she is put serves masculine interests. The woman is not her own agent. Less a partner of Faust than his prize, the spoils of the game he is playing, she meekly follows down her fated path. Nor does her story require much attention. Goethe makes it the lightest of sketches, correctly assuming that the audience will fill it in with details gleaned from the tabloids and from the general understanding of what good girls are like—they are demure, believe in God, covet jewelry, etc. The devil might have written the script. Yet Gretchen's very ordinariness, her representative quality as a representative abandoned woman, eventually leads to a glorious destination. Only when her individual character has been completely effaced, in the final scene, can she be revealed in her aspect as the "Ewig-Weibliche"—the Eternal Feminine, or what some today might call a To-tal Woman. Gretchen exists for a purpose, to draw us upward, "us," in context, plainly referring to men. To draw men upward is why she was created. Goethe does not intend to patronize women with such distinctions; he obviously considers them superior, if secondary, creatures. Yet men and the motives of men control the plot. Faust lives in a masculine world, and the purpose of Gretchen and of all abandoned women in that world is to teach men what they are.

The lesson may also be taught in more negative terms. Poets with less elevated notions of femininity than Goethe's often assign abandoned women a different role: to pull men down. "The emotional, passionate nature of the female in wild abandon is a terrible thing for man and his consciousness," according to Erich Neumann. "Deep down in the evolutionary stratum of adolescence, the fear of it still dwells in every man and works like a poison wherever a false conscious attitude represses this layer of reality into the unconscious." And even male poets who consciously favor women or raise them to the skies may recoil when sex comes in question. A rigid masculinity allows no unmanly weakness or sensuality to darken its dreams of feminine purity. In times of sexual repression, male poets guard the chastity of abandoned women as jealously as Sicilian husbands watch over a point of honor. Death itself may be preferred to a promiscuous mingling of sexes.

Wordsworth's Laodamia: Defining a Man

The case of William Wordsworth supplies a fascinating example. Few poets have ever depended more on the approval of women or condoled with them more—at least in theory. Moreover, his compassion for the suffering of women helped shape his poetic career. The great Wordsworthian style first ripened, in "The Ruined Cottage" (1797–99), through patient fellow-feeling with poor abandoned Margaret, whose life and infant pass away while she watches the road for a husband who will never return.

> I stood, and leaning o'er the garden gate
> Reviewed that Woman's sufferings; and it seemed
> To comfort me while with a brother's love
> I blessed her in the impotence of grief.

Wordsworth's phrasing subtly points the tale. Momentarily unmanned, the traveler unconsciously assumes the position of the suffering woman; he leans on the same gate where once she waited for news. The "it" that comforts him refers to his silent "review" of her life, an act of memory that seems identical with an act of blessing. But the deepest comfort stems from his ability to enter her feelings, imaginatively to join in "that secret spirit of humanity" which still pervades the empty cottage and unweeded garden. The man bends down to the woman. Recreating her story, he becomes a part of her.

Yet such recasting of the self into a woman's passive state does not come easily to a man. Wordsworth carefully spells out the conditions. The reason that the traveler leans on the gate is that his identification with the dead woman has resulted in "weakness" and loss of "power" (line 495); his grief is impotent to change anything; he loves her like a brother, not like a husband. In all these ways the poet has entered a halfway house, an unsexed state of being or pure humanity that relinquishes the self-control of manhood without arriving at the passive suffering of the woman or the ultimate passivity of the dead. To take on her nature he must give up a part of himself. I do not want to suggest that Wordsworth equates a woman with an impotent man. But the effect of "The Ruined Cottage," like that of such other crucial poems of abandoned women as "The Thorn" and "Ruth," depends on the extent to which a sympathetic man both can and cannot imagine the feelings of a woman. The male poet goes as far as he can. Indeed, the willingness of the young Wordsworth to entertain the most womanish, unmanly, or agitated points of view, even at the risk of looking ridiculous, is among his most admirable traits. But false notes frequently intrude. If Wordsworth found his best voice by adapting some cadences from abandoned women, his language still always reminds us that this is a man.

The later Wordsworth, however, had sterner ideas of manhood. He learned to resist the temptations of womanish feelings; he put behind him androgynous states of being. "Of all the men I ever knew," Coleridge said of this older poet, "Wordsworth has the least femineity in his mind. He is *all* man." The process of defeminization or disabandonment culminated in a poem that may be thought, according to one's taste, to end the poet's productive life or to inaugurate his later, more dutiful phase. "Laodamia" no longer receives much attention. Yet many readers once thought it among Wordsworth's best, and not the least of these admirers was the poet himself. Mrs. Alaric Watts records a visit when Wordsworth "asked me what I thought the finest elegiac composition in the language; and, when I diffidently suggested *Lycidas,* he replied, 'You are not far wrong. It may, I think, be affirmed that Milton's *Lycidas* and my *Laodamia* are twin Immortals.'" Mrs. Watts consented. Whatever one's opinion of this story, much better critics than she would have bowed to the judgment. Hazlitt, for instance, said that "Laodamia" "breathes the pure spirit of the finest fragments of antiquity. . . . It is a poem that might be read aloud in Elysium, and the spirits of departed heroes and sages would gather round to listen to it."

One wonders, however, what the spirits of departed *heroines,* had they been allowed to gather, would have thought of the poem. The question is by no means frivolous, since "Laodamia" derives from just such an Elysian gathering, the episode of the Mourning Fields (*Lugentes Campi*) where Aeneas finds the shade of Dido among other abandoned women whom love has wasted. Wordsworth singles out one passing shade for special attention: "Laodamia goes with them." But his treatment of this tortured woman hardly reflects a Virgilian attitude. Virgil specifically emphasizes that the heroines of the Mourning Fields are *victims* and describes Dido's own fate as unjust (*iniquo*). Wordsworth, in contrast, turns all his efforts toward demonstrating the eternal justice of the fate that such women suffer. The many critics who have praised the poem for its Virgilian spirit have tended to overlook the English poet's explicit intention to give the story "a loftier tone than, so far as I know, has been given to it by any of the Ancients who have treated of it." Wordsworth strains the music of Latin through a heavy filter (through its influence on Tennyson, "Laodamia" helped to create the Victorian Virgil). But more important, he perceives a dangerous impiety or *lowness* in the morality of the ancient sources. Hence he sets out to cleanse his dubious heroine, and thus to justify the ways of Jove to women.

The purification of "Laodamia" commences in the second stanza, a description of the heroine as she prays for her dead husband to come back to life. Wordsworth deliberately matches his vision of a poet-priestess against one of Virgil's great set pieces: the moment of the Sibyl's possession.

> *"deus, ecce, deus!" cui talia fanti*
> *ante fores subito non voltus, non color unus,*
> *non comptae mansere comae, sed pectus anhelum,*
> *et rabie fera corda tument, maiorque videri*

nec mortale sonans, adflata est numine quando
iam propiore dei. . . .
  "The god is here, the god!" As she speaks this
before the doors, suddenly neither face nor color is the same,
nor does her hair stay tied, but her breast heaves,
and madly her wild heart swells, and she looks taller
nor does she sound mortal, the sway of the god is
already breathing nearer. . . .

The woman resists the god. But Wordsworth tells another, more harmonious story. As smooth as marble, the English text crushes down the
Latin that supports it.

So speaking, and by fervent love endowed
With faith, the Suppliant heavenward lifts her hands;
While, like the sun emerging from a cloud,
Her countenance brightens—and her eye expands;
Her bosom heaves and spreads, her stature grows;
And she expects the issue in repose.

In both passages a male presence invades a female medium, enhancing
her stature. But a more enlightened religion has tranquilized the ancient
mysteries. In place of the raging Sibyl, Wordsworth sculpts a sunny and
dignified figure whose sudden change of color merely adds a glow of
matronly brightness. Her faith and love have blessed her with repose.
Wordsworth allows no touch of Virgilian fury: the mantic hysterical inspiration of the *vates* that surpasses any masculine understanding. Instead of fighting the god, the English Laodamia voluntarily lifts her hands
to him, and is rewarded by a magnification that might be attributed
equally to divine power or her own heightened spirits. This woman knows
her place. Thus, in her good fortune, she grows to exactly the height of
a man.

  Unfortunately Laodamia does not know when she is well off; she insists on being a woman. That deadly mistake accounts for the plot of the
poem. Wordsworth has picked a curious ancient legend as his source.
The story of Protesilaus and Laodamia, however well known in antiquity, has not come down to us in any definitive version, and it certainly
does not speak for itself. An oracle foretold that the first Greek soldier to
touch the soil of Troy would die; the hapless Protesilaus fulfilled the
prophecy by briskly disembarking and expiring; his bride Laodamia,
still virginal, mourned for him until the gods relented and let him return to earth for just three hours; at the end of that time Laodamia accompanied him back to the underworld. Wordsworth had always opposed
the sort of mindless classicizing verse that ransacks the past for dilapi-

dated myths, "A history only of departed things, / Or a mere fiction of what never was." Why then did he choose to tell this faded story?

Doubtless the theme of *duty* appealed to him. Protesilaus is above all a good soldier, ready to volunteer for the last detail simply because someone must. But Laodamia, not her husband, stands at the center of the poem, and duty is not her theme. Some poets have read her story as an emblem of love and faithfulness, the image of a woman striving to redeem death at the pledge of her own life. Male readers often take a prurient interest in the spectacle of female self-sacrifice. Yet Wordsworth focuses his attention elsewhere. The plot, as he conceives it, hinges on a fatal feminine slip, the desire of Laodamia to possess her husband in the body as well as the soul. As soon as Protesilaus appears she springs to grasp his "unsubstantial Form" in "consummation." Alas, like one of Milton's angels or Pope's sylphs his phantom only parts at her attack and reunites again. But the woman, aroused, persists.

> "No Spectre greets me,—no vain Shadow this;
> Come, blooming Hero, place thee by my side!
> Give, on this well-known couch, one nuptial kiss
> To me, this day, a second time thy bride!"
> Jove frowned in heaven: the conscious Parcae threw
> Upon those roseate lips a Stygian hue.

Protesilaus sternly warns her, at considerable length, to "control / Rebellious passion. . . . / Thy transports moderate; and meekly mourn." When she continues to hope, insisting on the mighty potency of love, "though his favourite seat be feeble woman's breast," the unsympathetic spirit plays his trump card: her selfish desire does not even deserve to be called love.

> "Learn, by a mortal yearning, to ascend—
> Seeking a higher object. Love was given,
> Encouraged, sanctioned, chiefly for that end;
> For this the passion to excess was driven—
> That self might be annulled: her bondage prove
> The fetters of a dream opposed to love."—

"Aloud she shrieked!"—not at his argument but at the reappearance of Hermes, come to take the dear shade back. Protesilaus goes, and Laodamia dies; "a trance of passion" carries her away. Whatever the mode of her death, the poet maintains, she must be considered a suicide. Immoderate passion has led to an excess even more shocking than the woman's desire for a "nuptial kiss": her willful defiance of the term that the gods have set on human life. And Wordsworth agrees with the gods.

Not all the poet's care and Virgilian pastiche can keep this version of the story from seeming inhuman. Wordsworth himself testified that the poem had "cost me more trouble than almost anything of equal length I have ever written," and the reasons are not hard to guess: anxiety about female sexuality had locked in mortal combat with the natural sympathy due an abandoned widow. Over the years the strain became manifest in increasingly harsh punishments meted out to the dead woman. The tenderness of the conclusion in 1815—

> Ah, judge her gently who so deeply loved!
> Her, who, in reason's spite, yet without crime,
> Was in a trance of passion thus removed

—eventually hardened, after several intermediary assessments, into a verdict with no appeal:

> Thus, all in vain exhorted and reproved,
> She perished; and, as for a wilful crime,
> By the just Gods whom no weak pity moved,
> Was doomed to wear out her appointed time,
> Apart from happy Ghosts. . . .

"As first written," Wordsworth explained to his nephew in 1830, "the Heroine was dismissed to happiness in Elysium. To what purpose then the mission of Protesilaus—He exhorts her to moderate her passion—the exhortation is fruitless—and no punishment follows. So it stood; at present she is placed among unhappy Ghosts, for disregard of the exhortation." Thus the poem, we may note, had a "purpose" and a "mission" for its author: to punish Laodamia for the "crime" of her active desire. To rebuke her womanish lack of "self-government" was why he told her story.

Wordsworth's piety here seems remarkably unsympathetic. But perhaps his motive may be clarified by comparing "Laodamia" to a source far more important than Virgil to its substance (if not to its style): *Heroides* 13, Laodamia's letter to Protesilaus. Wordsworth was grappling with Ovid. Most of the details of the heroine's passion respond to specific points in the Latin text. Thus the English Laodamia's attempt to clasp her phantom husband recalls the Latin Laodamia's fantasy of clasping his "weary body" when he returns; the "nuptial kiss" and "well-known couch" figure prominently in Ovid; and even Laodamia's swoon to death harks back to her fainting fit, in Ovid, when Protesilaus departs and her Roman vow to stay his comrade forever, whether he lives or dies. By transferring the heroine's *anticipation* of disaster, in the epistle, into her refusal to accept the *consequences* of disaster, Wordsworth has exchanged suspense and irony for a sense of inevitability. The poignant parting of Ovid's lovers—"I must break free, Protesilaus, from your embrace" ("solvor ab amplexu, Protesilae, tuo", line 12)—becomes a grim injunction in the English. Hence Wordsworth looks back at the tender and anxious passion of his source primarily to rebuke it. Fate cannot be altered, and hope must be quenched when the time for loving is over.

Wordsworth's rebuke of Ovid goes far beyond the correction of details. It touches on the essence of the heroic epistle: its substitution of a woman's way of imagining for a man's. Much of the pleasure of the *Heroides* depends on its ingenuity in retelling the great stories of legend from a woman's point of view. Thus Laodamia adapts the Trojan War to her own hopes and fears. It becomes a senseless squabble over a woman, an engine with no other purpose than to menace Protesilaus. The heroine takes no notice of male heroics. When she pictures a scene that closely resembles the famous Homeric parting of Hector and Andromache, she concludes that the warrior will fight more cautiously in order to return to his wife's arms (an image doubly ironic, since it is Hector who will kill Protesilaus). All notions of duty and glory vanish, and history itself assumes a feminine coloring. Ovid's own purpose here might be disputed. The epistle might be read as a satire against women, who are unable to understand the truth or values of the masculine world; or it might be read as a tribute to women's love, whose intensity reveals the hollowness of a life sacrificed to public standards of bravery and shame. Did Protesilaus's fine gesture have any meaning? Ovid does not commit his poem to answer one way or the other. Yet Wordsworth insists on the unequivocal value of the action: "For fearless virtue bringeth boundless gain." We must not be tempted to take the woman's side.

Even the structure of "Laodamia" confirms its rejection of the heroine's point of view. Wordsworth ends his poem not with the death and punishment of Laodamia but with a description (based on Pliny) of Protesilaus's tomb. Trees grown from out that tomb until, reaching the height at which the walls of Troy are visible, they wither at the top—"A constant interchange of growth and blight!" Evidently the poet considers this consoling, a sign that nature cares about his hero.

> —Yet tears to human suffering are due;
> And mortal hopes defeated and o'erthrown
> Are mourned by man, and not by man alone,
> As fondly he believes.

But the masculine nouns and pronouns remind us how little of this sympathy seems wasted on the woman. The trees, like a wilted phallus, witness the death of male aspirations. Yet they do not have much to do with Laodamia. *She* is buried elsewhere, and in any case might regard the symbolism more as a further irony or reproach than as a sign of compassion. The stoicism of the gods and Virgil and Wordsworth rewards heroes of its own stamp, not those victims who must pay for heroism without believing in it. Even in death she will get no satisfaction.

Nor is Laodamia allowed the comfort of dreaming. The poetry of the Latin epistle depends on the heroine's fantasy life, her ability to conjure up Protesilaus in his absence. Laodamia is ruled by her desire. In brilliant passages she imagines the ghost of her husband before her and makes love to his waxen image. Perhaps the appearance of the ghost signifies that Protesilaus has already died. Certainly it indicates the power of the abandoned woman's dreams and her readiness to believe in magic. She accepts an image for the truth; she sets her heart on fancies. So much of Laodamia's life consists of dreams that finally she loses her capacity to tell dreams from reality. That weakness makes her a woman; on this point at least Ovid and Wordsworth agree. But a far more disturbing implication follows: perhaps that weakness also makes her a poet. Wordsworth shrinks from this insinuation as if it were the plague. He forces the woman to face the ghost of her husband in the cold light of dawn, and snatches her dreams away.

By Ovid's standards, the association of poetry with the fantasies caused by unfulfilled sexual passion presents no threat. Though capable of mocking the enslavement of women to dreams, he also knows that men who would be poets must share a portion of that fantasy life. The skillful blend of uncontrollable, hallucinatory feelings with hard intellectual analysis is Ovid's stock in trade. But Wordsworth obeys quite different poetic gods. Protesilaus returns from Elysium, in his version, precisely in order to draw the line between a woman's mode of imagining and a man's. Reproaching Laodamia for her confusion of sexuality with love, he also implicitly censures Ovid for having failed to make the same distinction. Worse yet, Ovid has lent his authority to superstition. Wordsworth cannot accept the suggestion that the sources of poetry might be impure, that selfish passion or sexual longing might fuel them. Instead, he deliberately contrives a poem that distances the self—or the feminine side of the self—in every way. Ovid must be taught to speak in a loftier tone. The fires of abandoned women must be quenched by a man.

Thus Wordsworth proves himself manly. Perhaps his immediate motive for writing the poem, in fact, was to defend himself against reflections on his manhood. Donald H. Reiman has plausibly speculated that, just beneath the marble surface of "Laodamia," a secret may be buried: the poet's confession and justification of his sexual impotence. As the letters of William and Mary Wordsworth make clear, their marriage had been tender and passionate, at least until 1812. But the sudden death in that year of two of their children had strained the health of the Wordsworths and shriveled their pleasure in life. A shroud lay over their bed. Some lines added to *The Excursion* (and later canceled) seem painfully revealing: "To my Co-partner in this bitter loss / Support I could not yield, who did myself / Require support from others less disturbed, / Or

from the blank and calm of solitude. / Dark became doubly dark. . . ."
The Solitary is unable to touch his wife or ease her grief, and she dies.
Mary Wordsworth fared better. But if her husband's desire *did* wither
away the effect must have been devastating. A ghastly light breaks over
"Laodamia" when read in this context: "stern admonitions to a woman
to control her passions in the presence of a bodily lover who was yet only
the ghost of his former self." Was Wordsworth addressing his wife, and
did she consider herself chastised? We do not know. But whatever the
specific motive of the poet, his deeper urge seems to have been to define
the ways in which he was not vulnerable and was not a woman. Duty
must come before passion. He had proved that once to Annette Vallon
when, touching the soil of England, he had become dead forever to his
foreign bride. Now he would spell out the lessons: the comforts of sex
do not last; the sexes remain distinct.

Even Laodamia's abandonment and the pity owed her situation, therefore, serve mainly to steel the poet by contrast in the hardness of his own
sex. Women stand for desire and desire must be mastered. Hence Laodamia schools Wordsworth in the same virtue that Adversity, another
daughter of Jove, had once taught Thomas Gray: "what others are to feel,
and know myself a man." Men need to feel what others are precisely in
order to overcome those feelings. The later Wordsworth succeeds unequivocally in that objective. In "Laodamia" he manages to admonish and
correct not only his own womanish tendencies and his wife's but those
of the classical poets, Virgil and Ovid. Henceforth "no weak pity" will
move his ideal of poetry. Wordsworth's poem descends like an angel to
announce the triumph of spirit over body. And even his motive in raping
the Sibyl is just to uplift her sex.

Not many poets have held such rigid notions of masculinity. Perhaps
poetry profits from a better balance of genders. Wordsworth's own powers declined, according to most critics, from the moment when he began
to suppress his feminine "weakness" or sacrifice it to duty. Yet many
other male poets have also used abandoned women as emblems of what
men are not. The madwomen in the attic validate the better housekeeping
downstairs and at the office; Eve teaches Adam his strength. No cultures
have been more addicted to the poetry of abandoned women than those
in which the roles of men and women have traditionally been most dis-
criminated, as in ancient China or the Middle East. Poems can confirm
such roles. In the Mourning Fields, as in harems, the sexes are kept apart.

Pope's Eloisa: Defining the Human

Most men, however, prefer relations with women. By getting to
know the opposite sex, the male poet may discover not only how much
he differs but how much he and they have in common. Thus a second
motive for impersonating women may be the desire for self-recognition.

Byron uses Donna Julia, we have seen, not only to anatomize the difference between male and female hearts but to explore his own sense of abandonment. Both by contrast and similarity, she reminds him of intimate feelings and vulnerabilities that a merely masculine hero could never acknowledge. He writes her letter by recreating the style and openheartedness of his adolescence. Most sensitive male poets have used women in the same way: to trace their own steps and remind them of something in themselves. Crazy Jane is Yeats as he would like to be, in some moods at least, if only he could tear off the last tatter of his mortal dress and masculine dignity, and Ovid's Sappho is Ovid disrobed of shame. Such men enjoy distinguishing men from women, but they do not fear contamination from the other sex. Instead they hope for reciprocal understanding. Moreover, a full humanity will have to comprehend both sexes. According to the poet who taught Byron much of what he knew about women, "Heav'n, when it strives to polish all it can / Its last best work, but forms a softer Man"—that is, a man with a woman's virtues or a woman with a man's. The work of poets requires the same sort of polish.

Yet the line between self and other is easily frayed. In practice a male poet who approaches *too* close to a female identity—who fears that he may be in fact "a softer Man"—will often defend himself by exaggerating his masculinity (as actors who specialize in female impersonation sometimes find ways to signal us that they are "really" men). Certainly Alexander Pope availed himself of such defenses. Abusing such "Amphibious Things" as Sporus and Sappho, he attacks the confusion of sexual roles and defines himself entirely as a man. Pope likes to play the cavalier. Too delicate for rape, he takes his pleasure in verbal seduction and male supremacy. Meanwhile he guards against the danger of exposing himself to a woman and risking her scorn. "In Tasks so bold, can Little Men engage, / And in soft Bosoms dwells such mighty Rage?"

The answer to both questions, however, is yes. Despite his fears, Pope could engage the task of knowing a woman. He needed that knowledge for his poetry, and neither timidity nor dignity would stand in his way. For he had spied on the mysteries of the other sex and had forcibly entered (if not the Sibyl) the Spleen. Few men have paid such close attention to the dressing table, the card room, and the sources of feminine pride. Pope is intimately acquainted with "the moving Toyshop of their Heart," however rarely he acknowledges his own kinship with it. He prefers to judge those passions from outside. But once at least he put all his own heart into the portrait of a woman and then confessed her likeness to himself. In "Eloisa to Abelard," at the turning point of his career, he surrenders his male persona and allows his other sex to speak with her own voice.

That act of imagination—viewing the world through the mind and heart of an alien abandoned being—constitutes the unique vision of the poem. Not only does Pope imagine himself a woman, he also imagines the whole situation as feminine: a projection of woman's desire into the landscape and inscape. The opening lines already announce the theme.

> In these deep solitudes and awful cells,
> Where heav'nly-pensive, contemplation dwells,
> And ever-musing melancholy reigns;
> What means this tumult in a Vestal's veins?

A modern reader, unaccustomed to visualize or "paint" abstractions in the eighteenth-century style, might easily overlook the two rival female figures who dominate the scene: heavenly-pensive Contemplation and ever-musing Melancholy. We are meant to *see* these personifications through Eloisa's eyes. Indeed, the contrast between their two ways of seeing—Contemplation, presumably in the habit of a nun, whose eyes roll upward toward heaven; and the black goddess Melancholy, majestic in her wings and drapery, who broods upon the darkness or a letter—defines the basic tension of the poem: the heroine's double vision. From moment to moment Eloisa wavers. A trick of perspective can change the whole world.

Consider that celebrated descriptive passage in which Pope out-Ovids Ovid and out-Miltons Milton.

> The darksom pines that o'er yon' rocks reclin'd
> Wave high, and murmur to the hollow wind,
> The wandring streams that shine between the hills,
> The grots that eccho to the tinkling rills,
> The dying gales that pant upon the trees,
> The lakes that quiver to the curling breeze;
> No more these scenes my meditation aid,
> Or lull to rest the visionary maid:
> But o'er the twilight groves, and dusky caves,
> Long-sounding isles, and intermingled graves,
> Black Melancholy sits, and round her throws
> A death-like silence, and a dread repose:
> Her gloomy presence saddens all the scene,
> Shades ev'ry flower, and darkens ev'ry green,
> Deepens the murmur of the falling floods,
> And breathes a browner horror on the woods.

One picture replaces another. The pretty pastoral images of the first six lines, innocently dreamy, aid meditation by suggesting a perfect reciprocity among all the elements of nature. Thus the pines wave and murmur to the winds, the streams reflect the sky, the grots echo the rills, gales pant on the trees, lakes quiver when the breeze touches them. It is all very lulling; and even the conventional sexual undertones, planted in the feminized landscape with its gentle rises and hollows, its panting and quivering responsiveness, only confirm the maid's feeling of being at home in nature. But visionaries are susceptible to sudden changes of mood. The repose of Melancholy takes a more active form. She throws her presence around; she saddens and shades and darkens and deepens and breathes horror. Grots turn into caves and graves, and tinkling rills into falling floods. This goddess insists on her mastery over nature. Like the Sibyl or the Spleen, she is most at home in the underworld and converts the atmosphere to her own gloom and a deeper sexuality. After the fall, the world of pastoral love is stained by an obsession with longing and death and loss. Eloisa's sin of despair has darkened her soul. To imagine her rightly, Pope must blot his canvas and give her the power of bringing all nature down.

She also paints her love on heaven itself. One trick of perspective controls the poem as a whole: the superimposition of Abelard on God. Wherever Eloisa looks—a rock, a shrine, the sky, her heart—the face of her lover intrudes. Even at the moment of taking the veil, she cannot see anything else.

> Yet then, to those dread altars as I drew,
> Not on the Cross my eyes were fix'd, but you.

The verse repeats that effect for hundreds of lines. "Eloisa to Abelard" might be called a poem of ideas, but only so long as we understand "idea" strictly as a mental image or picture. Pope's heroine has little talent for abstractions. A literal-minded idealist, she hides her lover's picture in her heart, "within that close disguise, / Where, mix'd with God's, his lov'd Idea lies." Hence the dialectic of the poem pits two icons against each other—an unequal struggle, since Abelard, though absent and mutilated, still rules the senses with which she perceives him. Not even death will be able to cure her habits of reverie and hallucination. God wins the argument, but love makes better pictures.

Visions, ideas, images, and fancies. To some extent "Eloisa to Abelard" can be regarded as a sustained mad scene, in which the heroine encounters and shrinks from ghost after ghost that she herself has conjured up. Like Ovid's Laodamia, she clasps her arms around a phantom and wakes as it glides away. Again and again the same frustrating rhythm recurs. In the dark night of Eloisa's soul the air itself is peopled with visionary Abelards.

> What scenes appear where–e'er I turn my view!
> The dear Ideas, where I fly, pursue,
> Rise in the grove, before the altar rise,
> Stain all my soul, and wanton in my eyes!

> I waste the Matin lamp in sighs for thee,
> Thy image steals between my God and me,
> Thy voice I seem in ev'ry hymn to hear,
> With ev'ry bead I drop too soft a tear.
> When from the Censer clouds of fragrance roll,
> And swelling organs lift the rising soul;
> One thought of thee puts all the pomp to flight,
> Priests, Tapers, Temples, swim before my sight:
> In seas of flame my plunging soul is drown'd,
> While Altars blaze, and Angels tremble round.

The description comes to us, Brendan O Hehir has noted, through a veil of tears; it is the mist in Eloisa's eyes that makes the tapers swim and angels tremble. But not all her illusions are optical. Clearly she has internalized the scene and drawn the flames within. Hence the reader senses the images not merely through the woman's eyes but through her veins.

Pope enters his heroine's feelings. With extraordinary daring, he tunes his verse not only to blasphemy but to the melting or visionary swoon associated in his day with female orgasm. Like Tiresias he tries to experience the fantasies and the climax of a woman from inside. Almost inevitably this leads to an emphasis on her passivity and masochism even at the height of passion. Eloisa takes no active responsibility for her wanton ideas. Instead they pursue her and stain her and eventually damn her as if she were a helpless victim of rape by dreams. The controlling metaphor of the passage is human sacrifice, a mass that ends with blazing altars and the soul of the heroine drowned in seas of flame. Like Phèdre catching sight of Hippolytus (in Racine's play), the priestess becomes a victim of her own ritual. The line in which she falls, "Priests, Tapers, Temples, swim before my sight," is glossed by a likely source, Edmund Smith's version of Phaedra: "Priests, Altars, Victims swam before my Sight." Eloisa's act of yielding to Abelard, in visionary ecstasy, is identical with self-immolation. As hell yawns open, she surrenders her soul to "The torch of *Venus*" and turns into a holy martyr of sex.

Why should a male poet like Pope submit himself to such a passive dream? An interest in rape or voyeurism cannot be the whole answer, since (as compared with Ovid or Bussy-Rabutin, for instance) the English epistle seems relatively free from titillation. Pope does not reduce Eloisa to *deshabille;* her obsessions attract him more than her charms. To some extent that must be because they resemble his own obsessions. A "visionary" maid is not only one "given to visions" but one "envisioned," and Pope spent much of his time imagining women. Like Eloisa, he knew that he would not realize his dreams. As James Winn has shown, much of the poem consists of "a pastiche of phrases from Pope's earlier letters"; and by 1717 the poet's love life seems to have been almost wholly absorbed by visions of what he had lost or would never have. He no longer hoped for marriage. Yet transferring his obsessions to a woman could only compromise his ability to rise above them. "Eloisa to Abelard" is a claustrophobic poem. By writing from within the heroine's superheated frame of mind, Pope puts aside the calm, broad gaze at life he values as a man. What does he gain in return? Or, to collapse the issue of poetry into the issue of sex, in a phrase that balances Freud's: what do men *want?*

One possible answer is that they want to be real. Male poets, like other men, confirm the reality of their feelings through the echo of a woman's feelings, or the reality of sexual gratification through a woman's responsive excitement. "What is it men in women do require? / The lineaments of Gratified Desire." Women authenticate men. Thus Pope can trust his own emotions partly because he knows that Eloisa has aready felt them. Moreover, she is especially trustworthy because the story of her abandonment is based not on fiction but real life. "The heart naturally loves truth," said Samuel Johnson. "The adventures and misfortunes of this illustrious pair are known from undisputed history."

Unfortunately the history is no longer undisputed. We know that Pope's immediate source, John Hughes's English version of the letters, commits sentimental distortions; and even the Latin originals may be suspect. If Heloise *did* write her own letters, she had obviously consulted not only her heart but Ovid. Three hundred years before Pope, Jean de Gerson referred cynically to Abelard's "Heloydes." He was not wrong. Whatever their provenance, the letters come to us wrapped in literary traditions of abandonment and romance, an intertextuality in which we recognize the heart of a woman because it already resembles so many other texts. Pope knew that too. The relation of "Sappho to Phaon" to "Eloisa to Abelard" could hardly escape the attention of someone who tried his own hand at both. What he cared about, like any poet, was less the source of the document than its availability and reproducibility, its power to *confer* reality. Wherever she originated, Heloise passes her authority on to Pope. He proves himself real by showing that he can make a perfect copy of the woman and her letter—at least to those who judge by outward signs.

How far can signs be trusted? Much of the poem revolves around this question. Like other heroic epistles, "Eloisa to Abelard" builds its plot on the handling of letters—not only billets-doux but the letters of the alphabet. Though the sight of Abelard's handwriting rekindles Eloisa's passion, we learn very little about what he has written. Instead she invests her emotions in the physical appearance of his signature or *name*—a word constantly repeated. "Soon as thy letters trembling I unclose, / That well-known name awakens all my woes." She opens her soliloquy by kissing the name, and immediately afterward finds that Abelard's Idea will not stay hidden in her heart.

> Oh write it not, my hand—The name appears
> Already written—wash it out, my tears!
> In vain lost *Eloisa* weeps and prays,
> Her heart still dictates, and her hand obeys.

Pope creates an illusion of automatic writing. Abelard's name seems always already written, as if the words of the poem went straight from the heart to the page without any conscious volition. It is a magical view of language, like the thaumaturgy and animism with which Eloisa shapes her surroundings. In her world statues weep, a ghost calls in the wind, and the lover's spirit peers out from every moldering tower or cloud of incense. Such images animate the deadly rounds of the convent. A Freudian or Lacanian would not take long, I think, to identify the source of her compulsions, her need to animate the one thing that will never revive again, the one thing that could make her happy: Abelard's missing part. Even her final prayer for a signature carved on the tomb—"May one kind grave unite each hapless name, / And graft my love immortal on thy fame"—shows that she worships a fetish, the magic in names. But what is lost cannot be restored by vision.

The poet's question, however, is whether it can be restored by language: the act of writing in which both Eloisa and Abelard again spring to life. Pope hopes for reanimation. Copying the woman's letter, tracing her words, uniting his name with hers, he aims at total possession. Henceforth, like Lycidas and Laodamia, they will be twin immortals. The self-indulgence and self-reference of this act of appropriation become explicit in the closing lines, when Pope imagines Eloisa imagining Pope imagining Eloisa.

> And sure if fate some future Bard shall join
> In sad similitude of griefs to mine,
> Condemn'd whole years in absence to deplore,
> And image charms he must behold no more,
> Such if there be, who loves so long, so well;
> Let him our sad, our tender story tell;
> The well-sung woes will sooth my pensive ghost;
> He best can paint 'em, who shall feel 'em most.

The effect is a hall of mirrors or *mise en abîme*. The poet teases us into noticing his sorrows by reflecting them off his heroine, who reflects him in turn. Visionary reciprocity could hardly go further. Pope almost destroys the frame of his painting by insisting on a story of his own, a story that supplements Eloisa's and threatens to replace it. Readers are invited to go back over the poem and interpret it as the confession of some unutterable personal trauma (Pope hinted to more than one of his female correspondents that she was the cause of his grief). Yet the aesthetic principle stated in the final line is not only a wink to the reader but an affirmation that feeling can be transmuted into art. "Well-sung woes" can bridge the abyss that separates eras and lovers. Pope compensates Eloisa for her loss of Abelard by offering himself, and she rewards him by furnishing a sympathetic subject. Love may fail, but art and sympathy will last. The poet's hand obeys the heart of a ghost. A man *can* feel like a woman. Eloisa lives again.

Perhaps what Pope wants most from his heroine, in fact, is that she notice him. The majority of his early poems conclude with some gesture of self-reference, his poetic "signature." But "Eloisa to Abelard" exceeds the others by putting the words into the hand of an imagined other, a woman. Indeed, Eloisa's postscript seems to nullify her letter as a message to Abelard (who would surely have been puzzled by this talk of future bards). Instead she readdresses it to Pope, a more faithful lover. What more could any man want? Through mirroring the poet's own feelings, she verifies his immediate presence or existence. In that moment he changes from her scribe to her soul, an image fixed in the glass. Pope claims, in short, to have entered the mirror stage—absolute self-recognition. He sees himself at last, part woman, part man, and knows what he is.

Not every reader will agree with this analysis. Some, for instance, have glimpsed a phantom smile in the final passage, the poet waving to us as he intentionally distances himself from his heroine and her problems. A deconstructive reader might point out an aporia, the poet's admission of just that magical thinking or mystification which he has exposed in Eloisa. Thus the references to "joining" her griefs, to imaging, loving, telling, soothing, and above all painting and feeling, deliberately avoid the one operation for which evidence does exist: the process of writing. Despite their protests, Pope and Eloisa do *not* exist except in their words. Not all the visionary authority of an abandoned woman can certify the presence of the poet unless he has first slipped the lines into her hand. Vision itself depends on that verbal illusion. Eloisa cannot repair the missing piece of her lover, nor can Pope overcome his impotence and show us the earthly lover lurking at his heart. All we can know is the surface, an arrangement of letters that every new reader or writer will rearrange in turn. Moreover, Pope himself—a feminist reader might note—has made the mirror that reflects him. Male sentiment erects a screen to block out any female qualities—for instance, the intelligence and executive ability of the historical Eloisa—that it finds inconvenient to imitate. Even Pope's pity is only a mask for self-pity. And a biographer might add that the experiment of feeling like a woman did not last. In

retrospect the epistle closes a stage in Pope's career, a temporary tenderness replaced by more manly pursuits and aggressive designs. What
Eloisa confirmed for her poet in the long run may have been that he was
not formed to be a lover.

Yet once, at least, he had tried. In a curious way, all the arguments that
demonstrate the impossibility of bringing "Eloisa to Abelard" to a successful conclusion pay tribute to its success. For impossibility is what the
poem is about: the impossibility of vision creating reality, of desire reaching its object, or of men and women at last comprehending each other.
The Sibyl retains her secrets. Yet the poem is not despairing. As Eloisa
gazes into the future, she takes some comfort from the tears that will be
shed on her behalf. Perhaps "two wandring lovers" will come to the
Paraclete, lean sadly together with mutual pity, "And drink the falling
tears each other sheds." Or perhaps, amid "the pomp of dreadful sacrifice," if "some relenting eye" should be distracted from devotion by noticing Eloisa's and Abelard's relics, "One human tear shall drop, and be
forgiv'n." The emphasis on tears seems rather baroque (Crashaw helped
to influence these lines). But Pope has more in mind than contriving an
effect. Much of the epistle has depended on the torture and martyrdom
of Eloisa, as if she were a priestess sacrificed on her own altar. Numbly
wedding Christ again and again, she offers her body as "love's victim."
In this respect the poem is Eloisa's mass. But Pope redeems her with a
tear. He substitutes, for the flesh and blood of the Eucharist, a mass of
tears, a secular redemption based on sympathy. Men and women can
share each other's woes. The lovers who drink the emblems of their pity,
the eye whose teardrop proves that it is human, admit their own complicity in Eloisa's fall. Pope drops his tear and claims his forgiveness.
Thus he uses Eloisa to discover something that his own brilliance had
often disguised: his common and fallen human nature. Relinquishing his
superiority, he confesses himself a son of Eve, or even her daughter. A
knowledge of this part of himself, the weak and frustrated lover, the sensitive wounded soul, will follow him all his days. He wakes from his
vision a sadder and softer man.

The Bride of St. John of the Cross

Yet the rape of the Sibyl may entail a more extreme, more dangerous encounter with the other. The mortal who dares it may have to
abandon himself. While some men confirm their manliness and others
their human existence, a third sort of poet may try to submerge in the
woman—effacing himself in order to learn what she knows. The effort
is frightening. For the sake of such knowledge masculinity itself may
have to be sacrificed, at least provisionally, to be replaced by an identification with the female will. Men need strong motives to give up so much
of their sex. Curiosity drives them, and sometimes humility. But the

richest motive tends to be a desire to be possessed by the divine. Virgil has no better way of communicating with Apollo than through the Sibyl, and Yeats needs Leda's point of view in order to feel the feathered glory in all its power. Male gods love women best. Hence religious poets often approach the divine by wrapping themselves in the form of a woman. In the best such poetry the man surrenders so totally that he leaves no sign of pride or a self. Witness St. John of the Cross.

Each of John's three greatest poems—by common consent among the greatest erotic and religious poetry ever written—is told from a woman's perspective. Thus *Noche oscura del alma* ("Dark Night of the Soul") presents a speaker who has made her way to her lover through the dark; *Llama de amor viva* ("Living Flame of Love") describes the moment of intimate union as a woman experiences it; and the *Cántico espiritual* ("Spiritual Canticle") begins with a woman abandoned and ends with her looking forward to what her bridegroom is about to give her. Evidently John feels no shame. Whatever the allegorical significance of these situations, the passion that informs them is rendered with miraculous force and precision. There are no false notes and no lapses into prurience— only unspeakable rapture. That rapture can be quite unnerving. For Spanish men, traditionally bound to a cult of masculinity or *machismo*, the upside-down sex of their finest lyric poet induces some queasy feelings. Whole books about John have been written without a single mention of his erotic perspective. Others explain the woman's voice away. Yet John himself betrays no embarrassment. To a poet of his kind, nothing seems more natural than to adopt the style and feeling of abandoned women.

Learning to feel like a woman had made him a poet. An early biographer has left an account of the very moment it happened—an account we may take to be spiritually if not factually true. In 1578 John was being held prisoner in a tiny, filthy cell in the Carmelite priory of Toledo. Angered at his efforts to reform the order, the Calced friars scourged him, starved him, treated him with silence and contempt. He expected to die. Then, one dark night, he heard singing from the street below, a common love song. The voice was a boy's, but the story it told was a woman's.

> *Muérome de amores,*
> *Carillo. ¿Qué haré?*
> —*Que te mueras, alahé.*
> I am dying of love,
> Sweetheart. What shall I do?
> —Just go ahead and die.

Suddenly John realized his mission. He would become a poet, and his poems would show that the experience of that wounded woman held the key to salvation. Her sufferings figured his own degradation, yet the cruel sweetheart for whom she yearned was God. Sharing her loneliness, John too must appeal for love. The way lay open to him. A few months later, when he escaped from prison, he had already written most of his longest and finest work, the *Spiritual Canticle*. His life as a poet and saint commences from that time.

Like most such sudden conversions, this one had been well prepared. John had long since learned to listen to women. His ecstasy on hearing the street song may be explained, at least in part, by two voices that he heard weaving through it: the bride who cries to her bridegroom in the *Song of Songs,* and St. Teresa, who had taught him to read the true significance of the *Song.* Whether or not John had written poetry before, he knew the principles of typology and the varieties of love. Hence popular song fuses with Scripture, in his poems, and erotic love with divine. He comprehends the abandoned woman without difficulty as a type of the soul, and conceives no better fate for the soul than to be penetrated by its maker. A similar effect sustains many of St. Teresa's interpretations of Scripture. "So, my Lord, I ask Thee for nothing else in this life but that Thou shouldst 'kiss me with a kiss of Thy mouth'; and let this be in such a way, Lord of my life, that, even if I should desire to withdraw from this friendship and union, my will may ever be so subject to Thine that I shall be unable to leave Thee." Rapture and rape join in a total mystic surrender of the self. John was familiar with such willing abandon. He had assisted Teresa in her reform—the act that brought him to prison—and served as her confessor; and some of her unsurpassed longing for the nuptial kiss of God communicated itself to him.

Thus John regards poetry itself as feminine, the cry of a woman for a man, and identifies with that cry. He accepts the yearning and passivity of a helpless, dependent creature; he imagines his lover as infinitely masterful and strong. Moreover, he seems to have no difficulty envisaging his own body as a woman's in relation to his Lord, and opening it to invite possession. The *Spiritual Canticle* inhabits an utterly shameless feminine soul in its quest for fulfillment—literally, for being filled. The way to poetry, the way to God, pass through a woman's fallen flesh and blood.

To what extent should such poems be read as genuine expressions of sympathy with women, and to what extent as spiritual exercises that are interested in women only because of what they may be made to represent allegorically? The question is not easy to answer. One of John's great contemporaries, Luis de León, had recently been persecuted by the Inquisition for translating the *Song of Songs* into Spanish and insisting on its literal level; and John knew better than to make such claims either for the *Song* or for his own version of it. His own exhaustive commentary on the *Spiritual Canticle* shows a remarkable indifference to its story or

literal meaning. Instead he concentrates on the tropological interpretation, the marriage of Christ to the soul. Nor is this merely a matter of
prudence. As John's commentaries frequently remind the reader, "experience and knowledge" tend to "fail and deceive us." Without the spirit
of love and mystical wisdom, poetic figures and similes "will seem to be
absurdities rather than reasonable utterances, as will those comparisons
of the divine Canticle of Solomon and other books of Sacred Scripture
where the Holy Spirit, unable to express the fullness of His meaning in
ordinary words, utters mysteries in strange figures and likenesses." John's
poems require a similar understanding. As an interpreter he emphasizes
not the surface of the work but its doctrine, not the woman but what she
stands for.

Nevertheless the key to the poems is a woman. Only she can supply
the "poverty of spirit" and the passion that abandon all pride and set the
heart on the Word; only she knows how to infect all creation with the
pain of her loss. In order to understand the plenitude of God, John must
first imagine an uncreated world, the world as it would be if it lacked the
masculine principle of power. The *Spiritual Canticle* begins not with
something revealed but something hidden, not the Word but the absent,
unspoken word.

> *¿Adónde te escondiste,*
> *Amado, y me dejaste con gemido?*
> *Como el ciervo huiste,*
> *habiéndome herido;*
> *salí tras ti clamando, y eras ido.*
>
> Where have you hidden away,
> Beloved, and left me to moan?
> You fled like the hart
> Having wounded me; I followed on
> Calling you, and you were gone.

"In this first stanza," according to John's commentary, "the soul, enamored of the Word, her Bridegroom, the Son of God, longs for union with
Him through clear and essential vision. She records her longings of love
and complains to Him of His absence, especially since His love wounds
her. Through this love she abandoned all creatures and herself, and she
must suffer her Beloved's absence." Hence, sick unto death, she pursues
him wherever the trail leads, through the world of nature that, lacking
its Word, can only "keep stammering some something" ("un no sé qué
que quedan balbuciendo"; note the stammer on *que*). The first part of the
poem is dominated by a sense of something missing. Christ's Bride, like
Abelard's, searches the landscape endlessly for the signature of her lover.

Unlike Eloisa, however, the Bride of the *Canticle* receives the reward
for whose sake she has emptied herself. The Bridegroom comes and

comforts her, all nature speaks his presence, and spousal joy (as in the *Song of Songs*) crowns the final two-thirds of the poem. Giving herself without reserve, the Bride proclaims her willingness to sacrifice all other occupations to perpetual love.

> *Pues ya si en el ejido*
> *de hoy más no fuere vista ni hallada,*
> *diréis que me he perdido;*
> *que andando enamorada,*
> *me hice perdidiza, y fuí ganada.*
>   If, then, on the common
> From today I am no more seen or found,
> You will say that I am lost;
> That, wandering love-stricken,
> I lost myself, and was won.

The soul "rejoices and glories in having lost the world and herself for her Beloved." Indeed, her abandonment assumes a different aspect now, since properly interpreted it may be understood as a necessary stage on the journey to self-realization and eternal love. "He who desires to gain his soul shall lose it, and he who loses it for my sake shall gain it" (Matt. 16:25). Only those whose lovers have left them can appreciate the full bliss of reconciliation.

Yet the feminine way of abandonment does not lose its hold on the lovers even after they have been reunited. Salvation, for John, affords no overcoming of loneliness and solitude but only an intensification of the soul's isolation. Thus, in the remarkable last stanza of the *Dark Night,* the woman recalls the consummation of her love as if it were identical with the death of the self. Her senses suspended, she hovers in a spell of utter darkness, outside the world of memory and time.

> *Quedéme y olvidéme,*
> *el rostro recliné sobre el Amado;*
> *cesó todo, y dejéme,*
> *dejando mi cuidado*
> *entre las azucenas olvidado.*
>   I stayed there and forgot,
> My face reclined on my Beloved;
> Everything stopped, and abandoned,
> I abandoned my care
> Among the lilies forgotten.

In the dark she can no longer distinguish one moment from another or herself from her love. Forgetting and forgotten, abandoned and abandoning, she has lost the elementary grammar that allows one to differentiate mine from thine or the scent of lilies from some interior state (in the Spanish, of course, *my* face and *my* lover are simply *the*). She will never find her way back to self-possession.

The *Spiritual Canticle* carries the paradox of losing oneself to find oneself still further. Isolation and ecstasy combine. The final speech of the Bridegroom specifically compares his Bride to the turtledove of the *Song of Songs*, now come home to her mate; but not even her utmost contentment can assuage the loneliness and emptiness she inhabits like the air.

> *En soledad vivía,*
> *y en soledad ha puesto ya su nido,*
> *y en soledad la guía*
> *a solas su querido,*
> *también en soledad de amor herido.*
>   In solitude she lived,
>   And in solitude now has built her nest,
>   And in solitude is guided
>   By the solitary one who bears
>   Also in solitude the wound of love.

In a state of absolute grace, "the union of the soul with God in spiritual marriage" (according to John), the Bride and Bridegroom communicate perfect solitude to each other. Even her wound infects him. Christ, the abandoned and wounded son, loves those who share his poverty and rewards them with an increasing store of emptiness, his indifference to the things of this world. Nor does abandonment cease with death. Rather, the feminine soul recognizes her longing for an absent and invisible lover as the condition of her grace. "She formerly practiced this solitude, in which she lived, in trial and anguish because she was imperfect, but now she has built her nest in it and has found refreshment and repose in having acquired it perfectly in God." Understanding itself must vanish in that mystic moment. The repeated sound of "en soledad," like a drumbeat in the verse, emphasizes the futility of trying to vary the meaning of the single solitary Word.

Abandoned women listen to that word and most need its guidance. But the intensity of their need is not a sign of virtue. Quite the contrary. They stand for the human soul precisely because of their impurity and incompleteness. The logic of this feminizing of human experience is established by the Bridegroom himself, in a reminiscence that furnishes the poem with its doctrinal center.

> *Debajo del manzano,*
> *allí conmigo fuiste desposada;*
> *allí te dí la mano,*
> *y fuiste reparada*
> *donde tu madre fuera violada.*

> Beneath the apple tree,
> There you were betrothed to me;
> There I gave you my hand,
> And you were restored
> Where your mother was violated.

The cross redeems the forbidden tree of Eden, the Incarnation heals the sin of the first mother. Whether we interpret that mother as "Eve" or as "human nature" (John's own gloss), the moral seems clear: the corruption passed down from one female generation to another can be repaired only through an act of masculine charity, the Bridegroom's noblesse oblige in making his Bride an honest woman.

A scholarly controversy lies behind these lines. Their Hebrew original, in the *Song of Songs* (8:5), refers not to sex but to birth: "Under the quince tree I awakened you, / there your mother was in labor with you, / there she who bore you was in labor." Luis de León had pointed out the correct translation. But John resorts to the doubly corrupt text of the Vulgate: "there your mother was corrupted, / there she who bore you was violated." Rape upon rape. By substituting sexual assault for birth trauma, the Vulgate sharpens the legacy of guilt and torment that the Redeemer must touch with grace. But John has contributed a paradox of his own. In context, the "betrothal" surely implies another act of love or carnality. The Bridegroom has put his hand upon his Bride and redeemed her "where" her mother fell, in the vineyard of the body. Christ abides by the double standard. His own mother, like the Sibyl, has never been violated except by a holy spirit, and his own immaculate intercourse sets the soul free from the memory of its impure origin. The second coitus undoes the first. Through the mystic surrender of corrupt feminine nature to the active principle of the Lord, the "barriers between God and man which were built up through original sin" are now broken down. Ravishment makes amends for violation.

John puts a good face on this story. His commentary associates it at some length with Ezekiel, chapter 16, in which the Lord describes his espousal of Jerusalem, a ripe and beautiful woman whom he adorns until "the fame of your beauty went all over the world." Yet the allegory of the soul as a woman hungry for love undoubtedly causes some tension. In the passage of Ezekiel that immediately follows the part quoted by John, we learn what can happen to such women. "But you trusted to your beauty and prostituted your fame; you committed fornication, offering yourself freely to any passer-by for your beauty to become his." Ezekiel's parable seems motivated by a latent distrust (if not abhorrence) of women. How quickly their love turns into obscenity, adultery, abomination! John works hard to avoid such implications. He shows no sign of being repulsed by the physicality or sensuality of women, and he does not equate a woman in love with a whore. Yet his own allegory, like Ezekiel's, does tend to reduce the woman to a creature determined by sex, a creature whose corruption and salvation alike depend on her use by a man. If not "unclean," his speaker is certainly "frail." Thus the plot of the *Spiritual Canticle,* the literal sense or story to which John's prose pays so little attention, suggests a woman's utter incompetence to control her fate. All she can do is to lose herself in the hope of being found. A masculine spirit must take the initiative.

Most interpreters of the *Spiritual Canticle* would consider this focus on sexual matters marginal if not jejune. Mystical theology and union with the divine are not to be understood by a literal-minded preoccupation with whose body did what to whom. The sex of God is his secret. Yet the question of whether John succeeded in learning to love God as a woman loves is not irrelevant. It bears upon some crucial theological issues of the *Spiritual Canticle* as well as its place in poetic tradition. Many modern theologians have been disturbed by the inherent elitism and in-communicability of mysticism. They suspect John's sort of "emptying" or "selflessness" of concealing a latent, dogmatic egocentrism. Thus, according to Karl Barth, "There is nothing, nothing at all, to justify the belief that God has created us for the practice of this self-emptying, or that it has to be recognized and adopted as the way to reconciliation with God. . . . In a purely formal sense no one, not even a Spanish mystic, has ever really looked away from himself and beyond himself, let alone transcended himself in a purely formal negation." The soul cannot sub-merge itself in God, such critics would argue; it can only pretend to abandon the self in order to relocate its own desires and attributes within the godhead. Mystical union seduces the divine under the pretext of be-ing ravished.

Translated into secular terms, this argument might hint at an equiva-lent selfishness in John's apparent sympathy with women. The lover he pursues is Christ, a Christ created in his own image, and the Bride only the seductive means of bringing the Bridegroom close—a sort of Judas goat. A truly humble poet, after all, would hardly claim such intimacy with his Maker. Hence John's absorption in the female role might be branded merely strategic: the disguise of powerlessness a man wears in order to approach the true seat of power.

Such arguments can hardly be refuted by logic alone. Like the argu-ment that all apparent selflessness is selfish at heart, the argument that all male impersonations of women serve the man's needs is perfectly circu-lar. It is true that John seems to have taken an almost voluptuous pleasure in self-mortification. When, in a famous vision, he heard a picture of Christ addressing him: "What reward do you want for your service to me?", he replied, "Lord, to suffer for thy sake and be despised." Becoming a woman allows him to bear the cross. Yet to deny John his feminine vision, his Sibylline espousal of loneliness and rapture, would be to reject some feelings that both sexes share: not an urge for mastery but a longing for union, not the rise to power but the stillness as the senses *descend*. The *Spiritual Canticle* does not claim to know the godhead as a woman knows her lover; it only invites the coming of the God. The greatness of the poem consists in its representation of abandonment, an ecstasy forever deferred and retarded. The woman teaches the man that there are mysteries he will never capture.

Thus even in the nuptials at the end of the poem, as the lovers retire to a cavern to savor their mutual solitude, the Bride finds her fulfillment in memory and anticipation, not in a present love.

> *Allí me monstrarías*
> *aquello que mi alma pretendía,*
> *y luego me darías*
> *allí tú, vida mía*
> *aquello que me diste el otro día.*
>   There you will show me
> What my soul has sought after,
> And then will give me—
> There, you, my life—
> What you gave me the other day.

Allegorically, the soul expects the "essential glory, consisting in the vision of God's being," to which she was predestined in the eternal day of creation. In terms of sexual experience, however, the woman remains suspended between the two moments that give her life meaning: her moments of consummation. The poem remains there too. Merging less with the ravished soul than with a state of luminous sensual expectancy, John trembles on the brink of the mystery. (In this respect his confident prose commentaries might be thought a masculine forcing of a feminine poem.) The poetry subsists in that trembling.

What John requires from women, therefore, is not only weakness and poverty of spirit but a spirit loving and hopeful. The *Spiritual Canticle* and its sister poems could not have been spoken by a man; his self-sacrifice, as Barth implies, would appear too willful and individualistic. Instead the female speaker functions for John, as the Virgin for the human race, as a mediator whose tender impulses are totally unself-conscious. She is both inferior and superior, more vulnerable and more honest than any man. John does not stoop to women; he begs them to raise him up. And the poems that they bring him surpass the language of man precisely because they trust their meaning to something beyond them, a higher and greater power. Abandoned women define themselves by knowing their own incompleteness.

RILKE'S SIBYL: DEFINING A WOMAN

Can a male poet ask more of women? One further motive remains. A very few men have taken the voice of the Sibyl not to explore her sexual identity or her intimacy with a higher power, but simply because they admire her. Such poets look up to women. Attributing the Sibyl's eloquence less to the god within her than to her natural superiority, they ask for nothing better than to receive her blessing, sit at her feet, and devote their lives to her service. To become part female themselves is their greatest ambition. Or so, at least, they say.

No poet seems better suited than Rainer Maria Rilke to test the proposition that a man can sympathize with a woman; for Rilke ought by rights to have been born a girl. The story of his childhood is notorious. His mother wanted a child to replace her dead baby daughter, and when the next baby inconveniently came out a male she managed to suppress the unpleasant fact by dressing him as a girl, braiding his long locks, giving him dolls and kitchenware to play with, and protecting him from associating with any little boys. There is some evidence that the young René Maria internalized this parental preference and grew up thinking of himself as female, the lost daugher returned. At any rate he never lost his taste for dolls and feminine comforts. He did, however, learn what manhood means. At the age of ten, when his father decided he needed toughening, he was sent to a military academy; and though that terrible four-year ordeal did not quite kill him, it did succeed in breaking the maternal bond. Dresses were exchanged for uniforms—at least externally. Yet all his life Rilke was to feel more at home in the company of women than men.

The depth of Rilke's sympathy for women is to be judged less by outward circumstances, however, than by his absolute inner conviction of their moral superiority to men. Few themes recur so often in his work as the almost angelic virtues of the female heart. In comparison to what women know about life and love, men are no more than children. Indeed, abandoned women outrank even the other stars of Rilke's universe, the youthful dead. "What speaks to me of humanity, immensely, with a calmness of authority that makes my hearing spacious, is the phenomenon of those who have died young, and, still more unconditionally, purely, inexhaustibly: the woman who loves." By "the woman who loves," the context makes clear, he means "the woman whose love is unrequited." Reciprocated love, the mutual satisfaction of two crude appetites, interests him very little. Instead he returns compulsively and insatiably to a single figure: the woman transformed by suffering for a man unworthy of her. "They make lament for one alone, but the whole of nature unites with them: it is the lament for one who is eternal. They hurl themselves after him they have lost, but even with their first steps they overtake him, and before them is only God." Such women become divine. They go so far beyond men that the sexes can no longer speak with each other. In the best dialogues of love, women take both of the parts.

Hence the relationship of an abandoned woman and her beloved "brings to light," according to Rilke, "how very much on one side, that of woman, everything performed, endured, accomplished contrasts with man's absolute insufficiency in love. She receives, as it were—to put the matter with banal clarity—the Diploma of Proficiency in Love, while he carries in his pocket an Elementary Grammar of this discipline, from which a few words have scantily passed into him, out of which, as opportunity offers, he forms sentences, beautiful and ravishing as the well-known sentences on the first pages of Language Courses for Beginners." Love is a foreign language to men. They learn it—insofar as they ever learn it at all—by going to school to women.

Thus much of Rilke's career as a poet may be plotted on the points that he found and transcribed from women. Perhaps no other great male poet has ever been so fascinated by female authors, a devotion proved not only by his advocacy of their work but by his wonderful translations from Elizabeth Barrett Browning, Louise Labé, the Comtesse de Noailles, and above all the so-called Portuguese nun, "Marianna Alcoforado, that incomparable creature, in whose eight heavy letters woman's love is for the first time plotted from point to point, without display, without exaggeration or mitigation, as by the hand of a sibyl." (Rilke did not suspect the hand of a man, as modern scholars do, behind these sibylline leaves.) The agony of "Marianna" offers her translator an absolute confirmation of his own project as lover and poet: the conversion of all things into the Invisible. At the moment when the woman remade her pitifully uninteresting and inadequate fleshly lover into a pure internal possession—an essence of love uncontaminated by warts and silly excuses—she stood revealed as an archetypal Poet. "What else happened to the Portuguese nun, save that inwardly she became a spring?" Deprivation had taught her what the Sibyl always knew, the emptiness at the heart of every song. Rilke studies the poems of women to spy out a similar knowledge. He finds it in Sappho, "when she knew that nothing can be meant by union save increased loneliness; when she broke through the temporal aim of sex with its infinite purpose; when in the darkness of embracing she delved not for satisfaction but for longing." Abandoned women know those secrets by nature. Men must spend their lives at the task of translation.

Nor was it only in poetry that Rilke pursued the secrets of women. He could be, in fact, a very accomplished seducer. No biographer of the poet has quite faced up to the extent to which he depended on women not only for spiritual sustenance but for his daily bread. He made a living from loving. I do not want to accuse Rilke of being a gigolo. He was a poet first, and poetry, more than sex, supplied the interest with which he paid his way. Yet women were his capital. He wrote to them, of them, and for them; he practiced daily on their hearts like violins. And just as few days passed when he went hungry, so few days passed when he was not in love.

The results of this devoted pursuit of women, however, were somewhat peculiar. Rudolf Kassner, who claimed to be Rilke's only male friend, comments that he always showed "a special liking for what we are wont to call old maids. Not out of pity, . . . but because Rilke experienced women from within." Whether or not we accept the psychology, there is no doubt that abandoned women did attract the poet. But never for long. From the moment of their yielding he lost interest. Moreover, the testimony of some of the women themselves indicates that Rilke was not a very satisfactory lover. The act of love, however intense, served as a sort of preliminary to the deeper passions inspired by loss. Rilke seems to have *preferred* his women lonely or "sacrificed on the altar of love," as if abandonment were a service he performed for them. Perhaps he really thought it so. In "Don Juan's Selection" ("Don Juans Auswahl," 1908), Rilke imagines the greatest male lover given his charge by an angel: to make the sweetest women bitter. That is the function of a seducer. Though ignorant himself of love, he educates women's hearts by introducing them to solitude. Eventually all of them will be able to "surpass and outcry Heloise." Don Juan himself, by contrast, is rather pathetic; he may think that he does the selecting, but the truth is that he is selected. Abelard exists to produce a Heloise, and Juan to teach women to go beyond him. Rilke seems genuinely to have believed this. He also seems to have persuaded many of his women friends and patrons that, much as they loved him, they would be far better off in his absence.

Some women suffered from this treatment. But Rilke thought that he was suffering more. By creating a climate of abandonment around him, the poet steeps himself artificially in the dark knowledge on which poetry relies. He rapes the Sibyl in order to inspire her, so that he can catch her inspiration at second hand. Yet the problems raised by such behavior haunted Rilke for much of his life as a man and a poet. As a man he often had occasion to reproach himself for cruelty toward women, the vampirelike fascination with which he both caused and fed on their loneliness. But as a poet his cruelty extends toward the whole world, whose mystery must be heightened and violated to make it available to his own inner experience. A poet exploits the Other. At best he may reward the objects of his attention with death and forgetfulness, as Orpheus helped

Eurydice to become invisible by looking back at her. Rilke sacrifices everything to his art. Yet all he gains is a sense of obligation, the duty to
save things from the possessiveness of his love. As he complained on
more than one occasion, he lost the ability to enjoy nature when he began
regarding it as a "task"; things were always begging him to change them
into poems. Don Juan finally suffers more than his victims. He takes
their loneliness into himself and assumes it as his own burden.

A parable of this vision of the poet was sketched by Rilke in one of the
New Poems, the little-known "A Sibyl" ("Eine Sibylle," 1907). The sonnet derives from Michelangelo's Cumaean Sibyl on the Sistine ceiling,
and some of its strangeness may result from conflating the immortal
prophetess of legend with the artist's coarse peasant woman, broad-
shouldered and thick-footed, whose aging has not wasted her away but
encrusted her in bulky flesh. It is not easy to perceive her spirit. The Sibyl
exerts a power over Rilke related to the weary, unlikely lovers described
by Malte Laurids Brigge: "Aged women, grown hard, but with a kernel
of savoriness which they kept hidden. Uncouth, strong-grown women,
who, grown strong through exhaustion, let themselves become like their
husbands and who were yet entirely different inwardly, there where their
love had labored, in the dark." Yet not even Rilke dares intrude on such
a woman's solitude.

> *Einst, vor Zeiten, nannte man sie alt.*
> *Doch sie blieb und kam dieselbe Strasse*
> *täglich. Und man änderte die Masse,*
> *und man zählte sie wie einen Wald*
>
> *nach Jahrhunderten. Sie aber stand*
> *jeden Abend auf derselben Stelle,*
> *schwarz wie eine alte Citadelle*
> *hoch und hohl und ausgebrannt;*
>
> *von den Worten, die sich unbewacht*
> *wider ihren Willen in ihr mehrten,*
> *immerfort umschrieen und umflogen,*
> *während die schon wieder heimgekehrten*
> *dunkel unter ihren Augenbogen*
> *sassen, fertig für die Nacht.*

> Once, in a former time, they called her old.
> And yet she stayed and came to the same street
> each day. And then they changed the beat
> and told her age as if she were a wood
>
> by centuries. But still she stood
> each evening at the same place still,
> black as an ancient citadel
> high and hollow and burned out;

by words surrounded, which although unsought
against her will grew more and more in her,
forever flying round with circling cries,
while those already come back home once more
darkly beneath the arches of her eyes
waited, ready for the night.

The Sibyl does not speak. Like each of the *New Poems,* "A Sibyl"
strives to enter the innermost core of an object, reporting its essence as a
"thing" from within untouched by any embellishment or supervening
consciousness. Even persons, in this disinterested aesthetic, take on the
character of things. Thus the Sibyl gradually turns into an inanimate object, a black old burned-out citadel with nobody home inside. The curious detail of her "eyebows," in the penultimate line, reinforces the sense
of a fortress; her eyes are dark bow windows. Rilke seems awed by her
impassivity. Trying to imagine the inner condition or feelings of the Sibyl—
condemned to live *forever* without happiness, without expectation—his
mind staggers at the monotony and blankness of such a living death.
Better to leave her mystery alone.

The key to the mystery, and to interpreting the poem, seems to be the
meaning of the words "already again returned home." They roost in the
Sibyl like bats in a belfry, ready for the night. What will they say when
their time comes? One likely answer would be "death." That is what the
Sibyl of Cumae always broods on, according to Ovid, Petronius, and
T. S. Eliot: "when the boys said to her: 'Sibyl, what do you want?'; she
replied: 'I want to die.'" Death-in-life has long since petrified her soul,
and all that she can do is to prepare for night inwardly by accommodating her own darkness to the darkness outside. In this respect the poem
seems truly Gothic: the heroine is identical both with the castle that oppresses her and the death that awaits her.

The context of the Sistine ceiling suggests a second answer. To a casual
eye the sibyls might appear out of place there both as women and as
pagans, oddly interleaved among the Hebrew prophets. But Michelangelo was of course obeying the familiar tradition that credits the sibyls
with foretelling the coming of Christ. Ever since Virgil's Fourth Eclogue, the Sibyl of Cumae has represented the highest pitch of Christian
inspiration: a voice crying in the wilderness of antiquity, preparing the
way of the Lord. She prophesies the truth even without knowing the
meaning of her words. "A Prophet" and "Jeremiah," the poems that immediately precede "A Sibyl" in the *New Poems,* share the same theme, an
anguished need to voice the curses building within them. The Sibyl has
grown too old and weary for cursing. Instead she awaits the end of time,
when Christ himself will reappear and bring her timelessness its fitting
night. The fulfillment of her prophecy will ground her restless, flying
words in the one inevitable Word. Thus Rilke, without necessarily ac-

cepting the orthodox view of revelation, pays tribute to the Sibyl's intuition of a second coming. She triumphs over time and death and keeps her secret ready.

Yet a third reading seems still more characteristic of Rilke. Perhaps the words "already again returned home" refer to the one who always comes to animate the Sibyl at last: the god of poetry. In this version the dumb faithfulness of the old woman, steadfast at her station, readies her for her master Apollo. He alone can make sense of the words that cry and fly around her; he alone can give her a voice. She longs for possession. Indeed, by describing the empty Sibyl Rilke may intend to signify the longing of all the dumb things of the world for their poets. The world would be empty of meaning without its song. Thus Rilke himself is the agent within the Sibyl, the spirit that gives her expression. He renders her heavy body invisible and translates her into a poem. In this respect "A Sibyl" might be called a companion piece to the most famous of the New Poems, the "Archaic Torso of Apollo," in which the light streaming from the statue persuades the poet that he must change his life. The Sibyl offers her darkness. Yet she and Apollo are mates. Only when the invisible, shining god interpenetrates with the dim, inarticulate things of this world, only when the pure intensity of disembodied feeling merges with the vacant body of reality, can poetry find its voice. Neither Apollo nor the Sibyl can make a poem without the other. He needs her darkness as she needs his light.

As this analysis may indicate, however, the poet himself remains unsure of his position. With whom does he identify: the woman besieged by words, or the distant god whose arrival will crystallize their meaning? Is Rilke the passive instrument of poetry or an active and grasping principle that forces poetry on the Sibyl against her will? Or should we consider him a sort of go-between who brings the couple together and then retires? "A Sibyl" allows us to draw our own conclusions. It holds the woman in awe and yet implies that she is powerless to make a poem by herself. To become a poet, Rilke must go beyond her.

He never stopped putting words in the Sibyl's mouth. The great "Tenth Elegy," for instance, requires an ancient prophetess to interpret its trip through the world of death. In one of its aspects the poem is an eerie nightmare version of Aeneas's journey through the underworld, with none but a woman to guide him. Yet Rilke draws a landscape different from Virgil's: the Land of Lament. It is as if all the kingdom of the dead were one vast Mourning Fields, a place where abandoned women communicate their knowledge of grief to those who have passed over from the carnival of life. Here men become silent and women help them to die. The elders of this race are sibyls and prophets. But even here a man's perspective intrudes. The central figure of the "Elegy" is a dead young man; he shares the memories of the male poet; and when he finally parts from his instructress, he climbs (like Aeneas) to a higher place where she has never gone. Rilke does try to redress the balance. The "Elegy" concludes, like the *Spiritual Canticle,* with ecstasy imagined from a woman's point of view, a happiness that does not rise but *falls.* Even the sexual rhythm of the poem, insofar as a male poet can submit to it, obeys a woman's pleasure. Certainly Rilke rejects the heroic Virgilian image of rape. Yet not every woman would regard the office of Sibyl—or tour guide through the Land of Lament—as an ideal profession. The hours are too long.

In Rilke's view, in fact, they last forever. One final example may help to clarify how much he adores women and how much he demands of them, both the breadth of his sympathy and its limits. The "Requiem for a Friend" (1908) is among his most personal poems. He wrote it for Paula Modersohn-Becker (1876–1907), who was everything he admired: a sensitive woman, an artist, and someone who had died young. That admiration shines through the poem like a flame. Perhaps it is even too bright. Rilke's attitudes toward the living Paula Becker had been far more complex. When he had first met her, at the artists' colony Worpswede in 1900, he had been attracted to her still more than to her close friend Clara Westhoff. But the following year Paula married the painter Otto Modersohn, Clara married Rilke himself, and the relationships between the couples became strained. When Paula wrote to Clara suggesting that Rilke had engrossed too much of her love, leaving nothing for others, Rilke himself answered the letter with a torrent of self-justification: together he and Clara were standing guard over each other's solitude. The friendships and marriages cooled. Only after Paula's death, in the aftermath of childbirth, did Rilke's love for her fully rekindle, along with his appreciation of her importance as a painter. Thus many emotions mix in the "Requiem": jealousy and grief and anger and awe and regret. The poet tries, not quite successfully, to lay a ghost.

Much of the tension of the "Requiem" stems from Rilke's effort to make Paula face up to her responsibilities, as he sees them: her duty to be purely abandoned, purely artistic, purely dead. He suspects her of reluctance in leaving her life behind. Hence a good deal of the poem sounds less like an elegy than a polemic. Rilke attacks the enemies of art, who seem identical, at last, with all who cling to living. The principal carriers of this disease are men.

> *Doch jetzt klag ich an:*
> *den Einen nicht, der dich aus dir zurückzog,*
> *(ich find ihn nicht heraus, er ist wie alle)*
> *doch alle klag ich in ihm an: den Mann.*
> . . . .

> *Wo ist ein Mann, der Recht hat auf Besitz?*
>   Yet now I accuse:
> not that one, who drew you back from yourself,
> [I cannot pick him out, he's like them all]
> but I accuse them all in him: the Man.
> ....
> Where is a man who has the right of possession?

Possessive men like Modersohn, who try to persuade women that they are not abandoned, lure them into the creaturely world that kills. Thus Paula has been betrayed. Forgetting the detachment of her art, with its hard but beautiful lesson—"Women suffer; love means being alone"— she needs to be reminded how to let go. Rilke pries her fingers away from life. He will help her to vanish, if she will help him in turn.

> *Komm nicht zurück. Wenn du's erträgst, so sei*
> *tot bei den Toten. Tote sind beschäftigt.*
> *Doch hilf mir so, dass es dich nicht zerstreut,*
> *wie mir das Fernste manchmal hilft: in mir.*
> Do not come back. If you can bear it, then be
> dead with the dead. The dead are otherwise engaged.
> But help me still, if it does not distract you,
> as far-off things help me sometimes: in me.

Rilke prays to the woman for inspiration. Reversing the usual sexual roles and the Sibyl's position, he asks to be filled. Once again his acknowledgement of female superiority is unequivocal and absolute. Yet it is also disturbingly self-interested. The last two lines of the "Requiem" are dominated by "me." The poet does not want Paula back; he does not even want to think about her unless she will measure up to his idea of a woman. The real Paula, as the poem itself stresses, tended to be disappointing. She went her own way and was never abandoned enough; her greatest work was "somehow never done." Hence Rilke marks off his distance from women even in the act of honoring them. His need to learn from the Sibyl will always surpass his interest in her humanity. For unlike her he can never forget for one moment her proper sphere as a woman; and the effort to see her as a perfect woman and perfect victim inevitably strips her of all qualities save those he can put to use. He makes her face his own in the mirror of art.

Paula Becker came back once more. In *The Dream of a Common Language,* Adrienne Rich has imagined a verse letter from "Paula Becker to Clara Westhoff" (1975–76). This is a woman's version of friendship and art. As the title indicates, the names of Modersohn and Rilke fade into the background, and the men themselves seem mere interruptions in the women's essential life of love and work. Rich tries to undo Rilke's spell.

Paula, within the poem, dreams not only of her death but of the "Requiem," and points out its presumption in claiming a unique relationship with her. Rilke had less right than Clara to call himself Paula's friend. Hence the "Requiem" requires a countertruth, devoted not to Paula's status as an icon but to her actual experience. Men's fantasies may be beautiful; but what do they know about women?

> Rainer, of course, *knows* more than Otto knows,
> he believes in women. But he feeds on us,
> like all of them. His whole life, his art
> is protected by women. Which of us could say that?
> Which of us, Clara, hasn't had to take that leap
> out beyond our being women
> to save our work? or is it to save ourselves?
> Marriage is lonelier than solitude.

Whatever we think of the ideology behind these lines or their deliberate bleakness, they do represent a truth that few male poets have ever been able to state: women can exist without men and are often far better off without them. Rilke's attack on possessive love rebounds against him. Paula is not his possession, and what he feels and thinks may well be irrelevant to her story. When men come calling for help, living women as well as dead ones may be otherwise engaged. The Sibyl has a right to reject Apollo.

Indeed, according to Ovid's *Metamorphoses* it was exactly by saying no to Apollo that the Sibyl of Cumae became what she was. She would not submit to his love; he took revenge by letting her grow old. She has wasted away ever since. Yet despite her suffering, the Sibyl's resistance to men and their power has kept her a poet. Even when she has wasted so far that nothing remains but a voice, her voice will go on. No man possesses it, just as Rilke himself, in Rich's poem, can lay no claim to Paula Becker's voice. Apollo admits defeat. Archetypal poet though he may be, in his own realm, he must accept at last that certain regions of the Sibyl will be closed to him forever. She knows herself as he will never know her. Male poets can try to use women, but even the best such poets leave traces behind of themselves. Meanwhile the Sibyl is speaking. When we understand some of the words that she utters, what we hear is a woman alone.

6 "Could I be like her?" The Example of Women Alone

> Hast du der Gaspara Stampa
> denn genügend gedacht, dass irgendein Mädchen,
> dem der Geliebte entging, am gesteigerten Beispiel
> dieser Liebenden fühlt: das ich würde wie sie?

THE LEGEND OF GASPARA STAMPA

"Have you thought enough yet about Gaspara Stampa?" Rilke asks in a memorable passage of the "First Elegy"; and most of us probably admit at once that we have not. To tell the truth, not many readers have thought about Gaspara Stampa at all or even know who she is. Yet the question stirs feelings of guilt, for it demands a positive answer. We *must* begin to think about Gaspara Stampa, the poem insists, with that curiously intimate bullying at which Rilke excels (the *du* addressed so personally is both every reader and the poet himself)—we *must,* because many of the secrets of love and poetry take visible form in her. She is what every young woman needs to know.

> Have you thought enough yet
> about Gaspara Stampa, so that any girl
> whose lover has gone away might feel, from this more
> intense example of loving: could I be like her?

But what does being like Gaspara Stampa mean? What can we learn from her example? Rilke supplies some answers of his own. Yet the issue of what model an abandoned young woman ought to follow, her proper role in poetry and love, ought not to be left to a man. Too much depends on the answer. Thinking about Gaspara Stampa, we also think about the history of women's dreams: how poets and lovers have been imagined, and how they have imagined themselves. No one can tell us more about such imagining than the great women poets—not only Gaspara Stampa but Sappho, Li Ch'ing-chao, Emily Dickinson, Rosalía de Castro, Marina Tsvetayeva, and their many sisters. And it is their collective example—what it means to be like them—that is really worth thinking about.

To start with a crude, literal-minded question: just who *was* Gaspara

Stampa? It is easy to ask but hard to get satisfaction. Beginning where most readers do, with footnotes to Rilke, we soon feel that something is missing. Thus C. F. MacIntyre, in the most popular English version of the *Elegies*, offers no more than this: "A noble Milanese of the sixteenth century who loved and was deserted. She solaced herself with religion, poetry, and other lovers." Is this what every young woman ought to be like? MacIntyre seems to omit the gist of the matter. Moreover, he gets his facts wrong; for instance, Stampa was neither noble nor Milanese. But more significantly, he forgets to mention that she was a poet (solacing oneself with poetry is not quite the same thing as writing it). The story of love and desertion replaces the woman's own accomplishments. Compare this to another sort of footnote: "Perhaps the greatest woman poet of the Renaissance. A talented musician and classical scholar, she moved in the highest intellectual circles of Venice. The purity and sincerity of her *Rime* are said by Croce to be unrivalled in Italian literature."

That note will not be found in any edition of Rilke. One reason is that footnotes tend to follow tradition. To put it plainly, each annotator cribs his facts from the previous one, as MacIntyre copied from J. B. Leishman, and the whole procession subordinates Stampa's work to the man in her life. Thus one of Leishman's predecessors, Eugenio Donadoni, explains that "she was a poet almost against her will. She wrote for herself and for him: the sonnets were the letters of her correspondence, the brief and ardent pages of her inner diary." No wonder that Leishman brings in the verse only when he has finished laying on the pathos. "He finally left her and married. She consoled herself partly with other lovers and partly with religion, and died in 1554, at the age of thirty-one. The whole story of her love for Collaltino is recorded in some two hundred sonnets. . . ." She did not write poems, we note, she recorded her love. Nor did Rilke himself suggest that we ought to *read* Gaspara Stampa so much as *think* about her. If we knew too much, in fact, it might keep us from thinking about her in the right way, as a faithful, indelible victim. The historical woman cannot be allowed to interfere with the legend. Hence Rilke, his annotators, and his readers collaborate in reducing Stampa to an image of abandonment. She is more to be pitied than studied.

In this respect, a fascination with her love life rather than her art, Stampa does serve as a perfect example of the Woman Poet. She is best known, like Sylvia Plath, because of her fate, to which her work stands as witness. She lived for love and eventually died for it. Not even the best women poets have been able to escape this stereotype. Despite the evidence of history and her own poems, Sappho descends to posterity encumbered by Phaon, and the search for Emily Dickinson's lover continues. Legends of loss accumulate around the woman who writes. Like the oyster, she is assumed to secrete her pearls in order to cover up some hidden trauma. Indeed, this story is so well established that readers often fail to recognize a woman poet who is not sad and dead. The grief and early death of Gaspara Stampa confirm her vocation.

The legendary status of female authors, their relation to stories of love and loss and the prison of sex, helps to define a part of their difference from men. It is the difference between raping and being the Sibyl. A male poet who impersonates abandoned women need not, we have seen, forgo his own identity or private motives. Some of the interest of such poems will depend on what he captures from the other sex while retaining his own. Byron as Julia, Pope as Eloisa, St. John as the Bride, and Rilke as the Sibyl achieve rich effects by sympathizing with someone who is and is not themselves. Imagining a woman, Pope confides to us, is a feat in which a man has a right to take pride. But a woman who projects herself into an abandoned heroine may well have trouble keeping her distance. Even if the character she impersonates does not resemble her at all, she is likely to be credited less with imagination than with sincerity. However unfairly, women are supposed to know abandonment from within. Thus the popular view of the female author tends to identify her with her own heroines. Sometimes the two grow so close that they cannot be parted.

Many of the most famous women poets, therefore, seem to abide on a fine borderline between history and romance. Some are confused with their works, and some may never have existed at all. Consider the biography of that celebrated abandoned lady of Japan, "Ono no Komachi (mid–ninth century) Reputedly one of the greatest beauties of her age. Details of her life are few, but her beauty and her strong personality have made her the subject of a celebrated group of Nō plays." All the standard anthologies of poetry by women contain some verses attributed to her, and those tanka can certainly stimulate the imagination.

> There is no way to meet
> tonight, the moon is dark,
> I wake up wanting him,
> my breasts quiver with fire,
> flames scorch my heart.

As Kenneth Rexroth and Ikuko Atsumi note, "Her beauty may be legendary but her rank as one of the greatest erotic poets in any language is not." Yet who *did* write those poems? Was it an actual, beautiful noblewoman named Ono no Komachi, recording her own experience? Or the anonymous editor, perhaps a man, who compiled the collection in which they appear? Or simply "tradition," which always likes to assign a beautiful poem to a beautiful lady? The anthologies prefer to use her name; but Japanese scholars would rather not have to decide. The very notion of "authorship" seems irrelevant to such creatures of romance. Like "Heloise" and "the Portuguese nun," "Ono no Komachi" provides a glamorous label with which to merchandise dreams.

Gaspara Stampa did, I think, exist. Yet who she was remains a matter of doubt. Fiora A. Bassanese has recently documented some of the spectacular changes in Stampa's reputation, as well as the difficulty in separating fiction from reality. Even on their first appearance, in the year of the poet's death (1554), the *Rime* were wrapped in a legend: consecrated to her glory, edited by her sister Cassandra, and surrounded by a ring of encomiums. The laurels are laid on thick. A hostile reader might suspect that something is being covered up, for instance, by so much praise for this "new Sappho of our day, equal to the Greek in Tuscan language, / but chaster than she, and lovelier far"—considering Sappho's repute, to be chaster than she allows considerable leeway. Can we read another message between the lines? Probably not. Convention governs this volume in every respect, and no real woman peeps through the paragon.

In 1738 the legend of Gaspara Stampa took on new life when Antonio Rambaldo, one of Collalto's descendants, supervised a sumptuous edition of the *Rime* to honor his family's best-known conquest. No expense of money and poetry was spared on this romantic venture. It was Rambaldo who transformed Stampa into a noble Milanese and who speculated that her death had been caused not only by heartbreak but poison. Thus the count tells a racy story and simultaneously decorates his family tree with the corpse of a beautiful poet. "She was one of the most extraordinary and excellent women ever produced by benign nature." But the nineteenth century insisted on heightening the legend with still more lurid details. A set of pathetic love letters, trumped up by Luigi Carrer as the *Unhappy Love of Gaspara Stampa* (1851), became a best-seller and inspired many other biographical fictions, poems, and at least two plays. We hear the *Liebestot* behind them, and also a kind of sentimental sadism, the cast of mind that enjoys both torturing women and weeping over their pain. Poor Gasparina! "This woman who was the first to fashion with her flesh and her blood the modern myth of Love and Death." A woman so faithful and so unhappy, so haunted by death and spurned by the man she loved, seemed almost too good to be true.

She was not, in fact, quite so good. Though the legend of Gasparina has never yet died, the twentieth century requires a different sort of heroine; and even as Rilke was writing his "First Elegy," a scholar named Abdelkader Salza was preparing a portrait based on another model. Gaspara Stampa, he argued, was best seen as a high-class prostitute or "queen among whores" (as a contemporary sonnet had charged). Her acquaintance with the little world of the salon and the patron, her lovers, the ardor of her poems, the freedom of her life could not admit any other construction. All the rest was sentimentality. Thus Salza placed the

woman poet in another venerable tradition, exemplified by Veronica
Franco or the gorgeous Giuliettas who appear in Rousseau's *Confessions,*
Casanova's *Memoirs,* and the *Tales of Hoffmann:* the Venetian courtesan.
That lady of the night still lives, at least in literature, as the epitome of
sexual refinement. Like the geisha and the octaroon, her fantasy sisters,
she is associated with a taste for poetry, and she feeds men's imaginations.
But a touch of menace shadows the lovely picture, a hint of deceit or the
pox. The Venetian courtesan seems too good to be true. Her perfect
surface hides a witch or enchantress who can steal the soul. Through all
her poetry, the disillusioned lover eventually catches a glimpse of the
woman beneath.

Was Gaspara Stampa really a courtesan? The issue cannot be settled
with simple answers. It depends not only on how we select and interpret
the facts, but also on how we define a courtesan (like the "ruined" lady
of Hardy's ballad, the Renaissance *cortigiana* was often indistinguishable
from the finest woman of fashion). Yet however unanswerable, the question has totally dominated modern studies of Stampa. Scholars ride gal-
lantly into the fray as the challengers or champions of a lady's honor. It
is a curious spectacle. Surely literary scholarship has better things to do
than investigate how one sixteenth-century poet spent her nights. It
might, for instance, look instead at her poems. Moreover, the extreme
swings in Stampa's reputation, the remodeling of her image to suit the
fashions of each new generation, can induce a fit of vertigo. The angel
and whore seem equally unreal. Is there anything under the scandal and
wrangle and hype? Remembering that "stampa" means "print" or "the
press" in Italian, we might be tempted to conclude that she is nothing
but a media event.

We had better turn to the poems. Yet even when the work of the
woman absorbs us more than her sex life, something prevents us from
seeing her art clearly. Most critics praise Stampa, as Baudelaire praised
Marceline Desbordes-Valmore, exactly for being so *artless.* The "more
intense example" of the woman poet depends on passion, not art. She
follows her heart and forgets to obey conventions. Thus no one has ever
been able to write at length about Stampa's verse without using the word
"sincere." The obvious echoes of Petrarch in the *Rime,* the reliance on his
themes and forms and diction, are mentioned largely to insist on the
woman's essential difference. "Her naturalness, her sincerity, her abandonment to the emotions that swayed her, and the depth and force of her
passion, carried her beyond the limit of Petrarch's more studied expression." The master may supply the trappings of poetry, but the female
pupil makes poetry out of herself. Not even a sophisticated modern
scholar like Bassanese, who is so intent on divorcing the artist from the
legend, can pass over "the sense of a throbbing vitality, a human pres-

ence" in Stampa's work: "Produced in an era dominated by Petrarchan imitation and rhetoric, it stands out for its lack of affectation, its often unpolished voice of sincerity, and its emotional excesses." That is the way we praise a woman poet, for "spontaneous candor" or merely for being a woman. Perhaps the high point of such criticism was reached by Ada Negri, the "proletarian Sappho," who saw her own oppression mirrored in Stampa. "Woman, woman, woman, in love and stupid, on her knees and giving way in the unequal battle of love; but she was able to give living shape to her own human misery in the most perfect artistic sincerity ever achieved by any feminine creature in this world." Here is another sexual archetype—Gaspara Woman, Gaspara the Sincere. The poems enshrine a martyr to woman's truth.

THE ART OF GASPARA STAMPA

It was not the critics, though, who invented this image. Stampa herself had carefully fashioned and shaped it. In poem after poem she avows the sincerity of her passion and her want of art. Nothing is more typical of this poet than a confession that her powers have failed.

> *Quando innanti ai begli occhi almi e lucenti,*
> *per mia rara ventura al mondo, i' vegno,*
> *lo stil, la lingua, l'ardire e l'ingegno,*
> *i pensieri, i concetti e i sentimenti*
>   *o restan tutti oppressi o tutti spenti,*
> *e quasi muta e stupida divegno;*
> *o sia la riverenza, in che li tegno,*
> *o sia che sono in quel bel lume intenti.*
>   *Basta ch'io non so mai formar parola,*
> *si quel fatale e mio divino aspetto*
> *la forza insieme e l'anima m'invola.*
>   *O mirabil d'Amore e raro effetto,*
> *ch'una sol cosa, una bellezza sola*
> *mi dia la vita, e tolga l'intelletto!*
>
> When I come near those holy, shining eyes,
> the best good luck in all the world to me,
> style, language, ardor, ingenuity,
> ideas, sentiments and fantasies
>   all sink beneath the burden or take flight,
> and I am as one mute and without sense;
> whether because I feel such reverence,
> or else am so absorbed in that fair light.
>   Enough, there is no word that I can summon
> before that fatal face, to me divine,
> that ravishes my strength and soul as one.
>   O miracle of Love, and how refined!

that one sole cause, one lovely thing alone
should give me life, and take away my mind.

Eloquence claims to be speechless. Almost all the details of this sonnet
are borrowed from Petrarch. But it also refers to the archetypal poem of
a woman: Sappho's Second Ode. In each case the presence of the loved
one, divine as a god, reduces the poor lover or worshipper to the state of
a vegetable. We cannot prove that Stampa knew Sappho's ode. Its first
printing, in Francesco Robortello's edition of Longinus's *On the Sublime,*
appeared in the year of her death. But since Stampa moved in some of
the same circles as Robortello and was renowned beyond other women
for love of Greek as well as poetry, she might well have been told of
its existence earlier. At any rate, whether the sapphic strain came first-
hand or through such intermediaries as Catullus, Ovid, and Petrarch,
Stampa catches its symptoms: the progressive loss of faculties with which
the "miracle of love" ravishes the beholder, mortal and fainting and
senseless.

The difference, however, is that while Sappho loses her senses, Stampa
pleads the loss of her art. Each of the words in lines 3 and 4—style,
language, ardor, creative power, thoughts, conceits, and sentiments—
denotes a specific faculty of rhetoric, a skill extinguished by the beloved's
eyes. Her arsenal is depleted; henceforth she will never be able to "shape
a word." This is the death not of consciousness and life but of eloquence
and mind. Stampa asserts her weakness as an artist. Unlike Sappho, she
does not consider her poetry the passport to immortality that will redeem
the humiliations of love, but rather a helpless tribute to the man who
humbles her will.

Two paradoxes inform both this sonnet and most of Stampa's other
work, and each of them bears on the example she sets as an abandoned
woman poet. The first is the deliberate art she uses to announce that she
has no art. If love makes her "stupid," it does not rob her of rhymes.
Even her most personal confessions are couched in a familiar Petrarchan
style—for instance, the invasion of her heart by a shining image that
attacks through the eyes. It would be difficult to find an antithesis more
worn than the opposition of the heavenly beloved to the earthbound lover
(the sonnet seems to be taking place in church, as if she had gone there
to pay her devotions to him), or a more hackeyed poetic structure than
the balance of pleasure and pain in a seizure of love. Yet Stampa's artifice
can also be more subtle. Adapting the calendrical arrangement of Petrarch's *Canzoniere,* for example, she keys many of her poems to the
liturgy or a specific day of the year: her love is born on Christmas Day
and suffers its "martyrdom" at Easter. Adapting Petrarch's puns on Laura
(the laurel wreath) to her own Collaltino di Collalto, she often imagines

him as a high hill (*colle alto*) towering above her valleys. A skeptical reader might conclude that she wanted him primarily for the letters of his name. In any event, she swoons on schedule; the stages of her passion follow a master plan. Whatever the order in which the *Rime* were written, their arrangement plots an inexorable sequence from her first "virginal" stirrings to her rapture, betrayal, and final despair. Everything fits very neatly. Can it be that Gaspara the Sincere is also a product of art?

The paradox of artificial artlessness or contrived sincerity does not concern Stampa alone. In one form or another it has haunted most ambitious women poets. Women write about what they know, and what they know best, proverbially, is feeling. We expect our female artists to sound sincere, to count the ways of love, and we praise them for being unconscious. A traditional view of the division between the sexes in poetry would surely agree with Kingsley Amis, as he contrasts pretentious masculine texts with the ladies' titles: "I Remember You," "Love is my Creed," "Poem for J."

> We men have got love well weighed up; our stuff
>   Can get by without it.
> Women don't seem to think that's good enough;
>   They write about it,
>
> And the awful way their poems lay them open
>   Just doesn't strike them.
> Women are really much nicer than men:
>   No wonder we like them.

But the past few decades have soured such distinctions and revealed them as less flattering than patronizing. Not even Amis seems to think that women are so nice any more, nor do critics waste much time deciding whether Pasternak or Tsvetayeva is "nicer." A woman poet is likely to change the terms of comparison. Thus Gertrud Kolmar (1894–1943), in her beautiful meditation on "The Woman Poet" ("Die Dichterin"), contrasts men's comfort with abstractions to the burden of her own rigorous quest for truth of feeling.

> *Der Mann ist soviel klüger, als wir sind.*
> *In seinem Reden unterhält er sich*
> *Mit Tod und Frühling, Eisenwerk und Zeit;*
> *Ich sage: "Du . . ." und immer: "Du und ich."*
> A man is so much wiser than we are.
> He entertains himself in colloquy
> With Death and Spring, with Ironwork and Time;
> I just say "You . . ." and always "You and I."

The conversation of male poets with great eternal themes often contains a reflexive "sich" that hints they may be talking to themselves. But for the woman poet "her whole life is a single 'You . . .'"—the effort to speak honestly of what she feels. The painfully honest, personal style that Kolmar developed in love poems about being abandoned proved adequate to express another sort of affliction (she died at Auschwitz). A serious woman poet assumes a special burden when she strips her art of anything but "Du" and "ich." Far from unconscious, many women become obsessively self-conscious about their temptation toward playacting or emotional games. A poet who spends her life investigating love cannot help noticing when it does not ring true. Nor can a poet known for her sincerity be unaware of just how much it costs.

If love supplies the center of Stampa's art, therefore, the inability of that art to express love or win it becomes her constant theme. The strength of her feelings cripples her poetry and leaves her mute. In one respect the *Rime,* like many other poems by women, might be considered a sustained polemic against the treachery of language and the infirmity of the woman who loves. The wind blows her labors away like the leaves of the Sibyl (124). Collaltino does not pay attention. Yet it is less his indifference that she blames—at least on the surface—than the inadequacy of words to show him her soul. No matter how much she writes, she will never succeed in communicating the full force of her love or touching his heart. Thus Stampa's "sincerity" consists largely of discontent with her own rhetoric. The honest and passionate soul has no better way of expressing itself than by fainting and dying.

A second paradox follows from the first. It is what Stampa calls the "miracle of Love," a single cause that leads to a double effect: giving life and taking away the mind. The face of the beloved radiates a power both divine and fatal; to come near his eyes is at once the highest felicity and annihilating. Many of the *Rime* play with a similar irony. Indeed, a case can be made for reading them as an attack on Collaltino, whose "angelic" nature, too good for this world, destroys the mortal being it disdains to touch. "Every angel is terrible," as Rilke warns. Stampa's reverence masks a similar dread. By casting herself as a victim, she transforms her lover into a savage, inhuman god, a First Cause unwilling to take responsibility for the life he has created. Like other gods he prefers to remain in hiding or "happy among his hills" (*lieto ne' suoi colli*). Even his "holy, shining eyes" are ultimately impenetrable. They suck out her soul without returning her love.

In what sense, then, may the beloved be said to give her life? One answer, familiar to many abandoned women, would be simply that he provides a center of interest. So long as she loves Collaltino, no moment will be free of joy or pain. Not even the angels, Stampa argues, experience such a wealth of sensations. Obsession, masochism, martyrdom all prove that she is alive by stinging her awake; a dead body would not hurt so much. Thus her subject matter seems inexhaustible. A glance from the beloved makes her day, charging the empty hours with reverence and absorption, inspiring fits of amazement and plenty of sonnets. Eventually even his absence will perform the same function. When he does not come or does not write, her conjectures about his motives become a full-time occupation. In this regard her fall into love, like Eve's into sin, may be interpreted as fortunate, a passage to humanity or knowledge. Only abandoned women know what rapture means, that state in which the soul is wholly, perpetually immersed in the image of someone else.

If Collaltino's eyes give Stampa life, however, the man himself does not seem very important. Her spiritual growth depends on her love of love itself, the superiority of her passion to the constraints of modesty or any particular person. He is the mere occasion of that growth. In one of her most daring sonnets (91), Stampa makes a claim without precedent in Petrarchan tradition: she has gone beyond the beloved. This is the second miracle of love.

> *Quant'ei tutt'altri cavalieri eccede*
> *in esser bello, nobile ed ardito,*
> *tanto è vinto da me, da la mia fede.*
> *Miracol fuor d'amor mai non udito!*
> *Dolor, che chi nol prova non lo crede!*
> *Lassa, ch'io sola vinco l'infinito!*
>
> As much as he excels all other men
> in beauty, courage, and nobility,
> so much do I and faith surpass his ken.
> O miracle that none but lovers see!
> No one who has not tried it knows such pain!
> Yet weary, I alone conquer infinity!

Faith and pain have raised her to an understanding not to be comprehended by anyone who has not endured them. Thus Stampa exalts herself as a lover and poet. Not even the finest knight is worthy of such adoration. Her only equal is Amor himself, that ideal personification who figures in the *Rime* as largely as Collaltino. Viewed from so high a sphere, even Petrarch seems wanting.

Not many of Stampa's poems are so assertive. Yet the peculiar logic of the miracles of love, as she describes them, may help us to draw some preliminary conclusions about her example. The woman poet thrives on abandonment. She requires a lover, or at any rate the image of a lover, to supply her poems with a theme. But what gives her poems life, their special "miracle," is her realization that despite her weakness there is no one she can count on but herself. The beloved teaches her this by going away, or by offering nothing except some empty professions. Gradually she learns that most of his good qualities were her invention. But this allows her to recognize her own superiority. The weak know more than the strong, the vanquished see through the victors. The evidence of this power lies in the poems.

Another way to put this would be that Collaltino serves in place of a muse. Much of the most interesting feminist criticism of poetry, in recent years, has emphasized the problematic relation of women to the traditional myth of inspiration. The female daughter of memory who breathes into the male poet, wrapping him in a cloud of sexual confusion and longing until he takes up his pen and tries to impale her, exerts no spell over women. At one extreme she may even prevent women from writing. A poet who identifies with the Muse or Nature, the objects of desire, may find it impossible to regard herself as a subject. She ought to inspire poems, not write them. Some critics have used this dilemma to account for the literary inhibitions of women or to recommend a new model of inspiration in which the Muse transmits her power to women as mother or sister or lover. A more skeptical critic might suggest that the power of the Muse has been highly exaggerated, since many men have waited in vain for her coming and others have suffered from delusions of potency. We should not make too much of a symbol. Yet Stampa's "miracles of love" imply that another kind of inspiration may be available to the woman poet: not the Muse but the absent lover. The poem fills the empty space the beloved leaves behind; it represents the failure of nature and humankind. The *Rime* would not have been written had Collaltino proved faithful. Thus women poets create from a sense of loss; the myth, not of hope pursued, but of hope abandoned. To write such poetry requires a bitter knowledge. But Gaspara Stampa learned her lesson well.

Let us summarize some of that lesson. What is the example of the woman poet, and what does it mean to be like her? Whatever the truth may be, the pattern or stereotype has long been established. First, it means complicity with a legend: the poet has loved and suffered, and her poems reflect that story. Unlike the poems of men, they do not obey conventions but come from the heart. Thus, second, to be like her means being sincere. The strength of her love disavows an attention to art; her work is admired because of its truth to feeling. But, third, her beloved does not reciprocate those feelings for long. The woman poet is abandoned, and she makes her poems in order to protest her fate or to record and immortalize the pain of being alone. Finally, she is superior to men—and an example to women—precisely because abandonment has refined her soul. An expert at making something out of nothing, she graduates from love of a person to love itself, unmediated and absolute. Men stand in awe of her, and women can hardly think about her enough.

How many women poets follow that pattern? A great many do, I think. But like any poetic model or archetype, the abandoned woman poet influences not only those who conform to her example but those who deliberately violate it. The pressure on women to be sincere, for instance, has tempted some to elaborate ironies and contrivances, and the assumption that all women write about love has challenged some to declare that love means nothing to them. Examples exist to be broken. But the most disturbing implication of the pattern, for many women, is the way it assigns the poet a role as victim. Gaspara Stampa died young (like most of Rilke's heroines), and whether or not she died of a broken heart, she seems to talk of her own suffering as if it were natural and inevitable. The power of her work is bought at a terrible cost. Not every woman thinks it right or necessary. Yet to regard the abandoned woman as nothing but a victim is also an oversimplification. Some women follow the pattern aggressively, like Medea, to gain some self-respect or shut men out. They may even find some humor in the role. When Thomas Wentworth Higginson met Emily Dickinson, he was not sure whether the appropriate emotion should be pity or terror. Many later readers have felt a similar uncertainty. The mixture of weakness and strength, of victimization and power, accounts for much of the fascination of women's poetry—so fragile, and yet so hard. And it also accounts for many misunderstandings.

EMILY DICKINSON

Consider, for instance, a poem that even Dickinson's most fervent admirers have never been able to agree about. Some critics think it a masterpiece, others a mess. Fifty years ago R. P. Blackmur called it "in epitome the whole of her work," yet concluded that it "was not a poem but a private mixture of first-rate verse, bad verse, and something that is not verse at all." More recently Sharon Cameron has accused it of avoidance of feeling, confusion of meaning, and narrative breakdown. Other readers speak of its "consummate artistry." Perhaps the disagreement is not so surprising, since no one has ever been able to straighten out either the text or the syntax. But most of us will probably agree that the speaker has been abandoned, and that the poem describes her efforts to come to terms with it.

> I got so I could take his name—
> Without—Tremendous gain—
> That Stop-sensation—on my Soul—
> And Thunder—in the Room—
>
> I got so I could walk across
> That Angle in the floor,
> Where he turned so, and I turned—how—
> And all our Sinew tore—

I got so I could stir the Box—
In which his letters grew
Without that forcing, in my breath—
As Staples—driven through—

Could dimly recollect a Grace—
I think, they called it "God"—
Renowned to ease Extremity—
When Formula, had failed—

And shape my Hands—Petition's way,
Tho' ignorant of a word
That Ordination—utters—
My Business, with the Cloud,

If any Power behind it, be,
Not subject to Despair—
It care, in some remoter way,
For so minute affair
As Misery—Itself, too vast,
For interrupting—more—

On a first encounter, even the reader who has difficulty construing this poem—who cannot determine, for example, the grammar of the final sentence or the referents of the "it"s—is likely to feel its power. Despite the obscurity of meaning and story, the emotions drive through us like staples. Dickinson pictures herself as a martyr of love. Once the lover was here, in this room, on this floor. Then something happened, something stupendous and irretrievable—a parting. And since then life has consisted of varieties of pain: at first an agony like death, later numbness, and eventually a vast misery beyond definition or comfort. The disparity between the tiny objective details of the affair and their prodigious inner consequences—the sound of a name and thunder, a particular floorboard and the tearing of sinew, a letter box and a crucifixion—is rendered with a physical precision that puts us inside the vulnerable body of the speaker. The soul communicates its stop-sensation to the flesh.

How do the final three stanzas resolve this situation? Apparently they do not resolve it at all. Neither the speaker nor the poem can find a way out, and all the formulas for closure seem hollow. What significant action could the woman undertake? Her lover will not return; her pain will not vanish; she will not find the words to pray. Comfort remains in the conditional tense, and the conditions are not fulfilled. Again and again Dickinson's poems of martyrdom enact the same deliberate anticlimax, the same failure of recuperation. Misery is too vast to be interrupted, consolation will not come. "They say that 'Time assuages'— / Time never did assuage— / An actual suffering strengthens / As Sinews do, with age—." The only possible conclusion, for such experiences and poems, is a literal dying fall—"And I dropped down, and down," or "First— Chill—then Stupor—then the letting go—." Even the syntax seems unable to extricate itself from an endless run-on sentence that does not stop but merely runs out of breath. It resists our efforts to find the source of its power.

Not every critic has been willing to accept that frustration, and some have blamed the poem. "We feel that Emily Dickinson let herself go," Blackmur concludes, regarding that letting go as a sign not of artistic intent but of "desperate inarticulateness"; and according to Cameron the "rhythmic message of the last three stanzas . . . is 'I myself no longer wish to understand and therefore, of course, you must not either.'" To some extent these reactions have been based, like much criticism of Dickinson, on the use of bad texts. Blackmur was working (as he half suspected) from a ridiculous version of the poem that ended with the startling lines "Supremer than— / Superior to—," manuscript variants of "Not subject to" that an early editor had tacked onto the text. No wonder the conclusion seemed so inarticulate! But Cameron has also been misled, I think, by her uncritical acceptance of the better Johnson text. The final stanzas may be read as entirely regular, by Dickinson's standards, when printed as above. In this new or restored version, the appearance of mental and technical disintegration is replaced by a highly effective triplet—"Despair," "affair," "more"—in which the off-rhyme of the last word brilliantly conveys the speaker's inability to make a match with heavenly power. Dickinson's text draws the reader to the brink of misery and over; it does not lose control for a moment.

A proper text of the poem also confirms that it is written in Dickinson's favorite form: the hymn. Without accepting the faith of Isaac Watts or the Wesleys, she builds on their prosody, stanza, meter, and rhyme. But more precisely, what she prefers to write is an influential though neglected variant of the genre: the antihymn, a private meditation on one's inability to pray. This kind of poem, presumably a graft of eighteenth-century "night thoughts" onto the hymn, had been popularized by William Cowper and Coleridge, and American poets like Longfellow and Frances Osgood had long since naturalized it. But Dickinson carries it further than anyone. Sometimes with amazing pathos—"There came a Day at Summer's full, / Entirely for me"—sometimes playfully—"Some keep the Sabbath going to Church— / I keep it, staying at Home"—she molds the formalities of the hymn to the rhythms of her own spirit. "I got so I could take his name" clearly belongs with this poetic kind. Its suggestions of religious experience, its thunder and stigmata, raise expectations of a divine intervention in human affairs in order deliberately to frustrate them. The speaker lapses from grace; she goes through the motions of prayer but does not hope for any response. Hence the conventions of the hymn supply a perfect frame for her unbelief. Each stanza recalls a single empty form—a name without a presence, an angle without a turning, a box of unread letters, a God not personally experienced, a shaping of hands without prayer, a heaven without power or compassion—exactly to deny its relevance to her condition. The hymn is not sung but recanted.

Even a reader who grasps this form, however, may still not want to accept it. The discomfort that many critics once felt about Dickinson's eccentricities of style and technique, and that has been alleviated, to some extent, by a better understanding of her texts and her art, has now been displaced by an unease with what she seems to say. She seems to tell us that she is abandoned, and that she will stay abandoned. She also seems to find a virtue in it. Neither Blackmur nor Cameron, I suspect, would have been so ready to charge Dickinson's verse with incoherence had they been willing to accept the speaker's endurance of misery as adequate to the occasion. It is not only the structure of the poem that is on trial but the whole attitude toward life that it embodies. If "Emily Dickinson let herself go," as Blackmur says, she showed her weakness as a woman as well as a poet. And Cameron cannot credit the final retreat into misery except as a paralyzed refusal to deal with the rage or agony that must lie beneath: "The poem, though not, I suspect, intentionally, is about what it is like to trivialize feeling because, as is, feeling has become unendurable." A poet who faced her feelings would have arranged some "peripety," some satisfying reversal or resolution. Surely Emily Dickinson cannot have intended to say that she saw no way out of frustration.

The uneasiness goes still deeper. For many contemporary critics, the point that most needs explaining in "I got so I could take his name" and hundreds of other poems by Dickinson is the importance of that "he." In order to understand such poems at all, the reader must imagine or posit a beloved whose absence affects the poet (or "speaker") so violently that every aspect of her life has meaning only in relation to it. A part of her died when he left. But who is he? One obvious explanation would seek out some actual person whom Emily Dickinson loved and lost and spent her life regretting. But that explanation does not satisfy many scholars these days. There is not enough evidence for it (in spite of all the detective work and gossip), it is vulgar (as if any complex literary phenomenon could be explained merely by citing the right biographical item), and it is ideologically offensive (as if America's greatest woman poet could be reduced to a disappointed "spinster" or romantic cliché). Most scholars feel compelled to offer some alternative explanation. Thus "he" has been identified with Dickinson's father, her brother, her sister-in-law, some intimate female friend; with God or Christ or some other aspect of the divine (a plausible case can be made for reading "I got so I could take his name" as a version of Jacob's wrestle with the angel); with Dickinson's muse or animus or poetic precursors or daemon or genius; and many others. I do not mean to dismiss these suggestions out of hand. Many of them have produced illuminating readings of specific poems. Yet the identification of the "lover" with some preferred allegorical figure has the usual dangers of allegory: it tends to explain away the surface of the poem, its story or human immediacy; and it tends to substitute one privileged interpretation for the uniqueness and variety of many different poems. We do not resolve our discomfort about Dickinson's longing for some man by exchanging it for her thralldom to some abstraction.

A better way to deal with the charge that Dickinson let herself go might be to examine whether it is true. Does a poem like "I got so I could take his name" really end with a helpless display of feminine weakness? Textually and formally, I hope to have shown, it does not. But the issue is more than technical. If Blackmur was correct in claiming that the poem "represents in epitome the whole of her work; and whatever judgment you bring upon the epitome you will, I think, be compelled to bring upon the whole," then a good deal hangs on the question of its strength—not only technically but morally, intellectually, and emotionally. More reputations than Dickinson's are at stake. Most women poets have faced some of the same problems, and many have been accused of a similar weakness or passivity. If Emily Dickinson does not pass the test, what hope can there be for the others? Her more intense example bears the weight of a long poetic tradition.

Indeed, one answer to the question, who is he? would be that he is the same abandoning lover who has been leaving women poets from the beginning of time. As soon as Dickinson became a poet, his shadow came and went in her thoughts. Her own account of discovering her vocation points to one special source.

> I think I was enchanted
> When first a sombre Girl—
> I read that Foreign Lady—
> The Dark—felt beautiful—

The lady was Elizabeth Barrett, and the reference to her foreignness and darkness implies a train of associations. Robert Browning had been enchanted by the same qualities; partly because of them he called his future wife the "Portuguese." But another reason for that name was that, before he had met Miss Barrett, he had fallen in love with her poem, "Catarina to Camoens." Extremely popular in its time, and also a favorite of Dickinson, this rather sugary heroic epistle is addressed by a dying Portuguese beauty to the great poet who had once commemorated her eyes in a fa-

mous line. The Brownings treasured these associations and did not hesi-
tate to apply them to their own romance (perhaps a touch of the Portuguese nun also contributed to the sentiment). Yet Dickinson fell in love
with the darkness itself, so well suited to a somber girl. Learning to practice the magic of poetry, she identified with the exoticism, the obsessiveness, and not least the morbidity of the romantic heroine ("Catarina to
Camoens" also influenced Poe). Thus the Dark Lady of her poems is a
version of herself as abandoned woman. And every abandoned woman
depends on a missing lover.

Whoever else he may be, therefore, he fills a place in her verse as well
as her heart. The beloved inhabits the forms and conventions that Dickinson uses, her ideas, her language. As a matter of fact, he seems to
have made his first appearances in her work—"Heart! We will forget
him! / You and I—tonight!"—before any likely human candidate for the
"lover" had come on the scene. If the person had never existed (and
maybe he never did), Dickinson would have had to invent him. Her poetry required him for the faint suggestions of a story that enable her to
charge the simplest angle on the floor with infinite regret. Without ever
telling that story directly, the poet mines it for her deepest resources:
loneliness, pain, renunciation, courage. The phantom outline of a phantom lover confirms the authenticity of such emotions. The strength of
her verse at its best seems wedded to him.

Yet he himself keeps his distance. Like Stampa's Collaltino, Dickinson's unnamed and absent lover can be known only through his effects,
and most of those effects are destructive. The poet remembers him with
a surprising lack of tenderness, as the fallen Eve might remember the
Lord. Human and holy love seem equally remote, equally hard to pronounce. In this respect "I got so I could take his name" is perfectly symmetrical. The absence of the lover, in the first half, is balanced by the
absence of any consoling power in the second. (The equation becomes
still firmer if we accept the hypothesis that the beloved was an emissary
of God, such as the Reverend Charles Wadsworth—as some biographers
claim—or the angel who wrestled with Jacob.) Several time schemes
overlap in the poem: the time when he was there, turning on an angle;
the time when the memory of his presence still caused thunder, a stop-
sensation in the soul and breath; the time when that memory could be
borne and the floor could be crossed; and that indefinite time, encroaching into the present, when the speaker has discovered that her remedies
do not work and her suffering continues. The beloved has robbed her of
her mind—at least that part of the mind that enables one to forget the
past, to function, to prepare for the future.

Yet he also has given her life, for she no longer counts on him or
anyone else. The poem obeys an unusual imaginative logic: a chain of

images that depends not on the affair that once happened, the man who once left, or his action of leaving, so much on the internal sequence of feelings, the way that the woman passes from one state of existence to another. Abandonment has its own integrity. Hence the subject of the poem is not so much "getting over" as "getting so"—not becoming resigned to the situation but making it into a world. The passion of the abandoned woman begins to know itself only when its object has vanished and she is thrown back on her own resources. "The supper of the heart," Dickinson once wrote in a letter, "is when the guest has gone."

She feeds on misery. But the poem does not ask for our pity. The peculiar vulnerability of the envoi, as in so much of this poet's work, corresponds to a peculiar, fierce self-reliance. Perhaps the final lines even harbor a tacit pride or competitive edge. *My* misery, they suggest, despite its seeming insignificance, is too vast to be interrupted by the highest powers. Syntactically and spiritually, it vies with omnipotence. (Some readers have thought that the vast "Itself" refers to the Power behind the Cloud, but surely Misery has the better claim.) From this inner perspective, the poem does not trail off into incoherence but shuts the door, like the soul: "I've known her—from an ample nation— / Choose One— / Then—close the Valves of her attention— / Like Stone—." Dickinson does not invite us to share her feelings. The exact quality of her suffering, like the identity of the beloved, remains her secret. Thus we can regard her, if we wish, as a victim, the emotional wreckage left by a hit-and-run lover. But an alternative reading might emphasize the strength of her recusancy. The speaker will not serve. Rather than petition any God or human for mercy, she prefers to volunteer for a life of solitary confinement.

Her stubbornness reaches to language. The strength that readers have never denied Dickinson, the miraculous energy and virtuosity of her style, is related to her sense of abandonment. Like Gaspara Stampa, she likes to claim that all her words come "unsummoned," that she is no poet but only a sort of bird, that vision has left her speechless. Much of Dickinson's art consists of her fastidious refusal to take words for granted. She cannot bring herself to feel at home with "God" or his Word, to utter the word "faith," or even to adopt orthodox punctuation. Language as well as the lover may play her false. Though she can "take his name" in the sense of enduring to hear it, she cannot take it in the sense of possessing, as a bride takes the name of her husband, Jacob the name of the angel, a believer the name of the Lord. Those words are not hers. Neither is ordinary grammar. Even the tense modulates into a conditional or unspecified present, as all stages of the past collapse into an eternal condition without beginning or end. The formulas of poetry break against Dickinson's quest for the precise, incorruptible word. Not many poets would have had the daring to retain the puzzled and puzzling exactness of "turned—how" instead of the easier variant "let go," or the syntactical and lexical ambiguity of the nonrhyming "Tremendous gain" (is the gain the effect that his name once had upon her—a tremendous rush of blood—or her new ability to hear it without thunder?). Dickinson hardly ever fails to choose the wrong word—that is, the word that forces us to look again. Distrustful of art and language, she hesitates to lock the meaning up with any rhetorical key. The vocabulary of faith does not belong to the woman poet.

Out of that stubborn resistance to what is expected, however, she draws her own exclusive vocabulary. When formula fails, the poet is true to herself. Thus Dickinson acquires an idiom in which Despair and Misery can substitute for God and Faith, and "word" can rhyme with "cloud." She is comfortable with that language. In the long run, in fact, she may come to love it, if only because it is hers. One way of characterizing Dickinson's difference even from those male poets, like Cowper or Leopardi, whom she most resembles would be to note that she identifies with abandonment—not as an alien fate against which she must struggle, but as the source of her being. Much of the greatest poetry by women begins with the moment when Sappho faints. But we misinterpret that moment if we think it a sign of failure. What the woman poet discovers, in the aftermath of that love she can no longer claim, is how much remains to the one whom hope has deserted. The aftermath may feel like death. Yet it also allows the space she needs to write—a space too vast, in its desolation, ever to be interrupted. Not even God can intrude there; and men seem absurd. And there she is free to take any name that she wants.

This freedom is one of the secrets of the abandoned. Eventually, Dickinson tells us, they may grow to "love the Wound" that delivered them from ordinary life to the tremendous gain of heightened sensations. Abandonment sometimes smacks of a private vice, an addiction that tempts one to take his name for the sake of the thunder. Dickinson beautifully mixes pleasure and pain.

> Rehearsal to Ourselves
> Of a Withdrawn Delight—
> Affords a Bliss like Murder—
> Omnipotent—Acute—

Perhaps the victim of such murder is always the woman herself, exacerbating her memories not only to recall a lost happiness but perversely to savor the loss. The poet who constantly rehearses the scene of desertion may enjoy her ability, *this time,* to stay in control, yet even her bliss comes near despair and torture. *He* is not close enough to be touched by her feelings; their violence turns back on her. Moreover, the word "rehearsal" indicates the obsessiveness of her behavior, as if her martyrdom were a play that must be staged again and again. Yet Dickinson does feel omnipotent as a poet. Knowing the worst, she faces it down each day and steadily converts it into a mode of understanding. Her misery is magic. Seen from the outside it looks minute, worth scarcely a gesture of pity. But those who nurse it discover that it can grow forever. Once having "died," the woman poet can claim a mastery over life and death. Her sense of abandonment supplies her with a universal principle of explanation.

MARINA TSVETAYEVA
>   I am struck by the demoniac strength and abandon of
>   Tsvetayeva. Such women are prodigies.

Once we begin to regard the abandoned state of mind not as weakness but as potential strength, however, another set of questions arises. How well can abandoned women, abandoned poets, deal with the world? What are the practical consequences of their freedom? Is it inherently opposed to all conventional pieties and social norms? How adequately can it be adapted to different situations or different poetic kinds? What does it cost a woman to spend her life as a "more intense example of loving"? Must her strength itself be destructive? No single human being, and certainly no poet, can furnish us with answers to all these questions. Yet once at least a woman poet seems to have tried to live and write as if to test abandonment to its fullest. Not all the pain of Marina Tsvetayeva was self-inflicted, by any means. But even her "tragedy"—a word that none of her critics can resist—seems somehow to have been destined. She is a heroine of romance or legend trapped in history at its most sordid: the Queen of Abandonment. And she is also a poet who follows her principles wherever they lead her, whether to life or death.

Much of Tsvetayeva's career may be viewed, in fact, as a sort of acting out of the themes implicit in Dickinson: violent passion, poetic pride, alienation from the righteousness and optimism of her compatriots, despair and loneliness, a quest for the absolute, recusancy. The Russian poet did not keep these to herself. We have already heard her testify that at the age of six, under the influence of Pushkin's Tatyana, she dedicated her life to "unhappy, non-reciprocal, impossible love." What must be added is the contempt Tsvetayeva expressed for those who thought such passions could be restrained. In "Art in the Light of Conscience" (1932), she mocks the pusillanimous mentality of schoolteachers: "They give the older ones Tatyana's letter and are surprised when they fall in love (shoot themselves). They put a bomb in their hands and are surprised when it explodes." The poet herself is always explosive. She reads Tatyana's letter not as a document of private, introspective mourning but as a weapon or plan of attack. In the hands of Tsvetayeva the latent aggressiveness of Stampa and Dickinson—their "Bliss like Murder"—is cocked against betrayers and the faint of heart, all enemies of love.

Her enemies took their revenge. Though no one these days seriously doubts her greatness as a poet, Tsvetayeva remains the least known of the "four of us," Anna Akhmatova's famous phrase for the small circle who kept the Russian conscience and Russian poetry alive: Pasternak, Mandelstam, Tsvetayeva, and Akhmatova herself. Pasternak placed Tsvetayeva highest of all. Yet her death (in 1941) passed almost unnoticed, no selected edition of her poems appeared until twenty years later, and the first collected edition has just now been published. Translations are also sporadic. Only a small selection of the 160 items in *After Russia* (*Posle Rossii,* 1922–25), which many critics consider the best single book by any modern Russian poet, has ever been available in English. Most of this neglect may be accounted for quite easily by politics as well as by the inherent difficulty and untranslatability of much of the verse. Tsvetayeva herself had expected it.

> Amidst the dust of bookshops, wide dispersed
>   And never purchased there by anyone,
> Yet similar to precious wines, my verse
>   Can wait: its turn shall come.

Its turn *has* come. But Tsvetayeva was not merely prepared for neglect and hostility; she positively invited them. In 1921, in Moscow, this "rebel in head and womb" stood up at a public reading to praise the White Army and the Tsar. Almost ten years later, in Paris, she outraged the expatriate community by honoring the "Bolshevik" Mayakovsky with an amazing elegiac cycle. Neither Communist nor anti-Communist knew quite what to do with such willfulness. They preferred to pretend that she did not exist, and finally managed to make that pretense come true.

They did not, however, manage to keep her from writing. Despite incredible hardship and poverty, as well as the extremity of her emotional life, Tsvetayeva was one of the most prolific of modern poets. Perhaps that extremity even helped her work, as Nadezhda Mandelstam suggests: "Her willfulness was not just a matter of temperament but a way of life. She could never have reined herself in, as Akhmatova did. Reading Tsvetayeva's verse and letters nowadays I realize that what she always needed was to experience every emotion to the very utmost, seeking ecstasy not only in love, but also in abandonment, loneliness, and disaster." And Mandelstam generously adds that, in spite of the self-indulgence and indifference to the concerns of other people that accompany this uninhibited commitment to feeling, she herself is ashamed of never having been capable of the same wildness and freedom. Tsvetayeva aims this reproach at all the world. In "An Attempt at Jealousy," perhaps her best-known poem, she taunts a former lover with the comparative flatness of life after Marina: "How is your life with an *ordinary* / Woman? *Without* divinity?" All other women must seem pallid and tasteless, like store-bought goods or a plaster saint. The poet does not imply, to be sure, that she and the lover were happy together or could be again. She is not one to overestimate the pleasures of mere consummation. No one—not even Rilke— knows better than she that to possess someone or something reduces the object of desire to an earthly and boring normality, while the gods shield with lightning whatever we cannot have.

In retrospect, therefore, it seems almost inevitable that Tsvetayeva should have flowered as a poet just at the moment (in 1922) when she went into exile. Henceforth Russia itself would take its place among those distant, unfaithful lovers whom she could not live with or without (an attempted reunion in 1939 proved, as so often, a fatal mistake). She is not at home even in language. During the mid-1920s Tsvetayeva developed an original style of her own, often abrupt and compressed as a telegram. The image of telegraph wires, a tie to the homeland as well as a projection of the nervous system, occurs often in her work. It is as if the Russian language would have to be given a new urgency, an enigmatic directness like the messages of parting lovers, in order to survive. At the same time the poet inserts herself into the history and mythology of abandonment. To gloss all her references to abandoned heroines of literature would require a whole book—a book not unlike this one. Her tragic plays on Ariadne (*Theseus*, 1924; she later changed the title to *Ariadne*) and Phaedra (1927), her cycle of lyrics on Hamlet as seen through the eyes of Ophelia and Gertrude, her versions of Helen, Eurydice, Tatyana, the Snow Queen, and even Akhmatova, represent not only a summary of traditional accounts of the abandoned woman but a supreme effort to undo the tradition. Ophelia, for instance, exposes the prig in Hamlet, whose fear of passion (like Hippolytus's) marks him as more the cause of tragedy than its victim. Women have paid throughout time for the weakness of men. Thus Tsvetayeva builds a whole new poetics out of her sense of loss.

The ultimate triumph of this poetics is achieved in *Poem of the End* (*Poema kontsa*, 1924), which etches the end of an affair in fourteen caustic scenes, as the "lovers" walk around Prague on their last night together. Tsvetayeva captures the mood of the city, the sounds of the streets and cafes, as well as interior moods in their constant shifting, and brilliantly bleeds them together in the heightened consciousness of the woman and her dialogue with the man and herself. Even the language is stretched and falls into pieces. Thus in section 10 the word "separation" divides into four meaningless syllables, just as the couple divides into separate creatures. But the special quality of *Poem of the End* consists in its dread: the way that abandonment penetrates every emotion or statement or scene, filling the verse with innumerable false notes. No aspect of life can escape it. The suburbs remind the poet that people must always be moving somewhere else, the ghetto reminds her that all poets are Jews. Above all, love is abandoned. The poet's passion for the man she is losing seems indistinguishable from the sense of loss itself. It would be possible to argue that the woman's fear of what is about to happen has made her preternaturally sensitive to the tiniest signs of rupture and bad faith. But a more accurate reading, I believe, would interpret her despair and foreboding not as a prophecy of the future but as the essence of love in the present. "And so we live, forever taking leave." The phrase is Rilke's, of course, but on the basis of such phrases Tsvetayeva concluded that (Pasternak aside) only Rilke could match her strength. *Poem of the End* exhibits that strength on the verge. It uses the knowledge of parting—no less painful because of its inevitability—as a fundamental insight that makes sense of the modern world. Here Prague joins Moscow and Paris: stage sets with no room for a soul. And here the abandoned woman has her triumph. She becomes the type in which all honest exiles—all people who are not dead to feeling—may recognize themselves.

That was the message Tsvetayeva sent on her nerves. A year before, in a poem to Pasternak, she had expressed the depth of her exile, and her new-found poetic power, in a more explicit cry of rage and homelessness.

> Чтоб высказать тебе…да нет, в ряды
> И в рифмы сдавленные…Сердце—шире!
> Боюсь, что мало для такой беды
> Всего Расина и всего Щекспира!
>
> «Всё плакали, и если кровь болит…
> Всё плакали, и если в розах—змеи»…
> Но был один—у федры—Ипполит!
> Плач Ариадны—об одном Тезее!
>
> Терзание! Ни берегов, ни вех!
> Да, ибо утверждаю, в счете сбившись,
> Что я в тебе утрачиваю всех
> Когда-либо и где-либо *небывших!*
>
> Какие чаянья—когда насквозь
> Тобой пропитанный—весь воздух свыкся!
> Раз Наксосом мне—собственная кость!
> Раз собственная кровь под кожей—Стиксом!

Тшета! во мне она! Везде! закрыв
Глаза: без дна она! без дня! И дата
Лжет календарная...
                              Как ты—Разрыв,
Не Ариадна я и не...
                              —Утрата!

О по каким морям и городам
Тебя искать? (Незримого—незрячей!)
Я прòводы вверяю проводàм,
И в телеграфный столб упершись—плачу.

If I could speak to you . . . But no, in lines
And rhymes squeezed in . . . The heart is wider!
I doubt there's room enough for such misfortunes
In all Racine and in all Shakespeare!

"All wept, and if the bloodstream aches . . .
All wept, and if among the roses—snakes . . ."
But they lost only one—Phaedra: Hippolytus—
Ariadne wept for just one Theseus!

Torn into pieces! No seamark, no coastline!
Yes, I will get this straight, going astray,
That in you I lose everyone
Who some day or in some place *has not been!*

What else to expect—when through and through
You saturate—the air itself gets used to you!
Since Naxos is in me—my very bone!
Since underneath the skin my very blood is—Styx!

In vain! It is in me! All through! I make
My eyes shut: no bottom there, no day! Dates cross
The calendar with lies . . .
                              As you are: Break,
I am not Ariadne, no, but . . .
                              :Loss!

O, through what seas and cities can desire
Search after you? (Unseeing—the unseen!)
I see you off, confiding to the wire;
And with the telegraph pole to lean on—weep.

   The poem resembles a set of imaginary Chinese boxes, each one hold-
ing another kind of emptiness. Pasternak is not there to talk to. Poetry
cannot accommodate the full range of her unhappiness. Not even the
greatest poets have expressed what she feels. The usual sorrow of tragic
heroines, the weeping of Phaedra or Ariadne, is less than hers, since they
have lost a single lover while she has lost all her country and compan-

ions—even those who have not existed! The telegraph is a poor substitute for human contact. No one will hear her.

Three absences in particular shape the poem; and each of them, though a cause of despair, may also be viewed as a positive source of value. The first is Pasternak's. Tsvetayeva hardly knew him, yet here addresses him with the familiar "thou" (a form of speech she is said not to have used with her own husband and children). She had fallen in love with his recent book, *My Sister Life* (*Sestra moya zhizn'*, 1922), a collection of lyrics about a love affair; and the section called "Break" (*razryv*) in his *Theme and Variations* obviously moved her to give him the name of "Break." Nothing would be more precious than opening her heart to him. Lacking the chance, at the end of the poem, she weeps. Yet the absence of Pasternak also provides her with fuel. He saturates (or "impregnates") the air, and stands for all the might-have-beens—all those ideally sympathetic readers, all those fables of things and people too beautiful ever to have existed—that call forth poetic creation. Perhaps he even arouses her sense of competition: "Loss" goes further than "Break." Would his presence have proved as inspiring as his absence? Tsvetayeva herself thought not. Two poets so much alike would have canceled each other.

The second absence is within the poet herself. The reason that she cannot hold on to anything, the reason that she cannot even keep count (line 10) of how much she has lost, becomes clear in the fourth and fifth stanzas: loss is her essence, her entelechy, her principle of life. Naxos and Styx make up her bone and blood, and the disappearance of space and time when she closes her eyes confirms that she is ruled by Nowhere and Never. At the same time that inner life proves her a heroine. She wears the name of "Loss" like a medal of honor—even while it pierces her flesh. One of the most fascinating aspects of Tsvetayeva's poetry is the balance of pride and resentment with which she regards her own suffering. Not even Racine and Shakespeare seem adequate to such grief, and the concerns of Ariadne look petty by comparison. This poet is very proud. While hating those who have wounded her, she often seems to love the wound itself. Thus she spends her life searching for a remedy, and draws her poems from the failure of that search. Much of the best work in *After Russia* presents the speaker-heroine as a divided consciousness: wracked by torments that are intensely personal, yet already metamorphosing into a figure out of myth. She perceives herself during the change. To some extent this is the subject of the poem to Pasternak: the strange sensations of a living person as she feels her body turning into something inhuman—or wholly poetic. Whatever it costs her, "Loss" is supreme as a poet.

The final and perhaps the most important absence occurs in language. Tsvetayeva discards everything inessential. The poem first appeared in a

group of "Wires," and part of its effect depends on grammatical and syntactical contraction, a "squeezing" of the maximum meaning into the
fewest words. The rhythm is urgent, impatient. Even a reader fluent in
Russian may have trouble following the leaps of thought, in which tran-
sitions are typically implied rather than stated directly. English can hardly
reproduce the speed of this shorthand, virtually verbless notation. For
instance, the end of the second line, "Heart—wider!", not only dispenses
with the verb (Russian requires no articles, of course) but also with the
noun that, while dominating the first two lines, is never mentioned: the
feelings or confidences that she longs to speak, that formal writing con-
stricts, that only a heart is large enough to contain. Similarly, in the second stanza the opening words of line 7—"But only one"—must imply a
criticism of the preceding lines (though everyone suffers, as the quotation
suggests, the standard crosses of love involve only one beloved) as well
as a comparison with the speaker (*she* weeps for many more than one).
At the same time, Tsvetayeva reveals her impatience with the quotation,
and the prettiness of its consolations, by not pausing to finish the lines.
The abrupt punctuation here, the dashes and dots and exclamations, does
not indicate a stutter or hesitation so much as a furious rush of words.
The poet seems almost angry at language itself; it is too slow and stilted
to capture the pace of her mind. The heart is both wider and quicker.

The climax of these absences arrives in the last stanza, as the speaker
acknowledges that "you" may never receive her message. Their dialogue
has been quite imaginary. The untranslatable wordplay in the parenthesis
emphasizes the hopelessness of her search, the pursuit by the blind of the
invisible. All she can do is send off telegrams, confiding her hopes to the
wires. (Literally, she trusts the wires with "seeing-off," either a beginning or goodbye; the words for "seeing-off"—*provody*—and "wires"—
provoda—are related in Russian.) In the final line she has only the telegraph pole to support her, and weeps to herself. The mythological
heroine subsides into a vulnerable woman whom any passerby might
pity. Not even language helps; it breaks down into weeping. Thus the
momentary illusion of companionship that the poem entertains, its
"saturation" by another spirit, dissolves into the truth of loneliness:
Ariadne at the telegraph office.

Yet Tsvetayeva did not languish. Her later drama on Ariadne explicitly
affirms that the abandonment by "just one Theseus" was only a preparation for the divinity she found with Bacchus. Abandoned women learn
to talk to the gods, if only because there is no one else they can talk to.
Even their telegrams approach the status of high art. More practically,
the keenness of their sense of betrayal, their perception that every pleasure or sensation they enjoy may be happening for the last time, opens
their eyes to the poignance of every moment. Like Virgil, they recognize

the tears in things. Tsvetayeva dedicates herself to helping those things to pass. According to a later essay, "A Poet on Criticism" (1926), "A poet's most terrible, most persistent (and most honorable!) enemy is the visible world—an enemy he can conquer only by getting to know it. The poet's whole purpose is to put the visible in the service of the invisible." The sentiment sounds close to Rilke, her friend and correspondent at this time; the beautiful elegies they wrote for each other, he in June 1926 and she, on hearing of his death, early in 1927 ("New Year's Greetings"), both assume an almost perfect identity of views. But Tsvetayeva carries her commitment to abandonment still further. Not content to sympathize with the Sibyl, she insists on taking her over. "Could I be like her?" is a question no sooner asked than answered.

> Poets, we are—and that rhymes with pariahs,
> Yet still we burst our banks. Against the odds
> For god's sake we contend with goddesses
> And for the holy virgin with the gods!

This poet does not shrink from the terror of angels.

Tsvetayeva's fearlessness also extends to the Muse. In one of her most quoted poems, the beginning of her early cycle to Akhmatova (1916), she refers to her sister poet as a "Muse of Lament." Akhmatova returned the honor in "Four of Us" (1960), which uses Tsvetayeva's phrase as one of its epigraphs and therefore, by extension, as a way to describe her in turn. It is tempting to think of Tsvetayeva as a preeminent "Muse of Lament." But she herself rejected that characterization in a furious parable called "On Red Steed" (*Na krasnom kone*, 1921). Dedicated to Akhmatova, the poem may be interpreted (as Simon Karlinsky suggests) as a rebuttal to those critics who insisted on comparing the two poets. At any rate it deliberately spurns the Muse. Tsvetayeva will not follow such a passive and feminine goddess, the patron saint of dolls. Instead she is swept to the sky by a violent genius, the winged, red-steeded knight who demands that she sacrifice everything for her art. Ruthless as a male Valkyrie, he alone claims her and carries her to her fate. And though she will have to abandon whatever she owns, she gives her life to him and not to the Muse. That was how Tsvetayeva chose to tell her own story— not inaccurately. Her knight did not reward her by making her happy. But by teaching her not to fear and not to possess things, he did succeed in making her a poet.

She did not turn back. Only a year before her death, Tsvetayeva sharply criticized the final lines of Akhmatova's powerful "Lot's Wife," where the terrible predicament of the wife is compromised by a facile gesture of sympathy. It is not that Tsvetayeva fails to appreciate the pain of exile and the lure of looking back. But a sentimental view of the situation

ignores what Akhmatova's friend and rival knew best: life does not end
at the moment when a woman turns into salt. Perhaps salt expresses her
being. Thus much of Tsvetayeva's poetry begins where Lot's wife fin-
ishes, with the question of how to make life out of bitterness, deadlock,
and loss (one might argue that Tsvetayeva refuses to acknowledge that
Lot's wife had a soul *until* she had changed into salt). Flesh only gets in
the way of the soul and the poet. By contrast, salt preserves the wounds
of abandonment and keeps them hurting. Tsvetayeva is not afraid to hurt.
She inhabits her destiny as an abandoned woman, not willingly but with
a sense of inevitability, as the condition that makes her immortal. A
woman must be a martyr to be divine.

The Portuguese Nun

Is all this too melodramatic? A woman might be excused, surely,
for wanting to be something else, for trying as hard as she can not to
think about Gaspara Stampa and all her forsaken sisters. Moreover, Tsvetayeva's conception of poetry (not to mention life) might be thought too
extreme—or too Russian—to work for other people. Not all those who
choose martyrdom, or are chosen by it, become beautiful as a result.
Some women achieve poetic beauty through a process of intelligent control, nurturing rather than abandoning whatever they possess. And the
picturesque sorrow of beautiful losers seems often, like Stampa's virtue,
too good to be true. A cynic might accuse Lot's wife herself of only
posing. The strength of a statue resembles paralysis too closely for an
outside observer to jump to conclusions about whether it is held in place
by some internal power or merely by fear of moving. Women have
learned to distrust the temptations of martyrdom. Psychologically it can
be damaging; politically, vicious. The ideal abandoned woman depends,
for all her divinity, on the patriarchy she rejects and is rejected by. Her
pride and reserve, her fury, suit those who have caused that pain of hers
all too well; she removes herself from their sight. Nor does she set the
terms of her own career.

The dangers of abandonment as the model of a female career have been
sardonically described by La Rochefoucauld in the longest of his maxims, his anatomy of hypocrisy. One type of hypocrite, he says, "takes in
the whole world: that is the desolation of certain people who aspire to
the glory of a beautiful and deathless sorrow. When Time, which consumes everything, has consumed the sorrow they really felt, they do not
cease their tears, their wails, and their sighs, but adopt a lugubrious manner and try to give the impression that their unhappiness will only end
with their life. This mournful and tiresome vanity is generally found
among ambitious women. Since their sex closes for them all roads that
lead to glory, they struggle to gain celebrity by a show of inconsolable

grief." Whatever the cynicism and antifeminism of this analysis, it does
expose a trap that has claimed many victims: competitive suffering, the
will to seem more unhappy than anyone else. Ovid had set this pattern
for a heroine, and the popularity of the *Heroides* revived in the late seventeenth century. What distinguishes La Rochefoucauld's version, however, is his explicit connection of abandonment not only with hypocrisy
but with issues of power and ambition. He does not accuse women of
mistaking the proper road to glory—all other roads are closed—so much
as aspiring to something impossible. Ambitious women try to transform
their deprivation into a source of grandeur, permanent and compelling.
Yet since the essence of love, for La Rochefoucauld, consists of mobility,
the attempt to be steadfast in love is doomed to defeat—an honest failure
or hypocritical show. A career of abandonment may win a temporary
celebrity, but eventually decays into an art whose only object is decep-
tion. Though it "takes in the whole world," it will not fool sophisticated
lovers like La Rochefoucauld. They do not believe in miracles: a love that
lasts forever or a woman who earns her fame.

The danger of such careers may go even deeper. Even when an abandoned woman avoids hypocrisy—the word hardly seems pliant enough
to embrace Dickinson or Tsvetayeva—she still may appear to claim a
moral beauty. Her consciousness of pain becomes a mark of superiority,
as if to have loved and lost were itself a virtue. Men as well as women
bow down before it. Hence the best women poets are often objects of
worship. It is not so much Sappho's or Stampa's genius that is prized as
her extraordinary capacity for suffering. Enduring such loss, the sensibility of the poet seems refined almost out of existence. Even if the beloved were to reappear (as occasionally happens) communication with a
pure abandoned spirit would be impossible. Unhealthy consequences
may follow. For the poet herself, a career of abandonment builds a constantly rising pressure to enlarge and intensify her grief, heaping coals on
the fire in order to keep it alive. Not all poets survive that predicament.
For the reader, moreover, the poems that result may seem to disdain any
life that is less intense. Abandoned poems often convey a reproach, implied or direct, as if the reader were being accused of the same unfaithfulness and indifference as the lover. The shame induced in Nadezhda
Mandelstam by Tsvetayeva might breed resentment as well as admiration. Certainly lesser poets repel and embarrass the ordinary reader when
they exhibit their anguish in public as a sign of grace.

Nor can we ignore the hostility and anger with which many abandoned women express their love. Even when imploring their lovers to
come back, such poets do not seem to like them very much. One way of
reading Stampa's poems, we have noticed, would be as a covert attack on
Collaltino. Dickinson's lover looks so dim that we cannot tell for certain

whether it is a man, and when Tsvetayeva chose the *not-love* of Tatyana and Onegin as the model for her own future relations, she also chose an abiding contempt for Onegin's weakness as what might be expected from a lover. This effect should not be surprising. As many psychologists have recently argued, the dialectic of love and anger or passivity and aggression in women is historically determined, the inevitable result of women's dependence on men not only for sustenance but self-definition. In these terms, abandoned women act out the fear and hatred that other women suppress. Whether the poet passively turns her scorn against herself and withers into lassitude, or blames her affliction on the man who has betrayed her, she pays her tribute to the system that defines what a woman can do and be. Her passions are locked in the cell of a prison or convent; and there she scourges others or scourges herself.

The logic of this dilemma has never been worked out with more energy and precision than by a work that La Rochefoucauld himself may have inspired: the *Letters of a Portuguese Nun* (1669). We cannot be certain who wrote it. No Portuguese original has ever been found, and the best scholarly opinion now attributes the letters not to "Sister Mariana Alcoforado" but to a sophisticated Frenchman, Gabriel de Lavergne de Guilleragues. In any case the author has studied the heart of a woman where it lies most open, in the pages of Ovid and his classical French disciples. Those texts display a model of abandonment more ideal than any real woman could be. She is the creature of love. Deserted by her faithless chevalier, "Mariana" lives only in the letters that record her fears and torments, her resentment, and her gradual recognition that the man himself is pathetically unworthy of and irrelevant to the image of love that consumes her. The response that she did not win from her seducer has been amply indemnified by readers. Few women have ever been worshipped more. To catalogue Mariana's influence on later writing would require mention of most of the acknowledged experts on love. A small sampling might include Madame de Staël, Stendhal, and Rilke, who placed her even above Gaspara Stampa as a sublime revelation of the superiority of women to men and of "the irrepressible logic of the feminine heart" (Mariana is at her most radiant in Rilke's German translation). If a forgery, as La Rochefoucauld might have guessed, she is one who "takes in the whole world." What literary men have learned about women in love and women who write, in the past three centuries, they first learned largely from her.

Yet the Portuguese nun is not so easy to read. Perfect of her type, she reflects the tensions we have already seen in abandoned women and women poets: the art that disavows itself in the name of sincerity and the love that seems almost indistinguishable from hate. Part of the fascination of the letters has always been the contradictory spirit they reveal. We might define that conflict in various ways. In terms of conventional form, the letters represent an epitome of that Petrarchan mode refined and feminized by Stampa, the war between careless feeling and polished phrases. Mariana commands a peerless rhetoric. The "irrepressible logic" that so enamored Rilke may be analyzed as a triumph of style, in which the author's rapid shifts of mood and syntax draw us out of the exterior world into an inner recess of language, a pattern formed of a few obsessively repeated words and themes. Leo Spitzer has compared the five letters to the five acts of a Racinian tragedy, gradually building to a climax of self-realization. Nor does the recent discovery of an early manuscript with seven preliminary letters refute this argument. Whoever decided to publish the work as it stands deserves some credit for its artistic effect. By starting near the end, long after the affair has broken off, the *Letters* focus on a state of pure abandonment. Mariana's hope is past. We observe no conversation with the lover but only a dialogue of the self with the self.

Moreover, the work has a plot. Despite the monotony and airlessness of the nun's world, considerable suspense is generated by two questions about her psyche: will she ever discover the worthlessness of the man who torments her? and will she come to some self-understanding? The first question is answered with scornful assurance. Mariana touches her courtly lover where it hurts: "Your conduct was not that of a man of honor." But the second question arouses more doubts than answers. Like Pope's Eloisa, the nun can hope for nothing better than to fathom her own motives and find some peace; and more than one critic has praised her for achieving this resolution. Yet the turbulence of the final letter may be read as a deliberate contradiction of the tranquillity it purports to express. "But I want nothing more from you, I am a fool to repeat the same things again and again, it is necessary to leave you and think no more of you, I believe indeed that I will write you no more; am I obliged to render you an exact account of all my different sensations?" The fluttering prose betrays a woman who repeats her obsession even in the act of renouncing it. No doubt the last question is intended to be rhetorical, demanding a haughty *no;* but only time and her own heart will tell if that answer holds. The nun, the work, and the reader remain in suspense.

These tensions animate the *Portuguese Letters* and goad Mariana to write. While men have not hesitated to adore the purity and simplicity of her passion, her expression of those feelings is anything but simple. Again and again her words convey the perversity or masochistic pleasure of the love and pain that convulse her. It is not always clear whether she is boasting or complaining, ready to die from sorrow or luxuriate in it. The chevalier has educated her heart, and when he has gone she takes an advanced degree. "Why have you made me understand the imperfection and bitterness of an attachment that is bound not to last eternally, and the unhappiness that follows a violent love when it is not reciprocal, and why do a blind inclination and a cruel destiny take hold to fix us, usually, on those who would be responsive to someone else?" We never love the right people, or at the right time. That is Mariana's wisdom and the ground of her being. When she refers to her earlier happiness and fulfillment she is never convincing, but on the pleasure of self-sacrifice and the inevitability of abandonment she never lacks eloquent words. The economy of frustration, energized by atoms of shattered hope, drives the rhetoric on. Nor do readers find her mania unappealing. The sheer logic of the nun's predicament, and the almost giddy momentum of her rage, persuade us that the knowledge she has gained is true and that the residue of love, or love-hate mixed, is richer and more exciting than love itself.

Is "love" the right word for what Mariana experiences? The question may seem peculiar when directed to a figure who has often been considered the archetype or epitome of love, a figure chosen by Stendhal to open his book *On Love* as the defining type of *l'amour passion*. Without quibbling over terms, however, we might note that "passion love" describes her sensations in the text less accurately than "aftermath love," and that she begins her correspondence only at the point when the pain of separation has already yielded to a conviction that she has been betrayed. If this is love, it is an emotion to be experienced only in the absence of the beloved.

Other words seem more appropriate: the word "abandonment," of course, and especially the word "consciousness." The nun, like her readers, grows acutely conscious of each shade of feeling. Hence the process of continual self-analysis (however untrustworthy) replaces the ever-receding object of her affections. Trying to fathom her heart in all its tortured perplexity, Mariana becomes a sort of voyeur. Perhaps a similar effect, vicarious voyeurism, accounts for the delight with which male readers have responded to her despair. The *Letters* suggest that men know nothing of love, but encourage every man to suppose that at last he has been let in on the secret. Thus all the hostility addressed to the chevalier and others of his faithless kind reflects credit on the reader whose pity and understanding associate him with the superior insight of the victim. With what self-satisfaction Rilke assents to the verdict against his sex! "Man, as a lover, was done with, finished, outloved—if one may put it so considerately—outloved, as a glove is outworn." Having suffered so much, the nun is supremely knowing, and to communicate this knowingness seems the purpose of the *Letters*. That may be good internal evidence for suspecting that their author was a man.

Women have also adored the Portuguese nun. Yet the reactions of women have seldom been so free of criticism and indignation. To contemplate Mariana with the appreciative sympathy of a voyeur affords a rich pleasure; to value her as a model of feminine behavior may well induce rage. Even her heightened self-consciousness might be accused of catering to the enemy or acquiescing to the role of "superiority" that men assign women at so little cost. Yet the nun has one redeeming virtue: her unsparing and devastating candor. She does not let her lover off the hook, nor does she dissemble her pain. If men have treasured her for inspiring them like the Sibyl, women have warmed to her for speaking out. No nun's habit or feminine modesty is allowed to disguise her raw and outraged feelings. Far from taking all the blame for her own weakness, she threatens to avenge the chevalier's treachery with exposure or murder (whether authentic or not, the *Letters* did succeed in blackening the posthumous reputation of a prominent historical figure, Noël Bouton de Chamilly). Mariana's outspokenness relieves the female reader as well as herself. Despite the social conspiracy that allows men to exploit and abandon women under cover of darkness, she refuses to collaborate in a conspiracy of silence. All Europe will know of her grievance.

Thus the nun has passed her consciousness on to others. Adorable and pitiable to men, she may raise more complex emotions in women—anger and shame and scorn. The heroine is a fool as well as a saint. And by tracing the connection so logically and publicly, the author of the *Letters* provides a highly ambiguous pattern of thwarted romance. What is it women want? Would they prefer to stake their lives on a lover, or rather to know themselves? The former embodies conventional wisdom, the tradition that links the nun to her ancient sisters under the skin. But the latter suggests a way of breaking the chain. By violating the secrecy of the convent and inviting us into her motives, Mariana opens her passion to inspection. The reader does not have to like what she sees. Indeed, the nun seems by no means to like herself. The contempt she feels for the chevalier resembles the spite a woman might feel toward a mirror for reflecting her tear-streaked and ravaged face. Complaints so often repeated eventually sound boring even to her. Perhaps, like La Rochefoucauld, she has also become suspicious of her grief—so tiresome, so showy. Yet the public display of her emotions makes them available to others, whether for compassion or for cold-blooded scrutiny. All the clichés about abandoned women and their love—all that glorious claptrap—are exposed to a spotlight. They thus become a resource for other women. Having thought long enough about the Portuguese nun, some modern authors have turned their thoughts to getting rid of her. Her thin skin sensitizes women to what they have been and what they might no longer wish to be.

NEW PORTUGUESE LETTERS

Mariana's legend continues. The process of self-examination and self-exacerbation reached a further stage of development, in 1972, through publication of a modern classic of what we call "consciousness raising," the notorious *New Portuguese Letters*. The notoriety of this book is not incidental to its effect. Written by three Portuguese women, Maria Isabel Barreno, Maria Teresa Horta, and Maria Velho da Costa, the book rides on an internal excitement, a constantly refreshed sense of daring, terror, and scandal. The three Marias intend to disturb their readers. This too is brought to consciousness and regarded with frankness and irony. "The love of violating taboos as something that can one day be totally integrated within society is the truth behind this story and these crafty literary tricks of ours." Hence the arrest of the authors for their "outrage to public decency," the banning of their book, and the long trial that ended, amidst "the Revolution of the Flowers" in April 1974, with their complete vindication—the triumph of the new woman's right to free speech—all seem to confirm the theme and witness of the book itself: that acts of consciousness, however private, will force society to change. As Mariana came to know herself through accusing her chevalier, so the three Marias challenge the world in order to expose it and learn who they are.

The way to that knowledge passes through Mariana. The form of the *New Portuguese Letters* resembles Menippean satire in its melange of letters, poems, essays, and fictional sketches as well as in the range and freedom of its topics. From March to December 1971, each author tried to write something each week, and those pieces (dated but unsigned) are presented in chronological order. The results are of course uneven. But the work does achieve some focus through the text that it circles and conjures and plays with and tries to rewrite: the *Letters of a Portuguese Nun*. By using Mariana as a figure to think about and think through, the modern *Letters* suggest a warp in time, a curious haunted vision, even at their most daring moments. "Hence a number of motifs were already implicit in our choice of these letters as our 'inspiration': passion, feminine seclusion, and sisterhood; the act of writing; man and woman as strangers to each other; the couple; a national and personal sense of isolation and abandonment; hatred, separation, war; religious and moral prejudices and taboos; guilt; the pursuit of joy and pleasure; the community of the secluded; ingenuous love and sophisticated love letters; the constants of our national history . . . something of all this." Despite the limits of the nun's own perspective, her example opens onto an almost unlimited panorama of those problems that most concern contemporary women. The three Marias use the text of the letters like a stone splashed in a pond, whose ripples eventually reach the farthest horizon. Yet the stone itself, even when it disappears from view, is always felt as a dead weight in the center.

The relation of the *New Portuguese Letters* to the *Letters of a Portuguese Nun* might be described in three discrete but complementary ways. First, technically, the later work consists of a set of free variations on its precursor. From this point of view the interest of the new text depends on the fertility and ingenuity with which it can exploit the old one or turn it to some radical twist. Virtually every line of Mariana's letters appears in a different guise, developed, parodied, contradicted, or redressed. Between the forged pages of the original a whole array of fresh documents and forgeries has been inserted: anecdotes about nuns and witches, letters from the chevalier and other historical persons, elaborate punning games, two of the best-known "Sonnets from the Portuguese," surrealistic interludes, and occasional homiletics. The art of such a contraption does not require that all the pieces fit together or build to a climax but that each piece should respond, however indirectly, to some aspect of the primal theme, the nun's abandonment. Such art can be deeply subversive; it undermines our sense of an ordered world. Cumulatively, the boldness of the variations suggests the instability and unreliability of what has been described, whether the "facts" of Mariana's story or the morality that judges her. These objects of description can change at the whim of a writer. At the same time, the variations allow us to perceive a *discordia concors,* or sameness within difference: the oppression of women that remains constant no matter how much eras and forms may vary. The more outrageously each variation departs from the theme, the more will be the reader's pleasure in observing how things so very unlike—the confinement of a seventeenth-century nun and the "freedom" of a modern educated woman—may turn into a likeness after all. Such pleasure is the other side of pain.

The pain becomes more intense in a second connection of Mariana to her later sisters, the chain of genealogy. The *New Portuguese Letters* trace a descent from a fictional niece of Mariana through successive generations of women to the present time. It is as if the nun were reproduced from age to age without the participation of men. The point of this genealogy is made explicit in "Extracts from the Diary of Dona Maria Ana, Born Around the Year 1800":

> Beginning with Mariana, the first of us, I belong to the seventh generation, a spontaneous, philosophically minded offshoot of this female line, which has as its point of departure the worldly deeds of a nun, then goes on from that point, gradually becoming aware of itself, of its necessity for being—and hence a lineage opposed to the forgetting and the diluting, the rapid absorption of a scandal within the peace of the family circle and the reigning social order.

> If men create families and lineages in order to ensure that their names and property are passed along to their descendants, is it not logical for women to use their nameless, propertyless line of descent to perpetuate scandal, to pass along what is unacceptable?

The three Marias inscribe themselves in female rebels of each period, giving the lie to decency and orthodoxy wherever they reign. A woman's weapon is scandal, and men must fear scandal, since it threatens the legitimacy not only of what they think but of what they beget. Mariana's line of descent denies men their heirs. Thus the book presents a double chronology, the movement from the seventeenth century to the twentieth and from the beginning of an experiment in sisterhood to its result, and each movement is culminated by a reprinting of the *Letters of a Portuguese Nun,* which are shown to be not a historical anachronism but a permanent alternative to the reigning social order. Maria stems from Mariana, and once this genealogy has been drawn out there is no going back.

Together, these two sorts of connection—the willingness to regard all forms and institutions not as fixed but as arbitrary variations on the theme of gender, and the allegiance of women to a genealogical imperative or community of sisters that differs from communities of men—may be defined as the essence of "consciousness raising"; and a final relation between the old *Letters* and the new is furnished by their common emphasis on consciousness itself, or on the means of finding an identity. "Could I be like her?" The question signifies hope for Rilke, but for a modern woman might signify fear: the suspicion that all her progress leads back to Stampa and her paralysis. The three Marias find much to compassionate in Mariana but also much to despise—so much hypocrisy, "like the whining of a pitiful housemaid who is secretly happy at being abandoned." Yet they persist in counting the ways in which they resemble her. The object must be to name and root out the secrets of women, even those secrets so personal and intimate that to touch them seems to violate the soul. The search for an identity is ruthless. Impatient with all the standard models of female behavior, scornful not only of modesty and chastity but of undying, selfless love, the Marias pursue Mariana into her dreams and the core of her sex. There is no place they do not see her. And since she is perhaps a fiction, the three Marias do not blink at the possibility of seeing the heroine so clearly that at the center they may perceive nothing but a hole.

They focus their gaze, most of all, on the sex life of women. The scandal of this procedure is of course deliberate, and would have assured the fame of the *New Portuguese Letters* even if the government had not cooperated by repressing them. Nor do the authors refrain from hitting men below the belt. Much of the book mounts a direct attack, bitter,

cool, and often very funny, on the cult of machismo, exposed as a source
of pride that has more to do with fear and indifference toward women
than with any real pleasure.

> —By your orgasm
> senhora
> I remember you

> —The battlefield
> of your body
> the song of mine

> —By your tongue
> senhora
> I remember you

> —Sap in your mouth
> terror
> in your member

The repetitious formulas of the man, the knowing responses of the
woman that distinguish her enjoyment of love from his need to prove
himself, imply her superiority, not least because she does not gloss over
a loneliness unrelieved by the act of love. Cavaliers manage to avoid
thinking about this; they relieve themselves of anxiety by flourishing
their swords. But women are subtler; they are deceived by men only
when they first deceive themselves. The eroticism of the *Letters,* their
care to remind the reader that the pen obeys no phantom author, but
warm hands pulsing with the rhythms of flesh and blood and other
fluids, is crossed by signs of mockery and exhibitionism. Like Mariana,
the Marias contrive to be not only lovers but voyeurs. But exposing the
sex of men is all too easy. Spying on women presents a more interesting
challenge.

The results of this investigation are hardly conclusive. At the end of
the book the three Marias remain separate persons, each with her own
desires, and each uncertain about whether men or women (in the current
state of affairs) are equipped to satisfy those desires. A sort of postcoital
sadness hangs over the final pages. As the project dissolves, each woman
reenters her own isolation and experiences the poignance of separation.
Sexual freedom and companionship have not erased the history of Portugal or social and sexual injustice. Once having uncovered their secrets,
and laughed uproariously at them in public, the women acknowledge
how much is still obscure to them. The world intrudes again. Hence the
note of optimism on which the book ends is achieved in spite of a suspicion that nothing much has changed.

> And today (as so many other times), I confess to you my bewilderment at the world, my fear, my rage, my ravenous hunger for everything. O my love that is unflagging but futile!
> Misunderstanding things and people . . .
> And in all sincerity I say to you: we shall go on alone, but we will feel less forsaken.

The three Marias continue to love and support one another, but now their creative rapport recedes into a golden memory. What sustains them is not free love but aftermath love.

Indeed, as a revolutionary document the *New Portuguese Letters* pass on a paradox: a tradition or community of solitude. By returning to Mariana, again and again, the authors capture some of her desperate appeal. But each excursion also reminds them that the strength of her passion depends on its being thwarted, on the woman's being thrown back on herself. The three Marias will not allow the nun a hiding place. They stare at her sexuality until the mystique of abandonment looks as vain to them as it did to La Rochefoucauld. Yet their stare endures past the point of no return. Eventually their joint venture breaks down into a realization that the passion they have been analyzing is their own, and that it will persist despite their new ability to see through it. The aftertaste of the book is bittersweet. Comparing themselves at such length with Mariana, the Marias define not only their distance from her (at least they have been able to confide in each other) but also the ways in which she will always be part of them. They too have a love that remains unassuaged; they too have become conscious that abandonment corresponds to the soul in its moments of greatest power.

Many other women share that tradition. In the past few decades, as women have struggled to find more active models of living and writing, they have looked beyond the passive, suffering heroines of classical literature. The Portuguese nun is no proper sister, unless we find a revolutionary impulse in her speaking out. Now women must break down the walls. Indeed, the era since *New Portuguese Letters* has witnessed, in Portugal, a growing prominence of women in political life. There are other roles for ambitious women to play than the tearjerkers in which they were cast by La Rochefoucauld. Nor have literary women failed to profit from a new sense of opportunity and challenge. Yet Mariana still inhabits the present as well as the past. A woman poet who wishes to come to terms not only with the heritage of her sisters but with her own passions may still find a part of her identity in that lonely and eloquent figure. The memory of a more intense example of loving persists. Have we thought enough yet about her? I do not think that we have. Poems of abandoned women remain to be written.

Nor should the conflict between past and future models of the woman poet, between the old and new Portuguese letters, be simplified into a choice between dead and living ideas. Mariana continues to live in the three Marias. If women have become conscious of their own past victimization and the way that literature has exploited their pain, one source of that consciousness has been literature itself. Abandonment cannot be silenced. Gaspara Stampa teaches us by example, and one need not accept Rilke's interpretation to find her a type of many women. The woman alone may stand for more than herself. She offers a way of criticizing the structures of society that leave her out, the attitudes toward poetry that ignore the significance of her constant return. The poets who both describe and embody her remind us that life does not end when the cavalier rides away. New passions, a new poetics, may spring from the ruins of her love. We still need to think about her.

7 Aristotle's Sister: A Poetics of Abandonment

> Meanwhile his extraordinarily gifted sister, let us suppose, remained at home. She was as adventurous, as imaginative, as agog to see the world as he was. But she was not sent to school. She had no chance of learning grammar and logic, let alone of reading [Homer and Sophocles]. She picked up a book now and then, one of her brother's perhaps, and read a few pages.

IMAGINING ARIMNÈSTE

The silence of Shakespeare's sister, described so vividly by Virginia Woolf, has left a vast black hole in the canon of poets. But what words can express the silence of Aristotle's sister? To begin with, we cannot be sure that she ever existed. A few of the ancient accounts do mention a name, Arimneste, and scraps of tradition suggest that she may have helped raise her brother. Yet he never refers to her except as "Nicanor's mother," and the rest of the record is bare. No word of her own survives, of course. No word survives from any classic female theorist. Indeed, compared with Arimneste Judith Shakespeare and her kind seem quite talkative. Great women poets grace almost every national literature, and even if their acceptance depends upon their status as outsiders who express a countertruth or antitradition, they communicate well with readers and each other—a sorority of the abandoned. Nor can anthologies do without Sappho and al-Khansa and Dickinson and Nelly Sachs. Woolf's own novels have been absorbed by the canon. Yet the standard, large-scale anthology of *Critical Theory since Plato* does not find room in its 1,249 double-columned, small-printed pages for a word by her or any other woman. Unlike Shakespeare's sister, Aristotle's sister has yet to break her silence.

In one respect the exclusion of women from literary theory has been still more drastic than it appears. Most classic works of literature have taken at least occasional notice, after all, of women and their concerns. Ariadne, Eve, Antigone, and Dido haunt the imagination of the West; Shakespeare speaks for his sister by lending her the voices of Rosalind, Cleopatra, Lady Macbeth, and Lucrece. It would have been better had she spoken for herself, yet even these images not born of women can still provide women with mirrors (however warped) in which to study their features. But no one speaks for Aristotle's sister. The classic line of literary theory has hardly acknowledged the existence of two sexes, let alone the possibility that women might read and interpret literature in some way of their own. From Aristotle to Northrop Frye, women are assumed to be a subspecies of men. If Arimneste did pick up the *Poetics,* for instance, only chapter 15 would have offered her a chance for self-recognition, by distinguishing between good and appropriate characters. "Even a woman or a slave may be 'good,' though no doubt a woman is an inferior being and a slave beneath consideration. . . . A character may be brave, but it is not appropriate for a woman to be brave or clever." So much for brotherly love! Yet most poetics are not contemptuous but oblivious of women. The mainstream of theory glides over sexual issues without a ripple. Hence until quite recently theory knew only one gender—according to men.

In another respect the silence of Arimneste might be considered a rare piece of good fortune, at least for her later sisters. No dead hand of tradition grips feminist literary theory. Its time is the present. During the past few decades more and better criticism has been written by women than in all previous history. And much of that criticism fairly gleams, from a distance, with promise and daring. The canon itself cannot be immune from this change of air, this revolutionary wind blowing from resisting readers and madwomen unchained and Great Mothers and loaded guns. Like Lady Lazarus, Arimneste rises from her ashes. Surely some new poetics is at hand.

Close up the situation does not look quite so promising. Despite the brilliant achievements of feminist literary criticism and feminist literary history, few women as yet have cracked the precious, imposing bastions of literary theory. A classic woman's poetics has yet to be written. Many reasons have been offered to explain this, and some of them—for instance, male prejudice or the native good sense of women—undoubtedly deserve a hearing. But another reason seems still more plausible to me: the very lack of tradition that provides the opportunity. The best female literary theorists have grown up in the same schools of thought as men, and often they stand in the forefront of the most advanced critical cohorts. There are excellent female neo-Marxists, female semiologists, female Lacanians, female deconstructionists, female readers responding, antithetical females; and already some female postpoststructuralists have been glimpsed on the horizon. Nor do such women leave out of account—as might have been charged against an earlier generation—their own special problems in accommodating to a man's world. Indeed, much of the liveliest current theory explicitly sets out to show how women fit in: to prove that, despite Marx's own sexism, the alienated labor of women constitutes the prime example of class struggle in history; that phallus is not a masculine noun; that women respond to different signs from men; that the mischievous free-play of deconstruction exactly parallels the skepticism of every woman toward schemes of domination. I sympathize with such efforts. Yet I often hear in them a note of desperation.

They are desperate, I think, because they acknowledge no mothers. No school exists of neo-Arimnesteans, of neo-Diotimists. Thus female literary theorists tend to define themselves by rejecting the authority of the fathers, answering back for Eve. The strategy leads to some challenging questions: "What right has Adam to rule me?" "How should a Marxist deal with the protests of women?" But Adam and Marx come first. The boundaries of male-created, male-elaborated theories may be stretched to absorb the challenges of women, but no amount of stretching will put women at the center. At best the process leaves a space of her own to the daughter-disciple-rebel. And no established literary theory has yet been devised that builds from the ground up on women's own experiences of literature, on women's own ways of thinking. Even the most revolutionary feminist thought, it seems to me, has tended to ground its theory of revolution on masculine modes. In the absence of mothers, a father must raise the right issues. Yet historically men have shown no interest at all in a woman's poetics. There must be some better way.

That way exists, I believe. It has been carved out across the centuries by thousands of women, in the innumerable acts of response and commentary on which every poetics depends. For the absence of formal theory does not mean that women have never thought hard about literature. It only means that we must search out the evidence and use some imagination in putting it together. The outline of a woman's poetics is traced in poems and novels and plays, in essays and pamphlets and letters and diaries, and even in records of conversation. The line goes back, as we have seen, to Ur. From this point of view, the problem appears less Arimneste's failure to talk than our failure to listen. The documents where women's ideas about literature are already inscribed have only recently been opened for inspection, and much more digging remains to be done. Yet the fragments do cohere. A patient look at history reveals some consistent patterns in literary criticism by women, as well as some significant differences from the theories of men. As other voices join with Arimneste's, she begins to make herself understood. It is time to sketch her poetics.

No one voice can speak for every woman. A poetics of abandonment, like every other theory of poetry, requires a selection of texts and issues that casts light on part of the field and leaves another part to the shadows. Some women will always prefer Aristotle to Arimneste, and others may consider the choice irrelevant or offensive. The very notion of a woman's poetics involves some dangerous oversimplifications. By driving a wedge between the sexes, it might serve to perpetuate sexual stereotypes; by suggesting a uniformity or common interest among women, it might gloss over their genuine differences; by uniting women from many times and places, it might pretend that a poetics can escape the burden of history. These dangers are real. No attempt to sketch a woman's poetics can afford to ignore them.

Yet the risk seems worth taking. For Aristotle and his legion of successors have also paid a price for their neglect of Arimneste. Two consequences of this neglect have already been glanced at in my first chapter. By insisting on the rule of action and the authority of the canon, most theories of poetry have been forced to disregard some of the emotions and intensities that move readers most. They shut Ariadne out of their theories, and she returns to haunt them. Moreover, most theorists disregard not only abandoned women but also women poets. This is not accidental. A poetics that made room for women could no longer sanction a few genres fit for heroes, the epic and tragic modes, while discreetly dismissing the rest. Instead it would have to confront the vast anonymous body of poetry which women have traditionally created and appreciated as well as men. The definition of "literature," high and august, confirms a world of male privilege. By contrast, much of the poetry of women not only has been excluded from the canon but has directly expressed the frustration of being excluded. Hence the figure of the abandoned woman represents something more than the crosses of love. It stands for the pain of not being seen, of belonging to no one, of not being heard. A theory of poetry that does not recognize such pain is likely to be blind to half the human race.

The women who might have written another poetics are lost in the past. In more than two thousand years no one has been interested in Aristotle's sister. But I am interested now. A woman's poetics need not exclude a man's; it can help to complete him. Aristotle's sister was not his enemy but his ally. She still has much to teach us about poetry and about what discussions of poetry usually leave out. By using our imaginations to create her again, we can hope to repair a missing, vital part of our history and bring the abandoned back. Yet first we must do something that theorists have managed to avoid since the beginning of time. We must learn to listen to women.

Penelope's Silence

In the beginning was an aborted word. The first example of a woman's literary criticism in Western tradition, or more accurately the first miscarriage of a woman's criticism, occurs early in the *Odyssey*. High in her room above the hall of suitors, Penelope can hear a famous minstrel sing that most painful of stories, the Greek homecoming from Troy— significantly, the matter of the *Odyssey* itself. That is no song for a woman. She comes down the stairs to protest.

> "Phêmios, other spells you know, high deeds
> of gods and heroes, as the poets tell them;
> let these men hear some other, while they sit
> silent and drink their wine. But sing no more
> this bitter tale that wears my heart away.
> It opens in me again the wound of longing
> for one incomparable, ever in my mind—
> his fame all Hellas knows, and midland Argos."

It seems a reasonable request. But her words meet an immediate brutal rebuff from an unexpected source: her own son Telemachus.

> "Mother, why do you grudge our own dear minstrel
> joy of song, wherever his thought may lead?
> Poets are not to blame, but Zeus who gives
> what fate he pleases to adventurous men.
> Here is no reason for reproof: to sing
> the news of the Danaans! Men like best
> a song that rings like morning on the ear.
> But you must nerve yourself and try to listen.
> Odysseus was not the only one at Troy
> never to know the day of his homecoming.
> Others, how many others, lost their lives!"

Men like to hear the news; women must learn not to take songs so personally! And Penelope gives in. Marvelling at the wisdom of her son, she goes back to her room and cries herself to sleep.

Telemachus's words do not seem very much to the point. Penelope had not asked Phêmios to stop singing, after all, or to sing something fit for women; she only asked him to choose some other adventure. And to reproach her for not considering that others beside Odysseus had failed to come home seems irrelevant as well as cruel. The fact that others feel pain is hardly a reason for her not to feel it. Penelope cannot bear even to name her husband, but Telemachus seems to take pleasure in saying "Odysseus." By proclaiming his own indifference to pain, he argues just like a man. And that, of course, is the point. The scene has been contrived exactly to show his new maturity. He proves himself no longer a boy in the time-honored fashion, by rejecting any tenderness of heart and by putting down a woman. Henceforth he will be equal to the suitors.

In the manuscripts of the *Odyssey*, Telemachus's scolding of his mother concludes with four strong lines, suppressed by Aristarchus and omitted from the Fitzgerald translation. These lines are identical, except for a single word, with two other well-known Homeric passages: the speech in which Hector tells Andromache to return to her spindle, since the business of war and the *Iliad* is for men; and the later moment of the *Odyssey* in which Telemachus himself will tell Penelope that archery is man's affair, not woman's. But the single word makes a difference.

> "Go back within the house and see to your daily duties,
>   your loom, your distaff, and the ordering of your servants;
> for speech is man's matter, and mine above all others,
>   for it is I who am master here."

The crucial word is *mythos*, "speech" or "discourse"; and what Telemachus chides his mother for is thinking that she has a right to take part in the conversation—especially literary conversation. Like warfare or drawing a bow, *mythos* is barred to women.

This passage has exerted an irresistible attraction for male commentators. A short history of misogyny could be strung together from interpretations like those of the twelfth-century scholiast Eustathius. "Women are not forbidden entirely to speak, for women are talking animals, they have the faculty of talking, and indeed are rational creatures; but they must not give too much liberty to that unruly member, in the company of men. Sophocles advises well, 'O woman, silence is the ornament of thy sex'"; and the Pope-Fenton *Odyssey,* which quotes this wise counsel, cannot resist adding that "Madam *Dacier,* tho' she plunders almost every thing, has spared this observation." The snide reference to Madame Dacier is singularly pointed, since she had made her reputation as the first distinguished female critic in the history of Europe precisely by defending Homer's judgment against all his enemies. When her hero himself betrays her, the male critic hints, she can respond only by maintaining a most uncharacteristic silence. Many later female critics have been scarred by the same brand of masculine logic: a woman proves herself worthy of the faculty of speech through her prudence in never exercising it.

Not all women have been so prudent. Indeed, the first important work of literary criticism to defend the integrity of a woman's point of view begins specifically with the Homeric put-down. Germaine de Staël was no Penelope. In *Literature Considered in Its Relation to Social Institutions* (1800) she traces a theory of literature that takes the silence of Greek women as its founding, original fact. "Shameless prostitutes, slaves degraded by their fate, women secluded in their homes and unknown to the rest of the world, strangers to the concerns of their husbands, reared to have neither ideas nor feelings—this is all the Greeks knew of the ties of love. Even sons hardly respected their mothers. Telemachus orders Penelope to be silent and she leaves imbued with admiration for his wisdom. . . . Sorrow, tender and lasting grief, was not in their nature; it is in the hearts of women that enduring memories dwell. I shall often have the occasion to note the changes wrought in literature since the time women began to share the intellectual and emotional life of men." Madame de Staël demands her right to *mythos*. Directly contradicting Telemachus's doctrine, she argues that the exclusion of women from poetry fatally impairs the quality of its news. The health of literature depends on keeping the conversation open, making room for those ideas and emotions that women know best. Thus even the *Odyssey* itself defines its hero through his relations with women. If Penelope did not preserve the memory of Odysseus in her heart, he would remain forever a stranger and the epic would lose its pathos. The woman must have her share—not simply for the sake of justice, but for the sake of everything that will be missing from the story when Penelope does not speak.

The argument continues to the present. In the most authoritative modern discussion of Madame de Staël as a critic, the second volume of *A History of Modern Criticism,* René Wellek returns to the same passage and the same emphasis on conversation. "Details in Madame de Staël's literary history are often vague, wrong, or simply absent. Her discussion of Greek literature is almost grotesque. . . . The main offense of the Greeks is the low status granted to women: Telemachus ordering Penelope to be silent must have conjured the vision of some man giving the same order to Madame de Staël." Almost inevitably, it seems, the male critic comes round to Telemachus's manner of argument: women take literature too *personally.* The vision that caps the last sentence is entirely Wellek's invention. It is as if any judgment by a woman needs to be assigned some self-regarding motive to make it intelligible. New Critics consider themselves immune from such motives. They, of course, are objective, and so were the Greeks. Yet on reflection it seems far from clear that Madame de Staël would have been unjustified in associating herself with Penelope, just as Madame Dacier might have seen another Telemachus in Pope, or a current female critic in Wellek himself. Being deprived of *mythos* is not to be taken lightly. The command to be silent prevails over all others, in literary conversation, by shutting off the means of participation or appeal. Silence is not negotiable. And how else can a woman estimate what is missing in literature, after all, than by measuring it against what she herself has not been allowed to say?

A woman's poetics must begin, that is to say, with a fact that few male theorists have ever had to confront: the possibility of never having been empowered to speak. The right to *mythos* is the first law of literary creation; not even God could have created light without a word. And women have not been able to forget that law. Aristotle's sister could hardly have been unaware that he considered her inferior on exactly Eustathius's grounds, as in the *Politics:* "All classes must be deemed to have their special attributes; as the poet says of women, 'Silence is a woman's glory,' but this is not equally the glory of man." If Arimneste knew Sophocles' *Ajax,* she might have replied that the phrase (already an old saw) comes from the mouth of a crazed and violent man resisting his wife's efforts to calm him; to borrow the Homeric formula, vainglory and bloodlust are not the business of women. Yet men do not listen to reason when speech comes in question. Though Dante may have recommended the use of the vernacular in order to permit women as well as men to hear him, he becomes most uneasy when he reads in Genesis that "a woman, that is, the most presumptuous Eve, is found to have spoken before all others." The text needs correction. "But although in Scripture woman is found to have spoken first, it is nevertheless more reasonable for us to believe that man spoke first; for it is against what is fitting to think that such a noble act of the human race did not flow from the lips of man before woman." The moral could not be plainer: man was created to talk, and woman to listen.

A woman who reads and writes, therefore, implicitly challenges silence. The oppositions that inform so much traditional theory, the distinctions between the fictive and the real, literary and nonliterary language, poetry and prose, grammar and rhetoric, or even the signifier and the signified, tend to yield in women's theories to a prior distinction: the spoken and unspoken word. Sappho herself might have been kept from writing, nor did the greatness of her poems protect them from being burned. All works of literature exist against a ground of nonexistence. And women know this truth not through a chain of reasoning or metaphysics but as an urgent pressure on the brain. Before Virginia Woolf can address any other question about the great age of English literature, she must face the "perennial puzzle why no woman wrote a word" of it. Most theorists consider such questions beneath them, but that is where her theory starts. More than four thousand years earlier, when another great woman writer complained of her banishment from Ur, the image she used was the blurring of light by a sandstorm, her mouth choked with dust. Historically most women have lived in that storm. Hence female critics, even when aggressive and confident, rarely escape a certain dryness in the back of the mouth. The privilege of writing cannot be taken for granted; a woman who turns the pages of the canon can hardly fail to perceive how much of her is not there.

TAMAKAZURA'S PERSON

She also tends to look for what *is* there. The charge made by Telemachus and Wellek and almost every male critic between them, that women react to literature by thinking about themselves, is sustained not only by prejudice but by massive evidence from the writings of women. When Samuel Richardson's female correspondents implored him to spare Clarissa's life, they clearly felt their own lives were at stake. A literary theory based on such evidence cannot pretend to be impersonal. Most criticism that has made a difference to women, in our own time and others, has gained its ground precisely by identifying with the problems of literary women and taking them personally. Thus Kate Millett opens *Sexual Politics* by imagining herself one of those women trapped in the novels of Henry Miller, Mailer, and Genet; Ellen Moers reconceives Frankenstein's filthy creation as a woman delivering a stillborn child; Gilbert and Gubar gaze at the mad and outcast heroines of the nineteenth century as if into a mirror. The boundaries between truth and fiction or between reader, author, and character tend to blur in such readings. Women, male critics like to say, consistently fail to maintain "aesthetic distance."

An ingenious example both of the charge and of a proper rebuttal occurs in the famous discussion of fiction in part 3 of *The Tale of Genji*. Visiting his "foster daughter" Tamakazura (whom he is both protecting and trying to seduce), Genji finds her immersed in old romances where she searches for some parallel to her own situation. "'What a nuisance this all is,' he said one day. 'Women seem to have been born to be cheerfully deceived. They know perfectly well that in all these old stories there is scarcely a shred of truth, and yet they are captured and made sport of by the whole range of trivialities and go on scribbling them down, quite unaware that in these warm rains their hair is all dank and knotted. . . . I think that these yarns must come from people much practiced in lying.'" But Tamakazura comes back with a smart reply: "'I can see that that would be the view of someone much given to lying himself. For my part, I am convinced of their truthfulness.'" Her response to Genji's remarks, like her reading of the romances, applies them in the most personal way. The truth of fictions lies in the eye of the beholder: a seducer will naturally think them seductive, but an honest spirit can trust whatever they tell her. Women certainly have less to fear from romances than from men. And Genji, himself the creature both of romance and woman, laughs and good-naturedly concedes the point. Romances *are* true, he admits, both because they record the intimate details of life that slip through chronicles and because they present parables of good and evil, telling the reader how to live. Domestic truth deserves as much attention as the fate of princes.

Beneath the surface of the argument another subtle drama is enacted. When Genji rallies Tamakazura for being so absorbed by her romances, he clearly wants to redirect her interest to himself. A shining hero cannot bear a rival for the woman's mind and heart. Even in a situation where the man seems absolute master, he feels the threat of allowing her an inner life to which he has no access. Hence Genji's apparent curiosity about what Tamakazura is reading covers a brazen ulterior motive: he wants to insinuate himself into her dreams. "'But tell me: is there in any of your old stories a proper, upright fool like myself?' He came closer. 'I doubt that even among the most unworldly of your heroines there is one who manages to be as distant and unnoticing as you are. Suppose the two of us set down our story and give the world a really interesting one.'" And lest the reader mistake the intent of such "literary criticism," Lady Murasaki prefaces it with a crisp, revealing sentence: "He now seemed bent on establishing the uses of fiction."

If men use fiction for such worldly designs, however, women may use it precisely to claim a part of themselves that does not belong to the world. What Genji and Tamakazura contest is less her virginity than her self-consciousness. He tries to make her aware of her surroundings and appearance, of how she looks while she reads—her dank and knotted hair. She tries to preserve a private realm where he cannot follow, to lose herself in the unworldliness of the romances. Where else can she hide? The growth of those long prose fictions intended specifically for women, in medieval Japan as well as modern Europe, seems directly related to the need of women for a private space and time: a sanctuary where the person can be forgotten and the self remembered. The reader as well as the author requires a room of her own.

A literary theory true to women's experience, therefore, is likely to view "aesthetic distance" as a sham, a denial of women's rights to literature. A reader absorbed by a text finds her own identity there, and a man who tells her to stand back probably does so because he is after her place. When women come into question, male critics quickly expose the personal bias of their own judgments. Thus Wellek, like Telemachus and Genji before him, descends to personal remarks in order to accuse a woman of reading too personally—the argument *ad feminam*. From this point of view, it is men themselves who are responsible for the self-absorption of female readers, since men never allow women to forget their sex. Consider the outcome of Penelope's complaint. Curiously enough, she does get her way—not because anyone pays attention to her argument, but because of her sex appeal. The sight of her inflames the suitors so much that they fall to quarreling about which one will sleep with her first. Hence they drown out the minstrel and stop the song; Penelope has her wish. But sex has done the work of reason. Many debates between male and female critics seem to have the same structure: a logic that masks the real issues of power and desire. Small wonder, then, that so few women are willing to put their trust in any theory that fails to notice the importance of persons and sexes.

ARIMNESTE'S *OIKOS*

The exclusion of Penelope herself from the argument, however, may point another moral: works of literature are adapted to the audience they address, and women cannot assume themselves to be part of that audience. If a woman's literary theory cannot take the right to *mythos* for granted and cannot ignore the relation of literature to private life, neither can it leave matters of *community* out of account. Male critics often seem to regard the history of poetry as a sequence of heroic individuals, each of them sustained only by himself. And feminist critics have been tempted by the same mythology, emphasizing the ability of a few extraordinary women to rise above their place and time. But most women have always known better. Great poets go to school. They learn from their parents, their teachers, their peers; they catch the infection of poetry from those around them. Whatever the nature of Sappho's community of women—and scholars continue to disagree about it—her poems themselves record a society that cares about love and poetry and performance, that values intelligent women and saves their art. Not many later female authors have been so well supported. Hence the genius of Sappho can stir utopian longings, a vision of women in congress together, mutually sustaining and indifferent to any bonds but those of sisterhood. Certainly women require some sort of community. And a woman's poetics, more than a man's, must pay attention to the way that poets and readers have been schooled.

Consider, for instance, the kind of poetics that might have been conceived by Aristotle's sister. We shall assume that Arimneste had her share of *mythos*—that is, that she could read and write and was occasionally permitted to think and argue, at least in private. We shall also assume that, like other women, she had learned to take poetry personally, defining her identity in part by what she found there. These seem like modest assumptions (though only limited numbers of ancient women, we should remember, actually did read and write). Yet even so, the conditions for a poetics are far from satisfied. For we still do not know how much literature Arimneste was acquainted with or how well she had absorbed what Werner Jaeger calls *paideia:* that ideal unity of culture and education which, according to Greek thought, literature embodied. The *paideia* of Aristotle's *Poetics* is not in question. Much of its power derives from its easy familiarity with epic and tragic tradition, and still more from its sense of shared understandings and recognized ethical verities. The truth of *mimesis* can hardly be doubted by an audience that agrees about the nature of the thing imitated. Indeed, since the Homeric epics and great tragedies had taught that audience the nature of things in the first place, through Greek education, it is not surprising that Greek men should have found their masterpieces the image of truth itself.

Greek women may have been different. To begin with, they may not have been able to observe those great works of art. Whether women were admitted to the tragic festivals or recitals of epics remains a vexed question. In any case, few if any women went to school. Authors might be inspired by them or use them as examples, but did not have to count on their presence in a real or implied audience. Thus Madame de Staël may not have been far wrong when she accused Greek writers of catering almost entirely to masculine attitudes. The most interesting women in Greek literature tend to appear as outsiders, more a threat or a lure to the audience than a part of it. Their characteristic solitude and abandonment emblemize their distance from the group that watches them. Men thought about women, not with them. Certainly Aristotle did not philosophize for women; we have already seen that he regards them as a lower species. Hence his sister would not have been welcome to see herself in his work. Nor would she have found much place for her own truth in the *Iliad* or the *Oedipus*, even if she were allowed to view them. I do not imply that she must have been a rebel, only that she would have been most unlikely to belong to her brother's consensus. The ideal of the *polis* that still attracts so many scholars to the Greeks, an ideal enforced by the arts and by the public gatherings where men participated in communal rites, holds much less attraction for women. Their place was the *oikos* or household. Thus a woman's poetics must find its community elsewhere.

Indeed, for many women literature itself has served as a communion of the secluded and disenfranchised—not an occasion to affirm the general voice of the state or the will of the gods, but an interlude in which private feelings are shared. Not all good poems can fill an amphitheater. Sometimes they sound better around a well, where the women of Fez gather to sing what is on their minds—"I see a man who is dull / and boring like no one else"—or in a dressing room, where the women of Lesbos prepare the bride for her ordeal—"O Hesperus, you bring all things together"—or beside a bed, where the women of the Papago teach the dying the songs of the dead—"In the great night my heart will go out, / Toward me the darkness comes rattling. / In the great night my heart will go out." Such songs tell women who they are. They do not preach or shout, and often they thrive in intimate circumstances, as a girl chants to herself while skipping rope or a mother croons to her child. Even to eavesdrop upon them may seem to violate a confidence. They are not designed for publication. Anon. was a woman, as scholars have lately been reminding us, and much of the best literature by women has come to us draped in a veil. Yet Arimneste's poetics, unlike her brother's, would have had to listen carefully to Anon. From her she might have learned how much of poetry escapes official forms and public rituals, and so gained access to that secret society united not by myths of culture but by common experience and common suffering. A woman's poetics will be attuned to voices that it cannot name, so close to inner voices that at times they may sound like one's own.

The literary history of women suggests the plausibility of a view that joins writers and readers together in an anonymous community. Until the last few centuries, not many female authors achieved great names. Once again Virginia Woolf helps call attention to the social conventions (especially the equation of chastity with obscurity) that kept women under a cloud. "Currer Bell, George Eliot, George Sand, all the victims of inner strife as their writings prove, sought ineffectively to veil themselves by using the name of a man. . . . Anonymity runs in their blood. The desire to be veiled still possesses them." From this perspective, the invention of the printing press and the resulting opportunities for pseudonymity and secret reading constitute a crucial stage in the emancipation of literate women. An author can hide between the lines of print. Moreover, the thirst of presses for readers, and the becoming modesty with which women can read behind closed doors, gradually allowed a vast audience of women to discover the pleasures of literature and to demand the satisfaction of their desires. Such communities seldom meet in public, and even publication, for writers like Jane Austen, may have to take place under a veil. Yet no one can deny that Austen's readers make up a society—invisible, unknown to each other, but tied with threads of steel.

Furthermore, despite Woolf's justified resentment of the convention that "publicity in women is detestable," none knew better than she the costs of masculine privilege or the uses of anonymity. Eventually her hatred of the raw ego, its hunger for publicity and greatness, may have cost her her life. But a more positive view of the situation of women might emphasize the advantages of cutting texts free from names. Anonymous writers and anonymous readers can share their secret lives without fear of exposure. Historically, men have tended to use this cloak of namelessness for pornography; women, for expressing their real feelings. More recently, the fashionable critical skepticism about "works" and "authors," the insistence that all of us are swimming in a boundless sea of textuality or polysemous bliss, has suggested that all writing might be returned to its primal anonymous state, to be made use of as we will. But more than one moral can be drawn from such notions. Though many men have viewed the sea of textuality as fostering a radical independence, allowing every text a protean or pornographic shape to feed the reader's desire, some women have viewed it instead as promising a free sharing of meanings and interests, a place for meeting the world without defenses. To be at home in that sea would mean putting aside the fear of life without a name. More practically, it would mean reading texts not as performances but as silent conversations or webs of relationship to which each reader might bring her own confidences and impressions. The attempt to build a literary theory on principles of "affiliation" rather than "authority" has engaged many feminist theorists of late. It also reflects the way that many women have always read.

MADAME DE STAËL'S POETICS

The first European woman to construct her own poetics, in fact, consciously built it from relations and affiliations that go beyond author and text. Others before Madame de Staël had studied the "rapport" of literature with social institutions, but none had tried so ambitiously to associate the grand sweep of history with the intimate experiences of every reader—history as it affects the individual mind. The project she started has yet to be carried through. For what de Staël aimed at was nothing less than an alternative literary canon, adequate to the needs of women as well as men, that would define civilization not in terms of power, refinement, or national pride but as the communion of sensitive and enlightened beings—beings, needless to say, much like herself. This is the grand idea that unifies her work. We have already seen her contribution to the School of Abandonment from which Byron drew Donna Julia. But de Staël did not think abandonment an episode or interlude (or as Byron would have it, a regression) in the march of man's progress. Instead she thought it the cutting edge of progress. The perfectibility of the human species, she argues, culminates at its best in a sensitive soul, a soul aware of the fragility of its ties to others. When men and women are free at last to be themselves, they will still be bound together by love and death.

Thus a woman's poetics, as de Staël conceives it, addresses the fatal separation of *polis* from *oikos* that has marred European culture since the Greeks. With the breakdown of the *polis,* individuals have been imprisoned in "the circle of selfishness everyone wants to preserve as his inviolable asylum." In this desperate situation, only writings filled with sensibility can protect the reader from a cold and uncompassionate loneliness. "Such writings can draw tears from people in any situation; they elevate the soul to more general contemplation, which diverts the mind from personal pain; they create for us a community, a relationship, with the writers of the past and those still living, with men who share our love for literature. . . . And by feeling similar emotions I enter into some sort of communion with those whose fate I so deeply grieve." What sort of writings does she have in mind? Her "Essay on Fiction" proposes a modern canon: the *Letters of a Portuguese Nun,* "Eloisa to Abelard," *Clarissa, The Sorrows of Werther,* and above all *The New Heloise.* "Such works of fiction are in a class by themselves." They link all feeling people together in a human chain; they dissolve the distinctions among eras and social classes, among authors, readers, and fictional characters, and persuade the loneliest outcast that she is not alone. And they also appeal especially to women. As the social order and the sense of interdependence crumble, in modern times, the School of Abandonment offers to take their place.

Why should de Staël's poetics place such stress on abandonment? The reason is that poetry depends on passion, especially the passion of love, and love is known best through its torments. If women could only express what they feel, "this sublime sorrow, that melancholy grief, those all-powerful sentiments which enable them to live or die, would perhaps produce more deep emotions in the heart of the reader than all the transports to which the exalted imaginations of poets and lovers give birth." Love is the source of poetry, yet in the end it always resigns the lover to abandonment. This terrible logic stems from two root causes. First, the obsession with the loved one completely separates the lover from the rest of the world, leaving her "solitary and concentred." By making women indifferent to society or the ordinary decencies of life, love breaks those rules on which tranquillity and strength rely; a woman in love is "abandoned." Second, she will inevitably be abandoned in deadly earnest. Since the intensity of woman's love surpasses man's, and indeed may even become a spring of fear and disgust to him, the plot has a predictable outcome: he leaves, she stays and pines. "Alone in secret, our whole being is changed from life to death." The rest of her life may well be spent mourning or recreating the scene of her desertion. "How bitterly must a woman regret that she has ever loved." The secret story of the greatest passions—the love almost unknown to men—is always abandonment.

Abandonment may also provide a secret bond between authors and readers. The writings de Staël admires most invariably present an archetype of solitary abandoned pain, an Eloisa or Portuguese nun. Such figures are not only the victims of a plot but its authors; their act of writing sets the work in motion and produces the residue of passion that is its final effect. We look over their shoulders. At the same time they are emblems of authorship itself, its melancholy isolation and submission to dreams. If an author writes in order to disperse her phantoms and establish communion with other minds, the act of composition requires solitude and the imaginative recollection of past ecstasies and pains. The heart is most vulnerable then. But the reader is equally isolated, equally in thrall to dreams. Reading entails a constant sympathy or submission to the figures in the text. Hence the writing that moves us most, on de Staël's analysis, not only transmits images of absence and loneliness but issues from them. Poetry is a companion that makes the reader feel more alone. Doubling its solitude, she turns into a secret sharer. "Grief can only be assuaged by the power of weeping over our destiny, and of tak-

ing that interest in what concerns ourselves, so as to divide us in some
sort into two separate beings, the one of whom commiserates the other."
Thus the hunger for literary affiliations, the search for an absent friend,
finally throws the reader back on herself. She masters her grief only by
learning how to read it, as if it belonged to someone else. The sense of
abandonment that poetry consoles, therefore, it also confirms. The separation of author, character, and reader, like their communion, is an image
of that love that women pursue forever, at the cost of being forever
disappointed.

Not every woman will agree with de Staël's formulation. But most
women's literary theories, as well as women's preferences in literature,
have placed a similar strong emphasis on love and its discontents. Much
of this must surely be attributed to the historical oppression of women,
forbidden any interests that do not circle around some man, and therefore doomed to have some man betray them. Yet a considerable weight of
evidence suggests that concern with abandonment has deep psychological roots. While male fantasies and myths compulsively reenact the rise
and fall of Phaethon, his premature ambition and precipitate plunge, the
dreams of women tend to retrace the course of Demeter—the sunder-
ing, the long delay, eventual reunion, "all that pain." Recently psychologists have begun to stress the role in women's development of "separation
anxiety," a fear of being parted from others that is the female counterpart
to the male fear of intimacy in Freud's Oedipus complex. (A more extreme version of this theory would claim that separation anxiety also
dominates the infancy of men, as emblemized by the fact that all Oedipus's problems, as my first chapter argued, stem from his original abandonment by his parents.) The need to stay close to others, the difficulty
of sustaining and perpetuating ties of affection, preoccupy women from
infancy. Hence female growth, on this analysis, necessitates the complex
bargain of Demeter and Persephone: a balance between the worlds of
relationship and separation.

The truth of this theory is certainly open to question. Yet it does help
account for the internal tensions of much of the literature that has meant
most to women across the centuries. From Enheduanna to the three Marias, from Penelope and the *Heroides* through patient Griselda to Jean
Rhys, women have tended to identify with heroines who endure a long
season of loss. These models, one must admit, are often repulsive. To
modern eyes, the way that masochism becomes Griselda as she colludes
in her own victimization may seem to prove the virtue of impatience—or
rage, or revenge. Such rage has been put to use in current fiction, which
offers more active models of how to resent being hurt. Hence abandonment has gone out of style with critics (though not, of course, with the
vast audience that still devours popular romances). Good riddance, we

might say: "Well now that's done: and I'm glad it's over." Yet an aversion to images of female suffering should not blot out their role in making women strong. Much of the finest poetry by women has followed de Staël's prescription: abandonment steels the soul. Almost every national literature boasts at least one great woman poet of abandonment. These poets are survivors, and they speak for many women. When her reason for living has gone, survival demands that a woman learn new ways of enduring. "From that arid sadness which we feel when abandoned and forlorn, . . . we are rescued in some measure by those writings." De Staël was not alone in seeking such restoration. Women have sought it from writing throughout the ages; and it ought to appear again in a woman's poetics.

THE USES OF ARIMNESTE

It is time for Arimneste to try definitions. "Tragedy," she reads over her brother's shoulder, "is the imitation of an action. . . ." But something in that phrase does not sound right, and she goes off by herself to think again. Though history has abandoned her, I shall take the liberty of giving her some company: Sappho, Lady Murasaki, Christine de Pisan, Louise Labé, St. Teresa, Lady Mary Wortley Montagu, Madame de Staël, Margaret Fuller, Marina Tsvetayeva, Virginia Woolf, Simone de Beauvoir—and perhaps the Authoress of the *Odyssey,* the White Goddess, and the Wife of Bath. These women are necessary to Arimneste, for they know something that she has yet to learn—her silence can be broken—and thus can instruct her in the prior tragedy that consists not of acting and mirroring but of doing and saying nothing, or of looking in the mirror and finding no face there. Now she begins her poetics. "Poetry," she writes, "is the expression of a life, personal, incomplete, and proportioned to the self; employing whatever language and conventions one has been allowed to acquire; presented in fragments; and achieving, through sharing the emotions of loneliness and abandonment, a momentary sense of not being alone." She pauses and waits for examples. Eventually the murmur of women's voices—whispers at first, and then a many-languaged chorus—swells and inhabits the room. Her page begins to fill.

What use is this woman's poetics? It cannot compete, of course, with the brother's tradition. Nature and Aristotle are the same, as Pope and Frye remind us, not because the *Poetics* captured the whole truth about literature but because it established those critical conventions whose adaptations and transformations are identical with the history of theory itself, at least in the West. Nor can the poetics of Aristotle's sister conceivably satisfy all women. Not all women think alike. Moreover, insofar as Arimneste accurately represents the strategies of female authors within and against the dominant culture, she stands for a history of subordination and reaction that many women oppose more strenuously than they do the patriarchs themselves. The poetics I have tried to sketch remains within history, if only as a voice of dissent, and those who are trying to awake from that history may be forgiven for remembering Arimneste as one more bad dream. Yet her theory does have its uses. First of all, it reminds us not to confuse the relative silence of women, across the centuries, with a lack of intelligent convictions. Minds can survive in the dark. Moreover, the thought of a woman's poetics can help to create the sense of community that so many women have looked for and have not found. The history of poetry contains many sisters who not only wrote poems but read them. Arimneste has always existed. Imagining her modes of perception, we put women back into time.

A woman's poetics can also repair the balance of theory itself. One use of this way of thinking is that it reveals how much literary theory serves exclusively masculine interests. "Man" and "human" are not synonymous, and a poetics that takes differences of sex and gender seriously will raise some questions that men have preferred to ignore. When Aristotle located "the origin of the art of poetry" in man's "natural" pleasure in imitation and harmony, for instance, to what extent did his analysis presuppose a way of being at home in the world to which most women feel foreign? Abandoned women know that the world can shift too fast to be imitated, that the harmony of art is made to be broken. Hence their poetics obeys another law of nature, the unsatisfied craving of children who cry to be held. Much of the art of poetry, for men and women alike, originates in the primal need to relieve strong feelings by sharing them with others. Aristotle himself acknowledged this need in his reference to tragic catharsis, but he took it for granted. His sister, I think, could not. Most women know better than to suppose that feelings, when ignored, take care of themselves, or that the discharge of pity and terror can end any action. For abandoned women, the real story begins there. Hence a woman's poetics is likely to start not with means and objects and manners of imitation but with the needs that first give rise to a poem—a poetics of care and desire. The project deserves more attention. Women cannot claim exclusive rights, of course, to such a poetics, but they do bring one advantage to their questioning of theory: unlike men, they have never been able to identify the traditional forms and laws of literature with their own sense of the world.

Nor have they been able to count on being heard. Denial of *mythos* has sensitized many women to the privilege that sustains even the most revisionary or ironic theories of men: the privilege of being *important*. Literary theories acquire importance, as everyone knows, by establishing some relation (whether of continuity or confutation) with Plato,

Aristotle, St. Augustine, Descartes, Rousseau, Hegel, Marx, Nietzsche, Freud, or about a dozen other great names—almost all of them European, and all of them male. And the important fields of theory are metaphysics, epistemology, and the philosophy of language—fields in which no woman has ever become famous. Perhaps it is not surprising, then, that so many women insist on the priority of another set of questions about literature and literary studies: who is allowed to write and why? why is it that certain theorists are endlessly quoted, discussed, and imitated, while others of seemingly equivalent interest are hardly ever mentioned? on what principles are critics published by the best presses and journals, reviewed, assigned to reading lists, forgiven their errors of fact and judgment, footnoted, conjured with, anthologized, translated? whose interests are served by poetics? These are hard and annoying questions that have seldom been asked by male theorists. A woman's poetics is likely to take them to heart. If Penelope and Arimneste have been brought up to think their problems less important than those of Telemachus and Aristotle, they do have a right to inquire about the grounds of importance itself.

The final use of a poetics of abandonment, however, may bear less on theory than practice: it gives us new ways of reading. Abandoned women stand outside any familiar and comfortable view of poetic tradition. Some cultures have tried to deny their existence through stigma or censorship or even public burning. Sappho's survival, even in a mutilated and shredded form, is something of a miracle. Yet we have seen how much the scraps of Sappho mean to later generations. If abandoned women cannot be welcomed into the canon, neither can the canon keep alive without them. The *Aeneid* requires its Dido, if only to authenticate its hero's grief. But we might ask still more from such a figure. She can help us trace another story within the story, the story of abandonment that, however suppressed, insists on casting its shadow over the page. A woman's poetics infiltrates the classics. Once we have learned to read through Arimneste's eyes, we begin to notice how much her brother's poetics omits—not only women but the sort of poetry that might be true to their experiences. As we fill in those gaps with Sappho and her sisters, the *Poetics* itself starts to change.

Indeed, something peculiar has been happening lately to the classics. Some of them now seem less heroic and some less funny. Odd pages suddenly spring into sharp relief. Those scenes of cruelty to women, those obsessions with chastity and purity, those all-male debates about the nature and future of the human race, those sacrifices of feeling to duty no longer seem unimportant or irrelevant to the "higher" concerns of the work. An excluded figure peers in between the lines. Sometimes it resembles an abandoned woman who silently notes that no one is listening to her. Under her withering gaze, strong works can turn pale, as in the underworld, before a stone-faced Dido, Aeneas hears in his own excuses the lameness of the heroic mission to which he has sacrificed her. The woman's silence does not prevent her from controlling the scene. Attentive readers have lately begun to discover a similar presence lurking in many masterworks, a principle of contradiction or resistance to masculine authority that subverts the plot of the work or converts it to an antiheroic, ambiguous mode of feeling. In this regard Arimneste often reads more carefully than Aristotle; she seldom forgets to insert the missing woman.

She also chooses other works to read. The poetry of abandoned women is only a part of literature, but it stands in critical relation to the rest, exposing the complacent and remembering the forgotten. Hence Arimneste challenges the very definition of a classic. The concern often voiced about theory in our time, that all its sophisticated speculations and ruthless questioning leave the canon firmly in place—"An agony of flame that cannot singe a sleeve"—falls away from a woman's poetics. Its flames can scorch and burn, refining some authors and wasting others forever. Not even the most secret places—our language, our habits of reading—can be immune from that fire.

Arimneste is learning to speak; it is our turn to listen. Perhaps she has started now. I know that she has not finished.

Notes and Glosses

INTRODUCTION

xv   *no Penelope*   In *Heroines and Hysterics* (New York: St. Martin's Press, 1981),
Mary R. Lefkowitz cites Penelope as the best example of the way that
ancient poets "seem to have used female experience as a foil to the essentially destructive heroism their works were primarily intended to cele-
brate" (p. 1).

xvi   *Heroine with a Hundred Faces*   This sort of study has been attempted by
Paul Friedrich, *The Meaning of Aphrodite* (Chicago: University of Chicago
Press, 1978).

types of abandoned women   For the extensive taxonomy of abandoned love
worked out by Indian rhetoricians, see Lee Siegel, *Sacred and Profane Dimensions of Love in Indian Traditions as Exemplified in the* Gitagovinda *of Jayadeva* (Delhi: Oxford University Press, 1978), pp. 137–59.

xvii   *seduction and betrayal*   Elizabeth Hardwick, *Seduction and Betrayal: Women
and Literature* (New York: Random House, 1974), conveys an understand-
able impatience with the victimized heroines she examines. In one respect
the present book begins where she ends, with a view of other possibilities:
"When love goes wrong the survival of the spirit appears to stand upon
endurance, independence, tolerance, solitary grief. These are tremendously
moving qualities, and when they are called upon it is usual for the heroine
to overshadow the man who is the origin of her torment" (p. 207).

given up to   As the quotations in the *Oxford English Dictionary* indicate,
both senses of the word were current in Middle English. The restriction of
"abandoned" as given up to, or devoted to, only "things evil or opposed
to reason" is a later development; Gower (1393) could still write positively
of being "abandouned To Cristis feith."

xviii   *La Comtessa de Dia*   Peter Dronke, *Women Writers of the Middle Ages* (Cambridge: Cambridge University Press, 1984), pp. 103–5, stresses the countess's skill at analyzing her passion retrospectively, as in Ovid's *Heroides*.
On the contrast between male and female troubadours, see Meg Bogin,
The Women Troubadours (New York: Norton, 1980), pp. 63–76.

everything she perceives   Christine de Pisan's *Ballades, Rondeaux, and Virelais*,
ed. Kenneth Varty (Leicester: Leicester University Press, 1965), p. 7. As
Varty observes in his introduction, Christine is above all "the poetess of
love's ending and aftermath rather than of its budding and blossoming"
(p. xxvii).

xix   *bitter unending sorrow*   The "Lay de Dame" that concludes the sequence
       is a lament of 283 lines (Christine de Pisan, *Cent ballades d'amant et de
       dame,* ed. Jacqueline Cerquiglini [Paris: Bibliothèque Médiévale, 1982],
       pp. 132–40).

       courtly love   See Charity Cannon Willard, "Christine de Pizan's *Cent bal-
       lades d'amant et de dame:* Criticism of Courtly Love," in *Court and Poet,* ed.
       G. S. Burgess (Liverpool: Francis Cairns, 1981), pp. 357–64. Willard calls
       attention to Christine's analysis of "the psychology of relationships be-
       tween men and women" in "Lovers' Dialogues in Christine de Pizan's Lyric
       Poetry from the *Cent ballades* to the *Cent ballades d'amant et de dame,*" *Fif-
       teenth-Century Studies* 4 (1981): 167–80.

       like a woman   "If there should be men who also felt that desire for com-
       plete abandonment, upon my word, they would not be men" (Nietzsche,
       The Gay Science, no. 363; quoted by Simone de Beauvoir, *The Second Sex,*
       tr. H. M. Parshley [New York: Knopf, 1953], p. 642).

       "manly" resentment   Stephen Greenblatt, *Renaissance Self-Fashioning* (Chi-
       cago: University of Chicago Press, 1980), analyzes the paradoxes of power
       and sex in "They Flee from Me" and argues that Wyatt fashioned manliness
       "as his literary and social identity" (p. 154).

       Alas the while   Wyatt's *Collected Poems,* ed. Joost Daalder (London: Oxford
       University Press, 1975), p. 33.

xx   *according to Plato*   *Symposium,* 201d–212b.

xxi   *entirely mysterious*   The safest conclusion about the "Wife's Lament,"
       found in the Exeter Book, is that its authorship and intention are a "real
       puzzle" (Derek Pearsall, *Old English and Middle English Poetry* [London:
       Routledge & Kegan Paul, 1977], p. 56).

       the rhetoric of Otherness   Modern French thought about women has been
       dominated by the formulation that "he is the Subject, he is the
       Absolute—she is the Other" (Simone de Beauvoir, *The Second Sex,*
       p. xvi). This rhetoric remains in play even when the strategy of the author
       is to show its flaws, as in Jacques Derrida's *Éperons* (1976), tr. Barbara
       Harlow, as *Spurs* (Chicago: University of Chicago Press, 1979).

       men are not   A brilliant example is Hélène Cixous, "The Laugh of the Me-
       dusa," tr. Keith Cohen and Paula Cohen, *Signs* 1 (Summer 1976): 875–93.

xxii   *Tannhäuser*   Mario Praz, *The Romantic Agony,* tr. Angus Davidson (Cleve-
       land: World Publishing, 1956), p. 202.

       Death by Consumption   Robert Graves, *The White Goddess* (London: Faber
       & Faber, 1952), p. 429.

       occurred to anyone   Dorothy Van Ghent, *Keats: The Myth of the Hero,* ed.
       J. C. Robinson (Princeton: Princeton University Press, 1983), pp. 126–30,
       begins her analysis of the poem with a series of questions: "Who is the
       Belle Dame Sans Merci? . . . If she is 'without mercy,' why does she weep
       and 'sigh full sore' at the prospect of sending the knight to the same
       doom?" For answers, however, she looks not to the possible motives of
       the woman but to myths, archetypes, and "a purely subjective libido-
       symbolism."

xxiii *echo her feelings*   Nicolas P. Gross, *Amatory Persuasion in Antiquity* (Newark: University of Delaware Press, 1985), p. 69, offers a rhetorical analysis of abandonment: "in the rhetoric of abandonment a heroine such as Andromache or Dido seeks to restrain her husband or lover from a goal to which he is already committed. Consequently attempts to elicit an emotional response, the proof which Aristotle calls *pathos* (Rh. 1378a19), constitute the tradition's dominant argument."

xxiv *Anna Akhmatova*   Reported by Isaiah Berlin, *Personal Impressions* (New York: Viking, 1981), pp. 195–96: "Who punishes Anna? God? No, society; that same society the hypocrisy of which Tolstoy is never tired of denouncing."

xxv *better look elsewhere*   A good place to start would be Lynda Birke, *Women, Feminism and Biology: The Feminist Challenge* (New York: Methuen, 1986).

   like Britomart   see Lillian S. Robinson, *Monstrous Regiment: The Lady Knight in Sixteenth-Century Epic* (New York: Garland, 1985).

xxvi *Erich Auerbach*   "Figura" (1944), in *Scenes from the Drama of European Literature* (New York: Meridian, 1959), pp. 11–76.

CHAPTER ONE

1 *Peleus and Thetis*   Catullus 64 (*Peliaco quondam*). In a poem of 408 lines, the story of Ariadne occupies lines 52–264.

   takes in the world   In *The Idea of Lyric* (Berkeley: University of California Press, 1982), W. R. Johnson analyzes "the figure of Ariadne" in a set of poems, including Catullus 64, that express a "profound sense of isolation, the speakers' feelings of having cut themselves off from their authentic places in the world" (p. 154).

2 *its lesbian theme*   "I find it difficult to imagine him wishing to assume the love-sickness of Lesbian Sappho. Like his master Ovid, . . . Donne appears wholly uninterested in homosexual love" (Helen Gardner, in Donne, *The Elegies and the Songs and Sonnets* [Oxford: Clarendon Press, 1965], p. xlvi).

   come to light   Each of these cases of suppression or dubious provenance will be discussed in later chapters.

3 *nothing to be done*   Preface to *Poems* (1853), in *The Poems of Matthew Arnold*, ed. Kenneth Allott (London: Longmans, 1965), p. 592.

   passive suffering   W. B. Yeats, ed., *The Oxford Book of Modern Verse 1892–1935* (Oxford: Clarendon Press, 1936), p. xxxiv.

   arias in operas   I have discussed Donna Elvira as "Donna Abbandonata" in *The Don Giovanni Book*, ed. Jonathan Miller (London: Faber & Faber, 1988).

4 *warriors and heroes*   Leo C. Curran, "Catullus 64 and the Heroic Age," *Yale Classical Studies* 21 (1969): 169–92, argues for the fundamental irony of Catullus's attitude toward the warrior hero.

   great matriarchs   June Rachuy Brindel's novel, *Ariadne* (New York: St. Martin's Press, 1980), includes a bibliography of works supporting her representation of Ariadne as "the last Matriarch of Crete."

The Rape of Helen   This late Greek epyllion (ca. A.D. 500) offers a conspectus of ancient sources including Catullus. See the introduction to Pierre Orsini's edition, *L'Enlèvement d'Hélène* (Paris: Société d'Édition "Les Belles Lettres," 1972).

5   *highest poetic quality*   Matthew Arnold, "The Study of Poetry" (1880), *Essays in Criticism,* 2d ser., in Arnold's *Complete Prose Works,* ed. R. H. Super (Ann Arbor: University of Michigan Press, 1973), 9:170.

all that pain   John Milton, *Paradise Lost,* bk. 4, lines 271–72.

psychological novel   Thomas G. Bergin, *Boccaccio* (New York: Viking, 1981), p. 168, quotes versions of this common phrase from the Boccaccio scholars Vittore Branca and Francis MacManus. But Janet L. Smarr, *Boccaccio and Fiammetta: The Narrator as Lover* (Urbana: University of Illinois Press, 1986), p. 132, warns against reading the *Elegia di Madonna Fiammetta* as a novel of psychological analysis.

6   *on the deep sea*   Anonymous, *The Burning Heart: Women Poets of Japan,* tr. Kenneth Rexroth and Ikuko Atsumi (New York: Seabury, 1977), p. 137.

improvising to herself   The resemblances among poets of abandonment from different cultures may be sampled in *A Book of Women Poets from Antiquity to Now,* ed. Aliki Barnstone and Willis Barnstone (New York: Schocken Books, 1980), or *Women Poets of the World,* ed. Joanna Bankier and Deirdre Lashgari (New York: Macmillan, 1983).

many minds   Lady Gregory, "West Irish Ballads" (1901), reprinted in *Poets and Dreamers: Studies and Translations from the Irish* (New York: Oxford University Press, 1974), p. 54.

7   *taken God from me*   *Poets and Dreamers,* pp. 54–55. Lady Gregory reprinted this ballad, which she said was known both in the south and in Aran, on many occasions; for instance it is the first poem in *The Kiltartan Poetry Book* (1918).

8   *are laid*   Lady Gregory, *Poets and Dreamers,* p. 54.

keeps them down   Recent work on "Women in History" has been surveyed by Olwen Hufton (early modern Europe) and Joan W. Scott (the modern period) in *Past & Present* 101 (Nov. 1983): 125–57.

10   *Precisely for that reason*   *Tsvetaeva: A Pictorial Biography,* ed. Ellendea Proffer (Ann Arbor: Ardis, 1980), p. 77: "I named her out of romanticism and haughtiness, which rule my entire life. 'Ariadna! That is something to live up to!' 'Precisely for that reason.'"

in naked Bed   The quotations and information come from Isobel Grundy, "Ovid and Eighteenth-Century Divorce: An Unpublished Poem by Lady Mary Wortley Montagu," *Review of English Studies* (*RES*) 23 (1972): 423. Grundy was the first to publish this poem (pp. 424–26), which is also included in her edition, with Robert Halsband, of Montagu's *Essays and Poems and Simplicity, a Comedy* (Oxford: Clarendon Press, 1977), pp. 230–32.

m'Accuser, and Excuse   Montagu, "Epistle from Mrs. Y——," lines 59–62, in *RES* 23:425.

11   *may complain*   Ibid., lines 7–8.

loves what vanishes W. B. Yeats, "Nineteen Hundred and Nineteen."

history of Ireland J. C. Beckett, *The Making of Modern Ireland 1603–1923* (London: Faber & Faber, 1966), includes a good selective bibliography.

past the censor On Verdi's struggles against censorship, see D. R. B. Kimbell, *Verdi in the Age of Italian Romanticism* (Cambridge: Cambridge University Press, 1981).

petitions for advancement See the discussion of Ts'ao Chih, chapter 5, section 2, below.

12 *to a queen* *The World of Gwendolyn Brooks* (New York: Harper & Row, 1971), p. 43. "Queen of the Blues," which appeared in *A Street in Bronzeville* (1945), might be considered an ambiguous tribute to Langston Hughes's *Weary Blues.*

knew how to hear See the introduction to Michael G. Cooke, *Afro-American Literature in the Twentieth Century* (New Haven: Yale University Press, 1984), especially pp. 24–25,

to be himself "As a form, the blues is an autobiographical chronicle of personal catastrophe expressed lyrically" (Ralph Ellison, "Richard Wright's Blues" [1945], in *Shadow and Act* [New York: Random House, 1964], pp. 78–79).

13 *political implications* A standard account of "women's blues" in their context is Giles Oakley, *The Devil's Music: A History of the Blues* (New York: Taplinger Publishing, 1977), pp. 97–121.

He neglects to come E. M. Forster, *A Passage to India* (London: Edward Arnold, 1978), p. 72.

the Western view As G. K. Das points out in *E. M. Forster's India* (London: Macmillan, 1977), pp. 93–112, Forster was uneasy with Hindu rituals of worship, despite his deep sympathy with the figure of Krishna.

14 *her wasp* *A Passage to India,* pp. 274–81.

some human lover T. W. Higginson had trepidations about printing the poem: "One poem only I dread a little to print—that wonderful 'Wild Nights,'—lest the malignant read into it more than that virgin recluse ever dreamed of putting there" (*The Poems of Emily Dickinson,* ed. Thomas H. Johnson [Cambridge: Harvard University Press, 1955], 1:180).

numb to the world This rendering is based not on the (Rajasthani) original but on a collation of the following: A. J. Alston, *The Devotional Poems of Mīrābāī* (Delhi: Motilal Banarsidass, 1980), p. 70; Shreeprakash Kurl, *The Devotional Poems of Mirabai* (Calcutta: Writers Workshop, 1973), p. 56; Pritish Nandy, *The Songs of Mirabai* (New Delhi: Arnold-Heinemann, 1975), p. 53; and Usha S. Nilsson, *Mira Bai* (New Delhi: Sahitya Akademi, 1969), p. 57.

15 *biographical tradition* Ronald Stuart McGregor, *Hindi Literature from Its Beginnings to the Nineteenth Century* (Wiesbaden: Otto Harrassowitz, 1984), pp. 80–83, carefully summarizes the known facts. Much of the biographical tradition is challenged by Hermann Goetz, *Mira Bai: Her Life and Times* (Bombay: Bhavan, 1966).

Mira the mystic See T. L. Vaswani, *Saint Mira* (Poona: St. Mira's English Medium School, n.d.), and Baldoon Dhingra, *Songs of Meera: Lyrics in Ecstasy* (New Delhi: Orient Paperbacks, 1977).

women perceive Him differently John Stratton Hawley compares Mira Bai's vision of Krishna to the male poetic tradition, "Images of Gender in the Poetry of Krishna," in *Gender and Religion: On the Complexity of Symbols,* ed. C. W. Bynum, Stevan Harrell, and Paula Richman (Boston: Beacon Press, 1986), pp. 231–56.

earlier Jewish readings Marvin H. Pope summarizes the tradition of inter- pretations in his edition of the *Song of Songs* (Garden City, N.Y.: Double- day, 1977), pp. 89–112.

Sanskrit Song of Songs Pope compares the Hebrew and Sanskrit poems in *Song of Songs,* pp. 85–89.

love-in-separation Lee Siegel, *Sacred and Profane Dimensions of Love in Indian Traditions* (Delhi: Oxford University Press, 1977), pp. 137–59.

martyrdom Ibid., p. 146.

16   *Sumerian goddess Inanna* The "infinite variety" of the goddess is stressed by Thorkild Jacobsen, *The Treasures of Darkness* (New Haven: Yale Univer- sity Press, 1976), pp. 135–43.

hostility toward Ishtar Jeffrey H. Tigay, *The Evolution of the Gilgamesh Epic* (Philadelphia: University of Pennsylvania Press, 1982), pp. 68–71, specu- lates on some reasons for this antipathy.

great lady of ladies Line 60 in *The Exaltation of Inanna,* William W. Hallo and J. J. A. van Dijk (New Haven: Yale University Press, 1968), p. 22. I am indebted to this fine edition for both text and commentary, though I have varied at times from its translations.

Ishtar's love Ibid., pp. 6–7, 54–59.

17   *"these become you," he said* *Exaltation of Inanna,* line 108. My version fol- lows the suggestion of Hallo and van Dijk, p. 59, that Enheduanna has been invited to use the dagger and sword on herself. But S. N. Kramer, in his translation of the same work, "Hymnal Prayer of Enheduanna: The Adoration of Inanna in Ur," in *The Ancient Near East: Supplementary Texts and Pictures Relating to the Old Testament,* ed. J. B. Pritchard (Princeton: Princeton University Press, 1969), p. 145, associates the dagger and sword instead with the dervishes who use them: "*Eunuchs* were assigned to me—'These are becoming to you,' it was told me."

her array *Exaltation of Inanna,* lines 146–47.

one scholar notes Hallo, *Exaltation of Inanna,* p. 62.

brother and helper See *Inanna: Queen of Heaven and Earth,* by Diane Wolk- stein and S. N. Kramer (New York: Harper & Row, 1983), pp. 4–9, 143–46.

a woman's joy S. N. Kramer presents Inanna as "A Divine Model of the Liberated Woman," in *From the Poetry of Sumer* (Berkeley: University of California Press, 1979), pp. 71–97.

divine exaltation Hallo, *Exaltation of Inanna,* pp. 64–68.

18   *oneiromancy*   See ibid., pp. 59–60.

hapless Aegeus   Catullus 64, lines 188–248.

I eat men like air   Sylvia Plath, "Lady Lazarus," lines 79–84. On "the hypnotic, seductive, almost glamorous, almost magic energy that shimmers about women's best violence poems," see Alicia S. Ostriker, *Stealing the Language* (Boston: Beacon Press, 1986), pp. 149–63.

19   *we need of hell*   Emily Dickinson, "Parting" ("My life closed twice before its close"), Johnson no. 1732, in *Poems of Emily Dickinson*.

being left alone   John Bowlby's trilogy, *Attachment and Loss* (New York: Basic Books, 1969), is a standard account of the psychology of abandonment.

structural anthropologists   The influential accounts of Oedipus by Claude Lévi-Strauss have been translated in *Structural Anthropology* (New York: Basic Books, 1963), 1:213–18, and (1976), 2:21–24.

scapegoat or victim   René Girard, *Violence and the Sacred*, tr. Patrick Gregory (Baltimore: Johns Hopkins University Press, 1977), pp. 68–88. Girard opposes his reading of Sophocles' Oedipus to the "Freudian myth" of an Oedipus complex in a later chapter, pp. 169–92. He has returned to the Oedipus myth in *The Scapegoat*, tr. Yvonne Freccero (Baltimore: Johns Hopkins University Press, 1986), pp. 24–44.

20   *Women as well as men*   In *The Enigma of Woman: Woman in Freud's Writings*, tr. Catherine Porter (Ithaca, N.Y.: Cornell University Press, 1985), Sarah Kofman deconstructs both Freud's and Girard's readings of Oedipus and perceives woman or the mother as the answer to the Oedipal riddle.

social protest   Matilda Albert Robatto, *Rosalía de Castro y la condición femenina* (Madrid: Ediciones Partenon, 1981), p. 29.

archetypal Galician   Kathleen Kulp-Hill's useful introduction, *Rosalía de Castro* (Boston: Twayne, 1977), includes a description of Galicia, pp. 19–25.

an early feminist   See Robatto, *Rosalía de Castro*, pp. 29–48 et seq.

21   *loved and absent*   John Frederick Nims, in *The Poem Itself*, ed. Stanley Burnshaw (New York: Schocken Books, 1967), p. 164.

m'asombras   Rosalía de Castro, *Obras completas*, ed. V. García Martí (Madrid: Aguilar, 1966), p. 436.

beyond translation   Other translations and commentaries appear in Kulp-Hill, *Rosalía de Castro*, pp. 65–66; John Frederick Nims, *The Poem Itself*, pp. 164–65; and Nims's *Sappho to Valéry: Poems in Translation* (New Brunswick, N.J.: Rutgers University Press, 1971), p. 183.

22   *two possibilities*   Ricardo Carballo Calero analyzes the doubleness of the shadow in *Historia de la literatura gallega contemporanea* (Madrid: Editora Nacional, 1975), pp. 213–14.

also her fate   See Marina Mayoral, *La poesía de Rosalía de Castro* (Madrid: Editorial Gredos, 1974), pp. 88–108.

surrender to dejection   One standard study, by V. García Martí, is titled *Rosalía de Castro o el dolor de vivir* (Madrid: Ediciones Aspas, n.d.).

23   *mentioning the new*   "Am letzten Tage des Jahres (Silvester)" (1839); the text is printed and analyzed by Margaret Mare, *Annette von Droste-Hülshoff*

(London: Methuen, 1965), pp. 155–62. It should be noted that in a later poem, "Neujahrsnacht" (1842), the poet does look forward to the future. Cf. Coleridge's "Ode to the Departing Year" (1796).

the empty world again   Emily Brontë, "Remembrance" (1845). The original title of this poem, "R. Alcona to J. Brenzaida," attributes it to the heroine of the Gondal cycle.

acknowledging her feelings   In *The Last Courtly Lover: Yeats and the Idea of Woman* (Ann Arbor: UMI Research Press, 1983), pp. 130–34, Gloria C. Kline puts Yeats's struggle with Crazy Jane into a Jungian context.

24   *a fading vision*   "The mind in creation is as a fading coal. . . . when composition begins, inspiration is already on the decline, and the most glorious poetry that has ever been communicated to the world is probably a feeble shadow of the original conceptions of the poet" (Shelley's "Defence of Poetry," in *Shelley's Prose,* ed. D. L. Clark [Albuquerque: University of New Mexico Press, 1954], p. 294).

Falls the Shadow   T. S. Eliot, *The Hollow Men,* lines 78–82.

system of differences   Influential statements of a deconstructive view of language include Jacques Derrida's *Of Grammatology,* tr. G. C. Spivak (Baltimore: Johns Hopkins University Press, 1976), and "Différance," in *Margins of Philosophy,* tr. Alan Bass (Chicago: University of Chicago Press, 1982), pp. 1–27. It should be obvious, however, that the formulation in the text is my own and not to be attributed to any particular theorist.

25   *his own perspicacity*   Samuel Johnson, *Rasselas,* ch. 2.

like a deconstructionist critic   For examples of efforts to conflate deconstruction and feminism, see *New French Feminisms,* ed. Elaine Marks and Isabelle de Courtivron (Amherst: University of Massachusetts Press, 1980), and Jonathan Culler, *On Deconstruction* (Ithaca, N.Y.: Cornell University Press, 1982), pp. 43–64, 165–79.

I too dislike it   Marianne Moore, "Poetry." On Moore's struggle at "defining the genuine," see Bonnie Costello, *Marianne Moore: Imaginary Possessions* (Cambridge: Harvard University Press, 1981), pp. 15–37.

a portrait of the poetess   Sor Juana Inés de la Cruz, *Obras completas,* ed. Alfonso Méndez Plancarte (México: Fondo de Cultura Económica, 1951), 1:277. Octavia Paz comments on the poem in his magisterial *Sor Juana Inés de la Cruz o las trampas de la fe* (Barcelona: Seix Barral, 1982), pp. 392–93.

26   *shadow and nothingness*   "Es cadáver, es polvo, es sombra, es nada" (Sor Juana Inés de la Cruz, tr. Samuel Beckett, *Anthology of Mexican Poetry,* ed. Octavio Paz [Bloomington: Indiana University Press, 1958], p. 85).

truth with illusion   The once popular legend that attributed Sor Juana's renunciation of the world to abandonment by a lover has been replaced, in recent criticism, by attention to her strategies, as a woman writer within the church, against censorship and repression.

bronze and stone   Stephen Owen writes movingly about Li Ch'ing-chao's "snares of memory," her resentment at the burden of preserving the past, in *Remembrances* (Cambridge: Harvard University Press, 1986), pp. 80–98.

its intricacies   Hu Pin-ching, *Li Ch'ing-chao* (New York: Twayne, 1966), pp. 74–77. Though unsophisticated, this book remains the fullest study in English.

subtones, moods, and stresses   See Hu Pin-ching, *Li Ch'ing-chao,* pp. 17–26, and James J. Y. Liu, "Some Literary Qualities of the Lyric (*Tz'u*)," in *Studies in Chinese Literary Genres,* ed. Cyril Birch (Berkeley: University of California Press, 1974), pp. 133–53.

quite conventional   According to a later Sung dynasty writer, Wang Shuo, however, the poet was very daring in her use of colloquialisms: "Since time immemorial among the lettered women of cultured families there had never been one so completely defiant of convention as Li Ch'ing-chao." Quoted by Kai-yu Hsu, "The Poems of Li Ch'ing-chao (1084–1141)," *PMLA* 77 (1962): 525.

27   *with "sorrow"*   The problems of translating this famously untranslatable poem may be indicated by the second line, "Leng-leng ch'ing-ch'ing," in which the individual syllables, "Cold-cold clear-clear" (or "quiet-quiet") together form the compound word "lonely." Cf. Hu Pin-ching, *Li Ch'ing-chao,* pp. 37–38, and *Li Ch'ing-chao: Complete Poems,* tr. Kenneth Rexroth and Ling Chung (New York: New Directions, 1979), p. 31. The Chinese original faces an English version in *A Collection of Chinese Lyrics,* tr. Duncan Mackintosh, versified by Alan Ayling (London: Routledge & Kegan Paul, 1965), pp. 146–47.

clenched teeth   James J. Y. Liu, *Major Lyricists of the Northern Sung* (Princeton: Princeton University Press, 1974), p. 198.

28   *what can be expressed*   James J. Y. Liu notes that Chinese critics anticipated the modern Western preoccupation with "the paradoxical nature of language as the necessary but inadequate means of expressing the ineffable" (*Chinese Theories of Literature* [Chicago: University of Chicago Press, 1975], p. 55).

29   *many ingenious explanations*   Richard Jenkyns, *Three Classical Poets* (London: Duckworth, 1982), pp. 85–150, provides a thorough review of scholarship on Catullus 64 as well as a searching analysis of the work's self-presentation as a "masterpiece."

the story of Peleus and Thetis   An influential defense of the art of Catullus 64 was supplied by Friedrich Klingner, "Catulls Peleus-Epos," *Studien zur griechischen und römischen Literatur* (Zurich: Artemis, 1964), pp. 156–224.

biographical speculation   M. C. J. Putnam, "The Art of Catullus 64" (1961), reprinted by Kenneth Quinn, *Approaches to Catullus* (Cambridge: Heffer, 1972), pp. 225–65.

unintentional   It has been plausibly argued that Theseus's "amnesia" is deliberately induced by Dionysus, who has his own designs on Ariadne (Giuseppe Giangrande, "Das Epyllion Catulls im Lichte der hellenistischen Epik," *L'Antiquité Classique* 41 [1972]: 127).

30   *we who are abandoned*   See D. P. Harmon, "Nostalgia for the Age of Heroes in Catullus 64," *Latomus* 32 (1973): 311–31.

Attic kraters   See T. B. L. Webster, "The Myth of Ariadne from Homer to Catullus," *Greece & Rome* 13 (1966): 22–31.

Iacchus   According to Jane Harrison, *Prolegomena to the Study of Greek Religion* (Cleveland: World Publishing, 1959; first published 1903), pp. 540–44, "Iacchos" is the title or exclamation of Dionysos when he presides over the mysteries at Eleusis.

onomatopoeic verse   "Multis raucisonos efflabant cornua bombos/barbaraque horribili stridebat tibia cantu" (Catullus 64, lines 263–64). As Jenkyns demonstrates in *Three Classical Poets,* pp. 130–32, the passage seems indebted to Lucretius.

31   *savage voice*   According to David Konstan, *Catullus' Indictment of Rome: The Meaning of Catullus 64* (Amsterdam: Adolf Hakkert, 1977), p. 62, the arrival of Dionysus signifies that "Ariadne's love has turned to madness."

      worshipped together   The classic account of the union of Ariadne and Dionysus is C. Kerényi, *Dionysos: Archetypal Image of Indestructible Life,* tr. Ralph Manheim (Princeton: Princeton University Press, 1976), pp. 89–125.

CHAPTER TWO

32   *her letter*   *Don Juan,* canto 1, lines 1526–28, in Byron's *Complete Poetical Works,* ed. Jerome J. McGann (Oxford: Clarendon Press, 1986), 5:70. All further quotations from *Don Juan* are from this edition.

33   *vermilion*   *Don Juan* 1:1529–84.

34   *degrading sensuality*   Francis Jeffrey, *Edinburgh Review,* Feb. 1822, in *Byron: The Critical Heritage,* ed. Andrew Rutherford (London: Routledge & Kegan Paul, 1970), p. 203.

      go to school there   *The Letters of Percy Bysshe Shelley,* ed. Frederick L. Jones (Oxford: Clarendon Press, 1964), 2:567.

      If you search for passion   "Some Observations upon an Article in Blackwood's Magazine" (1820), in *The Works of Lord Byron,* ed. Thomas Moore (London: John Murray, 1833), 15:88. Pope's "Eloisa to Abelard" is discussed in chapter 5 below.

35   *in this production*   "Observations upon 'Observations'" (1821), ibid., 6:402.

      productions of human wit   Samuel Johnson, "Life of Pope," in *Lives of the English Poets,* ed. G. B. Hill (Oxford: Clarendon Press, 1905), 3:235.

      primarily on Ovid   See D. W. Robertson, *Abelard and Heloise* (New York: Dial Press, 1972), pp. 125–35, and Peter Dronke, *Women Writers of the Middle Ages* (Cambridge: Cambridge University Press, 1984), pp. 107–8. Though Robertson and Dronke differ sharply on the authorship of the letters, they agree on placing them in the Ovidian tradition.

      Renaissance best-sellers   George Turberville's translation of *The Heroycall Epistles* appeared in 1567, the same year as the first published book of poems by an Englishwoman, Isabella Whitney's interesting and neglected *Copy of a Letter by a Yonge Gentilwoman to Her Unconstant Lover.* See Richard Panofsky, "Love Poetry of Isabella Whitney, a Woman Author of the

English Renaissance," *New Mexico Highlands University Journal* 6 (April 1983): 1–8.

new lease on life   On the evolution of the "Ovidian wooing-story," see Robert Adams Day, *Told in Letters: Epistolary Fiction before Richardson* (Ann Arbor: University of Michigan Press, 1966), pp. 10–26.

36   *modern forsaken woman*   McGann suggests Jane Austen's *Persuasion* (vol. 2, ch. 13) as a source for Julia's letter (Byron, *Complete Poetical Works* 5:680).

create them   *Madame de Staël on Politics, Literature, and National Character*, tr. Morroe Berger (Garden City, N.Y.: Doubleday, 1964), p. 265. Throughout this chapter quotations of Madame de Staël are from this volume.

episode in that of men   Noted by Willis W. Pratt, *Byron's Don Juan* (Austin: University of Texas Press, 1957), 4:45. Watts's citation from *Corinne* is given in the same place.

perhaps, of any age   Byron's note to line 179 of *The Bride of Abydos* (1813), in *Complete Poetical Works* 3:436. Byron published a tribute to Madame de Staël after her death, as a note to canto 4, line 478 of *Childe Harold's Pilgrimage* (*Complete Poetical Works* 2:235–36).

sometimes listened   F. S. Frank, "The Demon and the Thunderstorm: Byron and Madame de Staël," *Revue de littérature compareé* 43 (1969): 320–43, and Ernest Giddey, "Byron and Madame de Staël," in *Lord Byron and His Contemporaries*, ed. C. E. Robinson (Newark: University of Delaware Press, 1982), pp. 166–77, both chart the ups and downs of this acquaintance.

37   *Byron owed something*   *Literary Women* (Garden City, N.Y.: Doubleday, 1976), p. 176.

performing heroinism   Moer's phrase. In an appendix to *The Style of "Don Juan"* (New Haven: Yale University Press, 1960), pp. 162–66, George M. Ridenour observes the possible influence of Corinne's "improvisation" on the mobile narrator of *Don Juan*.

male desire and fear   In "Narcissus Jilted: Byron, *Don Juan*, and the Biographical Imperative," in *Historical Studies and Literary Criticism*, ed. Jerome J. McGann (Madison: University of Wisconsin Press, 1985), pp. 143–79, Cecil Y. Lang argues that Juan's possession by Catherine the Great is a thinly veiled version of Byron's experience with Ali Pacha.

a yielding slave   *The Spirit of the Age* (1825), in *The Complete Works of William Hazlitt*, ed. P. P. Howe (London: J. M. Dent, 1932), 11:71.

pride were unavailing   *Lady Blessington's Conversations of Lord Byron*, ed. Ernest J. Lovell (Princeton: Princeton University Press, 1969), p. 26.

38   *emotional life of men*   Madame de Staël, p. 158.

powerful passions   Ibid., p. 143.

style of some writers   Ibid., p. 184.

influence can be recognized   Ibid., p. 144.

secrets of virtue   Ibid., p. 143.

protect Rousseau   To John Murray, 6 July 1821, in *Byron's Letters and Journals*, ed. Leslie A. Marchand (London: John Murray, 1978), 8:148. Cf. the letter to Murray of 25 Oct. 1822 (10:68).

39   *consented*   *Don Juan* 1:936.

      penned   *Don Juan* 1:524.

      Everything eloquent is true   *Madame de Staël,* p. 253.

40   *disappointed hope*   "Essay on Fiction" (1795), in *Madame de Staël,* p. 265.

41   *Song to David*   It is not certain that Byron knew Smart's poem. A common
      source is Lucretius, *De rerum natura* 2:1–13.

      his fall   *Don Juan* 1:1006–11.

      nothing further   *Don Juan* 1:1012–13. The suggestion of exhausted carnal
      knowledge and schoolboy betrayal might be taken to imply a homosexual
      first love. The evidence is thoroughly reviewed by Louis Crompton, *Byron
      and Greek Love* (Berkeley: University of California Press, 1985), pp. 63–106.

42   *any thing but angelic*   Medwin's *Conversations of Lord Byron,* ed. Ernest J.
      Lovell (Princeton: Princeton University Press, 1966), p. 61.

      that lame boy   Leslie A. Marchand, *Byron: A Biography* (New York: Knopf,
      1957), 1:78.

      till I was in love   Medwin, *Conversations of Lord Byron,* p. 60.

      confounded book of yours   9 June 1820, in *Byron's Letters and Journals* 7:117.

      and gaze, and sigh   "To Mrs. M——," *Poetical Works of Thomas Little Esq.,*
      in *The Works of Thomas Moore* (Leipzig: Ernest Fleischer, 1833), p. 381.

      so fond a lover   "To Julia," Moore's *Works,* p. 380. Ten of the poems are
      addressed to Julia, and she is "supposed" to be the author of some "Elegiac
      Stanzas."

43   *shall beat*   Byron, "To My Dear Mary Anne" (1804), in *Complete Poetical
      Works* 1:2. Byron wrote these verses at sixteen, when parting from Mary
      Chaworth.

      my boyish flame   Byron, "Well! Thou art happy," in *Complete Poetical Works*
      1:222. On the circumstances see Marchand's *Byron* 1:159–60.

      he loves but one   Byron, "Stanzas to [Mrs. Musters] on Leaving England,"
      in *Complete Poetical Works* 1:268.

      alarmed the poet   Marchand's *Byron* 1:430ff.

44   *a kind of quiet*   Byron, *Complete Poetical Works* 4:25.

      his revenge   In a crucial early scene of *Felix Holt, the Radical* (1866), vol. 1,
      ch. 5, George Eliot uses Byron's poem as an example of feeble wish-
      fulfillment. When Felix discovers Esther reading "The Dream," he rebukes
      her self-indulgent taste: "'The Dream'—he'd better have been asleep and
      snoring." The heroine's reformation, her call to a more serious life, begins
      at that moment.

      reversal of sexes   Byron's adeptness at such reversals is manifested by the
      ambiguous "Thyrza" poems in memory of John Edlestone, who had given
      him a cornelian. See Crompton, *Byron and Greek Love,* pp. 175–95.

45   *Former world and Future*   28 Jan. 1821, in *Byron's Letters and Journals* 8:37.

46   *best prescription*   Byron, *Complete Poetical Works* 5:680.

      to God from Man   This is the version given by T. G. Steffan and W. W.

Pratt in *Byron's Don Juan* (Austin: University of Texas Press, 1957), 1:131.

his own affairs   Doris Langley Moore analyzes Byron's sexual ambivalence in *Lord Byron Accounts Rendered* (London: John Murray, 1974), pp. 437–59.

47   *suit partout*   T. G. Steffan, *Byron's Don Juan,* vol. 1, *The Making of a Masterpiece* (Austin: University of Texas Press, 1957), p. 280.

one is not taken in   Ridenour, *The Style of "Don Juan,"* p. 79.

her finest hour   Cf. Leslie A. Marchand, *Byron's Poetry* (Cambridge: Harvard University Press, 1968), p. 173: "Her farewell letter, sentimental and ridiculous . . . is yet sincere and true."

visualizing sentiment   See Margaret Anne Doody, *A Natural Passion: A Study of the Novels of Samuel Richardson* (Oxford: Clarendon Press, 1974), pp. 216–40. The epistolary fiction of the eighteenth century often invites readers to picture letters as material objects; cf. Pope's "Eloisa to Abelard."

48   *derides our feelings*   According to Jerome J. McGann, *"Don Juan" in Context* (Chicago: University of Chicago Press, 1976), p. 125, "Julia is the first of a series of normative Romantic figures in *Don Juan* who stand as the symbols of Byron's quest to expose the reality of things existent."

with reaching   *Don Juan* 2:159–60. The final word is of course to be understood, as it is often printed, with a *t* in place of *a*.

49   *wolfish eyes*   Ibid., 2:575–76.

Julia's letter   Ibid., 2:590–92.

permanent reality   Jeffrey, *Byron: The Critical Heritage*, p. 203.

worthy of your genius   *Letters of Shelley* 2:567.

more suspicion   *Don Juan* 14:187–90.

50   *ridicule sentiment*   *Lady Blessington's Conversations of Lord Byron*, pp. 213–14.

always so to women   *Don Juan* 2:1585–94.

51   *his relations with women*   Jenni Calder offers a balanced view of "The Hero as Lover: Byron and Women," in *Byron: Wrath and Rhyme,* ed. Alan Bold (London: Vision Press, 1983), pp. 103–24.

sighs of adolescence   *Conversations of Lord Byron,* p. 196.

in common with Onegin   Quoted by Vladimir Nabokov in the introduction to his translation of *Eugene Onegin* (Princeton: Princeton University Press, 1975), 1:68, 72.

52   *related by antithesis*   See Sona S. Hoisington, *"Eugene Onegin:* An Inverted Byronic Poem," *Comparative Literature* 27 (1975): 136–52.

Tatiana or Julia   Nabokov's *Eugene Onegin* 1:72.

incorporate and surpass   Pushkin implicitly states his own ambition when he notes the immense superiority of Shakespeare to "this Byron who never conceived but one sole character (women do not have any character; they have passions in their youth; and this is why it is so easy to paint them), this Byron, then, has parceled out among his characters such-and-such a trait of his own character; his pride to one, his hate to another, his melancholy to a third, etc., and thus out of one complete, gloomy, and energetic character he has made several insignificant characters—there is no tragedy in that" (*The Letters of Alexander Pushkin,* tr. J. Thomas Shaw [Blooming-ton: Indiana University Press, and Philadelphia: University of Pennsylva-nia Press, 1963], 1:237).

preps for the role   Vladimir Nabokov provides thorough, opinionated notes on Tatiana's reading in his translation of *Eugene Onegin,* 2:338–59. My own translations are indebted to Nabokov, however little he would have approved them.

leading man   *Eugene Onegin,* Ch. 3, stanza 10.

your fate   *Eugene Onegin* 3:15.

June 1821   See Nabokov, *Eugene Onegin* 3:94–95. Pushkin and Onegin would have read the first two cantos of *Don Juan* in French, the Chastopalli translation (1820).

a parody   *Eugene Onegin* 7:24.

53   *End of novel*   "'Evgenii Onegin' (Pushkin i Stern)," in *Ocherki po poetike Pushkina* (Berlin: Epokha, 1923), p. 209. Shklovsky stresses the banality of the plot; my own formulation draws on John Bayley, *Pushkin* (Cambridge: Cambridge University Press, 1971), p. 265, and Bayley's introduction to Charles Johnston's translation of *Eugene Onegin* (London: Penguin Books, 1979), p. 15.

Nabokov notes   *Eugene Onegin* 2:399.

a young maiden's letters   *Eugene Onegin* 8:36.

54   *"affair" between the "lovers"*   J. Douglas Clayton, *Ice and Flame: Aleksandr Pushkin's* Eugene Onegin (Toronto: University of Toronto Press, 1985), associates Tatiana with the Princesse de Clèves in her chaste refusal to con-summate her love (pp. 128–31).

went to school to Pushkin   See Richard Freeborn, *The Rise of the Russian Novel* (Cambridge: Cambridge University Press, 1973), pp. 36–37.

Slavic madonna   Turgenev's and Dostoevsky's famous speeches at the dedi-cation of a monument to Pushkin (Moscow, 1880) have been translated by D. J. Richards and C. R. S. Cockrell, *Russian Views of Pushkin* (Oxford: Willem A. Meeuws, 1976), pp. 63–88.

the critical debate   The first chapter of Clayton's *Ice and Flame* provides a useful survey of criticism of *Onegin.*

55   *A lesson of loneliness*   Marina Tsvetaeva, *A Captive Spirit: Selected Prose,* tr. J. Marin King (Ann Arbor: Ardis, 1980), pp. 336–37.

not otherwise   Ibid., p. 338.

CHAPTER THREE

57   *dort an den Wolken*   Grillparzer's *Sappho* (1818), act 3, scene ii, lines 941–46, in *Sämtliche Werke* (Munich: Carl Hanser, 1960), 1:749.

the Tenth Muse   *Greek Anthology* 9:506.

inimitable grace   J. A. Symonds, *Studies of the Greek Poets* (London: Smith, Elder, 1873), 1:129–30.

Antipater of Sidon   *Greek Anthology* 7:15.

although she was a woman   *Rhetoric* 2.23.11. Aristotle is quoting Alcidamas to illustrate the argument from induction: "men of talent are honored everywhere," whatever their liabilities.

mascula   Horace, *Epistles* 1.19.28.

58   *Edith Mora*   *Sappho: Histoire d'un poète* (Paris: Flammarion, 1966). Useful surveys of scholarship include Helmut Saake, *Sapphostudien* (Munich: Ferdinand Schöningh, 1972), and J. F. Duban, *Ancient and Modern Images of Sappho* (Lanham, Md.: University Press of America, 1983). The most recent biography is Grytzko Mascioni, *Saffo* (Milan: Rusconi, 1981).

Sappho's reputation   The standard accounts are D. M. Robinson, *Sappho and Her Influence* (Boston: Marshall Jones, 1924), and Horst Rüdiger, *Sappho: Ihr Ruf und Ruhm bei der Nachwelt* (Leipzig: Dieterich, 1933).

Lobel-Page edition   *Poetarum lesbiorum fragmenta,* ed. E. Lobel and D. L. Page (Oxford: Clarendon Press, 1955).

59   *seem to myself*   No translation can do justice to more than a fraction of Sappho's ode, and no reader ought to mistake my version for the Greek poem itself. Since so much of the following discussion depends on noticing how various poets have adapted or distorted the text, however, it may be useful to consider some of the reasons for the impossibility of translating Sappho adequately. First, there is the condition of the text, which survives only in the version quoted by "Longinus" (at least six centuries after the poem was written). Editorial reconstruction is necessary to make some lines intelligible; for instance, what happens to the tongue in line 9 is far from certain, and the status of line 17 (discussed at the end of chapter 4 below) has led to endless, unresolved debate. Moreover, problems of textual transmission contribute to a second order of difficulty: establishing the context. Who are the speaker, the man, the "you"? What is the situation? Is the poem complete? In the absence of definite information, informed speculation must supply the answers. Hence the translator must decide the antecedent of "this" or "that" (*to*) in line 5—what is it that frightens the heart? Not even the most "literal" version can avoid such choices. Sappho's diction also presents special problems. Her Aeolic dialect can be obscure even to those who are fluent in classical Greek.

Even the translator who is quite sure what the words of the poem mean, however, will still find it impossible to render their poetic effect in another language. Greek meter is quantitative and no pattern of stresses can reproduce it; only a handful of English-speaking poets (chiefly Swinburne) have been able to approximate the rhythms of "sapphics," let alone their subtle variations. Richmond Lattimore's gallant attempt to preserve the sapphic stanzas of L.P. 31 (*Greek Lyrics* [Chicago: University of Chicago Press, 1960], pp. 39–40) illustrates another problem: the long Greek lines (three of eleven syllables each, one of five), well suited to the frequent polysyllables in Greek, require extraneous English words to fill out the meter. "Like the very gods in my sight is he who / sits where he can look in your eyes, who listens. . . ." Dead matter such as "very" (not in the Greek) slackens Sappho's pace. Nor is the word order of Greek—"appears to me that person equal to gods"—remotely translatable. As a consequence, English translators regularly adopt sequences of ideas and images quite foreign to the original. For instance, it is almost irresistible for an English speaker to climax the fourth stanza with "close to death" or "little short of dying" in the final line, while in Sappho the dying occurs in the previous line and the conclusion is reserved for "seeming" (an important distinction for those who point out that lines 1 and 16 begin with variations on the same word, *phainetai* or *phainom'*, "appears"). Such changes in word order inevitably warp the structure of the ode.

At the same time the translator must struggle—usually in vain—to keep the language fresh. Sappho's account of her symptoms has been repeated so often in poetry that most of the words that express them now seem trite. There is no good English word, for instance, to describe the location of the heart (line 6): "breast" and "bosom" are tired poeticisms, and "chest" is prosaic. Nor do such words as "roar" or "buzz" or "rumble" or "throb" or "drum" begin to convey the effect of the polysyllabic, onomatopoeic *epirrombeisi* (lines 11–12). No modern vocabulary registers the precise sensations of the Greek. But translators face a still greater hazard: capturing the *sound* of the ode. It is easier to acknowledge the beauty of Sappho's verse than to find equivalents in other languages. One example must suffice. The breathtaking acceleration of the ode after its first stanza pivots on the technique of polysyndeton (many conjunctions in close succession). In the Greek the effect is enhanced by the contrast between polysyllabic clauses and the brief (sometimes elided) words that connect them. In English this effect could be duplicated only by inflating words like "ears" and "eyes" into "soundboxes" and "opticals," or by ponderous circumlocutions. The translator has no choice but to substitute some other music for Sappho's.

Is translation hopeless, then? Only if we expect it to be the one right way. Of the more than one hundred versions of Sappho's ode that I have studied, many are fine poems, and almost every one clarifies some aspect of the Greek text. There is no one right way to read and interpret Sappho, let alone to translate her. But the inadequacy of any particular version (including of course my own) can be partly compensated by looking at many, to determine not only what has been lost by each but what has been saved.

60 *what the poem means*   The difficulty of interpretation is the starting point for fine readings by Garry Wills, "Sappho 31 and Catullus 51," *Greek, Roman, and Byzantine Studies* 8 (1967): 167–97, and G. Aurelio Privitera, "Ambiguità antitesi analogia nel fr. 31 L. P. di Saffo," *Quaderni Urbinati di Cultura Classica* 8 (1969): 37–80.

Plutarch   "Life of Demetrius" 38:2–5. The physician Erasistratus diagnoses love by watching Antiochus register each of Sappho's "telltale signs."

Lucretius   *De rerum natura* 3:152–58. For Lucretius such symptoms of terror prove the influence of the mind over the spirit and body.

the correct choice   Denys Page, *Sappho and Alcaeus* (Oxford: Clarendon Press, 1955), p. 22.

Wilamowitz's notorious theory   Ulrich von Wilamowitz-Moellendorff, *Sappho und Simonides* (Berlin: Weidmannsche Buchhandlung, 1913), pp. 56–61, 75–76.

competing with the man   K. J. Dover, *Greek Homosexuality* (Cambridge: Harvard University Press, 1978), p. 178. The diagnosis of "a perfect, 'text-book case,' anxiety attack" originated with George Devereux, "The Nature of Sappho's Seizure in Fr. 31 LP as Evidence of Her Inversion," *Classical Quarterly*, n.s., 20 (1970): 17–31.

61   *the Greek originals*   M. Marcovich, "Sappho Fr. 31: Anxiety Attack or Love Declaration?" *Classical Quarterly*, n.s., 22 (1972): 19–32, offers a detailed rebuttal of Devereux's reading; see also Mary R. Lefkowitz, "Critical Stereotypes and the Poetry of Sappho," in *Heroines and Hysterics* (New York: St. Martin's Press, 1981), pp. 59–68. These rebuttals are countered in turn by Guido Bonelli, "Saffo, 2 Diehl = 31 Lobel-Page," *L'Antiquité Classique* 46 (1977): 453–94, and Richard Jenkyns, *Three Classical Poets* (London: Duckworth, 1982), pp. 222–25.

if the man were reduced   Anne Pippin Burnett, *Three Archaic Poets: Archilochus, Alcaeus, Sappho* (London: Duckworth, 1983), pp. 229–43, interprets the man as a "faceless hypothesis."

Hölderlin read Sappho   "Geschichte der schönen Künste unter den Griechen," in *Sämtliche Werke* (Stuttgart: W. Kohlhammer, 1965), 4:204–5.

so do I   It is not my intention, however, to argue for the "universal" correctness of this reading or any other. My study of later interpretations of the Second Ode presumes that each may be valid for its own time, and that none (including my own) can be unequivocally "right."

62   *brazen sexual behavior*   See Dover, *Greek Homosexuality*, pp. 182–84, and Judith P. Hallett, "Sappho and Her Social Context: Sense and Sensuality," *Signs* 4 (1979): 451–54.

pantothen isa   *Second Idyll,* lines 106–10, in A. S. F. Gow, *Theocritus* (Cambridge: Cambridge University Press, 1952), 1:24.

used of dogs   Ibid., 2:54.

what they want   According to Devereux, however, in "The Nature of Sappho's Seizure," pp. 25–26, "Simaitha is not simply amorous, but also conflict- and anxiety-ridden," and her anxiety has "manifest homosexual overtones."

63   *the aggressor*   S. F. Walker emphasizes the boldness of Simaetha's passion in *Theocritus* (Boston: Twayne, 1980), pp. 95–98.

parody Sappho's words   On the relation between the two poets, see Roberto Pretagostini, "Teocrito e Saffo: Forme allusive e contenuti nuovi," *Quaderni Urbinati di Cultura Classica* 24 (1977): 107–18.

jealous rage   In his commentary on the *Second Idyll* in Theocritus, *Select Poems* (Basingstoke and London: Macmillan, 1971), p. 107, K. J. Dover anticipates his later reading of Sappho's "anxiety state caused, in her case, by homosexual jealousy."

64   *perdidit urbes*   The text is that edited by Kenneth Quinn, *Catullus: The Poems* (New York: St. Martin's Press, 1973), pp. 29–30. Line 8 is Gustav Friedrich's suggestion, *Catulli Veronensis liber* (Leipzig: B. G. Teubner, 1908), pp. 235–36.

      according to Swinburne   "Notes on Poems and Reviews" (1866), in *Complete Works,* ed. E. Gosse and T. J. Wise (London: Heinemann, 1925–27), 16:357.

      sequence to Lesbia   See Timothy P. Wiseman, *Catullus and His World* (Cambridge: Cambridge University Press, 1985), pp. 130–57; Kenneth Quinn, *Catullus: An Interpretation* (New York: Barnes & Noble, 1973), pp. 56–60; and Brian Arkins, *Sexuality in Catullus* (Hildesheim: Georg Olms, 1982), pp. 59–62.

      significant distortions   See D. A. Kidd, "The Unity of Catullus 51," *Journal of the Australasian Universities Language and Literature Association* 20 (1963): 298–308.

65   *the first troubadour*   D. E. W. Wormell, "Catullus as Translator," *The Classical Tradition,* ed. Luitpold Wallach (Ithaca, N.Y.: Cornell University Press, 1966), p. 193.

      reverses Sappho's direction   See Richmond Lattimore, "Sappho 2 and Catullus 51," *Classical Philology* 39 (1944): 184–87; Günther Jachmann, "Sappho und Catull," *Rheinisches Museum* 107 (1964): 1–33; and J. B. Itzkowitz, "On the Last Stanza of Catullus 51," *Latomus* 42 (1983): 129–34.

      some other poem   L. P. Wilkinson, "Ancient and Modern: Catullus LI Again," *Greece and Rome* 21 (1974): 82–85.

66   *ingenious solution*   Friedrich, *Catulli Veronensis liber,* p. 237.

      all their powers   Lord Lyttelton and W. E. Gladstone, *Translations* (London: Bernard Quaritch, 1861), p. 105.

      in the streets   Richard Deacon, *The Private Life of Mr Gladstone* (London: Frederick Muller, 1965), emphasizes Gladstone's work with prostitutes.

      to resume the fray   See Wills, "Sappho 31 and Catullus 51," pp. 193–97.

67   *arrangement of the Heroides*   The argument here is indebted to Howard Jacobson, *Ovid's* Heroides (Princeton: Princeton University Press, 1974), p. 409.

      a fallen woman   In a long and detailed analysis of Sappho's degradation by Ovid, Florence Verducci, *Ovid's Toyshop of the Heart:* Epistulae Heroidum (Princeton: Princeton University Press, 1985), argues that *Heroides* 15 is "at once an etiology of a fallen spirit and of a poet's fall" (p. 179)–the unmaking of Sappho as a poet.

      Sappho to Phaon   Like the majority of modern scholars since Daniel Heinsius (1629), I accept the authenticity of the "Epistula Sapphus" and would place it fifteenth and last in the collection (before the double letters) on the basis of circumstantial evidence. For a strong counterargument, however, see R. J. Tarrant, "The Authenticity of the Letter of Sappho to Phaon (*Heroides* XV)," *Harvard Studies in Classical Philology* 85 (1981): 133–53. Tarrant summarizes the evidence in *Texts and Transmission,* ed. L. D. Reynolds (Oxford: Clarendon Press, 1983), pp. 272–73.

in a play *Leucadia;* five lines on Sappho's leap are quoted by Strabo, *Geography* 10.2.9.

one scholar Gregory Nagy, "Phaethon, Sappho's Phaon, and the White Rock of Leukas," *Harvard Studies in Classical Philology* 77 (1973): 137–77.

came to overshadow The popularity of "Sappho to Phaon" dates from 1420 (only one medieval witness survives), *preceding* the recovery of the Second Ode.

some masculine help Heinrich Dörrie's fine edition, *P. Ovidius Naso: Der Brief der Sappho an Phaon* (Munich: C. H. Beck, 1975), surveys the biographical materials available to Ovid and discusses his remaking of Sappho's character (pp. 216–20).

68 *autobiography* Jacobson reads the epistle as "a parody of the very notion of the lover-poet" (*Ovid's* Heroides, p. 298), in which Ovid not only parodies himself but takes the leap, with Sappho, out of poetry.

Schiller's distinction *On Naïve and Sentimental Poetry* (1795). Schiller considers Ovid particularly artificial, sentimental, and immoral.

Pope's famous translation First published in 1712. These are the opening lines:

> Say, lovely Youth, that dost my Heart command,
> Can *Phaon*'s Eyes forget his *Sapho*'s Hand?
> Must then her Name the wretched Writer prove?
> To thy Remembrance lost, as to thy Love!

As the editors of the Twickenham edition point out, the first line derives less from Ovid than from earlier translations of Ovid's epistles by Aphra Behn and Sir Carr Scrope (1680) (*Poems of Alexander Pope,* ed. E. Audra and Aubrey Williams [New Haven: Yale University Press, 1961], 1:393). By promoting Phaon to "command" over Sapho, putting his name before hers, and even making her name "his," Pope reduces her to a wretched, dependent slave of her lovely youth.

69 *forced into Latin* The significance of this Latinizing of Greek tradition is emphasized in the Latin commentary by the fifteenth-century Italian humanist Angelo Poliziano (*Commento inedito all'epistola Ovidiana di Saffo a Faone,* ed. Elisabetta Lazzeri [Florence: Sansoni, 1971], pp. 14–22).

corpus inane rogos Ovid, "Sappho to Phaon," lines 109–116.

70 *freezing and burning* Longinus, *Peri Hupsous,* ch. 10. According to Denys Page, *Sappho and Alcaeus,* p. 27, "There are no such contradictions as the author alleges."

burned brighter On the "autodafés," see Mora's *Sappho,* pp. 146–50.

71 *full perfection* Mora describes the phases of rehabilitation in France (*Sappho,* pp. 153–67).

je ne meure From the second book of the *Amours: Les Oeuvres de Pierre de*

Ronsard, ed. Isidore Silver (Paris: Didier, 1966), 2:138. Henri Estienne, a friend of Ronsard, had printed Sappho's text in an edition of Anacreon (1554).

72   *by a mortal*   A more enthusiastic reading of this effect might be derived from Thomas M. Greene's observation that, for Ronsard and his circle, "poetry is an initiation into the divine immanence dwelling within mortal things" (*The Light in Troy* [New Haven: Yale University Press, 1982], p. 209).

Ronsard purchases sweetness   When Ronsard speaks of appropriating the qualities of the ancients, in "De l'election de son supulcre" (1550), he takes the "sweet" (*dous*) sound of Sappho (line 112).

retarded sonnet   In the same volume of the *Amours* (*Oeuvres* 2:119) Ronsard published *another,* looser version of the Second Ode in the form of a fourteen-line *chanson:* "Quand je te veux raconter mes douleurs . . . " The two versions are compared by K. R. W. Jones, *Pierre de Ronsard* (New York: Twayne, 1970), pp. 73–74.

73   *to take leave*   *Old Arcadia,* poem 32, in *The Poems of Sir Philip Sidney,* ed. William A. Ringler (Oxford: Clarendon Press, 1962), p. 66.

done to thee   John Donne, "Sapho to Philaenis" (1633), lines 51–52. Note the possible pun on "done." With the exception of Helen Gardner, most scholars accept the attribution to Donne.

wings more ample   *Don Juan* 1:331–34. McGann's commentary (*Complete Poetical Works* 5:676) incorrectly identifies the "Ode" as Sappho's "Ode to Aphrodite"; Longinus quotes the *Second* Ode. Despite Byron's discomfort with the image of the poetess as bluestocking, suicide, and lesbian— "Sappho the sage blue-stocking, in whose grave / All those may leap who rather would be neuter" (*Don Juan* 2:1635–36)—he expressed a better appreciation of the Ode in the love of Juan and Haidée (4:213–16):

> The world was not for them, nor the world's art
>   For beings passionate as Sappho's song;
> Love was born *with* them, *in* them, so intense,
> It was their very spirit—not a sense.

Byron also published a juvenile translation of Catullus 51 in *Hours of Idleness* (1807).

74   *war of words*   Anne Lefèvre, later Dacier, published her Greek and French edition of *Les Poésies d'Anacréon et de Sapho* in 1681. This and subsequent editions were critically examined by Bayle's article on "Sapho" in the *Dictionnaire historique et critique* (1697). Bayle's study of ancient references to Sappho leads him to deny the theory of the *two* Sapphos, and hence to cast aspersions on the virtue of the poetess.

vertuous or fortunate   John Lyly, *Sapho and Phao,* act 1, scene ii, lines 7–10. On Lyly's reshaping of Ovid to compliment the Queen, see G. K. Hunter, *John Lyly: The Humanist as Courtier* (London: Routledge & Kegan Paul, 1962), pp. 166–77.

loue could not violate   Lyly, *Sapho and Phao* 3:iii:108–13.

the learned woman   Carolyn C. Lougee, *Le Paradis des femmes* (Princeton: Princeton University Press, 1976), p. 29.

known as "Sappho"   Alain Niderst, *Madeleine de Scudéry, Paul Pellisson et leur monde* (Paris: Presses Universitaires de France, 1976), pp. 232–40, provides a key to "Sapho," "Phaon" (Pellisson), and other persons in the story.

75   *Sphere of her own Sex*   *Artamenes; or, The Grand Cyrus*, tr. F. G. (London: Humphrey Moseley, 1653–54), 2:104, 86. Subsequent quotations refer to this edition.

at least not troublesome   Ibid., 2:95, 97.

in love with some or other   Ibid., 2:118–19.

sexist mode of reading   The abilities of literary women are defended by "Sapho" in *Les Femmes illustres ou les harangues héroiques* (1642); though the work was published by Georges de Scudéry, the discourse of Sapho to Erinne has been attributed to his sister. See Nicole Aronson, *Mademoiselle de Scudéry* (Boston: Twayne, 1978), pp. 118–19, 128–29, and Mark Bannister, *Privileged Mortals* (Oxford: Oxford University Press, 1983), pp. 77–90.

76   *"dread" and "horrible"*   "Le tôme épouvantable . . . Le volume effroyable . . . de l'horrible Artamene" (Boileau's *Oeuvres complètes,* ed. Françoise Escal [Paris: Gallimard, 1966], p. 215).

a sort of beauty   Boileau, *Oeuvres complètes,* pp. 472–74. Ostensibly out of respect for Scudéry, the *Dialogue* was not published until after her death.

curse on romance conventions   According to Boileau himself, he had admired Scudéry's novels in his youth but later came to recognize their "puérilité." For the social basis of this attack, see Lougee, *Le Paradis des femmes,* pp. 104–5.

hazarder, etc.   Boileau, *Oeuvres complètes,* pp. 356–57.

77   *heterosexual love duet*   An early English version of the ode by John Hall of Durham (1652) represents the female speaker as falling in love with the *man* who "sits next to thee." It is thus *he,* "Beauteous as any Deity / That rules the skie," who dazzles the sight: "How did his pleasing glances dart / Sweet languors to my ravish'd heart." Hall's translation has been reprinted most recently by Duban, *Ancient and Modern Images of Sappho,* p. 171.

infallible secret   Boileau, *Oeuvres complètes,* p. 356. On Boileau's refocusing of Longinus, see Jules Brody, *Boileau and Longinus* (Geneva: Droz, 1958), pp. 42–53, 115.

phainom' [em' autai]   Those critics who emphasize that Sappho transcribes "a case of seemingness" (Burnett, *Three Archaic Poets,* p. 243) will note that Boileau omits any mention of "seems."

78   *agreeable*   Boileau, *Oeuvres complètes,* p. 416.

all of antiquity   "Rien vu de plus vif ni de plus beau dans toute l'antiquité." Quoted by D. M. Robinson, *Sappho and Her Influence,* p. 163, and by Mora, *Sappho,* p. 171.

tourments inévitables   Racine, *Phèdre* 1:iii:273–78.

79   *extremity of passion*   Page, *Sappho and Alcaeus,* p. 27.

giving their feelings a name   Marie-Odile Sweetser, "La Femme abandonée: Esquisse d'une typologie," *Papers on French Seventeenth Century Literature* 10 (1978–79): 142–78, traces the relation of Racine's heroines to contemporary attitudes toward women.

from guilt   See Bernard Weinberg, *The Art of Jean Racine* (Chicago: University of Chicago Press, 1963), pp. 256–66.

polluted with fluids   According to the statistical analysis of *Phèdre* in Charles Bernet, *Le Vocabulaire des tragédies de Jean Racine* (Geneva: Slatkine, 1983), p. 214, "the opposition of 'purity' and 'impurity' is at the center of the play."

80   *sinfulness of love*   In his preface to *Phèdre,* Racine stressed his own moral rigor: "The least faults are severely punished. The mere thought of crime is regarded with as much horror as the crime itself. The frailties of love are taken as real frailties. The passions are put on view only to show all the derangement they cause."

proper Christian woman   In *Les Martyrs* (1809) Chateaubriand uses both Sappho's Ode and Racine's version of it to make a similar point. When the heroine Cymodocée, not yet converted, suggests that Christians may forget that Love is the son of Venus, she notes the effect of burning fire and mortal cold in the veins (Chateaubriand appends both Boileau's and Racine's lines). But her Christian lover Eudore responds by declaring the superiority of Christian to pagan love, as evidenced by Cymodocée's own holy purity and chastity (*Oeuvres romanesques et voyages,* ed. Maurice Regard [Paris: Gallimard, 1969], 2:303–4).

Roland Barthes   "Dire ou ne pas dire? Telle est la question" (*Sur Racine* [Paris: Éditions du Seuil, 1963], p. 115).

steadily ascended   I have traced the eighteenth-century progress of Sappho in more detail in a paper delivered at the David Nichol Smith Seminars in 1986.

81   *a Reading*   *Spectator* 223 (15 Nov. 1711). Addison's influential account goes on to describe the Leucadian leap, which is treated with more fanciful detail in *Spectator* 233.

will possibly suffer   *Spectator* 229 (22 Nov. 1711). Addison compares Philips's version favorably with those of Catullus and Boileau.

the last words   In Philips's collected *Pastorals* (1748), the ode serves as the last poem in the book and is followed appropriately by "The End."

value of teasing   Pornographic variations on Sappho's Ode (interpreted both heterosexually and homosexually) were not uncommon in the eighteenth century; even Fanny Hill may have been influenced by Philips. *The Sappho-an* (anon., 1749), "an heroic poem of three cantos, in the Ovidian stile," describes "the pleasures which the fair sex enjoy with each other."

the past tense   When the highly respected Francis Fawkes translated the Ode in 1760, he used the past tense for the second stanza and then returned to the present. Philips's influence is especially obvious in stanza 3: "With subtle flames my bosom glows, / Quick through each vein the poison flows: / Dark, dimming mists my eyes surround; / My ears with hollow murmurs sound." The translation is reprinted in Richard Stoneman's anthology of classical translations, *Daphne into Laurel* (London: Duckworth, 1982), pp. 204–5.

82   *the much-imitated Ophelia*   In *Love and Freindship* (1790), the fifteen-year-old Jane Austen uses Sappho's Ode to parody the fashionable "frenzy fit" of her heroine: "My voice faltered, My Eyes assumed a vacant Stare, My face became as pale as Death, and my Senses were considerably impaired.—" (*Minor Works*, ed. R. W. Chapman [London: Oxford University Press, 1969], p. 100).

   unpitied die   *The Adventures of Roderick Random,* ed. Paul-Gabriel Bouce (Oxford: Oxford University Press, 1979), p. 227. Smollett's first published work seems to have been "A New Song" (1745), which suggests that, had Sappho possessed Celia's softer charms, "The worm of grief, had never prey'd / On the forsaken, love sick maid: / Nor had she mourn'd an happless flame, / Nor dash'd on rocks her tender frame." Random uses both this song and Sappho's Ode to woo Narcissa, the woman he eventually marries. In addition to its solipsism, Smollett's version of the Ode is notable for its depiction of *male* weakness; Random courts his lady by confessing his helplessness.

83   *the English Sappho*   The life of Robinson (1758–1800) was romantically recorded in four volumes of *Memoirs* (1801) published by her daughter. See also Marguerite Steen, *The Lost One: A Biography of Mary—Perdita—Robinson* (London: Methuen, 1937).

   Sappho dies   Mary "Perdita" Robinson, *Sappho and Phaon, in a Series of Legitimate Sonnets* (London: Gosnell, 1796), p. 42.

   Sappho's Last Song   Lamartine's "Sapho," an "élégie antique" (1815), essentially belongs to this genre, which derives at least in part from the death leap of Gray's "Bard." Lamartine surrounds his heroine, however, with chanting virgins of Lesbos, a cult of Venus that anticipates Baudelaire's "Lesbos."

   utter abandonment   "The Last Song of Sappho," in *The Poetical Works of Mrs. Felicia Hemans* (Philadelphia: Grigg & Elliot, 1839), p. 391. Madame de Staël was one of Hemans's favorite authors, and the influence of her *Sapho* (1811; published 1821) weighs heavily on "The Last Song."

84   *disdainfully runs away*   "Disdegnando sottragge," line 35. Leopardi noted his own identification with Sappho, a noble spirit imprisoned in an ugly body.

   made her a suicide   Kathleen Hickok, *Representations of Women: Nineteenth-Century British Women's Poetry* (Westport, Conn.: Greenwood Press, 1984), notes Hemans's identification with the forsaken Ariadne as the type of a lonely woman artist (pp. 146–48).

85   *painting of despair*   Charles Blanc, 1845, quoted by William Vaughan, *Romantic Art* (London: Thames & Hudson, 1978), p. 224.

   Sappho stands for both   Fragonard's *Sappho* (1774) and David's *Sappho and*

Phaon (1809) are paintings that contribute to the legend. See also Peter A. Tomory, "Angelica Kauffmann—'Sappho,'" *Burlington Magazine* 113 (1971): 275–76.

Phaon's girl still wanders   "Ebbi in quel mar la culla, / Ivi erra ignudo spirito / Di Faon la fanciulla" ("Ode all'amica risanata" [1802], lines 85–87). Glauco Cambon, *Ugo Foscolo: Poet of Exile* (Princeton: Princeton University Press, 1980), pp. 129–31, regards these lines as Foscolo's taking possession of his poetic heritage.

the graveyard line   For the influence of Gray on Foscolo, see Tom O'Neill, *Of Virgin Muses and of Love: A Study of Foscolo's "Dei sepolcri"* (Dublin: Irish Academic Press, 1981), pp. 40–41.

active, passionate artist   In *The Artifice of Reality* (Madison: University of Wisconsin Press, 1964), pp. 60–61, Karl Kroeber comments on the heroism of Foscolo's women: "without Cassandra (and Electra), we feel, there would be no Homer."

three times   A. Cipollini compares Foscolo's versions favorably with others, in Italian and other languages, in *Saffo* (Milan: Fratelli Dumolard, 1890), pp. 169–71.

86   *the sympathy of others*   *Essays on Petrarch*, in Foscolo's *Opere* (Florence: Felice le Monnier, 1953), 10:53. Foscolo's footnote cites *Corinne* as the example of an unsympathetic Sappho.

aimed at Madame de Staël   The identification of de Staël with a modern Sappho reflects Foscolo's awareness not only of the play *Sapho* but of a major influence on *Corinne*: Alessandro Verri's popular novel, *Le avventure di Saffo, poetessa di Mitilene* (1782). Verri was a friend of de Staël, and her choice of the name of the *second* Greek poetess cannot be accidental. The later assimilation of Corinne with Sapho is confirmed by Mary E. Hewitt's "Last Chant of Corinne," in *The American Female Poets*, ed. Caroline May (Philadelphia: Lindsay & Blakiston, 1853), p. 345.

Tacita, esangue   Foscolo, *Essays on Petrarch*, pp. 141–42.

87   *chills of dissolution*   Ibid., p. 141.

desperate love   Ibid.

the original   Ibid.

88   *fire in the blood*   Tennyson, "Fatima," lines 15–19:

> Last night, when someone spoke his name,
> From my swift blood that went and came
> A thousand little shafts of flame
> Were shivered in my narrow frame.

A Modern Sappho   (1849?) Arnold recasts the triangle of the Second Ode by imagining a woman who has lost her man to another woman—"Last night we stood earnestly talking together; / She entered—that moment his eyes turned from me!"—though the modern Sappho is consoled by reflecting that his passion will burn out and leave them united in world-weariness.

crooning "Alfred" Tennyson, "Eleänore," lines 132–39:

> . . . . soon
> From thy rose-red lips MY name
> Floweth; and then, as in a swoon,
>   With dinning sound my ears are rife,
>   My tremulous tongue faltereth,
>   I lose my colour, I lose my breath,
> I drink the cup of a costly death,
> Brimmed with delirious draughts of warmest life.

a weakness for that sound Tennyson's trances over his name furnish a starting point for A. Dwight Culler, *The Poetry of Tennyson* (New Haven: Yale University Press, 1977), pp. 1–4. Robert Bernard Martin, *Tennyson: The Unquiet Heart* (Oxford: Clarendon Press, 1980), pp. 84–85, notes the misery and fear such trances could induce. In this respect we might compare the mood of "Eleänore" with Sappho's "anxiety-attack."

89 *hysterics* From an article on "The Pagan School" (1852) in Baudelaire, *Oeuvres complètes,* ed. Claude Pichois (Paris: Gallimard, 1976), 2:46.

collaboration with friends Banville, Pierre Dupont, and Vitu. The set of parodies, *Fragments littéraires,* appeared in *Le Corsaire-Satan,* 24 Nov. 1845.

les soucis moroses Baudelaire, *Oeuvres complètes* 2:4.

Sapphos to come On nineteenth-century French Sapphos, see Mora's *Sappho;* pp. 188–95 set the contemporary context for Baudelaire's attitude toward "the Lesbian."

beauties of a woman Baudelaire, *Oeuvres complètes* 2:146–47 (1861).

monstrosity Ibid., p. 146. The praise for Desbordes-Valmore's innocent "nature" may be regarded, of course, as ironic. Rosemary Lloyd discusses the issues at length in *Baudelaire's Literary Criticism* (Cambridge: Cambridge University Press, 1981), pp. 190–202.

90 *lurid companion poems* "Femmes damnées," "Sed non satiata," etc. Baudelaire's stigmatizing of lesbians did not preclude him from identifying with their capacity for sin and damnation. When first announced in 1846, the *Fleurs du mal* was called *Les Lesbiennes.*

le poète Baudelaire, *Oeuvres complètes* 1:151, lines 56–60.

hermaphroditic Tamara Bassim, *La Femme dans l'oeuvre de Baudelaire* (Neuchâtel: Éditions de la Baconnière, 1974), pp. 188–200, describes the confusion of sexes in "Lesbos."

son blasphème Baudelaire, *Oeuvres complètes* 1:152, lines 66–70.

91 *reduce it to "her"* Baudelaire's revision; the line originally began "De Sapho qui." The change is ignored in some editions and translations of "Lesbos."

two brilliant exercises A fuller account of Swinburne's poetic debt to Sappho would have to include also the early fragment "The Nightingale," published by Georges Lafourcade, *Swinburne's "Hyperion" and Other Poems* (London: Faber & Gwyer, 1927), pp. 149–50, "Itylus," and especially "On the Cliffs."

92   *notion of lesbianism*   In an introduction to Swinburne's *Poems and Ballads;
       Atalanta in Calydon* (Indianapolis: Bobbs-Merrill, 1970), Morse Peckham
       argues forcefully that the "humiliating psychological bondage" described
       by Swinburne "is the inescapable and eternal condition of human exis-
       tence" (p. xxxv).

       the very greatest poet   Swinburne, *Saturday Review* 117 (1914): 228. Swin-
       burne used variations of these words on other occasions; cf. *Letters,* ed.
       C. Y. Lang (New Haven: Yale University Press, 1960), 4:123–24 (6 Jan.
       1880).

       to any man's   "Notes on Poems and Reviews" (1866), in Swinburne's *Com-
       plete Works,* ed. E. Gosse and T. J. Wise (London: Heinemann, 1925–27),
       16:358–59.

       but the poet   Ibid., p. 359.

       debase into English   A relatively Swinburnian translation of the Second Ode
       was performed by J. A. Symonds (1883):

>   Peer of gods he seemeth to me, the blissful
>   Man who sits and gazes at thee before him,
>   Close beside thee sits, and in silence hears thee
>   Silverly speaking,
>
>   Laughing Love's low laughter. Oh this, this only
>   Stirs the troubled heart in my breast to tremble.
>   For should I but see thee a little moment,
>   Straight is my voice hushed;
>
>   Yea, my tongue is broken, and through and through me
>   'Neath the flesh, impalpable fire runs tingling;
>   Nothing see mine eyes, and a noise of roaring
>   Waves in my ear sounds;
>
>   Sweat runs down in rivers, a tremor seizes
>   All my limbs and paler than grass in autumn,
>   Caught by pains of menacing death I falter,
>   Lost in the love trance.

       In Edwin M. Cox, *The Poems of Sappho* (London: Williams & Norgate,
       1925), p. 72.

93   *not death*   Swinburne, *Poems and Ballads,* p. 61.

94   *and grievous light*   Swinburne, "Anactoria," lines 129–36.

       a lover of pain   On the identity of love with sorrow in Swinburne's reading
       of Sappho, see Jerome J. McGann, *Swinburne: An Experiment in Criticism*
       (Chicago: University of Chicago Press, 1972), pp. 107–16.

       crueller than God   "Anactoria," lines 148–52.

       archetypal goddess-poet   The centrality of Sappho for Swinburne's theory
       and practice is argued by Meredith B. Raymond, *Swinburne's Poetics* (The
       Hague: Mouton, 1971), pp. 40–86.

95   *with death*   "Anactoria," lines 175–84.

       priority in suffering   Nina Auerbach notes Swinburne's worship of a transcendental female power in *Woman and the Demon* (Cambridge: Harvard University Press, 1982), pp. 104–5.

the insuperable sea   "Anactoria," lines 299–304.

96   *Egyptian coffins*   E. G. Turner, *Greek Papyri* (Oxford: Clarendon Press, 1968), pp. 21–34, 69–70, describes the excavations, and offers an example of the "perils run by the restorer" of Sappho.

pieces of words   Ronald Firbank's *Vainglory* (1915) opens with a reception honoring Professor Inglepin's recovery of a Sapphic fragment from Egypt: "Could not, for the fury of her feet!" The guests are puzzled. Brigid Brophy plumbs the episode in *Prancing Novelist* (London: Macmillan, 1973), pp. 439–50. Pierre Louÿs's influential *Les Chansons de Bilitis* (1895) purports to be an edition of remains by Bilitis, a contemporary of Sappho.

the opinion previously held   Arthur Weigall, *Sappho of Lesbos* (New York: Frederick Stokes, 1932), p. 322.

CHAPTER FOUR

97   *Sappho to Phaon*   Anonymous, 1982.

Sappho Lyonnaise   Labé was associated with Sappho in a Greek poem printed with her first works (1555); her first "Elegy" claims to have inherited the lyre that "used to sing the Lesbian's love"; and her lyrics have been haunted by the comparison ever since (they "express the joys and sufferings of love with the passion and sincerity of an ode of Sappho" [*Oxford Companion to French Literature*, 1959]).

Aphra Behn   The ambiguity attached to the name of Sappho is illustrated by Anne Wharton's poem "To Mrs. A. Behn" (1680?):

> May yours excel the matchless Sappho's name;
> May you have all her wit without her shame:
> 'Tho she to honour gave a fatal wound,
> Employ your hand to raise it from the ground.

Quoted by Angeline Goreau, *Reconstructing Aphra* (Oxford: Oxford University Press, 1980), pp. 244–45. A version of Sappho's Second Ode was attributed to Behn by Charles Gildon in *Chorus poetarum* (1694) and reprinted in the *Works* of Buckingham (1715) as if addressed by Behn to Buckingham in 1681. Montagu Summers prints the Gildon version in *The Works of Aphra Behn* (London: Heinemann, 1915), 6:390–91. But Behn was probably not the author, since the same version had been attributed earlier to W[illiam] Bowles in *Poems by Several Hands,* ed. Nahum Tate (1685), and later was reprinted with the title "On Madame Behn."

A short list of other British "Sapphos" might include Katherine Philips ("Orinda"), Anne Killigrew, Catharine Trotter, Elizabeth Thomas ("Corinna"), and Lady Mary Wortley Montagu.

the German Sappho   Anna Louisa Karsch (1722–91). Die Karschin, who signed many of her letters "Sappho," was a favorite folk-poet of Frederick the Great as well as such literary luminaries as J. G. Sulzer and Moses Mendelssohn. See *Die Karschin: Ein Leben in Briefen,* ed. Elisabeth Hausmann (Frankfurt am Main: Societäts-Verlag, 1933).

"modern Sappho" of France   Marie Anne Fiquet du Boccage (1710–1802) published an imitation of Milton, *Le Paradis terrestre* (1748) and a verse tragedy, *Les Amazones* (1749).

Sappho Lazia   Erichetta Dionigi Orfei, like her mother, Marianna Dionigi, wrote many poems about Lazio; see her *Alcune rime* (Orvieto: Pompei, 1830).

Rumanian Sappho   "Carmen Sylva" was the pen name of Elizabeth, Queen of Roumania from 1881 to 1916; her works include a poem, *Sappho* (Leipzig, 1880), and *Stürme* (Bonn, 1881), a volume of verse with sapphic imitations.

Sappho 1900   André Billy's coinage, in *L'Époque 1900* (Paris: J. Tallandier, 1951), adopted by Paul Lorenz, *Sapho 1900: Renée Vivien* (Paris: Juilliard, 1977).

98   *Saffo novella*   D. M. Robinson, *Sappho and Her Influence,* p. 142. Angelica Palli Bartolomei (1798–1875) was able to improvise verse (like Corinne) in many languages. Manzoni's "Versi ad Angelica Palli" (1827) begins "Prole eletta dal ciel, Safo novella" (*Opere* [Milan: Casa del Manzoni, 1950], 3:105). The presence of Lamartine makes the story especially piquant, since the French poet thought women too delicate to write lasting verse ("Madame de Staël," *Souvenirs et portraits* [Paris: Hachette, 1871], 1:220).

Women what they are   "The Prologue," lines 38–39, in *The Works of Anne Bradstreet,* ed. Jeannine Hensley (Cambridge: Harvard University Press, 1967), p. 16. Elizabeth Wade White, *Anne Bradstreet: "The Tenth Muse"* (New York: Oxford University Press, 1971), pp. 273–92, discusses Bradstreet's relation to earlier women poets.

since Sappho jumped   *The Flight of the Mind: The Letters of Virginia Woolf,* ed. Nigel Nicolson (London: Hogarth Press, 1983), 1:253.

silvery star   *The Complete Poems of Emily Jane Brontë,* ed. C. W. Hatfield (New York: Columbia University Press, 1941), p. 29.

a daughter of Venus   *Gondal's Queen: A Novel in Verse by Emily Jane Brontë,* ed. Fannie E. Ratchford (Austin: University of Texas Press, 1955), p. 47. Ratchford's note discusses the evidence for accepting the poem as Brontë's first.

99   *ascendant female star*   The "rich, almost pre-lapsarian undifferentiated sexuality" of starlight (in contrast to a violent phallic sun) in a late poem by Brontë, "Stars," is analyzed by Margaret Homans, *Women Writers and Poetic Identity* (Princeton: Princeton University Press, 1980), pp. 157–59. Homans's account of Brontë's problems in coming to terms with a masculine muse might be viewed as complementing, or showing the eventual failure of, Brontë's early effort to leave men out.

belong to Sappho   The Lobel-Page edition of Sappho's poems rejects the famous lines quoted by Hephaistion—"The moon has set, / and Pleiades, it is / midnight, time passes, I sleep alone" (Edmonds 111)—but they were universally known as hers in Brontë's time.

Unwept, untended, and alone   Christina Rossetti, *Verses* (London: G. Polidori, 1847), p. 24. Rossetti may have known Sappho secondhand, through Smollett's version in *Roderick Random*.

100   *not Miss or Mrs.*   Amy Lowell, *What's O'Clock* (Boston: Houghton Mifflin, 1925), pp. 127–28.

rather terrifying   Ibid., p. 136. The terror is related to the torture of creation by Jean Gould, *Amy* (New York: Dodd Mead, 1975), p. 319.

certain reticences   Lillian Faderman discusses Lowell's strategies of disguise in *Surpassing the Love of Men* (New York: William Morrow, 1981), pp. 392–99.

to discuss her art   William Drake, *Sara Teasdale: Woman & Poet* (San Francisco: Harper & Row, 1979), pp. 152–53, 188–89.

101   *even from herself*   Drake airs the evidence thoroughly in *Sara Teasdale,* and Ruth Perry and Maurice Sagoff, "Sara Teasdale's Friendships," *New Letters* 46 (1979): 101–7, show the intensity of her relations with women.

most people have done   Drake, *Sara Teasdale,* p. 97.

stately   Quoted by M. H. Carpenter, *Sara Teasdale: A Biography* (New York: Schulte Publishing, 1960), p. 171.

102   *windless, tideless sea*   Sara Teasdale, *Collected Poems* (New York: Macmillan, 1937), p. 39. "To Cleïs" first appeared in *Helen of Troy and Other Poems* (1911).

103   *for faithless Man expire*   Quoted by Emily Stipes Watts, *The Poetry of American Women from 1632 to 1945* (Austin: University of Texas Press, 1977), p. 35.

attaining the repose   "A Vision of Poets" (1844), lines 318–21, in *Complete Works of Mrs. E. B. Browning* (New York: E. R. Dumont, 1900), 2:322.

Ellen Moers   *Literary Women,* pp. 165–72.

I do love   Mary E. Hewitt, *Poems: Sacred, Passionate, and Legendary* (New York: Lamport, Blakeman, & Law, 1854). The collection also includes "Sappho to the Sibyl"; and Hewitt's "Last Chant of Corinne" echoes Madame de Staël's "The Last Song of Corinne," in turn a variation on "Sappho's Last Song."

100   *this explicitly*   Watts, *Poetry of American Women,* p. 80.

a vogue of Sappho   Jean-Pierre Jacques traces the progress of the sapphic cult in *Les Malheurs de Sapho* (Paris: Bernard Grasset, 1981). It should be noted that he distinguishes the historical figure, Sappho, from Sapho, the imaginary lesbian.

Barney had introduced her   There are thorough accounts of the affair by George Wickes, *The Amazon of Letters: The Life and Loves of Natalie Barney* (New York: G. P. Putnam's Sons, 1976), pp. 47–77, and Jean Chalon, *Portrait of a Seductress: The World of Natalie Barney,* tr. Carol Barko (New York:

Crown, 1979), pp. 53–86. Vivien herself left a thinly veiled memoir in her novel *A Woman Appeared to Me* (*Une femme m'apparut,* 1904). *Correspondances croisées* among Pierre Louÿs, Barney, and Vivien have been edited by Jean-Paul Goujon (Muizon: A l'écart, 1983).

monologues, and dramas *Poèmes de Renée Vivien* (Paris: Lemerre, 1923–24), 2 vols., has been reissued in one volume (New York: Arno, 1975), and Jean-Paul Goujon has edited Vivien's *Poésies Complètes* (Paris: Régine Deforges, 1986). Translations of individual books of poems include *The Muse of the Violets,* tr. Margaret Porter and Catherine Kroger (Bates City, Mo.: Naiad Press, 1977), and *At the Sweet Hour of Hand in Hand,* tr. Sandia Belgrade (Weatherby Lake, Mo.: Naiad Press, 1979).

made her cruel Susan Gubar discusses Vivien's appropriation of the sadistic male image of Sappho in "Sapphistries," *Signs* 10 (Autumn, 1984): 48–49. Swinburne's *Lesbia Brandon* seems to have been a particular influence, along with Baudelaire's "Femmes damnées" and "Lesbos" and Verlaine's "Sappho."

105 *mixed races* Vivien, *Sapho* (Paris: Lemerre, 1903), p. xi. Like Pierre Louÿs, Vivien espouses "Psappha" as the correct, Dorian form of the name, as if the true poetess were not Greek but prehistoric.

onto her idol Elyse Blankley describes the creation of a visionary Lesbos in "Return to Mytilène: Renée Vivien and the City of Women," in *Women Writers and the City,* ed. Susan M. Squier (Knoxville: University of Tennessee Press, 1984), pp. 45–67.

of the strophe Vivien, *Sapho,* p. xi.

A travers la mort Ibid., pp. 11–14. Vivien includes the Greek original, a prose paraphrase, and Catullus 51.

106 *something "odd"* Verlaine's "Art poétique" (1882), line 2.

incompletion Mora's *Sappho,* p. 200—a good technical analysis.

erotic manicheism Ibid., p. 199.

need to be punished See Faderman, *Surpassing the Love of Men,* pp. 362–63. Vivien's "Litanie de la haine" ("Litany of Hate") makes this theme explicit.

107 *looking in a mirror* Colette's touching sketch of Vivien (1928) is included in *The Pure and the Impure,* tr. Herma Briffault (New York: Farrar, Straus & Giroux, 1967), pp. 79–98.

as a Sappho "Battle of Marathon" (1820), in *Complete Works of Mrs. E. B. Browning* 1:2.

Not Sappho, Sacco Muriel Rukeyser, *Collected Poems* (New York: McGraw-Hill, 1978), p. 3.

108 *reborn Greek spirit* Thomas B. Swann, *The Classical World of H.D.* (Lincoln: University of Nebraska Press, 1962), pp. 109–21, discusses HD's use of the fragments. A contemporary essay by HD, "The Wise Sappho" (1920), has been published with her *Notes on Thought and Vision* (San Francisco: City Lights Books, 1982).

book-knowledge of them   Letter to Harriet Monroe (1912), in *The Letters of Ezra Pound 1907–1941,* ed. D. D. Paige (New York: Harcourt, Brace, 1950), p. 11.

straight as the Greek   Ibid. On Pound's invention of "H.D. Imagiste" see Barbara Guest, *Herself Defined: The Poet H.D. and Her World* (Garden City, N.Y.: Doubleday, 1984), pp. 40–46.

not those of an imagist   HD's disentangling from Pound as she developed a personal, "secret doctrine of the image" is a central theme of Janice S. Robinson, *H.D.: The Life and Work of an American Poet* (Boston: Houghton Mifflin, 1982), pp. 62–77. See also L. S. Dembo, "H.D. *Imagiste* and Her Octopus Intelligence," in *H.D.: Woman and Poet,* ed. Michael King (Orono, Maine: National Poetry Foundation, 1986), pp. 209–25.

Sigmund   HD, *Tribute to Freud* (Boston: David R. Godine, 1974), p. 88.

woman-centered epic   Alicia Ostriker discusses HD's remaking of herself in *Writing like a Woman* (Ann Arbor: University of Michigan Press, 1983), pp. 7–41.

they could not follow   Rachel Blau DuPlessis describes HD's struggle against "romantic thralldom" to men in "Family, Sexes, Psyche: An Essay on H.D. and the Muse of the Woman Writer," in *H.D.: Woman and Poet,* pp. 69–90.

Ariadne with Sappho   "The Islands" (1921), in HD, *Collected Poems 1912–1944,* ed. Louis L. Martz (New York: New Directions, 1983), pp. 124–27. Martz comments on the association of Ariadne's anguish with HD's, p. xiv.

109   *deep center of her poetry*   Martz, in HD's *Collected Poems,* p. xxii.

see anymore, people   Quoted by Susan S. Friedman, *Psyche Reborn: The Emergence of H.D.* (Bloomington: Indiana University Press, 1981), p. 44.

biologically, no   HD, *Tribute to Freud,* p. 152.

not always right   Friedman reviews HD's disagreements with Freud in *Psyche Reborn,* pp. 121–54.

unmixed with evil   H. T. Wharton, ed., *Sappho* (New York: Brentano's, 1920), p. 112.

110   *fiery tempered steel*   HD, *Collected Poems,* pp. 131–32.

sequel to the Second Ode   Swann compares HD's verse to the Ode in *The Classical World of H.D.,* p. 113.

come away scorched   In "The Wise Sappho," HD reads the Second Ode as a study in burning by "this woman whom love paralysed till she seemed to herself a dead body yet burnt, as the desert grass is burnt, white by the desert heat" (p. 64).

instrument or muse   "She is indeed rocks set in a blue sea, she is the sea itself, breaking and tortured and torturing, but never broken. She is the island of artistic perfection" (HD, "The Wise Sappho," p. 67).

111   *not been lost on men*   Gubar's "Sapphistries" comments on the influence of

HD's fragments (especially "Fragment 113") on the imagist aesthetic, pp. 53–55.

Hugh Kenner   The Pound Era (Berkeley: University of California Press, 1971), pp. 54–75.

as Ezra Pound did   Pound's relation to Sappho is complex. He studied her, often praised her, and used her to create brilliant technical effects, as in the sapphics of "Apparuit," where traces of the Second Ode may be discerned amidst the lusher spirits of romance. "Blessed be Sappho who has shown you a path towards Truth," Dorothy Shakespear wrote him in 1911 (*Ezra Pound and Dorothy Shakespear: Their Letters: 1909–1914,* ed. Omar Pound and A. W. Litz [New York: New Directions, 1984], p. 58). He also regularly recommended comparing her to Catullus, as in "I gather the Limbs of Osiris" (1912), *Selected Prose 1909–1965,* ed. William Cookson (London: Faber & Faber, 1973), p. 41. Yet in fact he seems to have preferred Catullus; see Pound's *ABC of Reading* (New York: New Directions, 1960), pp. 47–48.

the hyacinth girl   T. S. Eliot, *The Waste Land,* lines 35–42.

From the narrow between   Guy Davenport, *Sappho: Poems and Fragments* (Ann Arbor: University of Michigan Press, 1965), no. 20.

112   *purple flower to earth*   Wharton, *Sappho,* p. 104. In this edition, the lines on the hyacinth are cited under "Epithalamia," no. 94, and the Hesperus fragment is no. 95.

a man   See James E. Miller, *T. S. Eliot's Personal Waste Land* (University Park: Pennsylvania State University Press, 1977), pp. 70–76.

to feel or communicate   A. D. Moody comments on the "painful ambiguity" of the passage, the "centre from which the entire poem radiates," in *Thomas Stearns Eliot: Poet* (Cambridge: Cambridge University Press, 1979), p. 81.

the lion's tooth   W. B. Yeats, "Crazy Jane grown old looks at the Dancers."

go on forever   Eloise Knapp Hay emphasizes that the passage recalls "a moment without issue" in *T. S. Eliot's Negative Way* (Cambridge: Harvard University Press, 1982), p. 54.

drown in nostalgia   Hugh Kenner interprets the passage as a fantasy of a drowned girl, part of "The Death of Europe," in *The Invisible Poet: T. S. Eliot* (New York: Ivan Obolensky, 1959), p. 161.

113   *A Muse their Sire   Letters of Ezra Pound,* p. 170.

female passions   Tony Pinkney, *Women in the Poetry of T. S. Eliot: A Psychoanalytic Approach* (London: Macmillan, 1984), reads the passage on the hyacinth girl, and much of Eliot's other work, as a Strindbergian expression of "misogynistic and psychotic themes" (p. 105).

114   *Why do you never speak   The Waste Land,* lines 111–12.

Nothing   Ibid., lines 121–23, 126. In the manuscript of *The Waste Land,* ed. Valerie Eliot (New York: Harcourt Brace Jovanovich, 1971), p. 18, the answer to this question was "I remember / The hyacinth garden." Pinkney,

Women in the Poetry of T. S. Eliot, suggests that this is one of many transformations of women into doomed and drowned Ophelias.

What thinking   *The Waste Land,* line 113.

115   *fascinated by Sappho*   See Paul Mariani, *William Carlos Williams: A New
World Naked* (New York: McGraw-Hill, 1981), pp. 709–12.

H.D. and Ezra Pound   Quoted by John C. Thirlwall, "William Carlos
Williams' 'Paterson,'" *New Directions* 17 (1961): 253. Thirlwall slightly
misquotes his own earlier interview with Williams, *New Directions* 16
(1957): 8, where the text reads "I early abandoned. . . ."

fall of the beat   William Carlos Williams, *I Wanted to Write a Poem* (Boston:
Beacon Press, 1958), pp. 92–93.

Sappho had to give   Thirlwall interview, *New Directions* 17:292.

to instruct me   *Sappho: A Translation by William Carlos Williams* (San Francisco: Poems in Folio, 1957). Williams's comments accompany an elegant
printed broadsheet of the poem.

of dying   William Carlos Williams, *Paterson* (New York: New Directions,
1963), p. 253.

official British translations   Williams, *Sappho*.

116   *Tumults in my Breast*   As Emily Mitchell Wallace points out in an informa-
tive essay, "A Musing in the Highlands and Valleys: The Poetry of Grat-
wick Farm," *William Carlos Williams Review* 8, no. 1 (Spring 1982): 31–32,
Williams depended mainly on the prose translation by W. Hamilton Fyfe,
included in the Loeb edition of Aristotle, vol. 23. But he also read other
versions, including J. A. Symonds's, and had probably seen the "official"
translations, Philips's among them, in H. T. Wharton's edition of Sappho.

avoided all roughness   *Paterson,* p. 253. Wallace, "A Musing," pp. 31–32,
describes Post's assistance to Williams. In *Assault on Mount Helicon* (Berkeley: University of California Press, 1984), p. 282, Mary Barnard, a friend
of Williams, records the opposition of her own translations of Sappho to
such notions of "tinkling." When her *Sappho* appeared in 1958, Williams
sent his approval (Wallace, p. 40).

she put it down   Thirlwall interview, *New Directions* 17:292.

defiance of authority   *Paterson,* p. 144.

a damn thing   Thirlwall interview, *New Directions* 17:292.

in one poem   Ibid.

insertion of "dry"   The word does not appear in Williams's first published
version.

Joseph Riddel   *The Inverted Bell* (Baton Rouge: Louisiana State University
Press, 1974), pp. 167–70.

117   *a question I was asking*   *Paterson,* p. 258.

you will appear   *Paterson,* p. 148.

another person   *Spectrum* 1, no. 3 (Fall 1957): 57.

I love myself more   William Carlos Williams, *Pictures from Brueghel* (New

York: New Directions, 1962), p. 65. According to Charles Doyle, *William Carlos Williams and the American Poem* (New York: St. Martin's Press, 1982), p. 146, some drafts of *Paterson* include a version of this poem.

with another person   *The Waste Land,* ed. Valerie Eliot, p. 104. The line is not assigned to a speaker, but clearly belongs to the husband in the variation on p. 106, "If it is terrible alone, it is sordid with one more."

118   *a girl like Robert Lowell*   Randall Jarrell, *Poetry and the Age* (London: Faber & Faber, 1955), p. 230. Jarrell is commenting on "The Mills of the Kavanaughs."

breathe or speak   Robert Lowell, *Phaedra* (London: Faber & Faber, 1963), pp. 24–25.

arbitrary disconnection   John Crick, *Robert Lowell* (Edinburgh: Oliver & Boyd, 1974), p. 71, cites the passage to illustrate "a post-Freudian Phèdre" pushed "in a quite Websterian direction." George Steiner had found the same touch of a Websterized Racine in Lowell, "Two Translations," *Kenyon Review* 23 (1961): 717–18.

electric rage   *Phaedra,* p. 8.

withdraws or dies   Robert Lowell, *Imitations* (New York: Farrar, Straus & Cudahy, 1961), p. 3.

119   *once pined to share*   Ibid., p. 4. Norma Procopiow, *Robert Lowell: The Poet and His Critics* (Chicago: American Library Association, 1984), pp. 96–97, points out that Lowell has chosen fragments that change Sappho's voice to a version of his own, gloomy or suicidal.

I sleep alone   "Sappho," in Robert Lowell, *Notebook 1967–68* (New York: Farrar, Straus & Giroux, 1969), p. 94.

120   *omnivorous and self-absorbed*   Adrienne Rich makes the case against Lowell's "merciless masculinity" in *American Poetry Review* 2 (Sept.-Oct. 1973): 42–43.

female poets of his time   As early as 1947, Lowell praised Elizabeth Bishop and Marianne Moore for their "bare objective language" and honesty (*Sewanee Review* 55 [Summer 1947]: 498). His foreword to Sylvia Plath's *Ariel* (New York: Harper & Row, 1966), p. vii, calls the poems "personal, confessional, felt." The patronizing implications of such tribute have been noted by many critics, e.g., Alicia Ostriker, *Stealing the Language,* pp. 1–2.

Plath's favorite word   Ted Hughes, "The Chronological Order of Sylvia Plath's Poems," *TriQuarterly* 7 (Fall 1966): 88. *A Concordance to the Collected Poems of Sylvia Plath* by Richard M. Matovich (New York: Garland Publishing, 1986), however, lists only one use of "ecstasy."

121   *spare but musical*   Mary Barnard, *Assault on Mount Helicon,* p. 282.

directness of speech   Mary Barnard, *Sappho: A New Translation* (Berkeley: University of California Press, 1958), p. 102. Barnard acknowledges her debt to Pound and his approval of her efforts ("Yuz—vurry nize—only grump iz yu didn't git to it 20 years ago") in *Assault on Mount Helicon,* pp. 282–83.

the planes of rhetoric   "Discourse on Poetry," in Salvatore Quasimodo,

Complete Poems, tr. Jack Bevan (New York: Schocken Books, 1984), p. 234. Barnard credits Quasimodo's translations of Sappho with inspiring her to try an equivalent "in living, not lexicon English" (*Assault on Mount Helicon,* p. 281).

surfeit of words   Quasimodo's translation of the Second Ode (1944) is notable for its economy (compare it, for instance, with Foscolo's version quoted above):

> *A me pare uguale agli dèi*
> *chi a te vicino cosí dolce*
> *suono ascolta mentre tu parli*
>
> *e ridi amorosamente. Subito a me*
> *il cuore si agita nel petto*
> *solo che appena ti veda, e la voce*
>
> *si perde sulla lingua inerte.*
> *Un fuoco sottile affiora rapido alla pelle,*
> *e ho buio negli occhi e il rombo*
> *del sangue alle orecchie.*
>
> *E tutta in sudore e tremante*
> *come erba patita scoloro:*
> *e morte non pare lontana*
> *a me rapita di mente.*

(*Lirici Greci* [Milan: Mondadori, 1967], pp. 16–19.) Barnard achieves a similar streamlining, though she supplies an extraneous "title" (*Sappho,* no. 39):

> He is more than a hero
> He is a god in my eyes—
> the man who is allowed
> to sit beside you—he
>
> who listens intimately
> to the sweet murmur of
> your voice, the enticing
>
> laughter that makes my own
> heart beat fast. If I meet
> you suddenly, I can't
>
> speak—my tongue is broken;
> a thin flame runs under
> my skin; seeing nothing,
>
> hearing only my own ears
> drumming, I drip with sweat;
> trembling shakes my body
>
> and I turn paler than
> dry grass. At such times
> death isn't far from me

J. V. Cunningham   "My Fires and Fears Are Met: Sappho, Longinus, and the Rhetorical Tradition," *Antaeus* 40/41 (Winter/Spring 1981): 442–58. Cunningham's translation seems to me among the best in modern English:

He is, I should say, on a level
With deity, the man who sits over
Against you, and attends to the nearby
Sweetness of your voice

And charm of your laughter. I tell you
It frightens the quick heart in my breast.
For, soon as I look at you, there is
No voice left to me.

My tongue has been fractured, a thin fire
Instantly runs underneath my skin,
My eyes cannot see anything, and
My ears re-echo.

I am in a cold sweat, a trembling
Seizes me all over, and, pallid
As range grass, I think I am almost
On the point of death.

122   *totally opposed to us*   Marguerite Yourcenar, *Fires,* tr. Dori Katz and Yourcenar (New York: Farrar, Straus & Giroux, 1981), p. xiii.

  are sacred   Yourcenar, *With Open Eyes,* tr. Arthur Goldhammer (Boston: Beacon Press, 1984), p. 52.

  a vocation   *Fires,* p. ix.

  missing their suicide   Ibid., p. 129.

  sad mania   Ibid., p. xxi. In "Sapphistries," Susan Gubar reads the story more tragically, as a parable of "the lonely isolation of the woman artist" or "the utopian grandeur of the lesbian aesthetic project in the modernist period" (p. 61).

  sacred psalmody   *With Open Eyes,* p. 164.

123   *je connais la mort*   Yourcenar, *La Couronne et la lyre* (Paris: Gallimard, 1979), p. 75.

  slack or artificial   Ibid., p. 72.

  those in love   Ibid., p. 70.

124   *human behavior*   Ibid., p. 73.

  a "Right On" woman   Sue Schneider, "Thinking Back Lesbian," in Sidney Abbott and Barbara Love, *Sappho Was a Right-On Woman* (New York: Stein & Day, 1973), p. 7.

125   *a lost stanza*   On efforts to fill the lacuna, see Salvatore Nicosia, *Tradizione testuale diretta e indiretta dei poeti di Lesbo* (Rome: Edizioni dell'Ateneo, 1976), pp. 121–40.

  approach the girl   "The obvious completion of her line of thought is that she must brace herself to bear all the symptoms that batter her in the girl's presence, *because she means to enter that presence, to bear that obliterating proximity*" (Garry Wills, "Sappho 31 and Catullus 51," p. 190).

CHAPTER FIVE

127   *Is need*   Wallace Stevens, "The Sail of Ulysses," in *The Palm at the End of the Mind* (New York: Knopf, 1971), pp. 392–93.

128   *spur in her breast*   "Ille fatigat / os rabidum, fera corda domans, fingitque premendo"; "ea frena furenti / concutit et stimulos sub pectora vertit Apollo" (*Aeneid* 6:79–80, 100–1).

night, and false dreams   The Cumaean Sibyl was priestess of Apollo, but Virgil made her priestess of Hecate (and hence the underworld) as well. In *Cumaean Gates* (Oxford: Blackwell, 1936), pp. 31–32, W. F. Jackson Knight argues that Virgil was restoring an older tradition of ghostly sibyls who belong to the earth and caves. John Pollard emphasizes the originality of Virgil's conception in a memorial lecture for Jackson Knight, *Virgil and the Sibyl* (Exeter: University of Exeter, 1982).

Virgil himself   The poet's later reputation as a Christian prophet derives, of course, from the Fourth Eclogue, which takes its inspiration from the Cumaean Sibyl.

that rule below   *Aeneid* 6:264–67.

a "young fate"   On the genesis of "La Jeune Parque," see Valéry's "Memoirs of a Poem," in *The Art of Poetry,* tr. Denise Folliot (New York: Pantheon, 1958), pp. 100–32.

129   *the great creators*   W. B. Yeats, Introduction to *The Winding Stair and Other Poems* (1933), in *Collected Poems* (London: Macmillan, 1950), p. 537.

projecting it onto a woman   "For reasons that deserve exploration, the plight of the deserted woman seems to strike the poet with a greater urgency than that of the despairing male in the early work" (Gerhard Joseph, *Tennysonian Love* [Minneapolis: University of Minnesota Press, 1969], p. 46).

not even a name   This is literally true; no character is named in Pär Lagerkvist, *The Sibyl,* tr. Naomi Walford (New York: Random House, 1958).

130   *the most interesting form of modern poetry*   Ezra Pound, "Chinese Poetry," *To-Day* 3, no. 15 (May 1918): 93.

of all things   Conrad Aiken, *Collected Poems* (New York: Oxford University Press, 1970), p. 905.

the clear autumn   Pound, *Personae* (New York: New Directions, 1950), p. 132; first published in *Cathay* (1915).

play Conan Doyle   Pound, "Chinese Poetry," *To-Day* 3, no. 14 (April 1918): 55–56.

131   *no direct reproach*   *Personae,* p. 132.

to make a translation   Pound, "Chinese Poetry," *To-Day* 3, no. 14, p. 54.

autumn moon   Wai-lim Yip, *Ezra Pound's* Cathay (Princeton: Princeton University Press, 1969), p. 66. Yip notes that step(s), dew(s), and stocking(s) may be singular or plural. Fenollosa's version of this poem has not been preserved.

equally valid   Ibid., p. 68. Yip's own translation of "Jade Steps Grievance," *Chinese Poetry* (Berkeley: University of California Press, 1976), p. 382, prefers "she."

Chinese scholars   Arthur Cooper summarizes the Chinese detective work in his translation of *Li Po and Tu Fu* (London: Penguin Books, 1973), pp. 112–13.

132   *my thoughts of you*   Yip, *Ezra Pound's* Cathay, pp. 66–67n.

welfare of the people   Cooper, *Li Po and Tu Fu,* p. 29.

best English poem   Hugh Kenner, *The Pound Era,* describes Pound's Chinese translations as the invention of "a new kind of English poem" (p. 218).

projected onto the woman   Ronald Bush argues that Pound has subtly modified Li Po's original to hint at the wife's "suppressed ambivalence" ("Pound and Li Po: What Becomes a Man," in *Ezra Pound among the Poets,* ed. George Bornstein [Chicago: University of Chicago Press, 1985], pp. 40–42).

lonely and sensitive woman   Hans H. Frankel illustrates the obsession of Chinese poets with "lonely women" in *The Flowering Plum and the Palace Lady* (New Haven: Yale University Press, 1976), pp. 56–61.

133   *what place will take me in*   My translation is based on the Chinese, but I have consulted the versions by George W. Kent, *Worlds of Dust and Jade* (New York: Philosophical Library, 1969), p. 60; Hugh Dunn, *Ts'ao Chih* (Taipei: China News, 1970); Ronald C. Miao, in *Sunflower Splendor,* ed. Wu-chi Liu and Irving Y. Lo (Garden City, N.Y.: Doubleday Anchor, 1975), p. 47; and Anne Birrell, *New Songs from a Jade Terrace* (London: Allen & Unwin, 1982), p. 66. The title of the poem, "Seven Sorrows," is obscure, but Frankel offers several interpretations, pp. 229–30.

banishment from court   David T. Roy, "The Theme of the Neglected Wife in the Poetry of Ts'ao Chih," *Journal of Asian Studies* 19 (Nov. 1959): 30. Hans H. Frankel expresses skepticism about such biographical readings, and recommends a more structural analysis, in "Fifteen Poems by Ts'ao Chih: An Attempt at a New Approach," *Journal of the American Oriental Society* 84 (1964): 1–14.

master and slave   K. P. K. Whitaker, "Tsaur Jyr's Luohshern Fuh," *Asia Major,* n.s., 4 (1954): 40. "Tsaur Jyr" is another transliteration of Ts'ao Chih.

134   *somebody Poor*   Blake, "The Human Abstract," in *Songs of Experience.*

What's Hecuba to him   *Hamlet,* act 2, scene ii.

he is a man   Marilyn French reads *Hamlet* as a questioning of male legitimacy in *Shakespeare's Division of Experience* (New York: Summit Books, 1981), pp. 145–58.

suppress everything womanish   In *Hamlet's Absent Father* (Princeton: Princeton University Press, 1977), Avi Erlich interprets Hamlet's repudiation of Hecuba as an effort at "throwing away the good mother and adopting the bad" (p. 173), thus mastering his fear of becoming a "sexually perverted passive male" as well as his fear of women.

135   *supplement the Heroides*   See Peter Dronke, *Women Writers of the Middle Ages* (Cambridge: Cambridge University Press, 1984), pp. 107–39.

Ovid had opened   Epistles from Paris to Helen and Helen to Paris begin the series of double letters that supplement the *Heroides;* their authorship is disputed. Thomas A. Kirby, *Chaucer's Troilus: A Study in Courtly Love* (University, La.: Louisiana State University Press, 1940), opens with Ovid, pp. 3–13.

trial for infanticide Eudo C. Mason, *Goethe's* Faust: *Its Genesis and Purport* (Berkeley: University of California Press, 1967), pp. 67–73, reviews the evidence for this theory, with considerable skepticism.

136 *not all critics do* Jane K. Brown, *Goethe's* Faust: *The German Tragedy* (Ithaca, N.Y.: Cornell University Press, 1986), pp. 97–116, analyzes Gretchen as an illusory figure whose story reveals the ambiguity of the sentimental love tradition.

why she was created "Women," Goethe told Eckermann (22 Oct. 1828), "are silver dishes in which we lay golden apples. . . . The female characters in my works have all come off well, they are all better than those we run across in real life."

into the unconscious Erich Neumann, *The Origins and History of Consciousness,* tr. R. F. C. Hull (Princeton: Princeton University Press, 1969), pp. 57–58.

137 *impotence of grief* William Wordsworth, "The Ruined Cottage," lines 497–500, in Jonathan Wordsworth, *The Music of Humanity* (London: Nelson, 1969), p. 48.

spirit of humanity Ibid., line 503. As Jonathan Wordsworth points out, the passage also serves as a transition from the pain of Margaret's fate to the distance and comfort of the Poet's acceptance of that fate (pp. 98–101).

bends down to the woman Kenneth R. Johnston comments on the inappropriateness of such "sexual or romantic undertones" in *Wordsworth and* The Recluse (New Haven: Yale University Press, 1984), pp. 44–51.

poems of abandoned women Barbara A. Schapiro, *The Romantic Mother* (Baltimore: Johns Hopkins University Press, 1983), pp. 119–29, views Wordsworth's "image of the abandoned woman," and particularly Margaret, as the means by which the poet "faces his feelings of rage and loss and yet confirms his faith in the mother and her love" (p. 129).

all man The Table Talk and Omniana of Samuel Taylor Coleridge, ed. T. Ashe (London: Bell & Sons, 1909), p. 339.

138 *among Wordsworth's best* For a survey of opinions, see Richard D. McGhee, "'Conversant with Infinity': Form and Meaning in Wordsworth's 'Laodamia,'" *Studies in Philology* 68 (1971): 357.

twin Immortals Alaric Alfred Watts, *Alaric Watts: A Narrative of His Life* (London: R. Bentley, 1884), 1:240. The visit occurred ca. 1825. "Indeed," Mrs. Watts continues, "it was difficult to differ from him on any question of poetical criticism."

to listen to it From *The Spirit of the Age,* in *Complete Works of William Hazlitt,* ed. P. P. Howe (London: Dent, 1932), 11:90. Cf. 16:253.

Laodamia goes with them "his Laodamia / it comes", in *Aeneid* 6:447–8.

a Virgilian attitude Douglas Bush, *Mythology and the Romantic Tradition in English Poetry* (Cambridge: Harvard University Press, 1937), p. 64, notes the difference between Virgil's sympathy for Dido and Wordsworth's severity toward Laodamia.

treated of it   Fenwick notes, in Wordsworth's *Poetical Works,* ed. E. de Selincourt (Oxford: Clarendon Press, 1952), 2:518. Even Harold Bloom, one
of the few modern critics to have read "Laodamia" closely and intelligently,
exaggerates its fidelity to Virgil, as when he comments that a few of Wordsworth's most lofty and lifeless stanzas, "with Tennyson's *Tithonus,* . . . are
the closest in English to the spirit and manner of Virgil" (*The Visionary
Company* [Ithaca, N.Y.: Cornell University Press, 1971], p. 191). As
Bloom's own later work has repeatedly argued, a poet's apparent homage
to one predecessor (Wordsworth's to Virgil) may mask his anxious struggle
against another (Wordsworth's against Ovid).

the Victorian Virgil   The adjective chosen by Wordsworth to praise Tennyson's poems in 1845—"Their diction . . . seems singularly stately"—
corresponds to the famous conclusion of Tennyson's "To Virgil": "Wielder
of the stateliest measure / ever moulded by the lips of man." Earlier Virgils,
such as Dryden's, were far less stately.

139   *propiore dei*   *Aeneid* 6:46–51.

the issue in repose   Wordsworth, *Poetical Works* 2:267.

any definitive version   Euripides' lost tragedy, *Protesilaus,* was probably the
standard classical treatment of the myth. The "jumble of evidence" about
Ovid's sources for *Heroides* 13, Laodamia to Protesilaus, is discussed by
Howard Jacobson, *Ovid's* Heroides, pp. 195–98.

140   *fiction of what never was*   Preface to *The Excursion* (1814), in Wordsworth,
Poetical Works 5:4.

a good soldier   Wordsworth doubtless intended a political message. Composed in October 1814 (after the defeat and abdication of Napoleon but
before his return from Elba), "Laodamia" implicitly praises the soldiers
who had given their lives for their country and rebukes the antiwar party
(Whigs) for its lack of will. Laodamia's weakness associates her with the
Whigs. In "Ode: 1814" (composed after Waterloo, in January 1816), the
spirit of Saint George instructs English women in a proper response to
"their martyred Countrymen":

>"Haste, Virgins, haste!—the flowers which summer gave
>   Have perished in the field;
>But the green thickets plenteously shall yield
>   Fit garlands for the brave,
> That will be welcome, if by you entwined;
>
>. . . . .
>   [your stern Defenders] in due time shall share
>Those palms and amaranthine wreaths
>Unto their martyred Countrymen decreed,
>In realms where everlasting freshness breathes!"

>   (lines 37–41, 49–52)

Laodamia fails to understand the political necessity for Protesilaus's sacrifice; she ought to be twining wreaths in honor of his patriotic example,
instead of trying to undo it.

a Stygian hue   Wordsworth, *Poetical Works* 2:269.

opposed to love   Ibid. 2:271.

141   *I have ever written*   Fenwick notes, in Wordsworth, *Poetical Works* 2:519.

intermediary assessments   Ibid., 2:271–72n. De Selincourt also prints another version supplied by Buxton Forman (2:532), but the provenance is suspect.

disregard of the exhortation   March 1830, in *The Letters of William and Dorothy Wordsworth,* ed. Alan G. Hill (Oxford: Clarendon Press, 1979), 5:215–16.

grappling with Ovid   Bush dismisses the influence of the *Heroides* on the grounds that "Ovid's heroine, while not without pathos, comes dangerously close to comedy" (*Mythology and the Romantic Tradition,* p. 62). But this characteristic Ovidian mixture of responses may have been just what spurred Wordsworth to reply.

whether he lives or dies   *Heroides* 13:148, 105–7, 23–24, 159–64.

142   *woman's point of view*   According to L. P. Wilkinson, "Greek Influence on the Poetry of Ovid," in *L'Influence grecque sur la poésie latine de Catulle à Ovide* (Geneva: Fondation Hardt, 1956), "The feelings of a woman's heart had been expressed in poetry by Sappho and Erinna and Sulpicia, and imagined by Euripides and the Comic poets; but no poet known to us had conceived them with the mixture of sympathetic understanding and detached amusement that we find in Ovid. In the Heroides the sympathy naturally predominates" (p. 232).

his wife's arms   *Heroides* 13:137–48.

As fondly he believes   Wordsworth, *Poetical Works* 2:272.

143   *his waxen image*   *Heroides* 13:109–14, 151–58.

different poetic gods   John Hollander, *The Figure of Echo* (Berkeley: University of California Press, 1981), argues that the description of Protesilaus is mediated through Milton's devils, as if "Wordsworth were clinging to the demonic prefiguration of classical antiquity in the culture of Pandemonium" (p. 94).

a loftier tone   In *Ovid's Toyshop of the Heart,* Florence Verducci points out that Wordsworth's handling of Ovidian materials in book 7 of *The Prelude* (the "Beauty of Buttermere") is "selective: chaste, discreetly laundered, even bleached" (p. 17).

sexual impotence   Donald H. Reiman, "Poetry of Familiarity: Wordsworth, Dorothy, and Mary Hutchinson," in *The Evidence of the Imagination,* ed. Reiman, Michael C. Jaye, and Betty T. Bennett (New York: New York University Press, 1978), pp. 164–70.

144   *Dark became doubly dark*   Wordsworth, *Poetical Works* 5:98n.

his former self   Reiman, "Poetry of Familiarity," p. 170. Jean H. Hagstrum, *The Romantic Body* (Knoxville: University of Tennessee Press, 1985), p. 88, regards Reiman's hypothesis of impotence as "melodramatic and unproven, indeed unprovable," and notes that "there was worry about a pregnancy for Mary after her great grief" (not a conclusive argument, since the worry was expressed by *Dorothy* Wordsworth).

know myself a man   Thomas Gray, "Ode to Adversity" (1742), line 48.

145   *forms a softer Man*   Alexander Pope, "To a Lady. Of the Characters of Women" (*Moral Essays* 2), lines 271–72. Most recent critics interpret the phrase as a sexist or androcentric reminder that "the best that even the ideal woman can aspire to, is to become 'a softer Man'" (Brean S. Hammond, *Pope* [Atlantic Highlands, N.J.: Humanities Press International, 1986], p. 193). See also Felicity A. Nussbaum, *The Brink of All We Hate* (Lexington: University Press of Kentucky, 1984), pp. 156–58.

confusion of sexual roles   G. Douglas Atkins discusses the problematics of "Becoming Woman" in *Quests of Difference: Reading Pope's Poems* (Lexington: University Press of Kentucky, 1986), pp. 99–146.

such mighty Rage   Pope, *The Rape of the Lock,* canto 1, lines 11–12.

Toyshop of their Heart   Ibid. 1:100.

146   *a Vestal's veins*   "Eloisa to Abelard," lines 1–4, in the Twickenham edition of the *Poems* of Alexander Pope, *The Rape of the Lock and Other Poems,* ed. Geoffrey Tillotson (New Haven: Yale University Press, 1962), 2:319.

ever-musing Melancholy   Jean Hagstrum analyzes Pope's figure of Melancholy in *The Sister Arts* (Chicago: University of Chicago Press, 1958), pp. 218–20.

out-Miltons Milton   David Fairer interprets "Eloisa to Abelard" as "a *psychomachia* engaged upon Miltonic terms," in which the "divine" and "base" imagination war for the heroine's soul (*Pope's Imagination* [Manchester: Manchester University Press, 1984], pp. 25–52).

on the woods   "Eloisa to Abelard," lines 155–70.

147   *bringing all nature down*   In *The Figure in the Landscape* (Baltimore: Johns Hopkins University Press, 1976), pp. 71–73, John Dixon Hunt emphasizes the influence of Eloisa's feelings over what her eye sees, and compares the description to a plate in Cesare Ripa's *Iconologia*.

but you   "Eloisa to Abelard," lines 115–16.

his lov'd Idea lies   Ibid., lines 11–12.

has conjured up   Patricia Meyer Spacks stresses the morbid self-indulgence of this effect in *An Argument of Images: The Poetry of Alexander Pope* (Cambridge: Harvard University Press, 1971), pp. 234–40.

Like Ovid's Laodamia   Reuben Brower deftly illuminates Pope's use of Ovid in *Alexander Pope: The Poetry of Allusion* (Oxford: Clarendon Press, 1959), pp. 74–84.

148   *Angels tremble round*   "Eloisa to Abelard," lines 263–76.

Brendan O Hehir   "Virtue and Passion: The Dialectic of 'Eloisa to Abelard,'" in *Essential Articles for the Study of Alexander Pope,* ed. Maynard Mack (Hamden, Conn.: Archon Books, 1968), p. 335.

Victims swam before my Sight   Cited by Tillotson, *The Rape of the Lock and Other Poems,* p. 342. Evelyn Hooven compares "Racine and Pope's Eloisa," *Essays in Criticism* 24 (1974): 368–74.

Bussy-Rabutin The racy version of the letters (1687) by Roger de Rabutin, Count of Bussy, forms the basis for Pope's own source, John Hughes, *The Letters of Heloise to Abelard* (1713), reprinted in the edition of Pope's "Eloisa to Abelard" by James E. Wellington (Coral Gables: University of Miami Press, 1965).

one "envisioned" Johnson's *Dictionary* cites Pope's line to illustrate the first meaning of "visionary": "Affected by phantoms; disposed to receive impressions on the imagination." But the second meaning is also relevant: "Imaginary; not real; seen in a dream; perceived by the imagination only."

Pope's earlier letters James Winn, "Pope Plays the Rake: His Letters to Ladies and the Making of the 'Eloisa,'" in *The Art of Alexander Pope,* ed. Howard Erskine-Hill and Anne Smith (New York: Barnes & Noble, 1979), p. 102.

149 *Gratified Desire* William Blake, "The Question Answered" (page 103 of his *Notebook*).

undisputed history Samuel Johnson, *Lives of the English Poets,* ed. G. B. Hill (Oxford: Clarendon Press, 1905), 3:235.

Abelard's "Heloydes" Cited by D. W. Robertson, *Abelard and Heloise* (New York: Dial Press, 1972), p. 155.

many other texts Gillian Beer deftly places "Eloisa" in traditions of writing about women, "'Our Unnatural No-voice': The Heroic Epistle, Pope, and Women's Gothic," *Yearbook of English Studies* 12 (1982): 125–51.

awakens all my woes "Eloisa to Abelard," lines 29–30.

150 *her hand obeys* Ibid., lines 13–16.

immortal on thy fame Ibid., lines 343–44.

restored by vision On Eloisa's alienation from nature, see Wallace Jackson, *Vision and Re-Vision in Alexander Pope* (Detroit: Wayne State University Press, 1983), pp. 53–66.

who shall feel 'em most "Eloisa to Abelard," lines 359–66.

151 *cause of his grief* Maynard Mack, *Alexander Pope: A Life* (New York: Norton, 1986), p. 326.

a mask for self-pity Ellen Pollak, *The Poetics of Sexual Myth* (Chicago: University of Chicago Press, 1985), argues that "Eloisa" indulges in "a voyeuristic male appropriation of female eroticism in the service of a phallocentric ordering of desire in which both excess and lack are figured as female" (p. 186).

did not last Mack, *Alexander Pope,* p. 330. Pope later parodied the form of the heroic epistle in "Mary Gulliver to Captain Lemuel Gulliver" (1727), in which the language of Eloisa is used to lament the husband's preference for a sorrel mare.

152 *a successful conclusion* My analysis largely ignores the extensive critical debate over the question of whether Eloisa finally attains self-understanding or serenity. Opposing views are represented by Murray Krieger, *The Classic Vision* (Baltimore: Johns Hopkins University Press, 1971), pp. 83–

272 NOTES AND GLOSSES

103—con—and Hoyt Trowbridge, *From Dryden to Jane Austen* (Albuquerque: University of New Mexico Press, 1977), pp. 135–53—pro.

Crashaw The reference to Crashaw's "Alexias," noted in the eighteenth century, is cited in *The Rape of the Lock and Other Poems,* p. 347.

redemption based on sympathy See David B. Morris, *Alexander Pope: The Genius of Sense* (Cambridge: Harvard University Press, 1984), pp. 131–51.

153 *erotic perspective* The omission has been remedied by Eugene A. Maio, *St. John of the Cross: The Imagery of Eros* (Madrid: Playor, 1973), but with reference only to Plotinian Eros, not to sexuality.

a poet of his kind The standard work on John's poetry is Dámaso Alonso, *La poesía de San Juan de la Cruz* (Madrid: Consejo Superior de Investigaciones Científicas, 1942).

early biographer Jerónimo de San José (1641). The source of the story is unknown, but much information about John was gathered as evidence for sanctification (he was beatified in 1675). See Colin P. Thompson, *The Poet and the Mystic* (Oxford: Oxford University Press, 1977), p. 29.

alahé Gerald Brenan tells the story in *St. John of the Cross: His Life and Poetry* (Cambridge: Cambridge University Press, 1973), pp. 32–33.

154 *Song of Songs* José L. Morales, *El "Cantico espiritual" de San Juan de la Cruz* (Madrid: Marto, 1971), details the influence of the *Song* on John's work.

St. Teresa The doctrinal convergence of the two Carmelite saints is the subject of E. W. Trueman Dicken, *The Crucible of Love* (New York: Sheed & Ward, 1963).

unable to leave Thee "Conceptions of the Love of God," ch. 3, in *Complete Works of Saint Teresa of Jesus,* tr. E. Allison Peers (London: Sheed & Ward, 1957), 2:382.

literal level See Manuel Duran, *Luis de León* (New York: Twayne, 1971), pp. 90–96.

155 *strange figures and likenesses* *The Collected Works of St. John of the Cross,* tr. Kieran Kavanaugh and Otilio Rodriguez (London: Nelson, 1966), p. 408.

y era ido St. John of the Cross, *El cántico espiritual,* lines 1–5. Good texts and translations are available in Brenan, *St. John of the Cross,* and John Frederick Nims, *The Poems of St. John of the Cross* (Chicago: University of Chicago Press, 1979). On the considerable textual problems of the poem, see Roger Duvivier, *La Genèse du "Cantique spiritual" de Saint Jean de la Croix* (Paris: Société d'Édition "Les Belles Lettres," 1971), pp. xxxiii–lxxix.

her Beloved's absence St. John of the Cross, *Collected Works,* p. 416.

stammer on que See Jorge Guillén, Language and Poetry (Cambridge: Harvard University Press, 1961), p. 99.

156 *y fuí ganada* *Cántico espiritual,* lines 101–5. I have adopted Brenan's text, which modernizes spelling and punctuation and adds one stanza from the codex of Jaén to the Sanlúcar manuscript (*St. John of the Cross,* pp. 154, 222).

for her Beloved St. John of the Cross, *Collected Works,* p. 525.

157 *de amor herido* *Cántico espiritual,* lines 171–75.

spiritual marriage St. John of the Cross, *Collected Works,* p. 544.

perfectly in God Ibid.

violada *Cántico espiritual,* lines 141–45.

158 *A scholarly controversy* My analysis both of the controversy and of the stanza is indebted to Judy B. McInnis, "Eucharistic and Conjugal Symbolism in *The Spiritual Canticle* of Saint John of the Cross," *Renascence* 26 (Spring 1984): 125–28.

through original sin St. John of the Cross, *Collected Works,* p. 500.

causes some tension "Under this heavy burden of allegory," according to Jorge Guillén, "poetry has difficulty in subsisting" (*Language and Poetry,* p. 113).

159 *incommunicability of mysticism* Jean Baruzi, *Saint Jean de la Croix et le problème de l'expérience mystique* (Paris: Félix Alcan, 1924), remains a useful study.

a purely formal negation Quoted by Colin Thompson, *The Poet and the Mystic,* p. 159. Much of Thompson's evaluation of John's theology, pp. 146–72, emerges from his argument with Barth.

true seat of power Mary E. Giles contrasts John's mysticism with that of a woman in "Take Back the Night," *The Feminist Mystic* (New York: Crossroad, 1982), pp. 39–70.

be despised José C. Nieto, *Mystic, Rebel, Saint: A Study of St. John of the Cross* (Geneva: Droz, 1979), p. 80. Nieto provides a very thorough analysis of John's Christology.

160 *el otro día* *Cántico espiritual,* lines 186–90.

God's being St. John of the Cross, *Collected Works,* p. 555.

lost daughter returned The standard account is by Rilke's son-in-law, Carl Sieber, *René Rilke: Die Jugend Rainer Maria Rilkes* (Leipzig: Insel-Verlag, 1932).

161 *the woman who loves* "Die Liebende" (letter to Annette Kolb, 23 Jan. 1912, in Rilke's *Briefe* [Wiesbaden: Insel-Verlag, 1950], 1:345). I have used the translation by J. B. Leishman, *Duino Elegies* (London: Hogarth Press, 1957), p. 148.

162 *only God* Rilke, *Sämtliche Werke* (Frankfurt am Main: Insel-Verlag, 1966), 6:924. The English version is from *Notebooks of Malte Laurids Brigge,* tr. M. D. Herter Norton, in Rilke's *Prose and Poetry,* ed. Egon Schwarz (New York: Continuum, 1984), p. 139.

Courses for Beginners *Briefe* 1:346–47 (*Duino Elegies,* p. 149).

hand of a sibyl *Briefe* 1:346 (*Duino Elegies,* p. 148).

sibylline leaves The *Portuguese Letters* will be discussed in the following chapter. Rilke's preface to his translation is reprinted in *Sämtliche Werke* 6:999–1002, and his praise for the Comtesse de Noailles as the epitome of the woman who loves is in the same volume, pp. 1016–20.

became a spring   Rilke, *Sämtliche Werke* 6:925 (*Prose and Poetry,* p. 139).

but for longing   Rilke, *Sämtliche Werke* 6:930 (*Prose and Poetry,* p. 143).

biographer of the poet   The fullest account is that of Donald Prater, *A Ringing Glass: The Life of Rainer Maria Rilke* (Oxford: Clarendon Press, 1986).

163   *from within*   W. L. Graff, *Rainer Maria Rilke* (Princeton: Princeton University Press, 1956), p. 179.

satisfactory lover   Claire Goll, Rilke's "Liliane," volunteers some lurid details in her memoirs, *La Poursuite du vent* (Paris: Olivier Orban, 1976); her earlier essay, *Rilke et les femmes* (Paris: Falaize, 1955), had been more romantic. It should be noted that many other women found him adept at love.

outcry Heloise   "Heloïsen / überstehn und überschrein" (Rilke, *Sämtliche Werke* 1:617).

in his absence   Among the many memorials of Rilke by women, Magda von Hattingberg, *Rilke and Benvenuta,* tr. Cyrus Brooks (New York: Norton, 1949), is notable for its romantic spirit, and Lou Andreas-Salomé, *Rainer Maria Rilke* (Leipzig: Insel-Verlag, 1928), for its mixture of sympathy and analysis.

fed on their loneliness   Graff analyzes the complexity of Rilke's Don Juanism in *Rainer Maria Rilke,* pp. 169–79.

164   *Orpheus helped Eurydice*   Rilke's "Orpheus. Eurydike. Hermes" (1904), in *Sämtliche Werke* 1:542–45, pictures the translation of Eurydice into darkness and immortality.

change them into poems   The "Ninth Elegy" may be read as an expression of this theme, and it continues through the *Sonnets to Orpheus.*

Sistine ceiling   On the background of the poem see Hans Berendt, *Rainer Maria Rilkes Neue Gedichte* (Bonn: H. Bouvier, 1957), pp. 212–13.

in the dark   Rilke, *Sämtliche Werke* 6:833 (*Prose and Poetry,* p. 81).

für die Nacht   Rilke, *Sämtliche Werke* 1:568.

165   *disinterested aesthetic*   Walter A. Strauss discusses the theory of the "thing-poem" in "Rilke and Ponge: L'Objet c'est la poétique," in *Rilke: The Alchemy of Alienation,* ed. Frank Baron, E. S. Dick, and W. R. Maurer (Lawrence: Regents Press of Kansas, 1980), pp. 63–93.

I want to die   Petronius, *Satyricon* 48; used as the epigraph for *The Waste Land.* An alien creature in the Latin text, the Sibyl talks in Greek.

coming of Christ   See Edgar Wind, "Michelangelo's Prophets and Sibyls," *Proceedings of the British Academy* 51 (1965): 47–84.

A Prophet   The relation of "Ein Prophet" to "Eine Sibylle" is particularly close: "Und in seinem Innern richten / sich schon wieder Worte auf, / nicht die seinen" (Rilke, *Sämtliche Werke* 1:566; "And in his recesses are / prepared already again the words, / that are not his").

its fitting night   Anthony Stephens, *Rainer Maria Rilke's 'Gedichte an die Nacht'* (Cambridge: Cambridge University Press, 1972), pp. 137–62, discusses Rilke's complex use of "Nacht" as a possible mediator between immanent and transcendent being.

166 *orthodox view of revelation* Rilke suppresses two crucial details of Michelangelo's Cumaean Sibyl: her prominent breasts, which suggest the "celestial milk" that is "the future food of salvation" (Wind, "Michelangelo's Prophets and Sibyls," p. 68), and the massive book from which she is reading, which suggests the conversion of Sibylline leaves into Christian doctrine. Hence the poem deliberately empties the prophecy of its content. Rilke's early effort to make a Christ of his own may be studied in *Visions of Christ,* ed. Siegfried Mandel, tr. Aaron Kramer (Boulder: University of Colorado Press, 1967).

sibyls and prophets "Tenth Elegy," line 72.

167 *an ideal profession* It may be worth noting that in the most authoritative study of the *Elegies,* Jacob Steiner, *Rilkes Duineser Elegien* (Bern: Francke, 1969), the index entry for "Frau" directs the reader to "Mutter, Mädchen, Liebende"—a fair commentary on Rilke's priorities.

far more complex The relations between the two artists are the subject of a full-length study by Heinrich Wigand Petzet, *Das Bildnis des Dichters* (Frankfurt am Main: Societäts-Verlag, 1957).

self-justification *Paula Modersohn-Becker in Briefen und Tagebüchern,* ed. Günter Busch and Liselotte von Reinken (Frankfurt am Main: S. Fischer, 1979), pp. 307–11.

to lay a ghost Robert Hass discusses the raw and morbid emotions of the "Requiem" in his introduction to *The Selected Poetry of Rainer Maria Rilke,* tr. Stephen Mitchell (New York: Random House, 1982), pp. xxvii–xxxiv.

168 *auf Besitz* Rilke, *Sämtliche Werke* 1:653, 654.

in mir Ibid., p. 656.

169 *a countertruth* "Paula Becker to Clara Westhoff" was reprinted in an epilogue to *The Letters and Journals of Paula Modersohn-Becker,* ed. J. Diane Radycki (Metuchen, N.J.: Scarecrow Press, 1980), pp. 328–30. The epilogue also contains a translation of Rilke's "Requiem" by Lilly Engler and Rich, pp. 319–27.

lonelier than solitude Adrienne Rich, *The Dream of a Common Language* (New York: Norton, 1978), p. 43.

her voice will go on Ovid, *Metamorphoses* 14:129–53.

CHAPTER SIX

170 *dass ich würde wie sie* Duino Elegies, "First Elegy," lines 45–48.

Rilke supplies some answers In *Three Women Poets* (Lewisburg, Pa.: Bucknell University Press, 1987), which offers translations of poems by Stampa, Louise Labé, and Sor Juana Inés de la Cruz, Frank J. Warnke concludes that "Rilke has commented on what is truly in the text"—the transcendent divinity of the woman who loves (p. 55).

171 *other lovers* Duino Elegies, tr. C. F. MacIntyre (Berkeley: University of California Press, 1961), p. 7n.

said by Croce   Benedetto Croce, *Poesia popolare e poesia d'arte* (Bari: Laterza, 1946), pp. 366–75.

man in her life   Stephen Mitchell continues the tradition in glossing Stampa for his fine recent translation of the "First Elegy": "An Italian noblewoman who wrote of her unhappy love for Count Collaltino di Collalto in a series of some two hundred sonnets" (*Selected Poetry of Rainer Maria Rilke*, p. 318).

inner diary   Eugenio Donadoni, *Gaspara Stampa* (Messina: Principato, 1919), p. 41.

two hundred sonnets   *Duino Elegies*, p. 108.

172   *"Nō plays"*   From the *Country of Eight Islands: An Anthology of Japanese Poetry*, tr. Hiroaki Sato and Burton Watson (Garden City, N.Y.: Doubleday Anchor, 1981), p. 632.

greatest erotic poets   Kenneth Rexroth and Ikuko Atsumi, eds. and trs., *The Burning Heart: Women Poets of Japan* (New York: Seabury Press, 1977), p. 141.

who compiled the collection   On the provenance of the *Kokinshū* (the court anthology that is the source of Ono no Komachi's *waka*), see Shuichi Kato, *A History of Japanese Literature*, tr. David Chibbett (Tokyo: Kodansha International, 1981), pp. 126–36.

173   *Fiora A. Bassanese*   *Gaspara Stampa* (Boston: Twayne, 1982).

lovelier far   "Di Giulio Stufa a Benedetto Varchi" (1554), in *Gaspara Stampa and Veronica Franco, Rime*, ed. Abdelkader Salza (Bari: Laterza & Figli, 1913), p. 193.

benign nature   Quoted by Bassanese, *Gaspara Stampa*, p. 23.

Love and Death   G. A. Borgese, *Studi di letterature moderne* (Milan: Fratelli Treves, 1915), p. 27.

queen among whores   "Gaspara Stampa fui, donna e reina / Di quante unqua p......"; quoted by Salza, "Madonna Gasparina Stampa," *Giornale storico della letteratura italiana* 62 (1913): 73.

174   *Giuliettas*   Rousseau's captivating Giulietta was in fact the same person as the brassy Giulietta undraped by Casanova; and the hint of corruption that Rousseau imagined in her may have served as the source for Hoffmann's soul-stealing Venetian beauty.

Venetian courtesan   See Georgina Masson, *Courtesans of the Italian Renaissance* (London: Secker & Warburg, 1975), pp. 145–68. In *Lives of the Courtesans: Portraits of the Renaissance* (New York: Rizzoli International, 1987), pp. 54–55, Lynne Lawner uses Stampa as the perfect type of an "honest courtesan" (*cortigiane oneste*, as opposed to prostitutes, *cortigiane di candela*).

a lady's honor   Bassanese summarizes the argument and leans toward the conclusion that the freedom of Stampa's life can be explained by her activities as a professional musician (*Gaspara Stampa*, p. 31).

look instead at her poems   This was already Croce's suggestion in *Conversazione critiche* (Bari: Laterza & Figli, 1924) 2:230–33.

artless Baudelaire, *Oeuvres complètes,* ed. Claude Pichois (Paris: Gallimard, 1976), 2:146.

echoes of Petrarch Luigi Russo, "Gaspara Stampa e il Petrarchismo del '500," *Belfagor* 13, no. 1 (1958): 1–20, analyzes Stampa's departures from her Petrarchan models.

Petrarch's more studied expression Eugene Benson, *Gaspara Stampa: A Venetian Sappho* (Boston: Roberts Brothers, 1881), p. 14.

175 *emotional excesses* Bassanese, *Gaspara Stampa,* p. 123. Bassanese's later article, "Gaspara Stampa's Poetics of Negativity," *Italica* 61 (1984): 335–46, presents a more subtle view of the poet as a deliberately "failed petrarchist" whose confession of inferiority "allows her a degree of freedom to subvert traditional order" (p. 343).

in this world Quoted by Abdelkader Salza, "Madonna Gasparina Stampa e la società veneziana del suo tempo," *Giornale Storico della Letteratura Italiana* 70 (1917): 58. Translated by Bassanese, *Gaspara Stampa,* pp. 40–41.

tolga l'intelletto Stampa, *Rime d'amore* 28, in *Rime,* ed. Salza, p. 19. The narrative of the sequence is accentuated by descriptive headings; here, "In front of him she is full of confusion."

177 *colle alto* See Bassanese, *Gaspara Stampa,* pp. 73–74; other Petrarchan influences are analyzed in the same chapter, pp. 74–81.

we like them Kingsley Amis, "A Bookshop Idyll," in *A Case of Samples* (London: Victor Gollancz, 1956), p. 55.

Du und ich "Die Dichterin," lines 22–25. The German text is accompanied by an English translation in *Dark Soliloquy: The Selected Poems of Gertrud Kolmar,* tr. Henry A. Smith (New York: Seabury Press, 1975), pp. 54–57.

178 *a single 'You'* "Ihr ganzes Treiben ist ein einzig: 'Du . . .'" (Kolmar, "Die Dichterin," line 17).

Auschwitz Smith provides biographical information about Kolmar in *Dark Soliloquy,* pp. 3–52. Kolmar herself drew a connection between her fate as an abandoned woman and her fate as a victim of the Holocaust; see especially the letter quoted on p. 52.

attack on Collaltino Justin Vitiello, "Gaspara Stampa: The Ambiguities of Martyrdom," *Modern Language Notes* 90 (1975): 58–71, interprets the *Rime* as a sustained, subtle rejection of the passive, abstract male by the active, vital female poet.

Rilke warns "Ein jeder Engel ist schrecklich" ("First Elegy," line 7).

179 *vinco l'infinito* Gaspara Stampa, *Rime,* ed. Salza, p. 52. Bassanese contrasts the claim with Petrarch's, *Gaspara Stampa,* pp. 106–7.

180 *see through the victors* Donata Chimenti Vassalli analyzes Stampa in terms of this tension, "Emancipazione e schiavitù in Gaspara Stampa," *Osservatore Politico Letterario* 18, no. 9 (1972): 70–85.

myth of inspiration Influential musings on this problem include Sandra M. Gilbert and Susan Gubar, *The Madwoman in the Attic* (New Haven: Yale

University Press, 1979); Margaret Homans, *Women Writers and Poetic Identity* (Princeton: Princeton University Press, 1980); and Joanne Feit Diehl, "'Come Slowly—Eden': An Exploration of Women Poets and Their Muse," *Signs* 3 (1978): 572–87. It is not coincidental that each of these studies responds to a model of male inspiration based on Harold Bloom's "anxiety of influence," concentrates on the situation of women in the aftermath of romanticism, and uses Emily Dickinson as a test case.

181   *pity or terror*   See Richard B. Sewall, *The Life of Emily Dickinson* (New York: Farrar, Straus & Giroux, 1980), pp. 563–67.

not verse at all   R. P. Blackmur, "Emily Dickinson: Notes on Prejudice and Fact" (1937), in *The Recognition of Emily Dickinson,* ed. C. R. Blake and C. F. Wells (Ann Arbor: University of Michigan Press, 1964), p. 223.

narrative breakdown   Sharon Cameron, *Lyric Time* (Baltimore: Johns Hopkins University Press, 1979), pp. 58–61.

consummate artistry   David Porter, *The Art of Emily Dickinson's Early Poetry* (Cambridge: Harvard University Press, 1966), p. 173. The same phrase occurs in Paul J. Ferlazzo, *Emily Dickinson* (Boston: Twayne, 1976), p. 70.

182   *For interrupting—more—*   A facsimile of this text appears in *The Manuscript Books of Emily Dickinson,* ed. R. W. Franklin (Cambridge: Harvard University Press, 1981), 1:231. In Thomas H. Johnson's standard edition of *The Poems of Emily Dickinson,* 3 vols. (Cambridge: Harvard University Press, 1955), the poem is no. 293. My text replaces "call" with "called" (line 14) and changes the lineation of the last two stanzas, which Johnson gives as follows:

> And shape my Hands—
> Petition's way,
> Tho' ignorant of a word
> That Ordination—utters—
>
> My Business, with the Cloud,
> If any Power behind it, be,
> Not subject to Despair—
> It care, in some remoter way,
> For so minute affair
> As Misery—
> Itself, too vast, for interrupting—more—

183   *with age*   Poems, Johnson no. 686.

down, and down   Poems, Johnson no. 280.

the letting go   Poems, Johnson no. 341.

desperate inarticulateness   Blackmur, "Emily Dickinson," p. 222.

you must not either   Cameron, *Lyric Time,* p. 60.

tacked onto the text   *Further Poems of Emily Dickinson,* ed. M. D. Bianchi and A. L. Hampson (Boston: Little, Brown, 1929), pp. 183–84.

better Johnson text   Despite my disagreement with Johnson, his recognition of Dickinson's added words as *variants* was a fundamental advance in editing. In that respect Vivian R. Pollak's attempt to put each word back in, even at the cost of rhythmic and semantic chaos, seems distinctly regressive (*Dickinson: The Anxiety of Gender* [Ithaca, N.Y.: Cornell University Press, 1984], p. 179n).

printed as above   No text of a Dickinson poem can be regarded as definitive, in the absence of her own instructions for publication. But neither can the manuscript be substituted for editorial decisions about her probable intentions. My own text is based on the assumption that formally Dickinson's poems seldom fall apart, though much of her skill depends on small but brilliant departures from regularity.

the hymn   See Thomas H. Johnson, *Emily Dickinson: An Interpretive Biography* (Cambridge: Harvard University Press, 1955), pp. 84–88, and David Porter, *Dickinson: The Modern Idiom* (Cambridge: Harvard University Press, 1981), pp. 98–104.

Cowper and Coleridge   Cowper's influence on poetry by nineteenth-century American women in general, and by Emily Dickinson in particular, deserves far more study; his reclusive life and high moral standards provided a much-admired model for women, and Dickinson knew and used the *Olney Hymns*. A high proportion of Coleridge's poems end with an alienated prayer. In *Dickinson and the Romantic Imagination* (Princeton: Princeton University Press, 1981), pp. 50–54, Joanne Feit Diehl stresses Dickinson's "formalistic subversion" of Coleridge's "Frost at Midnight" into a sort of nightmare; but Coleridge too was well acquainted with nightmares.

Longfellow and Frances Osgood   Longfellow, e.g., "Christmas Bells" or "Weariness." On Osgood's relation to Dickinson see Emily Stipes Watts, *The Poetry of American Women* (Austin: University of Texas Press, 1977), pp. 125–37. Cheryl Walker, *The Nightingale's Burden* (Bloomington: Indiana University Press, 1982), places Dickinson against and outside the tradition of poets like Osgood (pp. 87–116).

Entirely for me   Poems, Johnson no. 322.

staying at home   Poems, Johnson no. 324.

184   *recanted*   Shira Wolosky, *Emily Dickinson: A Voice of War* (New Haven: Yale University Press, 1984), reads "I got so I could take his name" as a blasphemous or defiant prayer (pp. 118–21).

unendurable   Cameron, *Lyric Time,* p. 60.

some actual person   William H. Shurr, *The Marriage of Emily Dickinson* (Lexington: University of Kentucky Press, 1983), hypothesizes a love affair in which "I got so I could hear his name" furnishes "concrete details about their meetings" (p. 68).

alternative explanation   See *Feminist Critics Read Emily Dickinson,* ed. Suzanne Juhasz (Bloomington: Indiana University Press, 1983), especially the essays by Karl Keller, Joanne A. Dobson, and Adalaide Morris.

185   *upon the whole*   Blackmur, "Emily Dickinson," p. 223.

felt beautiful   Poems, Johnson no. 593.

a favorite of Dickinson   Jack L. Capps, *Emily Dickinson's Reading* (Cambridge: Harvard University Press, 1966), p. 84.

186   *their own romance*   See Gardner B. Taplin, *The Life of Elizabeth Barrett Browning* (New Haven: Yale University Press, 1957), pp. 128, 234. "Catarina to Camoens" (1844) furnished the title of *Sonnets from the Portuguese*.

You and I—tonight   *Poems,* Johnson no. 47, ca. 1858.

biographers claim   Shurr argues the case for Wadsworth in *The Marriage of Emily Dickinson*, pp. 142–70.

187   *the guest has gone*   *The Letters of Emily Dickinson,* ed. Thomas H. Johnson (Cambridge: Harvard University Press, 1965), 2:452.

Like Stone   *Poems,* Johnson no. 303.

reaches to language   The essays by Margaret Homans, Cristanne Miller, and Joanne Feit Diehl in *Feminist Critics Read Emily Dickinson* all emphasize her disruptions of traditional uses of language and ideas about language.

188   *Omnipotent—Acute—*   *Poems,* Johnson no. 379. The danger and fascination of such bliss are explored in Adrienne Rich's influential "Vesuvius at Home: The Power of Emily Dickinson" (1975), in *On Lies, Secrets, and Silence* (New York: Norton, 1979), pp. 157–83.

189   *Such women are prodigies*   Nadezhda Mandelstam, *Hope Abandoned,* tr. Max Hayward (New York: Atheneum, 1981), p. 465.

impossible love   Marina Tsvetaeva, *A Captive Spirit: Selected Prose,* tr. J. Marin King (Ann Arbor: Ardis, 1980), p. 336.

when it explodes   Marina Tsvetayeva, "Art in the Light of Conscience," tr. Angela Livingstone and Valentina Coe, *Russian Literature Triquarterly* 11 (Winter 1975): 256.

190   *highest of all*   Ronald Hingley, *Nightingale Fever* (New York: Knopf, 1981), p. 36. The four poets and their interrelations are the subject of Hingley's book.

its turn shall come   Translated by Vladimir Nabokov, *TriQuarterly* 27 (Spring 1973): 93.

head and womb   Hingley, *Nightingale Fever,* p. 117.

elegiac cycle   Ibid., pp. 160–61. Tsvetayeva's brilliant critical appraisal, "Epic and Lyric in Contemporary Russia: Mayakovsky and Pasternak" (1932), has been translated by Anya M. Kroth, *Russian Literature Triquarterly* 13 (1976): 519–42.

loneliness, and disaster   Mandelstam, *Hope Abandoned,* p. 462.

191   *style of her own*   Simon Karlinsky, *Marina Cvetaeva: Her Life and Art* (Berkeley: University of California Press, 1966), pp. 193–99, discusses the daring new achievement of *Posle Rossii*.

undo the tradition   See Antonina Filonov Gove, "The Feminine Stereotype and Beyond: Role Conflict and Resolution in the Poetics of Marina Tsvetaeva," *Slavic Review* 36 (1977): 231–55.

fourteen caustic scenes   Elaine Feinstein has translated thirteen of the poems (omitting the eleventh) in *Selected Poems of Marina Tsvetayeva* (Oxford: Oxford University Press, 1981), pp. 48–70.

192   *forever taking leave*   The last line of Rilke's "Eighth Elegy."

match her strength   Karlinsky, *Marina Cvetaeva,* p. 73.

193   *plachu*   "Provoda" ("Wires") no. 2, in Tsvetayeva's *Stikhotvoreniia i poemy v piati tomakh* (*Collected Poetry in Five Volumes*), ed. Alexander Sumerkin (New York: Russica, 1983) 3:58. I am indebted to the commentary on this poem by Peter France, *Poets of Modern Russia* (Cambridge: Cambridge University Press, 1982), pp. 132–36. David Campbell offers a verse translation in *Seven Russian Poets* (St. Lucia: University of Queensland Press, 1979), p. 55.

194   *husband and children*   Hingley, *Nightingale Fever,* p. 129. On Pasternak's relations with Tsvetayeva, see also Guy de Mallac, *Boris Pasternak: His Life and Art* (Norman: University of Oklahoma Press, 1981), pp. 97–99, and Elaine Feinstein, *A Captive Lion: The Life of Marina Tsvetayeva* (London: Hutchinson, 1987), pp. 124–35.

thought not   "I couldn't live with you, Boris, not because I don't understand you, but because I do" (10 July 1926, in *Letters Summer 1926* by Pasternak, Tsvetayeva, and Rilke, tr. Margaret Wettlin and Walter Arndt [San Diego: Harcourt Brace Jovanovich, 1985], p. 176).

195   *syntactical contraction*   On this effect see France, *Poets of Modern Russia,* pp. 135–36, and Barbara Heldt, "Two Poems by Marina Tsvetayeva from 'Posle Rossii,'" *Modern Language Review* 77 (1982): 679–87.

196   *service of the invisible*   Tsvetayeva, "A Poet on Criticism," tr. Paul Schmidt, *TriQuarterly* 27 (Spring 1973): 116. Ieva Vitins discusses the poet's otherworldliness in "Escape from Earth: A Study of Tsvetaeva's Elsewheres," *Slavic Review* 36 (1977): 644–57.

friend and correspondent   The correspondence is collected and annotated in *Letters Summer 1926.*

New Year's Greetings   "Novgodnee." Tsvetayeva's effort to hold Rilke back from nonbeing by identifying with him is the burden of a remarkable essay by Joseph Brodsky, *Less than One* (New York: Farrar, Straus & Giroux, 1986), pp. 195–267.

with the gods   Tsvetayeva, "Poety" ("Poets"), part 2, stanza 4, in *Stikhotvoreniia i poemy* 3:68.

Simon Karlinsky   *Marina Cvetaeva,* p. 210. Karlinsky has recently strengthened his interpretation in *Marina Tsvetaeva: The Woman, Her World, and Her Poetry* (Cambridge: Cambridge University Press, 1986), pp. 102–4.

not to the Muse   Anya M. Kroth, "Androgyny as an Exemplary Feature of Marina Tsvetaeva's Dichotomous Poetic Vision," *Slavic Review* 38 (1979): 563–82, stresses the poet's defiance of sexual dualism, and a similar refusal to categorize Tsvetayeva in terms of gender motivates Zhanna Ivina, "With the Grandeur of Homer and the Purity of Sappho . . . ," in *Women and Russia,* ed. Tatyana Mamonova (Boston: Beacon Press, 1984), pp. 155–63.

gesture of sympathy   Hingley, *Nightingale Fever,* pp. 108, 233. "Lot's Wife" is printed and translated by Stanley Kunitz and Max Hayward, *Poems of Akhmatova* (Boston: Little, Brown, 1973), pp. 76–77.

197   *Akhmatova's friend and rival*   See Jane A. Taubman, "Tsvetaeva and Akh-

matova: Two Female Voices in a Poetic Quartet," *Russian Literature Triquarterly* 9 (Spring 1974): 355–69.

198   *inconsolable grief*   La Rochefoucauld, *Maximes* 233 (1678), in *Oeuvres complètes* (Paris: Gallimard, 1964), p. 434, tr. Louis Kronenberger, *Maxims* (New York: Stackpole, 1936).

lovers like La Rochefoucauld   See Louise K. Horowitz, *Love and Language* (Columbus: Ohio State University Press, 1977), pp. 29–49.

199   *self-definition*   See Harriet G. Lerner, *The Dance of Anger* (New York: Harper & Row, 1985).

No Portuguese original   Portuguese critics have tended to speculate that the French text is a translation from Portuguese, though "sometimes, it is true, a trace of French reason seems to mingle with the ingenuous Portuguese sentiment" (Aubrey F. G. Bell, *Portuguese Literature* [Oxford: Clarendon Press, 1922], p. 264).

Guilleragues   This is the verdict of the standard modern edition, *Lettres portugaises, Valentins et autres oeuvres de Guilleragues,* ed. F. Deloffre and J. Rougeot (Paris: Éditions Garnier Frères, 1962). But the issue has not been settled, and is carefully left open by the editors of the facsimile, *Un manuscrit des Lettres d'une religieuse portugaise: Leçons, interrogations, hypothèses,* ed. Jean-Pierre and Thérèse Lassalle (Paris: Papers on French Seventeenth Century Literature, 1982). In "Writing like a Woman," in *Women and Language in Literature and Society,* ed. Sally McConnell-Ginet, Ruth Borker, and Nelly Furman (New York: Praeger, 1980), pp. 284–99, Peggy Kamuf reviews the questionable assumptions about gender and writing that have led critics to prefer a male or female author, and advises a reading of the text unburdened by surmises about who wrote it.

French disciples   The influence of the *Heroides* on early European fiction, including the *Portuguese Letters,* is the starting point of Robert Adams Day, *Told in Letters* (Ann Arbor: University of Michigan Press, 1966). As Marie-Thérèse Hipp points out, in *Mythes et Réalités* (Paris: Klincksieck, 1976), pp. 54–55, the *Letters* mark an important passage from memoirs to the novel—assuming the authorship of someone other than the nun herself.

the feminine heart   Rilke, letter to Annette Kolb, tr. Leishman, *Duino Elegies,* p. 149.

200   *Racinian tragedy*   Spitzer's essay on *Les Lettres portugaises,* originally published in 1954 in *Romanische Forschungen,* has been translated by David Bellos in Leo Spitzer, *Essays on Seventeenth-Century French Literature* (Cambridge: Cambridge University Press, 1983), pp. 253–83.

seven preliminary letters   In *Un manuscrit des Lettres d'une religieuse portugaise.*

a man of honor   *Lettres portugaises,* p. 66.

different sensations   *Lettres portugaises,* p. 69. As with Pope's "Eloisa," critics have differed about whether the nun has finally freed herself from her obsession. Louise Horowitz, *Love and Language,* pp. 125–43, thinks that she has, though only by admitting the failure of her art. Jean H. Hagstrum, *Sex and Sensibility* (Chicago: University of Chicago Press, 1980), pp. 112–17, finds her still wavering in doubt; she yet might break her vow. Janet G. Altman, *Epistolarity* (Columbus: Ohio State University Press, 1982), notes the nun's new strength or independence, but "it seems prob̦able that closure is being purchased at the expense of repression" (p. 152). Peggy Kamuf, *Fictions of Feminine Desire: Disclosures of Heloise* (Lincoln: University of Nebraska Press, 1982), throws the question back on the "interpretive choice for readers who would put something in the blank that follows it" (p. 65).

201   *responsive to someone else*   *Lettres portugaises*, p. 64.

       a glove is outworn   *Duino Elegies*, p. 149.

202   *speaking out*   In *Fictions of Feminine Desire*, Peggy Kamuf argues that Mariana's text signals a desire to break outside the domain of the chevalier and the cloister. "Retrieving that desire from beneath the screen of the opposing fantasy of her passive victimization has been the work of these letters" (p. 63).

       de Chamilly   See the introduction by Deloffre and Rouget to *Lettres portugaises*, pp. viii–xiv.

203   *tricks of ours*   *The Three Marias: New Portuguese Letters*, tr. Helen R. Lane (Garden City, N.Y.: Doubleday, 1975), p. 359. All page numbers in the text refer to this translation.

       public decency   "Translator's Preface," in *New Portuguese Letters*, p. 7.

       force society to change   In "Political Power and the Portuguese Media," in *In Search of Modern Portugal*, ed. L. S. Graham and D. L. Wheeler (Madison: University of Wisconsin Press, 1983), Ben Pimlott and Jean Seaton connect the literary battles, including the case of the "Three Marias" and culminating with Spínola's *Portugal e o futuro*, with the overthrow of the government. "There has seldom been a clearer declaration of the political power of the written word" (p. 49).

       something of all this   *New Portuguese Letters*, p. 400.

204   *forged pages of the original*   The three Marias are aware that the "original" itself may be a forgery, though a "classic" of Portuguese literature (the letters were translated into Portuguese in 1812). This scene of inauthenticity reinforces their sense of skepticism about the history of Portuguese women.

205   *what is unacceptable*   *New Portuguese Letters*, p. 193.

       reprinting   "The Portuguese Letters," in Donald E. Ericson's imperfect translation, appear as an appendix to *New Portuguese Letters*.

       at being abandoned   *New Portuguese Letters*, p. 45.

206   *in your member*   Ibid., pp. 137–38.

207   *feel less forsaken*   Ibid., p. 395.

       women in political life   According to Diana Smith, in *Portugal in the 1980's*, ed. Kenneth Maxwell (Westport, Conn.: Greenwood Press, 1986), p. 19, since 1974 there "seems to be a powerful release of energy among young Portuguese women. The inertia and the ennui of an older group of middle-

or upper middle-class Portuguese women is in radical contrast to this new trend."

CHAPTER SEVEN

209   *a few pages* Virginia Woolf, *A Room of One's Own* (New York: Harcourt, Brace & World, 1957), p. 81. I have substituted Homer and Sophocles for Horace and Virgil, Woolf's choice of the texts unread by *Shakespeare's sister.*

Nicanor's mother The phrase occurs in Aristotle's will, preserved by Diogenes Laertius. Anton-Hermann Chroust, *Aristotle* (London: Routledge & Kegan Paul, 1973), 1:76–81, records the few known facts and inferences about Arimneste.

Critical Theory since Plato Ed. Hazard Adams (New York: Harcourt Brace Jovanovich, 1971). Significantly, the later anthology *Critical Theory since 1965,* ed. Adams and Leroy Searle (Tallahassee: Florida State University Press, 1986), includes *six* women, though the retrospective "Appendix" puts neither Woolf nor any other woman among its eighteen added men.

210   *some new poetics* Elaine Showalter's useful survey of the recent past and possible future of feminist poetics, "Feminist Criticism in the Wilderness" (1981), has been reprinted with other challenging essays on women, literature, and theory in *The New Feminist Criticism,* ed. Showalter (New York: Pantheon Books, 1985).

deserve a hearing Sniader Lanser and Evelyn Torton Beck, "[Why] Are There No Great Women Critics? And What Difference Does It Make?", in *The Prism of Sex,* ed. Beck and Julia A. Sherman (Madison: University of Wisconsin Press, 1979), pp. 79–91, offer a brief in defense of women critics.

211   *how women fit in* Josephine Donovan provides a generous survey of various schools of feminist thought in *Feminist Theory: The Intellectual Traditions of American Feminism* (New York: Ungar, 1985).

schemes of domination Many of these points of view are ably represented in *New French Feminisms,* ed. Elaine Marks and Isabelle de Courtivron (Amherst: University of Massachusetts Press, 1980).

women's own ways The effort to remedy this situation has been the starting point for much influential criticism, such as Mary Ellmann, *Thinking about Women* (New York: Harcourt Brace Jovanovich, 1968), and Patricia A. M. Spacks, *The Female Imagination* (New York: Knopf, 1975).

opened for inspection The extraordinary growth of scholarship on women writers, in the past few decades, has made a book like this one possible; these notes record only a part of my debt.

212   *genuine differences* The case for a more eclectic view of feminist theory has been made by Annette Kolodny, "Dancing through the Minefield: Some Observations on the Theory, Practice, and Politics of a Feminist Literary Criticism," *Feminist Studies* 6 (Spring 1980): 1–25.

213   *lost their lives* Homer, *Odyssey* 1:337–55, tr. Robert Fitzgerald (Garden City, N.Y.: Doubleday, 1961), pp. 23–24.

214 *Homeric passages* *Iliad* 6:490–93; *Odyssey* 21:350–53.

master here Samuel Butler's translation (1897), *The Authoress of the Odyssey* (Chicago: University of Chicago Press, 1967), p. 20.

literary conversation Carolyn G. Heilbrun comments on Penelope's position as an "outsider" in *Reinventing Womanhood* (New York: Norton, 1979), pp. 40–41.

this observation Alexander Pope, *The Odyssey of Homer* (New Haven: Yale University Press, 1967), 1:54n.

215 *life of men* *Madame de Staël on Politics, Literature, and National Character,* tr. Morroe Berger (Garden City, N.Y.: Doubleday, 1964), pp. 157–58.

to Madame de Staël René Wellek, *A History of Modern Criticism: 1750–1950* (New Haven: Yale University Press, 1955), 2:221, 222.

216 *the glory of man* Aristotle, *Politics* 1:13. Susan G. Bell has gathered Aristotle's remarks on women in *Women: From the Greeks to the French Revolution* (Stanford: Stanford University Press, 1980), pp. 17–21.

before woman *Literary Criticism of Dante Alighieri,* tr. Robert S. Haller (Lincoln: University of Nebraska Press, 1973), p. 6.

challenges silence Tillie Olsen's *Silences* (New York: Delacorte Press/Seymour Lawrence, 1978) is a powerful indictment of the forces that keep women from writing.

perennial puzzle Woolf, *A Room of One's Own,* p. 71.

choked with dust Enheduanna, *The Exaltation of Inanna,* tr. W. W. Hallo and J. J. A. van Dijk (New Haven: Yale University Press, 1968), p. 25.

217 *spare Clarissa's life* See William B. Warner, *Reading* Clarissa: *The Struggles of Interpretation* (New Haven: Yale University Press, 1979), pp. 158–71.

Kate Millett *Sexual Politics* (Garden City, N.Y.: Doubleday, 1970).

Ellen Moers *Literary Women* (Garden City, N.Y.: Doubleday, 1976), pp. 90–99.

into a mirror Sandra M. Gilbert and Susan Gubar, *The Madwoman in the Attic* (New Haven: Yale University Press, 1979), pp. 15–16, analyze Mary Elizabeth Coleridge's "The Other Side of a Mirror" as a poem "central to the feminist poetics we are trying to construct," in which the woman "has an invincible sense of her own autonomy, her own interiority." This is a moving interpretation. Victorian readers, however, would have been more likely to view the poem as the confession of an abandoned woman, whose mirror conjures up "the ghost of a distracted hour" when some secret affliction of love and grief drove the speaker to despair, "And in her lurid eyes there shone / The dying flame of life's desire, / Made mad because its hope was gone."

their truthfulness Murasaki Shikibu, *The Tale of Genji,* tr. E. G. Seidensticker (New York: Knopf, 1978), p. 437.

218 *the uses of fiction* Ibid., p. 438.

219 *so well supported* Catharine R. Stimpson discusses the special problems that women have faced in developing a sense of community in "Ad/d Feminam: Women, Literature, and Society," in *Literature and Society,* ed. E. W.

Said (Baltimore: Johns Hopkins University Press, 1980), pp. 174–92.

did read and write   Susan Guettel Cole discusses the evidence in "Could Greek Women Read and Write?" in *Reflections of Women in Antiquity,* ed. Helene P. Foley (New York: Gordon & Breach, 1981), pp. 219–45.

Werner Jaeger   Paideia: The Ideals of Greek Culture, 3 vols., tr. Gilbert Highet (New York: Oxford University Press, 1962). As Jaeger notes in relation to the *Odyssey,* "the real areté of woman is beauty—naturally enough: men are valued by their intellectual and physical excellence" (1:22). The "naturally enough" manifests Jaeger's identification with Greek values.

220   *a vexed question*   See Sarah B. Pomeroy, *Goddesses, Whores, Wives, and Slaves: Women in Classical Antiquity* (New York: Schocken Books, 1975), p. 81.

went to school   Plato's famous vision, in the *Republic* (book 5), of a utopia where women would be educated to serve as Guardians, remained of course a fantasy. Significantly, there is no section on education in the translations of primary sources by Mary R. Lefkowitz and Maureen B. Fant, *Women's Life in Greece and Rome* (London: Duckworth, 1982). Plato and other philosophers, however, had female disciples; and outside of Athens—most notably in Sappho's Mitylene—some women did educate others in arts and letters.

appear as outsiders   The use of female characters to expose contradictions in Greek society is stressed by Helene P. Foley, "The Conception of Women in Athenian Drama," in *Reflections of Women in Antiquity,* pp. 127–68.

less attraction for women   Eva Cantarella discusses women's systematic exclusion from the *polis* in *Pandora's Daughters: The Role and Status of Women in Greek and Roman Antiquity,* tr. Maureen B. Fant (Baltimore: Johns Hopkins University Press, 1987), pp. 38–51.

boring like no one else   Anonymous, *A Book of Women Poets,* ed. Aliki Barnstone and Willis Barnstone (New York: Schocken Books, 1980), p. 100.

my heart will go out   Anonymous, ibid., p. 424.

221   *anonymous community*   See Janet M. Todd, *Women's Friendship in Literature* (New York: Columbia University Press, 1980), and Nina Auerbach, *Communities of Women: An Idea in Fiction* (Cambridge: Harvard University Press, 1978).

possesses them   *A Room of One's Own,* p. 87.

detestable   Ibid.

polysemous bliss   Many of Roland Barthes's influential essays, including "The Death of the Author" and "From Work to Text," are included in *The Rustle of Language,* tr. Richard Howard (New York: Hill & Wang, 1986).

more than one moral   Alice A. Jardine surveys the feminist (and antifeminist) implications of recent French theory in *Gynesis: Configurations of Woman and Modernity* (Ithaca, N.Y.: Cornell University Press, 1985).

without defenses   See Marcia Landy, "The Silent Woman: Towards a Feminist Critique," in *The Authority of Experience,* ed. Arlyn Diamond and Lee

R. Edwards (Amherst: University of Massachusetts Press, 1977), pp. 24–25.

222   *affiliation* *Writing and Sexual Difference,* ed. Elizabeth Abel (Chicago: University of Chicago Press, 1983), includes essays by Abel and Judith Kegan Gardiner debating an object-relations theory of literary criticism.

much like herself Madelyn Gutwirth, *Madame de Staël, Novelist: The Emergence of the Artist as Woman* (Urbana: University of Illinois Press, 1978), offers a spirited defense of de Staël's "heroic claim to the realm of culture as a province for women" (p. 308). See also Vivian Folkenflik's excellent introduction to her selection and translation of de Staël's writings, *An Extraordinary Woman* (New York: Columbia University Press, 1987).

man's progress Wellek, *A History of Modern Criticism* 2:221, remarks that her "emotionalist theory is combined, rather incongruously, with a belief in perfectibility, a frantic faith in progress, which clashes oddly with her taste for melancholy and her admiration for Ossian." The combination is not incongruous, however, but the founding logical principle of her theory.

deeply grieve *Madame de Staël,* Berger, p. 151.

a class by themselves Ibid., p. 265.

223   *give birth* De Staël, *Letters on the Works and Character of J. J. Rousseau* (London: Robinson, 1789), p. 18. The context is Rousseau's comment on Sappho, who was then in the process of being reinterpreted as a romantic suicide.

life to death De Staël, *A Treatise on the Influence of the Passions* (London: Cawthorn, 1798), p. 142.

has ever loved Ibid., p. 154. Jean Starobinski traces the logic by which love leads to suicide in "Suicide et mélancolie chez Mme de Staël," *Preuves* 16 (Dec. 1966): 41–48.

submission to dreams Marie-Claire Vallois stresses the heroine's ability to use authorial discourse for her own purposes—"The role of the Sibyl, her body in a trance applying herself to voicing Apollo's oracles, is thus used in a subversive and playful way"—in "Voice as Fossil: Madame de Staël's *Corinne or Italy:* An Archaeology of Feminine Discourse," *Tulsa Studies in Women's Literature* 6 (Spring 1987): 47–60.

224   *commiserates the other* De Staël, *The Influence of Literature upon Society* (London: Colburn, 1812), 1:68.

love and its discontents Peggy Kamuf, in *Fictions of Feminine Desire,* uses a canon not unlike de Staël's in order to trace structures "working to appropriate and disguise the force of a woman's passion" (p. xvi).

the course of Demeter See Robert May, *Sex and Fantasy: Patterns of Male and Female Development* (New York: Norton, 1980).

separation anxiety *Separation* (New York: Basic Books, 1973), the second volume of John Bowlby's trilogy *Attachment and Loss,* contains an appendix on "Separation-Anxiety: Review of Literature," pp. 375–98.

the infancy of men The assumption that gender relations derive from preoedipal experience, influentially argued by Nancy Chodorow, *The Reproduction of Mothering* (Berkeley: University of California Press, 1978), is shared by many of the contributors to *The (M)other Tongue: Essays in Feminist Psychoanalytic Interpretation,* ed. S. N. Garner, Claire Kahane, and Madelon Sprengnether (Ithaca, N.Y.: Cornell University Press, 1985).

preoccupy women   The case for a separate female model of psychological and moral development has been made by Carol Gilligan, *In a Different Voice* (Cambridge: Harvard University Press, 1982).

open to question   Anne Fausto-Sterling demonstrates the lack of scientific evidence for most theories of gender difference in *Myths of Gender: Biological Theories about Women and Men* (New York: Basic Books, 1985).

225   *I'm glad it's over   The Waste Land,* line 252.

by those writings   De Staël, *The Influence of Literature upon Society* 1:67.

Pope and Frye   Alexander Pope, *An Essay on Criticism,* lines 135, 645–52; Northrop Frye, *Anatomy of Criticism* (Princeton: Princeton University Press, 1957), pp. 14–15, and "Nature and Homer," in *Fables of Identity* (New York: Harcourt, Brace & World, 1963), pp. 39–51.

satisfy all women   See Jane Marcus, "Still Practice, A/Wrested Alphabet: Toward a Feminist Aesthetic," and Josephine Donovan, "Toward a Women's Poetics"; both articles appear in *Tulsa Studies in Women's Literature* 3 (Spring/Fall 1984): 79–97, 99–110.

226   *care and desire*   Julia Kristeva has done much to construct such a poetics, for instance in *Desire in Language,* tr. Thomas Gora, Alice Jardine, and Leon S. Roudiez (New York: Columbia University Press, 1980), and *Tales of Love,* tr. Leon S. Roudiez (New York: Columbia University Press, 1987).

227   *less funny*   Wayne C. Booth discusses his own turn away from Rabelais's humor in "Freedom of Interpretation: Bakhtin and the Challenge of Feminist Criticism," *Critical Inquiry* 9 (Sept. 1982): 45–76.

228   *the missing woman   Gender and Reading,* ed. Elizabeth A. Flynn and Patrocinio P. Schweickart (Baltimore: Johns Hopkins University Press, 1986), gathers a set of essays that found feminist literary theory on the responses of readers.

singe a sleeve   Yeats's "Byzantium," line 32.

Index